Touchpoints

Books by T. Berry Brazelton, M.D.

On Becoming a Family: The Growth of Attachment Before and After Birth

Infants and Mothers: Differences in Development

Toddlers and Parents: Declaration of Independence

Doctor and Child

To Listen to a Child: Understanding the Normal Problems of Growing Up

Working and Caring

What Every Baby Knows

Families, Crisis, and Caring

Going to the Doctor

Touchpoints Birth to Three: Your Child's Emotional and Behavioral Development
Revised with Joshua D. Sparrow, M.D.

By T. Berry Brazelton, M.D. and Joshua D. Sparrow, M.D.

Touchpoints: Three to Six: Your Child's Emotional and Behavioral Development

The Brazelton Way Series

Understanding Sibling Rivalry

Mastering Anger and Aggression

Feeding Your Child

Toilet Training

Sleep

Calming Your Fussy Baby

Discipline

By T. Berry Brazelton, M.D. and Stanley I. Greenspan, M.D.

The Irreducible Needs of Children: What Every Child Must Have to Grow, Learn, and Flourish

By T. Berry Brazelton, M.D. and Bertrand G. Cramer

The Earliest Relationship: Parents, Infants, and the Drama of Early Attachment

T. Berry Brazelton, M.D.

Revised with
Joshua Sparrow, M.D.

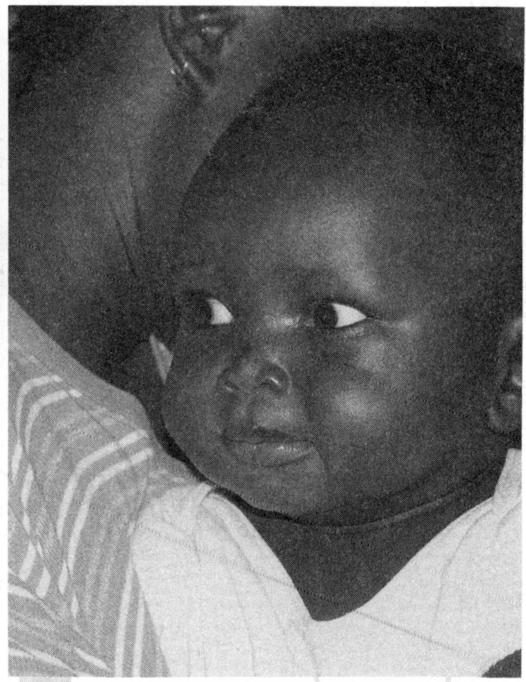

Touchpoints
Birth to 3

Your Child's Emotional and Behavioral Development

Second Edition

A Merloyd Lawrence Book
DA CAPO LIFELONG BOOKS
A MEMBER OF THE PERSEUS BOOKS GROUP

Disclaimer
This book is meant to complement, not substitute for, the advice given by your child's pediatrician. It should not be used as an alternative to appropriate medical care. The authors have exerted every effort to ensure that the information presented is accurate up to the time of publication. However, in light of ongoing research and the constant flow of information it is possible that new findings may invalidate some of the data presented here. Before starting any treatment or new program, you should consult your pediatrician about your own child's health, symptoms, diagnosis, and treatment.

Da Capo Press books are available at special discounts for bulk purchases in the U.S. by corporations, institutions, and other organizations. For more information, please contact the Special Markets Department at the Perseus Books Group, 11 Cambridge Center, Cambridge, Massachusetts 02142, or call (800) 255-1514 or (617) 252-5298, or email special.markets@perseusbooks.com.

Published by Da Capo Press
A Member of the Perseus Books Group
http://www.dacapopress.com

Text design by Lisa Diercks
Typeset in Minion.

A CIP record of this book is available from the Library of Congress.

10 ISBN 0-7382-1049-8
13 ISBN 978-0-7382-1049-0
10 9 8 7

Photography, preceding spread: ***Steven Trefonides, Janice Fullman, Dorothy Littell Greco, Michel Egron-Polak***

Photography Credits

Michel Egron-Polak, *pages v left, 1, 120, 189, 198, 214, 284, 323, 347, 366, 383*

Janice Fullman, *pages iv, pp. 2, 15, 25, 105, 133, 166, 184, 210, 213, 239, 252, 265, 272, 291, 306, 310, 319, 331, 338, 362, 392, 419, 443, 444, 452*

Dorothy Littell Greco, *pages 93, 255, 279, 359*

Marilyn Nolt, *pages v right, 37, 57, 114, 174, 300, 424*

Steven Trefonides, *pages 177, 234, 294, 325, 341, 349, 385, 402, 407, 423, 437, 449, 457*

Luz Arboleda, *pages 30, 83*

Elizabeth Carduff, *pages 53, 151, 430, 434*

Lisa Diercks, *page 467*

Hornick-Rivlin Studio, *page xvi*

Lisa Treacy, *page 372*

Alexa Trefonides, *page 126*

Barbara Wood, *page 415*

To our families

Contents

Acknowledgments

The authors are very grateful to Fred Francis, managing editor at Da Capo Press, for guiding the book through production; to Lissa Warren, our publicist at Da Capo, for nurturing us and helping us promote the books; and to Merloyd Lawrence, our magnificent editor and friend. What treasures!

Introduction to the Second Edition

In the first edition of this book, I laid out a map of infancy developed from four decades of pediatric practice in Cambridge, Massachusetts, and research at Children's Hospital, Boston. Since its publication in 1992, much more has been learned about young children's development, and our world has become an even more complex and challenging one in which to raise them. In the years that followed, I have worked with child psychiatrist Joshua Sparrow (whom I have asked to help me revise this book) and others at the Brazelton Touchpoints Center in Boston to bring my approach in working with young families to healthcare and childcare professionals around the country, from Harlem to Puget Sound. Now, many hospitals, clinics, childcare centers, preschools, and other institutions serving families with young children have been using my preventive, strengths-based model and have joined a national network of more than seventy Touchpoints Collaboratives. This work has introduced us to families of every kind, in just about every state in our nation. They have taught us much about the pressures on families today and the strengths they rely on to face them.

Back in the 1990s, the human side of medicine was being dismantled by the managed care experiment that we now all know failed to contain healthcare costs. But since then, our field has begun to rediscover the therapeutic importance of relationships, and more and more pediatric healthcare providers are taking up the touchpoints approach to families to rehumanize their work, and to make it more fun!

For years, families have struggled with the demands of dual careers or single parenthood. More recently, certain technological advances have made it easier for some parents to work at home—often a mixed blessing. Some workplaces have introduced more family-friendly policies, such as quiet, private places to pump breast milk and flexible hours to attend family events. (Many more still must do so.) An upswing in downsizing and outsourcing has forced increasing numbers of parents, though, to work without benefits like these (or even healthcare coverage for their children), while the shortage of affordable, high-quality child care persists.

Though we still aren't investing adequately in early childhood education, great strides have been made in understanding how very young children learn and how their brains develop. With our new knowledge comes new pressure (much of it from marketers) on parents to stimulate their infants—in just the "right" ways—earlier and earlier. But children learn more from the full complexity of their spontaneous interactions with parents than from any prepackaged program.

Meanwhile, progress in pediatrics has proceeded apace, and specialists are saving ever smaller premature infants and other desperately imperiled young lives. Modern-day ultrasounds offer unprecedented windows into our unborn children's worlds, and fetal surgery can sometimes even repair defects that they reveal. Yet we continue to miss out on many other opportunities for prevention, and we now face new challenges in the current epidemics of asthma, autism, and obesity. Though we still have no cures for these, there is progress. However, the resources have not been dedicated to making new treatments available to every child who needs them.

Since the first edition of this book, it has become harder for parents, even in so-called developed nations, to promise their children a safe world. Man-made disasters, added to the natural ones, and new forms of terrorism have forced parents—and children—to find new strategies for coping, and new strengths. Still, we can promise our children that we will be truthful with them about the challenges of our world, and that we will each do what we *can* do to protect them. As my own children grew older, I began to realize—as do many parents (who eventually join the PTO or coach after-school sports)—that to protect their futures I would need to turn my attention to whatever small part I could do for other people's children too. In these uncertain times, we can give our children hope by modeling—with our own small acts of generosity—the ways that they, too, can do what they *can* to help. Such gestures reassure them that they belong to a community that cares. We can also approach their development as a series of opportunities to instill in them the self-control, self-respect, and sensitivity to others that they will need in order to be resilient and to make their own contribution one day to bettering our strained world.

In the face of these new threats and ever-greater technological prowess, a new trend seems to be gathering steam. As demands on families' time together threaten to pull them apart, many are reaffirming traditional forms of family intimacy. For instance, we've now recognized that the alleged nutritional equivalence and convenience of formula do not make up for all the natural advantages of breast milk. Breast-feeding is not simply a better way of nourishing a baby, it is one of nature's most potent means of cementing the mother-infant bond as they interact with each other in the pauses between bursts of sucking. Also, co-sleeping, long a traditional practice, has begun to gain popularity. More recently, another return to more intimate parent-infant rituals has surfaced in the area of early toilet training. "Elimination communication" is a new term for the traditional practice of carrying a baby close throughout much of the day, which allows parents to respond to babies' physical cues when they need to urinate or move their bowels. Family mealtimes are now also finally being reclaimed as we rediscover the importance of family relationships for healthy nurturance (including the prevention of childhood obesity). These and other "new" trends, it seems to me, affirm a heightened sense of urgency for families to restore intimacy in the face of uncertain times, and to defend it from childrearing techniques imposed by commercial culture and the demands of the workplace.

The map of behavioral and emotional development that I have called "Touchpoints" has been refined over years of research at Children's Hospital in Boston and at other sites around the world. It is designed to reassure parents that they can navigate the predictable spurts in development, and the equally predictable issues that they raise, with the resources that they can find within themselves, their communities, and their cultures. Unlike yardsticks of physical development (the heights, for instance, that parents take such pride in marking off on door-frames), this map has many dimensions. Emotional, behavioral, motor, and language development all occur at their own pace but also affect each other. A child's advances in any one of these areas are preceded by temporary backslides, or regressions, in the same area, or another. The cost of each new achievement can temporarily disrupt the child's progress—and the whole family's stability. Yet each of these disruptions also offers parents a chance to reflect, consider a change in direction, and grow along with the child.

The concept of "touchpoints" is a theory of the forces for change that drive a child's development. Though they may be expressed differently in different cultures, touchpoints are universal. This is because they are for the most part driven by the predictable sequences of early brain development, especially in the first three years of life, the focus of this book. Since the first edition of *Touchpoints,* scientific advances in our understanding of this process have begun to confirm the connections between the behavioral developments (and underlying brain development) and the regressions that I observed for so many years in my practice.

Just before a surge of rapid growth in any line of development, for a short time, the child's behavior seems to fall apart. Parents can no longer rely on past accomplishments. The child often regresses in several areas and becomes difficult to understand. Parents lose their own balance and become alarmed. Over the years, I have found that these predictable periods of regression can become opportunities for me to help parents understand their child and solidify my relationship with them. The touchpoints become a window through which parents can view the great energy that fuels the child's learning. Each step accomplished leads to a new sense of readiness for the next. When seen as natural and predictable, these periods of regressive behavior are opportunities to understand the child more deeply and to support his or her growth, rather than to become locked into a struggle. A child's particular strengths and vulnerabilities, as well as temperament and coping style, all come to the surface at such a time. What a chance to get to know a small child as an individual! Parents who achieve this understanding at each regression can feel even more proud of their parenting.

When the first edition of this book was published, parents everywhere reached out to tell me that they too had noticed these ups and downs in their own children's development. Many pediatricians also reported that they found they could predict when parents would be most likely to call with a new worry about a temporary backslide. "Was it teething, or was the child ill?" parents would fret. Pediatricians learned to rely on the calls that would come a few weeks later saying that the child had settled down after taking his first step or overcoming some other predictable developmental hurdle. If the pediatrician had offered this as a likely explanation at the time of the crisis, parents expressed newfound confidence in their collaboration.

A Dutch ethologist, Frans Plooij, told me that he had observed a similar pattern of growth spurts and regressions in chimpanzee infants and mothers!

"Why do you sound so surprised?" he asked. "Ninety-eight percent of their genes are the same as ours." Unlike humans, the chimp mothers didn't call their pediatricians when their infants regressed. But they often appeared to predict these changes, isolating their babies from the pack before the male chimps became annoyed with the intensified crying and clinging. After reading *Touchpoints,* scientists from a variety of fields reassured me that many kinds of important changes in nature unfold in this way, with disorganization an inevitable precursor for reorganization at a new and more complex level.

Part 1 of this book describes these touchpoints in the areas of behavioral and emotional growth, showing how they affect many aspects of the child's life, such as sleep, feeding, toilet learning, motor achievements (such as walking), communication, self-esteem, and self-control. The issues they raise are laid out just as they emerge in office visits with parents, from the prenatal visit with an expectant mother and father to the checkups for infants to the annual visits with the older child. Parents' questions appear at predictable times. Their concerns about how to handle these disruptive regressions lend focus to our visits. If I can help parents understand the developments in the child that contribute to troublesome behavior, each visit becomes more valuable. Parents become able to make decisions about their role in the child's temporary struggles. A caring professional can use such times to reach into the family system, offer support, and prevent future problems.

Part 2 takes up those specific issues of child rearing in the first years that can challenge development, including several that extend beyond age three. (For these, see also Brazelton and Sparrow, *Touchpoints Three to Six,* listed in *Further Reading.*) "Problems" such as sibling rivalry, crying, tantrums, waking at night, fears, emotional manipulations, lying, or bedwetting may be inadvertently reinforced when parents attempt to control situations that really belong to the child. I try to show how parents can see these various kinds of behavior as part of the child's struggle for autonomy, and how they can remove themselves from the struggle and thus defuse it.

The chapters in Part 2, written for parents who see themselves or their child getting stuck in an issue, are designed not only to help them avoid getting locked into overwhelming worry and even destructive interactions but also to know when to seek help if their efforts fail. They are not meant to be comprehensive and are intended only to help parents distinguish between normal variations in behavior and problems that require expert help.

Part 3 examines the ways in which children's development is affected by those around them. Each close relationship—with mothers, fathers, grandparents, friends, other caregivers, and the child's doctor—contributes to the child's emotional and behavioral growth. The more that parents can foster these relationships, the more allies a child will have on the journey toward autonomy—which, of course, none of us ever fully attains, nor would we want to!

In my experience, no developmental line in a child proceeds in a continuous upward course. Motor development, cognitive development, and emotional development all seem to proceed in a jagged line, with peaks, valleys, and plateaus. Each new task a baby learns is demanding—it requires all of the baby's energy, as well as that of family members. For instance, when a year-old baby is learning to walk, everyone pays a price. The baby is up and down at the side of the crib all night, coming to full waking at every light-sleep cycle, crying out for help every three to four hours during the night. Since the first edition of *Touchpoints,* scientists have begun to think that there may be a good reason why babies so predictably wake up more often in the weeks before they learn to walk. It turns out that a baby spends more time in light sleep—and is more likely to awaken—during this period than at any other. It is thought that in this state the brain "records" the memories of each small movement that will soon be sequenced into the baby's first step!

As understandable and auspicious as the baby's middle-of-the-night awakenings may be, everyone else's sleep is still disrupted. A parent's first response to a touchpoint like this is often to worry that the child might be sick. The child's doctor is sure to hear about it. In the daytime, the baby cries out in frustration every time a parent or sibling walks by. When a parent turns her back, the frustrated baby collapses into a frantic heap. A child's learning to walk is costly to everyone's peace of mind. Once a parent knows that there's no medical problem, irritation is the next understandable reaction. A small amount of this may even help push the child along. The child who has finally learned to walk becomes a different person, face aglow with triumph. Everyone in the family settles down. The next phase in development will be spent in consolidating and enriching this last achievement. A toddler will learn to walk holding a toy, to turn around while walking, to squat, to climb stairs. In this phase, the child won't be so unpredictably volatile. The pressure is off—until the next spurt.

Each of these spurts and the regressions that precede them are key moments for pediatricians and nurse practitioners interested in playing an active role as part of the family system. Parents are likely to meet a child's regression with anxiety and an attempt to control the behavior at the very time when the child is searching for a new sense of autonomy. This can reinforce any "deviant" behavior and prolong it as pattern or habit. Understanding these touchpoints helps prevent such difficulties from getting locked in. At such times, I find that I can offer parents choices in behavior. If their own strategies have ended in failure or in anxiety, they are ready to look for alternatives. When parents come with such concerns, I first respond not with advice or pat reassurance but by sharing my observations of the child's behavior, things I think the parents can see too. That way, they know that we are starting from the same place. Insights into this behavior become our shared language. At such times, parents are often more open than ever, and more vulnerable. I can use my relationship with the family—our shared experience—to help them uncover their underlying worries. By pointing out the reason for the turmoil and the predictable outcome in development, I am able to respond to their concerns in a positive and helpful way. If parents can understand the child's powerful need to establish his or her own autonomous pattern, they may be able to break a vicious cycle of overreaction and conflict.

Balancing a child's need for containment and limits with his need for autonomy is not always a rational matter for parents. We are all likely to become mired in situations that call up powerful childhood memories or, as child expert Selma Fraiberg said, "ghosts from our own nursery." Patterns of parenting learned from our parents loom over us, pressing us to respond irrationally. Parents don't make mistakes because they don't care, but because they care so deeply. Caring revives issues from the past. Passion creates determination, which may supersede judgment. As I pointed out in my book *The Earliest Relationship,* written with Bertrand Cramer, by bringing these ghosts to consciousness, we are able to strip them of their power. We, as parents, can then make more rational choices about how to handle our child's disturbing behavior.

Learning to parent is made up of learning from mistakes—as well as from successes: Parenting is a process of trial and error. When something goes wrong, parents must rethink their approach in order to remedy the situation. Mistakes and wrong choices stand out and grab you; successes do not. Rewards for "right choices" are deep and quiet: having a child cuddle in your arms to be crooned to, or announce proudly, "Look, I did it myself!"

In recent years we have been learning more and more about the importance of individual differences in children. As I wrote in my book *Infants and Mothers,* babies' individual temperaments, or styles of interacting with and learning about the world, can heavily influence the way they pay attention to and absorb the parents' guiding stimuli. Their temperaments also profoundly influence the parents' reactions to them from the moment of birth. While a child cannot be seen as born with a fixed nature, neither is the environment all-important in shaping a child. These inborn individual differences mean that the chronology of development suggested in the following chapters must be adapted to the reader's own child.

Each parent's own style and temperament must also be respected. Two parents cannot be expected to react the same way at the same time to the same child—nor should they. Their own differences in temperament and experience should make their reactions different if the parents are true to themselves. Each situation demands a custom-made decision if it is to be a "right choice"—that is, right for the child and right for each parent. However, it is important to note that what parents do at any point may not be as critical as the emotional atmosphere that surrounds their action. This becomes even more complicated when parents must face yet another point of view from anyone else who cares for the child.

Parenting can be lonely. Most new parents are insecure and wonder whether they are doing as well as they can with their children. As a pediatrician, I have always felt a responsibility to anticipate the issues that I know will arise, and to help parents find opportunities for learning to understand their children. I want to be an active part of each family as a unique system and to try to help as family members interact with each other and readjust to stresses or to each new level of learning in any one of the individuals making up this system.

When I began to practice, I found I was sometimes bored by the routines of shots, weight and height checks, and physical exams. For me, the excitement lay in the developmental issues that the children presented and that the parents raised with deep concern at each visit. Such concerns as fitful sleep, food struggles, or bedwetting were uppermost in parents' minds when they brought a healthy child for a checkup. If I was ready to listen and to share ideas with them, they were eager and grateful to discuss their side of these issues. While we talked, I observed the child's play and way of handling my examination. Through many such observations, I learned to form an idea of each child's temperament and stage of development. Then, I could predict for the parents the issues that might arise in each of the areas we discussed—feeding, sleeping, thumb sucking, toilet training, and so on. When I could predict their conflicts, and when I could help them understand the child's issues, our relationship deepened. Each visit became more exciting for me and more rewarding for them.

Shared experiences such as these are valuable both to the parents and to the physician. When parents bring the child for a later visit, they and the doctor have a chance to reevaluate any earlier predictions. If the predictions have held, they know they are on the right track. Mistaken predictions are also revealing. Parents and physician can then examine (1) the biases that shaped the predictions in the first place; (2) the strength of the defenses of the family, which may have hidden certain vulnerabilities and underlying issues; and (3) the relative strength of the physician-family relationship, which determines how much a family can trust the physician and reveal their concerns openly. At each subsequent touchpoint, these become clearer, and the ability to predict of both parents and physician will sharpen.

When I discuss the concept of touchpoints with parents and describe the role a pediatrician, nurse practitioner, or family physician can play in interpreting the regressions and spurts of development with parents, many tell me that their own doctors are more interested in assessing physical growth and dealing with illness. Parents often feel that doctors may not want to answer their questions, when actually, we sometimes don't know how. Though progress has been made, pediatric training is based largely on the medical model, with its emphasis on disease, and still often fails to help doctors learn to identify a child's strengths, and a family's. Doctors also often don't receive the training they deserve to learn how to collaborate with families to build strong therapeutic relationships. "Managed" care makes this more difficult when it treats doctors as technicians who are too costly to deploy except in the most limited roles in which skills that only they possess are required. As a result of efforts to reduce the art of medicine to algorithms, doctors are taught to teach and to tell, and to make up for lack of time with brochures that are unlikely to be read, instead of to listen. This may save time in the short term, but families' most important concerns and questions may be pushed aside.

In many "managed" care settings, families see a different doctor at every visit, as if the doctors were interchangeable and their relationships with families unimportant. This was supposed to have saved money, but healthcare costs have only gone up since "managed" care took over, and much of the increase has gone to paperwork and other administrative costs of this inefficient system.

The power of the therapeutic relationship has been demonstrated by medical research over and over. With its loss, the quality of health care is gravely compromised. If the costs of neglected prevention, missed diagnoses, and bad outcomes are factored in, the magnitude of this lost opportunity is even more daunting. Neither pediatricians nor parents should put up with this.

Pediatricians have a unique opportunity to listen to new parents and support the birth of new families. If these relationships are protected by our healthcare settings, pediatricians can use this special, shared experience to cement families through the predictable crises for years to come. In our program at the Brazelton Touchpoints Center in Boston, we try to fill the gaps left by medical education and our current healthcare system. We train medical professionals to reexamine their interview style, to share observations of each child's development, and to encourage parents to share the feelings that are part of learning to nurture. We ask them to reconsider whether they really can accomplish their agenda without welcoming that of each family.

In recent years, the field of child development has continued to blossom despite shriveling funding, with new research in areas such as early brain development, parent-child attachment, the abilities of the newborn, genetic and environmental influences, and temperament. Pediatric training has often lagged in assimilating these advances. Much of this new knowledge can give pediatricians rare insight into the unique development of *each* child. When they share these observations with parents, and invite parents to share theirs, it will greatly solidify the parent-physician relationship. I have found that parents who know I understand their child can forgive me for all kinds of delays or frustrations in our work together. They see me as their ally in providing the best environment we can for their child. They share their own mistakes, their own concerns. We are a team.

Knowledge of the map of development in each of the developmental lines —motor, cognitive, and emotional—makes a "compleat pediatrician." For those who can appreciate the powerful, universal neurodevelopmental forces behind the struggle to learn to walk, or the passionate conflict between "yes" or "no" in the second year, which leads to temper tantrums, both pediatrics and parenting become a delight. Every office visit can then be a window, offering the perennial excitement of watching each child grow and master the great tasks of the first few years. We need more pediatricians trained to understand and enjoy this aspect of their practice. Through our work at the Brazelton Touchpoints Center (and its national network of healthcare, social service, and educational institutions serving families of young children around the country), which offers this training, and through this book, I hope to transmit these shared joys, the rewards of a lifetime of caring for parents and children.

Touchpoints

part one
Touchpoints of Development

1. Pregnancy: The First Touchpoint

In the last few months of pregnancy, expectant parents become aware of the activity of the baby-to-be and the reality of the huge adjustment that lies ahead. The seventh month is the ideal time for a first visit to the physician who will care for the baby. By now, parents know they will need a pediatrician and advocate for the baby and are eager to share their hopes and concerns. Later than this in the pregnancy, I find mothers-to-be more concerned about the fast-approaching experience of delivery and less available to talk to me about the baby. Fathers will become involved in childbirth education classes by the eighth month. Their role in the delivery process will then be uppermost in their minds.

At seven months, parents are still dreaming of the baby. They wonder who this child will be. I can help uncover and share their dreams and anxieties with them. This is the first "touchpoint" and an opportunity for me to form a relationship with each parent before there is a baby between us. The visit can have lasting effects. When fathers come to my office at this time, even for ten minutes, I can be sure that 50 percent of them will be present at each subsequent visit throughout the baby's first year. Eighty percent will come in for at least four visits. A father who feels wanted in a pediatric office knows he can express his importance to his baby's well-being. Fathers say to me, "So far, no one else has really spoken to me about this. They only talk to my wife. But it's my baby, too. When you asked me to come in and to be a part of the interview, I knew you realized that." A father's vulnerability, his hunger to be included, makes this visit a valuable touchpoint for both of us.

When busy mothers-to-be call for an appointment in pregnancy, they say, "My obstetrician says I should come to meet you *before* I deliver. Is that really necessary?" This question often shields a number of anxieties that may be interfering with her interest in getting to know her pediatrician in advance. I can honestly answer, "Yes, it is very important for us to meet before we have a baby to concentrate on. I want to know you and your concerns ahead of time so we can share them." "Oh, well then, when can I come?" she will say cautiously. At this point, I express my interest in meeting the baby's father as well. If she hesitates again, I simply suggest that she ask him before making the appointment.

When the parents-to-be do come in together, the father tends to retire to the background. Since I feel strongly that we should be urging fathers to be equal participants in their babies' care, I ask him to pull his chair up to my desk. As he does, he looks to his wife for permission. I point this out and use the opportunity to introduce the notion of "gatekeeping"—a new name for very old feelings. All adults who care about a baby will naturally be in competition for that baby and may try to exclude others or have more say than others in caregiving, thus acting as a "gatekeeper." Competitive feelings are a natural component of sharing the care. Each adult strives to do each job more skillfully for the infant or small child than the other. For the mother and father, this competition is fueled by passionate attachment to the child. Such feelings are present in other members of the family as well. They can unconsciously influence grandparents' behavior and lead them, without intending harm, to criticize the sensitive new parents. Doctors and nurses also compete with parents in this way when they criticize them and fail to recognize their expertise. Schoolteachers are also likely to compete with parents. All this gatekeeping is predictable and represents caring on both sides.

If the competition does not interfere with the child's best interests, it can fuel passionate caring. But as we will see later in this book, the urge to exclude the other parent can create friction in the family if parents aren't aware of it. For instance, when a new mother starts to breast-feed, fathers and grandmothers may say, "The baby's crying again! Are you sure you have enough milk?" As a new, vulnerable father begins to diaper his new baby, his spouse is likely to say, "Darling, that's not quite the way you do it," or when he settles in to give a bottle for the first time, she may say, "Hold her this way, and she'll be more comfortable"—innocuous remarks on the surface, but ones carrying an unsettling message. If fathers are to participate, both parents must be prepared for this subtle competition. They'll need to learn to expect these differences and to bring them to the surface to talk them over. This is the best way I know for parents to keep these differences from invading their relationship and confusing the child.

First-time parents have universal doubts and questions: "How will we ever learn to become parents? Will we have to be like our parents?" With these questions come concerns about the baby. "Suppose we have a damaged child? Will it be our fault? How can we ever face such a thing?" Parents-to-be often have dreams at night about the various defects they have seen or heard of. With busy days to divert them, they may not let themselves worry, but these fears are likely to crop up at night. The dreams stir up attachment and help to prepare prospective parents for the possibility of a less-than-perfect baby. A pregnant woman and her spouse dream of three babies—the perfect four-month-old who rewards them with smiles and musical cooing, the impaired baby, who changes each day, and the mysterious real baby whose presence is beginning to be evident in the motions of the fetus.

Prenatal Diagnosis

Fortunately, we have an ever-growing number of prenatal tests available to help identify a fetal health concern early. For example, in the first trimester, a mother can be tested for HIV/AIDS so that she can be treated and transmission to the fetus can be prevented. Antibody Rh-Negative testing early in pregnancy also allows for critical life-saving preventive measures to be taken. Other first-trimester tests include Cystic Fibrosis screening, Alpha-Fetoprotein Test (AFP—to screen for neural tube defects such as spina bifida), and Triple or Quad-Screen Test (for Down Syndrome). When specific inherited diseases are a concern, chorionic villus sampling (CVS) may be done at 9–11 weeks instead of waiting until 16–18 weeks for an amniocentesis. There are also more and more genetic tests for parents-to-be to choose from if either one has a heritable disorder in his or her family.

Of course the decision to undergo any of these tests, and the wait—however long or short—for the results, can be frightening, even overwhelming. A few of the available tests provide less than certain results, so that expectant parents may still harbor concerns about their baby's health at the pediatric prenatal visit in the last trimester. They may be reassured by third-trimester testing such as an ultrasound, or a more detailed ultrasound procedure known as a "biophysical profile." If a health concern should require that a baby be delivered early, there are several tests of fetal lung maturity that help determine when it is safe to do so, or what extra help will be needed. (See *Useful Addresses and Web Sites* for more information.)

Preparing for Birth

The work of the last part of pregnancy prepares parents for the crisis of birth. The parents' attempt to imagine the baby-to-be—fearing an impaired one, dreaming of a perfect one—mobilizes the emotional energy they will need to fall in love with the real one. All this inner turmoil loosens up old habits, opening parents to the job of rebalancing their lives, and prepares them for the sacrifices that all parents learn to make.

In the short interview we have together, my questions are simple ones. I am looking for the feelings below the surface, which will give me an opportunity to know this family better.

"How do you plan to deliver your baby?"

"We are going to childbirth education classes. I want to be in control as much as possible. I don't want any medication, if I can help it; I want to deliver my baby naturally—without anesthesia."

At this point, the mother-to-be may have questions about how medication and anesthesia affect her baby. I explain that labor seems to alert the fetus and serves to awaken the baby after delivery, whereas many types of medication have the opposite effect. The longer medication can be postponed, the more alert and responsive the baby will be. She knows this already, so what we are really sharing is our mutual concern for the baby. I hope she sees that I will join her in wanting a responsive baby, and that I am ready to address any other concerns she might have about labor and delivery. I want her to know that I also share her concerns about pain management during labor, and I encourage both parents-to-be to master the techniques for relaxation, paced breathing, focusing, and touching that they will learn in their childbirth education classes.

This is where a father can help. He can work with his wife or partner to follow the lessons of the childbirth classes in managing her pains and support her in postponing medication. Depending on the approach of the obstetrician, the father may have to help the mother be firm in declining offers of medication. Well-documented research shows that having someone present who can actively support the mother during labor and delivery, such as a labor companion (*doula*), can shorten a woman's labor and help her postpone or avoid medication, one of the main goals of childbirth classes.

While explaining this, I try to listen for any sign that the parents-to-be may want to ask more questions. "What will a cesarean section do to the baby, if it becomes necessary?" "What are the effects of epidural anesthesia?" "Will I feel like a failure if I have anesthesia?" By discussing these questions with me, parents-to-be can become clearer about their goals and the depth of their fears.

A cesarean section is often performed to protect the baby, but its effects on the baby are not yet well understood. (Research compiled by Childbirth Connection, formerly known as the Maternity Center Association, suggests that babies born by cesarean section may be at higher risk for respiratory distress at birth, but less likely to sustain nerve injuries at birth than those born by vaginal delivery.) In the past, infants delivered by cesarean section without labor were watched in a special nursery for twenty-four hours since they were expected to be sleepier and less able to cough up their mucus. If that is true (and it hasn't been carefully studied), it might be attributed to the fact that labor does wake a baby for the immediate adjustments after birth. Medication given to mothers during labor and before a cesarean section crosses the placenta to affect the baby's behavior for several days after birth. In my observations using my Neonatal Behavioral Assessment Scale (NBAS), when medication for the mother was carefully managed babies born by cesarean section were less responsive for the first day than a group of babies whose mothers delivered them vaginally and without pain medication. But these effects were gone after twenty-four hours, and the baby's subsequent courses were no different.

Medication given less cautiously during labor may have a more lasting influence on babies' behavior. Medicated babies are sleepier and more difficult to rouse. They stay alert for shorter periods, and their responses to human stimuli are also more short-lived. If a mother is aware of these effects, she can make up for them by working harder to keep her new baby alert, particularly at feeding times. If she's not, she may see her baby as quiet and more sluggish than expected or feel that she is failing when she tries to nurse her difficult-to-rouse infant. This early image might become self-perpetuating. I urge a mother to postpone medication as long as possible and to have as little as possible. If medication becomes necessary, she must be aware of the effects and plan to rouse the baby more vigorously—at feedings and for play—until the medication wears off several days later.

Although the rising rate of cesarean sections over the past several decades is a national concern, they can sometimes make a big difference for the better. The fact that we can detect a baby's difficulty during labor with external fetal monitors or, after the mother's membranes are ruptured, internal fetal monitors, placed on the baby's scalp, means that we detect more distress signals and earlier ones than we were able to before the use of monitors. As a result, obstetricians can often intervene before the baby suffers any real brain damage. While the resulting cesarean section is not without risks, and is harder on the mother physically and psychologically, the goal is to protect the baby from brain injury caused by too little oxygen (hypoxia) during a stressful period of uterine contractions and poor oxygen supply from the placenta. This may prevent some cases of cerebral palsy, although there are many causes of this condition, and only about 10 percent are due to oxygen deprivation during delivery. A physician must help parents understand the reasons for a cesarean section and be alert for feelings of disappointment and failure. In the prenatal visit I can encourage parents to work for a natural labor and delivery, but at the same time to avoid burdening themselves with the belief that there is only one way for their baby to come into this world. (For more information, see American College of Obstetricians and Gynecologists, International Childbirth Education Association, Lamaze International, Childbirth Connection, and InterNational Association of Parents and Professionals for Safe Alternatives in Childbirth in *Useful Addresses and Web Sites* and Klaus, Kennell, and Klaus in *Further Reading.*)

Breast or Bottle

When I ask about feeding the baby, I listen for the reasons behind whichever choice the parents will make. Before most women began returning to work so soon after having a baby, I expected parents in my practice to choose breast-feeding. I added my strong support, and we discussed the preparation for it. But for many years now, it has seemed to me that more mothers-to-be who plan to go back to work after a few months have been choosing bottle-feeding. There are, of course, practical concerns about breast-feeding on the job, but when I have inquired further, some have expressed their fears of getting too attached to the baby, whom they will have to leave in someone else's care. When I can help mothers to be open with me, and with themselves, they can sort out their goals more clearly. My role as their supporter and the baby's advocate gives them the safety to explore their decision. I will be able to help them attach to their baby with either choice.

I am prejudiced in favor of breast-feeding because of its health advantages for baby (for example, protection against infection—including ear and upper respiratory infections—and milk allergies) and mother (more rapid weight loss after pregnancy, decreased incidence of breast and ovarian cancer and of diabetes) and its importance in strengthening the parent-infant relationship. But I can help parents who choose or must resort to the bottle to make feedings as deeply rewarding a time for communication with the baby. Breast milk has so many advantages—it's perfect for a human baby. No babies are allergic to breast milk (though a baby will on rare occasions react to something the mother has eaten that comes through in her milk). The ratio of protein and sugars is ideal, and breast milk is loaded with antibodies that will boost the level of immunity with which the baby is born. Babies receive immunity from their mothers across the placenta, but this immunity to infection will diminish over the next few months unless breast milk keeps the level up. Besides lessening the dangers of infection, breast-feeding is ideal for other reasons as well. One is that mothers find the closeness in communication while nursing a baby so delicious.

At this visit, I mention to women who plan to breast-feed that it may hurt when they begin. The baby's suck reflex can be amazingly strong. Mothers tell me that their breasts go into spasms at first and hurt until the milk starts flowing. The spasms are thought to be due to the enlargement of the milk ducts. I reassure mothers-to-be that after a few initial feedings the spasms will stop, and the resultant feeling will be pleasure.

There are conflicting points of view about whether mothers-to-be can successfully prepare their nipples ahead of time. They would do well to buy a good book on breast-feeding (see Huggins in *Further Reading* and La Leche League in *Useful Addresses and Web Sites*) and also consult their physician. In my own experience of having helped mothers over the years, I have found that light-skinned women are more likely to get sore and to have cracked nipples unless they toughen them up beforehand. To do this, a woman should wash her hands and breasts with mild soap, then gently massage the nipples between the fingers twice a day. She should rub a little harder as time goes on but *not* hurt them. It's better to prevent cracked nipples than to have to treat them. (Note: Some experts caution against nipple stimulation in mothers at risk for premature labor since theoretically it could cause uterine contractions. All mothers-to-be should consult their midwives or obstetricians before trying this technique.)

While I respect the concern of working women about the difficulties of breast-feeding when returning to their jobs, we might still discuss ways to keep that option open. We can discuss the possibility of pumping breast milk while at work and, after the baby is four to six weeks old, of having the father (or another caregiver) use a bottle of this breast milk for a supplementary feeding. This way a father can have a chance to nurture, while the mother can still enjoy coming home after a hard day's work to put the baby to breast—and get close again. We can also discuss the fear of separation that accompanies this attachment to the baby. Meanwhile, as we talk, the parents and I are establishing a closer relationship. They see that I want to support their choice and their attachment to the new baby.

For the mother who wants to breast-feed, I can offer other practical suggestions, such as being prepared to wait several days after delivery for her milk to come in, and feeding for short periods at first to help her nipples toughen up—all the while offering my support as she prepares for the new job. Meanwhile, in this first visit I hope she will express any concerns about her ability to feed, as well as to tend the baby in all areas. By discussing feeding now, we are making it easier to face feeding issues together as they come up later on.

Circumcision

I always ask the father at least one question that I know he'll feel strongly about: "Will you have your baby circumcised if it's a boy?" This is a sure way to bring out his involvement. If he asks my opinion, I can give him the pros and cons while encouraging him to take responsibility for that decision. I want him to feel that it is his and that we can make it work for him and the baby. The decision to circumcise or not should be a personal one, or one that takes into account the father's culture and religious beliefs. Though some studies have suggested preventive advantages to circumcision such as reduced risk of urinary tract infections in the first year and foreskin infections that sometimes occur in preschool-aged boys, some experts and organizations—among others, the American Academy of Pediatrics—have taken the position that current evidence does not offer *medical* grounds for circumcision, unless, of course, there is a specific condition requiring it—such as a foreskin that is too long or too tight, both uncommon. Certainly a painful procedure for a newborn, circumcision can disrupt sleep, EEG (electroencephalogram) patterns, and other behavior patterns for twenty-four hours. However, local anesthetic procedures can quite safely prevent much of the pain and disruption seen previously.

Circumcision should be a family decision. Most important is the father's role in participating in the child's future. I think a father should make the choice for his son. This may be the first time that he experiences a deep possessive feeling about the baby-to-be. Most fathers want their boys to be like themselves. A father may worry that when his little boy compares himself to his daddy later on, a difference will be hard to explain. But a little boy's inevitable comparison of his penis size to his daddy's will call up questions in any event, so differences can't ever be altogether avoided. I feel this question is of deep significance to a male, and the father's choice needs to take his emotional reactions into account. This discussion and his decision will draw the father into thinking more about his future baby. If I show my support for him, he will feel freer to turn to me for advice later on.

The Physician as Advocate for the Baby and the Family

To care for babies, their families must be cared for too. At the prenatal visit, I am likely to hear about the family constellation. There are many new kinds of families. I want each one to feel respected and backed-up by me.

If the mother is a single parent, she will need extra help in her new, demanding role. As she raises her fears, I can assure her that I will assume a more actively supporting role. Raising a child alone is likely to be difficult, but it can be done well, and I assure her that I will be ready to guide her whenever she wants me to.

A common challenge for single parents seems to be letting the baby become independent. At each stage of autonomy, when babies are still vulnerable, it is easy to overpower their search for their own way of doing things by showering them with too much attention and too much direction. All of this comes from caring, which is critical to the child, but a single mother may need someone to say, "Let your child go. Let her get frustrated. Let her work things out for herself. In the long run, if you can do this, it will be *her* achievement, not yours." No parent really wants to hear this kind of advice, so I warn a single parent that I will be saying it for the child's future benefit, and hers. Discipline can also be hard for a parent alone. When the child teases incessantly, a whole day can feel like one long struggle. In the second, difficult year, she will need to offer firm limits and may need my support to do so. I urge her to surround herself with any family members who are nearby. If she has no extended family close by, I suggest that she find a support group of other single parents who can offer each other emotional backup for day-to-day crises.

Families in which both parents work full-time outside the home also deserve special attention at a prenatal visit. I want the mother and father to know that I'll stand up for them as they seek what they, as parents, need from the workplace. I also want to be sure they've planned for the supports they'll need to do the best job they can for this baby. As mentioned earlier, I will try to help them work out breast-feeding, if they decide to do that. I'll want to find out if one or both parents will be able to stay at home long enough to give the baby a good start. Are there grandparents nearby who can help in a crisis? What are the pressures of their jobs, and how will they share the baby's care? Are they aware of the importance of the first few months as a time for adjusting to a changed way of life, for the mother to recover from any postpartum letdown or depression, for them both to accept the deepening responsibility to their new family? Have they looked for the quality child care they'll need when they both must return to work? In many communities it has become necessary to reserve a spot before the baby is even born.

Learning about a new baby—her individuality and remarkable responsiveness—will take time and energy. As the family's advocate, I will be encouraging the parents to immerse themselves in adjusting to this initial period. Their own development as nurturing adults is as critical to the baby's future as is their adjustment to the baby's need for them. Parents today who need to maintain their jobs in the workplace need to plan. I want them to fight to stay home with a new baby for the first precious months. While I don't see myself as directing their decisions, they may need my help in laying out priorities for care and determining the times when the baby will need them most. We know now that the first three to four months are a critical time. Can they free up this time? Can they save up to afford it? Will the price at the workplace be too great? They need to face this decision *now.* I wish that more employers in our country would value parents' commitment to nurturing their families at this critical time.

Parents-to-be find it hard to face the issues, often because of the pain of separation which they can experience ahead of time. We need to face that pain together so they can be free in this period to invest their energy in learning to attach to the fetus and baby-to-be. In my experience, helping parents recognize their ambivalence and their tendency to deny the future pain of separation makes these issues more manageable when the time comes.

While it may seem almost magical that parents and a doctor can form a close relationship in such a short time, they can. The parents' hunger to understand what is ahead creates an openness about themselves that cuts across the usual barriers. Their hunger and vulnerability, the results of a tumultuous inner transition, make possible a wonderful burst in their adult development. This giant step toward their own maturity is the main focus of this first touchpoint between parents and their baby's physician or nurse practitioner.

Drug Exposure and Prenatal Deprivation

Today, parents are very aware of the dangers to the fetus of tobacco, alcohol, drugs, many medications (even over-the-counter ones), infection, and poor nutrition. During our first visit I try to learn as much as possible about any exposures, so that I can guarantee the parents that I will evaluate the baby with these in mind. I also can promise to share any concerns with them from the very first exam. When parents are able to share their concerns, I can usually allay them right away or at birth. At least we can address them together. The now widespread knowledge of the risk to the developing fetus of tobacco, alcohol, and drugs raises deep concern among many pregnant women and fathers-to-be. Some couples may have exposed the fetus to one of these before they were aware of the pregnancy. Then, they are bound to worry that the critical early stages of fetal development may have been disrupted. Fortunately, when they occur very early, the most severe exposures will usually result in spontaneous abortion. Parents-to-be will be reassured to learn that they can still make a big difference in their baby's health, especially in the second and third trimesters, by avoiding these substances.

Heavy exposure before birth to alcohol, tobacco, or narcotic drugs can cause a number of problems. Exposure to some substances can interfere with fetal brain development. A smaller brain can result. Poor nutrition adds to the developing fetus's vulnerability to these insults. Though the newborn brain has remarkable capacity to recover, long-term effects on brain function may result.

At birth, babies exposed in utero to an addictive substance may go into withdrawal. They may at first be slow to respond to stimuli, unreachable, and struggle to maintain a sleep state. When such babies do respond, they may shoot to an equally unreachable crying, thrashing state. They can be so volatile that they appear to have no state in which they can take in information from the environment, digest it, and respond appropriately. They are not only unrewarding to their already stressed mothers, but they give back only negative or disorganized responses. They can be extremely difficult to feed and to settle for sleep. Parents of such babies need all the help they can get in caring for these very challenging babies. Later, these children may need extra help to develop their capacity for attention and learning. This, we have learned from many studies, may also be true for some other fragile babies—for example, those who are undernourished in the uterus due to a compromised placenta.

If we can identify babies affected by intrauterine deprivation or toxin exposure, we can institute a program of early intervention. The long-term follow-up studies done so far suggest that a nurturing environment sensitive to the easily overloaded nervous systems of these babies can often bring about amazing recoveries. But we need to start intervention as early as possible.

If I can establish a trusting relationship with parents-to-be in this first visit, they are much more likely to share any such health concerns, exposures, or untoward events with me. We can discuss their fears of having damaged the baby. For withdrawal from an addiction, we can institute a program that will help protect the baby.

Parents deserve to know about any variation in behavior that could make parenting their new baby more difficult. I do not believe in protecting them from such observations; they know anyway. I feel that the rehearsal for an impaired baby that all expectant parents go through in fantasy helps prepare them for any problem they will encounter in their baby. When I meet parents during pregnancy, my role is to encourage this sort of preparation and to explain as fully as possible what I will watch for in the baby.

The Developing Fetus

One of my major goals with expectant parents is to begin to establish the notion of the individuality of each baby and that baby's behavior. To do this, I press parents to talk more about how they experience the fetus as a person. "Have you a picture of this baby as a person in your mind?" Mothers who have noticed the fetus's behavior will wonder whether, if a fetus is active, it means an active baby, or if quiet, a quiet one.

There is some correlation between fetal activity and the baby's behavior. The way a fetus responds to stimuli may be significant. Some startle more easily than others. Many parents report that the fetus gets very active when they go to bed at night. There does seem to be an inverse relationship: When the mother is active, a fetus is likely to be quiet. The baby's activity increases when she quiets down. Already, the fetus is learning to cycle between sleep and active states (see chapter 2). This tuning in to cycles of rest and activity is a preparation for the rhythms a baby will follow later. A fetus has short cycles of rest and activity. The mother's own cycles of activity and sleep are already entraining the fetus to longer cycles of rest and responsiveness. This entrainment is reflected at birth in the baby's cycles.

Mothers-to-be have long believed that they are influencing the unborn baby by what they do and how they do it. This can lead to concerns. "If I'm tense, will I have an anxious baby?" While I can't answer that question, I point out that nearly all pregnant women experience some tension and anxiety.

Severe or prolonged stress may lead to certain hormonal changes in mothers (for example, increased cortisol levels) that can be transmitted through the placenta. Some studies have correlated these levels (secondary to depression or anxiety) with increased risk of premature birth. Poorer performance on tests of newborn behavior may also result. However, fetuses may adapt to tension in the uterine environment and may even learn to deal with these stresses by becoming quiet and controlled, or more and more active. The main job for a mother will be to adjust to whatever kind of baby she gets.

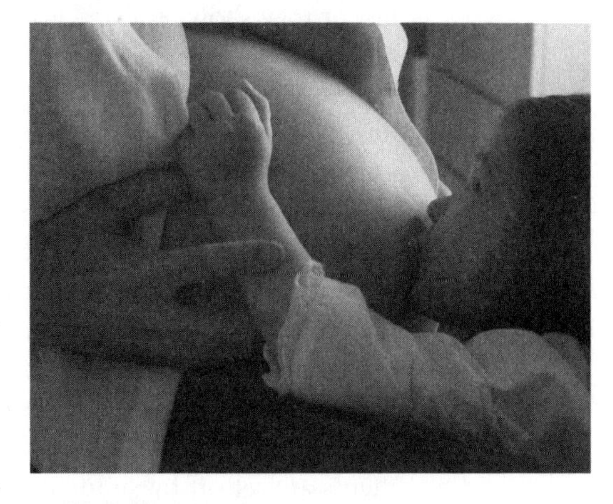

Parents work in the last trimester of pregnancy to understand their baby-to-be. They pay conscious and unconscious attention to the movements and the behavior of the fetus. Parents today realize that the fetus can hear and does respond to stimuli around the mother. Many fathers talk to and sing to their baby in the last three months of the pregnancy in an effort to get close to her before delivery. Some parents say their newborns recognize the cell-phone ring they heard over and over before birth! One mother who is a pianist told me, "I knew my baby could hear because she seemed to dance in rhythm with my music. What I didn't realize was that she was learning from it as well. I practiced a particular phrase in a Chopin waltz over and over the last few months of pregnancy. She always seemed quiet in the uterus when I played it. For some time, after she was delivered, I had no chance to play. When she was three months old, she was lying in her playpen by the side of my piano. I started practicing again. As I played through the waltz, she was playing on her back, looking at her mobile. When I got to that particular phrase, she stopped playing, and turned to me, looking surprised, as if 'There it is again!' I know she recognized it and remembered it. I was amazed. Now, I hope she'll be a musician."

The behavior of a fetus is complex and predictably rich in responses. But when the fetus is stressed by malnutrition, toxins, or a poor placenta, its behavior will reflect this by becoming restricted. Such a fetus will not show the same complex responses to auditory, visual, and kinesthetic (movement, positional changes) cues that a healthy fetus does. We have known for some time that the nature of the fetus's movements can help to diagnose stress. For example, when there is too much activity, or if the fetus is not responsive to the mother's movements or moves too little, with no response to external stimuli, one needs to worry. These aberrations should be reported to the obstetrician for assessment of the fetus's well-being.

A fetus's heart rate can be measured and assessed for signs of stress. If the fetus is stressed by too little oxygen, the heart rate will become too slow or too fast or may show repeated gradual slowings. An obstetrician can tell by signs like these whether the parents-to-be need to worry. If these stresses are judged to be endangering the fetus toward the end of pregnancy, the baby can be delivered prematurely and cared for as it continues to develop outside the uterus. As we learn more, we hope that parents can be alerted to some of the danger signs and become even better observers of the fetus's well-being. Fetal movements after a stress, such as a loud noise or a bright light, give us a window into the fetus's capacity to respond. But no fetal behavioral assessment scale has yet been perfected and tested, though an important ominous observation occurs when the fetus does not move even in response to stimulation. A mother-to-be can become aware of her fetus's alert and sleep states and how they cycle through the day and night. In an alert state, fetal movements are set off by sudden changes in light or noise and they may even be smoother. In sleep, any jerky movements are random and not necessarily related to outside stimuli.

When there is a concern in the third trimester that the fetus is too still, an expectant mother may be taught by her obstetrician or mid-wife to perform "kick counts" to keep track of fetal movements. Sometimes fetal non-stress tests (NSTs) and even contraction-stress tests (CSTs) are performed at 32 weeks or later to be sure that a less active fetus is continuing to grow and thrive in the uterus.

We have been slow in recognizing the amazing complexity of the fetus, just as we were previously slow in respecting the newborn's amazing capacities. Several researchers in France and the United States have studied the fetus's capacity for learning, in particular from auditory messages. Anthony De Casper, at the University of North Carolina, has shown that fetuses store complex songs and stories when they are repeated in the last three months of pregnancy. As the musical mother in my practice observed, after delivery babies recognize familiar sounds and respond with increased attention to them. Babies apparently do have memory for this prenatal learning.

Certain kinds of learning seem to occur in the uterus. In our research at Children's Hospital in Boston, we visualized fetuses with ultrasound machines. We found we could tell when they were asleep or awake. We could also identify at least the following four states of consciousness (see chapter 2 for such states in the newborn).

In *deep sleep* the fetus is predominantly quiet. If there are any movements, they are in the form of discrete jerks. In this state the fetus is unresponsive to most stimuli.During *light sleep,* or *REM (rapid eye movement) sleep,* movements are rare. When they occur, writhing or stretching movements predominate. These are smoother than deep-sleep movements and slightly organized. Still not very responsive to stimuli, the fetus can be roused, but with difficulty. Periodically, there are jerky movements—kick-kick-kick or bang-bang-bang of one arm—or respiratory efforts repeated in sequences of four to eight movements.

The *active alert* state is felt as the fetus climbs the uterine wall. If the fetus reacts to stimuli from the outside, the response will be that of quieting. Afterward, high activity will be resumed. This state occurs at predictable times during the day, usually when the mother is resting and is tired. The most common time for this state occurs at the end of the day. Parents know when it is coming and know what will change it—for instance, if they go out at night, the active period may be postponed until they get home.In the *quiet alert* state the fetus will be inactive, as if listening. Movements are smoother and more organized. In this state fetuses are especially responsive to outside stimuli. In our research we presented six- and seven-month-old fetuses in the quiet, alert state with various stimuli. Using a loud buzzer placed eighteen inches from the abdominal wall, we sounded a short buzz six to eight times. This caused a predictable set of reactions in the eight fetuses we studied. The first buzz caused the fetuses to jump. The second buzz resulted in less startling. By the fourth buzz, the fetuses had stopped startling and had become immobilized. A few had respiratory jerks of their abdomens, but no other response. By the fifth buzz they would often bring one hand up close to the mouth, sometimes to insert a thumb or finger. Then they would turn away from the buzzer to relax. No more responses. We thought these fetuses had adapted, or "habituated," to these negative stimuli.

Next, we shook a rattle next to each mother's abdomen. We thought the uterus might be too noisy for the fetuses to hear it. But as soon as we rattled it, the fetuses would turn in the direction of the rattle, as if waiting for the next signal. As we continued with discrete rattles, the fetuses would continue to be quietly attentive. They were already showing the capacity to attend to appealing stimuli and to turn away from distressing ones.

We also tried a series of very strong light stimuli, flashed in each fetus's line of vision. We first determined which way each fetus was facing. The first few stimuli caused slow startles. Then, the babies would bring their hands up to their mouths and faces. They'd turn the head away from the stimulus and again, all movements would cease, as if they had habituated to the strong light and gone into a sleep state. Then, using a pinpoint light on another part of the mother's abdominal wall over the uterus, we noted that the fetus moved slowly to turn in the direction of the pinpoint light, as if focusing on the spot where the light stimulus came through. Once again, the fetuses seemed to be protecting themselves from intense stimuli and to attend to more subtle ones.

When one fetus became active and seemed upset, my colleague Dr. Barry Lester placed both hands on the mother's abdomen. He started rocking the fetus, which calmed it down. At this point, the mother expressed the thoughts of all of us: "I didn't know babies were so smart so early!"

When I quote this research to parents-to-be, they begin to tell me stories of how they'd noted this already. When I confirm their observations, they give them more attention and credence. As one mother said to me, "When I went to a Bach concert, she danced in rhythm with the music. When I went to a rock concert, she danced entirely differently. She got wild. *I* knew she could hear already. It has just taken you researchers a long time to catch up with what parents have known all along."

With improving ultrasound technology, parents-to-be are getting increasingly revealing glimpses of their baby well before birth. What had once been a primarily medical procedure has become a highly personal window into a family's future. Though the baby still remains largely unknown, the mystery and dreaming have given way to early familiarity. Before a child is even born, some parents find themselves saying, "I think she has my chin," or "Last time we saw her, she was all curled up and sucking her thumb!" Family photo albums now often include ultrasound images of the new baby before she is born!

A New Alliance

Once the expectant couple and I feel close enough to each other, I ask more about pertinent medical history. As they tell me about diseases or congenital defects in the family, we know we are sharing fears that are bound to surface. If there is a problem in any part of her family, any caring pregnant woman will fear a replication in her baby. If a father has a parent or relative with heart disease or a chronic disease, he is bound to wonder whether this will be a tendency in his baby. Irrational fears can erupt in the middle of the night. If parents tell me of these, I can become part of the defense system they use to cope with fears. If I am aware of the pertinent family history and the parents' anxiety, I can address these openly when I examine the new baby in their presence later on.

When we have discussed the hopes and fears common to all caring parents-to-be, and when I have established my role as that of a concerned participant, we have established an important initial relationship. I want new parents to know ahead of time when and how I can be reached for routine calls, for emergencies, and of course for news of the baby's birth. Ideally, a pediatrician will want to be notified as soon as possible in order to examine the newborn in the first twenty-four hours and to share the baby's behavior with both new parents before they leave the hospital. Parents should ask how to reach the doctor after hours or on weekends, or someone else if he or she is unavailable. They'll want to know if their pediatrician reserves a portion of each day to squeeze in urgent office visits for symptoms that shouldn't be put off. Many pediatricians set up "call hours" at the beginning or end of each day for parents to phone in with their urgent questions. After they return home from the hospital, the calls parents make at my routine call-in hour every morning, as well as their first visit to my office at two to three weeks, will give me a chance to participate actively in their adjustment to the new baby. Often, for example, I can help a mother when she needs help with breastfeeding, or when parents have difficulty with formula.

Ideally, the visit during pregnancy will leave parents and doctor with a feeling of trust and of intimacy for facing the next important touchpoint. While this first meeting need not take very long, it is one of the most valuable opportunities for any new family and their physician.

2. The Newborn Individual

THE SECOND TOUCHPOINT—THE NEXT TIME I HAVE A CHANCE TO PARTICIPATE in the growth of a new family—is the exciting moment when, together with the parents, I examine their baby soon after birth.

Evaluating a Newborn's Responses

Evaluation of a newborn has long been a routine part of pediatric care. The first physical assessment of the baby's color, breathing, heart rate, muscle tone, and activity, known as the Apgar score, is done moments after birth. This is an assessment of the newborn baby's ability to respond to the stresses of labor, delivery, and the new environment. As such it does not predict the baby's future well-being but reflects more what the baby has encountered during delivery. It involves the assignment of two points for each of the five items on the test if they are optimal, or one if they are okay, to produce a total score (with ten being the highest). To evaluate the baby more thoroughly, a physical and behavioral assessment is done within the first days by the pediatrician or other specialist in newborns on the staff of the hospital. At this time, the baby is evaluated for physical health and for his responsiveness to being fed and nurtured.

The Neonatal Behavioral Assessment Scale (NBAS), now used in hospitals worldwide, is designed to evaluate the kind of person the newborn is. It assesses the baby's behavioral repertoire as he responds to human and nonhuman stimuli. The way his states of consciousness (deep and light sleep, drowsy, alert, fussy, and crying states) affect his responses—and vice versa—reveals his ability to adjust to his new environment. With the help of a number of colleagues, I developed this scale to assess responses and reflexes in a twenty-minute interaction with the baby. Unlike other medical tests, our assessment treats the newborn as an active participant, and the score is based on his *best* (rather than average) performance. We have been refining the NBAS for more than thirty years and have been adapting it to evaluate premature and small-for-date babies as well as to reflect intrauterine influences on fetal development.

The most important use of the NBAS has been to share the baby's behavior with parents to sensitize them to the abilities and amazing variety of responses already present in their baby. Every parent worries, "Is my baby okay?" When we can elicit the baby's best performance, parents' anxieties can be addressed and usually dispelled. We have found in many studies that new family bonds can also deepen during this rich, though brief, encounter. A newborn's behavior seems designed to capture new parents. His tiny, strong grasp, the way he nuzzles deliciously into the angle of a neck and shoulder, and the way he looks into a parent's face with his searching eyes all reach out to a father or mother hungry to hold and learn to know him.

In the NBAS, I like to start with a sleeping baby so that I can test his ability to maintain a deep sleep state. I try to examine the baby in each of the six states of consciousness. As the baby moves from one state to another, I look for his ability to respond to stimuli, both alluring and repelling, in each state. The stimuli I use include a soft rattle, a bright light, a loud bell, a red ball, and the human voice and face.

The first step, while the newborn is still asleep, is to test his response to a light, and then to a rattle, and a bell, shone or sounded several times. The purpose of this is to measure his capacity to shut out disturbing stimuli. This tests his ability to habituate, that is, to decrease his level of responsiveness when intrusive stimuli are presented repeatedly. It helps me know whether this baby will be able to shut out unnecessary environmental stimulation. Some infants have a "raw" nervous system due to stress before or during birth. These hypersensitive infants cannot shut out stimuli and must respond over and over, mercilessly. They will need a very protected environment similar to those needed for premature infants.

The first stimulus is a bright flashlight shone for two seconds through the baby's closed lids. After his initial startle subsides, I shine the light a second, a third, and as much as a tenth time. The first few times, the baby will demonstrate responses by startling and moving his whole body; his arms and his legs will jump, but each time these movements should decrease. By the fourth light stimulus, there is usually little or no movement. His breathing becomes deep and regular again. His face softens. His whole body returns to relaxed sleep. The baby has habituated to the light. Next, I try a rattle about ten inches away from his ear. Again, he rouses with a startle, and his whole body may move. The second rattle might produce a second big startle and a whimper. But by the third or fourth rattle there is likely to be a diminished response with very little movement. Later, subsequent rattles cause only a flutter of his eyelids and a grimace that subsides. Soon, the baby is no longer responding and seems to be in quiet sleep with deep breathing again. If the bell is used last, in consecutive, one-second bursts, it may produce only a couple of responses initially; then the infant relaxes into a successful, deep sleep. He has proven his ability to maintain a sleep state even in a chaotic environment. A baby who can habituate in this way has built-in resources.

Premature or Stressed Babies

When babies are premature or have been stressed in the uterus, they cannot shut out repeated stimuli. They respond to each rattle, each bell, or each bright light. One can observe how costly this is for them. They will frown and their color may even change, for their heart rates and respiration speed up with each stimulus. They may make attempts to quiet themselves by arching away or by bringing a hand up to their mouths. If they can't manage the repetitious stimulation by going into sleep, they may have to build up to a crying, thrashing state. Crying also can serve to shut out stimulation, but it, too, can be costly for a fragile baby (see also "Prematurity").

When I find a baby who has real difficulty in shutting out stimuli, I let the parents know and plan to follow him for a period to watch for evidence of his resiliency. If he becomes more proficient over time, the problem may have been due to a stress at delivery, which many babies undergo, or perhaps to the effects of medication or anesthetic given to his mother at delivery. If the hyper-reactivity persists, I worry about whether he will have a difficult time later, overreacting as he tries to assimilate information from the environment. The ability to shut out unimportant stimuli is necessary for all of us in order to focus on the particular information that matters to us. Increased activity can become one way a baby discharges the overwhelming overload of too many incoming stimuli.

Parents of a hypersensitive baby can help him develop an effective threshold for screening out unimportant information. They can cut down on stimuli; for example, they can arrange a quiet room at home, with subdued light, and use low-pitched, soft voices or reduce the visual or tactile stimuli, especially at feeding times or when they want to play with him. We have even found that some babies can tolerate being looked at *or* touched *or* picked up —but only one of these at a time. Once the baby subsides, another modality can be added. Gradually, all of them can be put together at once, but in a low-keyed way and with respect for the baby's easily overloaded nervous system. A baby's behavior will show when he feels bombarded. With patience, parents of a hyper-reactive baby can teach him how to take in and manage information in short bursts and how to manage by taking time out. Knowing of their baby's needs early will help them respond appropriately to that baby. Over time, he'll get better and better at managing for himself.

After this part of the testing is complete, I begin to undress the baby gently, observing his reactions to being handled. I want to observe and score how long he takes to go from sleeping to rousing. As he rouses, I will assess and record his pattern of coming to a semi-alert state and then to fussy and wide-awake states. The way a baby moves from one state to another is likely to be a predictor of his style or temperament. A baby who moves slowly from one to another, and who can hold on to an alert or a sleep state, is already demonstrating a marvelous capacity to manage his world. If he moves rapidly, shooting between states, unable to stay in any one, he will need a patient parent's quiet help to learn to develop his own controls. It will take time—a year or more. A pediatrician can help such parents chart the baby's progress and can support them in their demanding job. Holding and carrying him, swaddling him, or encouraging thumb sucking or use of a pacifier may help him learn to master these transitions from one state to another.

A baby who cannot control state transitions is at the mercy of a raw, immature nervous system. Some easily irritable newborns are recovering from maternal medication. As noted in chapter 1, women who smoke, drink alcohol, or expose their babies to narcotics in pregnancy may have babies who are irritable and either hypo- or hypersensitive as they recover from the effects of these drugs. With narcotics, they may also experience a period of withdrawal. Babies whose mothers have had to use medication at delivery can be quiet for the first several days but then react with irritability after that. This period of irritability is likely to be short-lived, and it won't really reflect the baby's future personality. To help him, a parent can provide a quiet environment, protecting him from bright lights, loud noises, and unnecessary handling. While an irritable baby can be trying for new parents, they needn't blame themselves. Instead, if parents can recognize this as the temporary result of the baby's immature, oversensitive nervous system, they can help him gradually learn ways to calm himself.

Once the baby is undressed, I can assess his state of nutrition and hydration. I look for good skin color and an ample fat reserve underneath his soft, slightly fuzzy skin. A baby who has been stressed in the uterus may have wrinkled, peeling skin and a worried expression. He will look like a weary, little old man, as if his time in the uterus had begun to tire him. Once he's rehydrated and fed after delivery, he will gain weight and lay down fat, his skin will improve, and his drawn face will fill out to look pudgy, babyish, and beautiful.

Checking a Newborn's Reflexes

Now that the baby has been awakened, I can test his reflexes and all of his waking responses. As the baby lies in front of me undressed, I watch for smooth movements of his arms and legs. I watch to see whether he can maintain good skin color even though he's unprotected. At the end of each stretching movement, he may have a short period of jitteriness of both legs, and his arms may come together in a startle. I stroke his feet to produce reflexes. When I stroke his inner sole, he grasps my finger with his toes. When I stroke the outer side of his sole, he spreads his toes out in a *Babinski reflex.* I test him for active knee jerks and for firm muscle tone of his legs and arms.

Given a forefinger to grasp in each hand, a newborn can be pulled up slowly to sit. As he comes up, his head will lag, but he will use his neck and shoulder muscles to try to bring his head up to the midline. When he is sitting, his eyes pop open like a doll's, and he may even begin to look around. Parents will gasp with admiration. If a newborn's head continues to hang backward and he is unable to right it, I check further into his muscle tone. I know from the reflexes that I've tested whether the baby's muscles are intact and strong. But his shoulder girdle's response as he is pulled to a sitting position tells me how responsive he will be to being handled by his parents.

To elicit the *walking reflex,* I lean the baby's body forward across one hand, planting his feet firmly on the bed. He will begin to step first with one foot, then with the other, in a kind of slow jog. Not only is this great fun to watch,

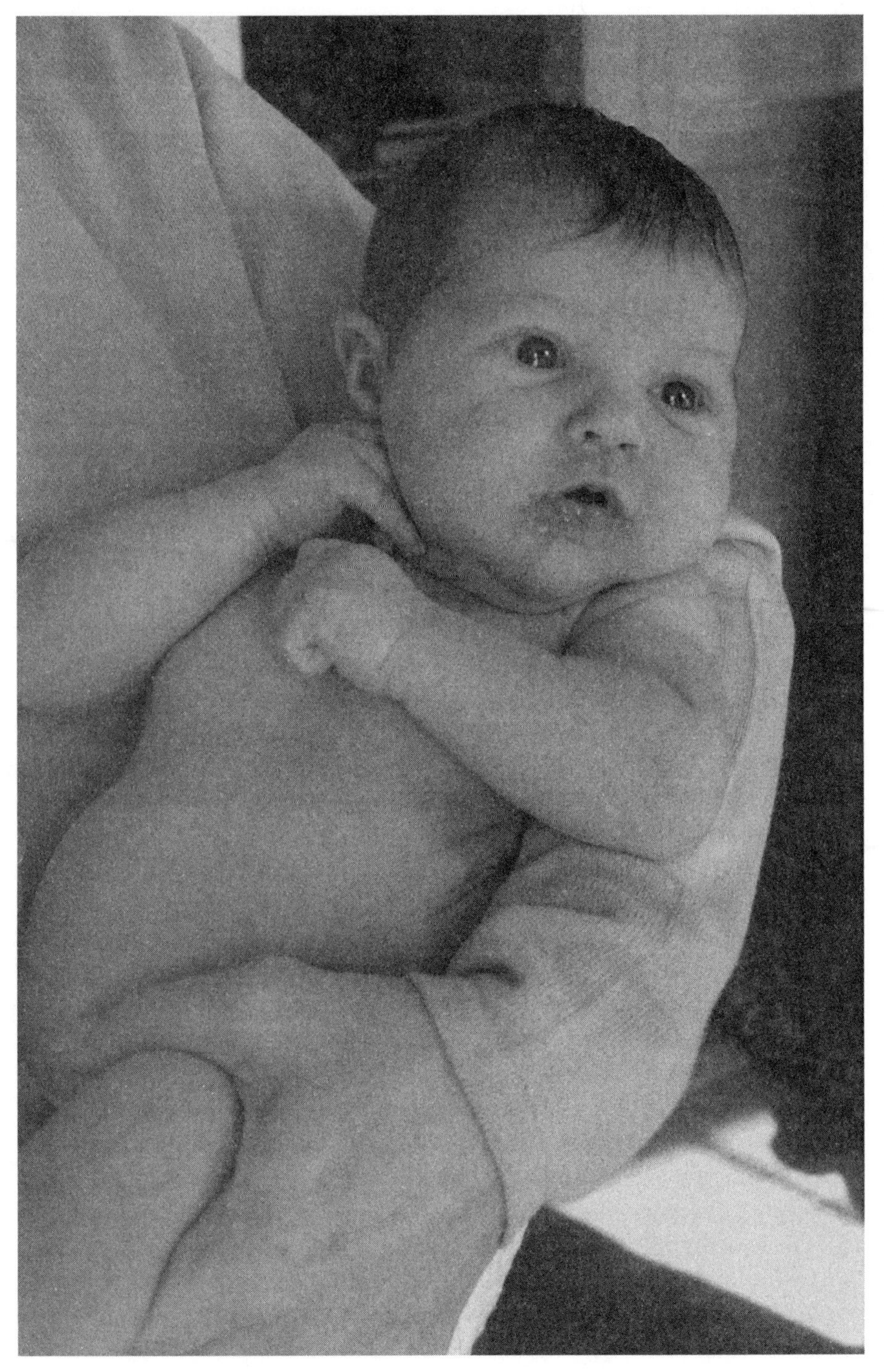

The baby's whole face brightens and his whole body participates in this state of attention.

but it offers parents a sense of the potential for the future, compressed into this perfect little being. Nothing I as a caregiver can say will be as convincing to parents as this powerful, wordless repertoire.

A baby who has had a brain hemorrhage or an episode of too little oxygen at birth may not be able to produce all of these responses. So it is a relief when parents can see them all performed. If a baby is delayed or weak, or *too* active, I will need to examine the baby a few days later to be sure that they are improving over time. If the reflexes appear more normal by then, I won't worry. Many infants perform sluggishly in the period after birth as they recover from the usual stresses of labor and delivery. If the delays persist, we must look for a reason, such as a depressed nervous system, for which there can be help. But I want to start early. Now we know that early intervention for a disorganized or impaired baby can make a significant difference in how much he recovers. From the earliest age, he can learn either patterns of success in overcoming difficulties or patterns of failure, which will add to his problems. Parents who worry about their child's development should pursue an assessment and join into an early intervention program. This not only helps the baby develop his best potential but also offer worried parents the support and understanding that will encourage their participation in his recovery.

When I lay the baby down on his back again, he will begin to squirm and to startle. A baby on his belly can settle himself by nestling into the bedclothes. On his back, he's at the mercy of startling and flailing legs and arms. While he's in this position, I can test for the important *protective reflexes.* If I place a soft cloth over his eyes and nose, holding it gently by my fingers on each side of his nose, he will thrash. Though his airway is not obstructed, he will arch his head, turning it from side to side to throw off the cloth. He will bring one hand, then the other, up to his head, swiping across his face to push off the cloth and keep his airway clear. Babies are not likely to smother unless bedclothes are pulled over their face and airways. Only a sick infant will not resist having face and nose covered. Nevertheless, babies' breathing while asleep should be protected by keeping loose bedclothes and pillows out of their cribs and using firm mattresses. Also, the American Academy of Pediatrics recommends that babies be placed on their backs for sleeping. This is because of the very uncommon risk of sudden infant death syndrome (SIDS), which appears to happen more often when infants sleep on their stomachs. SIDS, however, is still not yet fully understood.

The head arching and the hands coming up to push off the cloth are both examples of an intact nervous system in a full-term baby. As we pointed out, if the baby is too sedated by maternal medication, or if he is premature, all of his motor patterns will be markedly diminished. If he has had brain damage, his motor activity will be disorganized, and his ineffective attempts to perform all these behaviors become clues to the fact that he's in trouble. We must go to work to help him recover!

The *rooting reflex* appears if you touch a newborn on either side of his mouth. He will turn in the direction of the touch, searching for the "breast" with his mouth. When you give a newborn your finger to suck on, you can tell a lot about his *sucking* coordination. You can feel at least three different kinds of milking reactions. The front of his tongue laps on the part of your finger nearest his mouth. The back of his tongue begins to massage the middle of your finger. Finally, he will begin to pull on the tip of your finger with his esophagus. All three mechanisms quickly become coordinated in a healthy, alert newborn baby. If he is immature, they are slow to do so. Nurses know that such a baby may not be ready to suck on a bottle, so they must feed him with a tube. As he matures, these three necessary sucking reflexes start to pull together and he is able to suck on the breast or bottle.

A sleepy baby may not be able to coordinate his sucking and will need to be roused before he gets started. After a parent awakens him, the baby will need to be soothed into a calm and focused state. Simply looking into his eyes, or speaking softly and steadily to him as he lies in his mother's arms, may be enough. His chin against his mother's breast, and his nose pointing toward her nipple, give him important cues. He's likely to reach above the nipple with his upper lip all by himself, leading to a comfortable latch-on: His gums should always make contact with the areola, not the nipple itself, to avoid injuring it. He should be able to breathe, and swallow, without causing his mother pain. If she is in pain, or he is not getting any milk, she can try adjusting his position with the slightest tug on his chain. If it hurts a lot, she should insert a finger into the corner of his mouth to release his grip *before* pulling him to one side to try again. Both baby and mother often need a little practice before getting the latch-on position right.

If he's too drowsy in the first days to get started on his own, a parent can first stroke around his mouth and then give him a finger to suck on. After jiggling it in his mouth gently to elicit all these responses and then feeling them becoming coordinated, the parent or nurse will know he is ready to go to the breast. If that doesn't work, I have found that it can be helpful for the mother to flatten the areola so the nipple protrudes between her two fingers; it will then go into the *back* of his throat to set off an effective sucking mechanism.

Lactation consultants have many other helpful approaches. The most potent sucking reflex is at the back of the tongue. When all three reflexes begin to pull together, the mother's milk will let down and the process is on its way. After a few helping efforts, the baby will learn how to do it for himself. Also, this will ensure that the baby's mouth will press on the mother's areola rather than on the nipple itself. This will be less likely to cause a cracked nipple and interfere with successful breast-feeding. One of my colleagues, pediatrician Constance Keefer, suggests these steps for successful breast-feeding:

Place the baby in a reclining position, parallel to the ground, and belly to belly with the mother. Bring the baby gently to the nipple, facing it. Wait for an alert state, and stroke his cheeks gently, using the reflex response that results to get him to open his mouth as wide as possible. Gently help him get as much of the areola as possible into his wide-open mouth. When his lips are wide and tucked in (like a fish mouth) he is ready to start sucking.

When I turn a newborn's head to one side, he produces a *tonic neck reflex*—a fencing-like response in which the baby's body arches away from the face; the arm toward which the face is turned stretches out, and the other arm flexes up by his head. Flexion on one side of his body and extension on the other may help him lateralize his movements in the future, that is, make them one-sided instead of symmetrical. Interestingly enough, reflexes are useful in labor. As the baby turns his head in response to contractions, he sets off a series of writhing reflexes, which contribute to delivery by stimulating the mother's uterus. Later in infancy, this same reflex will help him use one arm to reach for a toy and to suppress the other arm. The development of a dominant side for coordinated activity is helped by the underlying tonic neck reflex.

Another of my "toys" in this assessment is a shiny red ball about two inches in diameter. When I hold it about twelve to fifteen inches in front of an alert newborn's eyes, he will fix on it slowly and follow it back and forth and sometimes even upward for as much as a thirty-degree angle. He follows it with jerky movements of his eyes, his head turning slowly from side to side. This tells me that he not only can see but also can maintain an alert state for himself and respond with appropriate motor activity. His whole face brightens and his whole body participates in this state of attention to the visual stimulus. Vision is already important to him.

If I then present my face at the same distance, his face will become alert and mobile. He can follow my face back and forth. The newborn follows the human face differently from a nonhuman stimulus. Not only is he likely to be more intensely involved with the face, but his own face becomes active, too.

With a red ball or the rattle, his expression will be static and "hooked." With a human face, his mouth and his own upper face will wrinkle and move slowly, as if in imitation. In such an alert state, some babies will indeed imitate what they see. They will even open their mouths to stick out their tongues when you put yours out. This has been documented by several researchers, especially Andrew Meltzoff at the University of Washington in Seattle. He sees this as a first sign of the way the baby's behavior can be shaped by the important people around him.

If I talk gently, the newborn's interest in my face will increase. Some babies can follow me smoothly backward and forward, up and down, for several excursions before losing interest. As the baby watches me, his mouth and face move in rhythm with my voice. By this point in the assessment, if he is responding and even sticking out his tongue, most parents are ecstatic. The newborn's many skills, and especially his clear preference for human faces and voices, fill them with anticipation.

There is an important mutuality here. Parents seem to have an expectation for the kinds of behavior with which a newborn is equipped. When the baby's skills and ways of communicating are confirmed, parents gain more confidence in their own ability to understand and care for their infant. Our studies have shown that after such a shared assessment, the mother and the father are significantly more sensitive to their own baby's behavioral cues at one month, and they remain more responsive throughout the first year.

Sooner or later during this examination, of course, a baby is likely to become upset. At first, it may be just a whimper, but when he is left undressed and not held, his activity will begin to increase. As he moves, he begins to startle. These startles, or *Moro reflexes,* consist of his throwing out his arms, arching his back, grimacing, and then crying out. When there is nothing to grab, or no one to hold the baby, each startle sets off more startles. Soon, the baby will be very upset, with constant flailing activity and a persistent, demanding cry. When parents watch this, they can hardly contain themselves. They feel a great urge to help him, as do I. At this point, I explain that I want to see what it takes to help him contain himself. I like to know him when he cries as well as I know him when he's quiet. In this way, the parents and I can learn to help calm him when he needs it.

The baby may try to turn his head to one side to get his thumb up to his mouth, suck on it, and quiet himself. If I talk firmly and soothingly in one ear, he may stop the frantic thrashing to listen briefly. Then he may begin to cry again, but less insistently. I hold both hands on his chest to contain the startling movements. This time, as I talk to him, he is more likely to quiet

himself. His body will soften and he may bring his hand up to his face, turn his head slightly, perhaps insert one finger in his mouth, and attend to my voice, his face alert.

If he doesn't quiet to my voice and my containment, I pick him up to hold and rock him. If that doesn't work, I might give him his finger or a pacifier to suck on. At each step, we learn how this particular baby can be consoled and how much he will contribute to consoling himself.

A baby who can't get himself under control or can't use help in controlling himself will be difficult for his parents. A baby who is irritable and easily upset may need to be swaddled (with hands free and close to his mouth so that he can learn to suck them), carried, or rocked. These maneuvers help contain his startles, which would throw him into an anguished state otherwise. When he is contained, he can pay attention and can learn to calm himself over time. Meanwhile, he will need to be handled with a smooth, gentle approach.

There are other reflexes that are exciting to see and to understand in an infant. For example, when you stroke a newborn's cheek or put your finger in his palm, he will bring his fist up to his mouth and try to insert his finger. This is the *Babkin,* or *hand-to-mouth, reflex* that serves him later to suck on his fist or fingers. If you stroke along the side of the newborn's spine while he is held under his belly over your hand, he flexes his whole body to the side that is stroked; when you switch to the other side, he flexes to that—a swimming reflex results. We've inherited this reflex, known as the *Gallant response,* from our amphibian ancestors. It too may help him squirm his way through the birth canal. In the *crawling reflex,* when the newborn is placed on his abdomen he flexes his legs under him and starts to crawl, picking his head up to turn it and to free it from the bedclothes. He is likely to bring his hand up to his mouth to suck on it and to settle down in a cozy position.

Learning Your Baby's Style

As I share a newborn's responses to the rattle, the bell, the red ball, and various kinds of handling with his parents, I describe the states of consciousness we are seeing and what they represent in terms of the baby's internal organization. We look for clues to his style of managing this new world. Parents who can understand the cycle of six states that we mentioned earlier (deep and light sleep, drowsy, alert, fussy, and crying states) as the baby's way of controlling his internal and external world are already able to understand their baby. The cycling of these states over a twenty-four-hour period becomes a window into the predictable behaviors that parents will encounter as they take care of the baby. Understanding the way a newborn actually manages his own environment gives caregivers and parents respect for his competence.

A major goal for sharing all these responses and reflexes is to identify the individual strengths and vulnerabilities of a newborn that parents will need to understand, and even possible early clues to his particular temperament. Babies have widely differing styles of handling responses to stimuli around them, in their need for sleep, and in their crying. They differ in how they can be soothed as well as in their responses to hunger and discomfort, to exposure to temperature changes, to handling, and to interaction with caregivers. The task for parents is not to compare these characteristics with some other baby's, but to watch and listen for their own baby's particular style. As we saw in the last chapter, the parents may have had a preview of this style before birth.

One part of the outside world that the baby has already experienced is the sound of his parents' voices. With a quiet, alert baby, we can test this during the hospital visit. I hold the baby up with his head in one of my hands, his buttocks in another, while he is looking at the ceiling. When I talk gently to him, he turns to my voice and searches to find the source. When he finds my face and mouth, he brightens. Then I get his mother to stand on his other side and to compete with me, talking to him gently. Any baby will choose the female voice, turn to her, find her face, and brighten. Each time I do this, the new mother will reach for her baby to cuddle him closely and talk to him: "You know me and my voice, don't you?" she might say. This predictable but powerful newborn response helps to cement their relationship.

When fathers are present, I try the same procedure with them. In most cases (80 percent) the baby will turn to his father's voice instead of mine. If he doesn't turn toward his father's voice, I tip his head. My interest is not in "testing" the newborn at this point, but in strengthening the father's tie to him. The father will then do just what the mother did—reach out for his new baby, exclaiming, "You know me *already*!" as if it were a miracle.

Adults who are trying to get a baby's attention automatically pitch their voices at a higher level. Babies are probably conditioned in the uterus to the female pitch of their mother's voice and are more responsive in that high-pitched range. In every sensory modality, the baby will have a preferred range. When you stroke a baby slowly and gently, you soothe him. When you pat him rapidly, in a staccato way, he alerts or startles. The same goes for visual responses. If you move slowly, he can follow your face. If the movement is too abrupt or the stimulus is more than eighteen inches away, he can only stare, not adjust or focus.

Many parents do not need these explanations to help them understand the wonderful complexity of their newborn. Nevertheless, sharing the first assessment of their baby with a professional gives them an opportunity to ask questions and to unload concerns they may have. As I examine the newborn's behavior with parents, my goal is therefore twofold. One goal is to alert them to the astounding array of abilities with which the newborn is equipped. I know that they will observe his behavior with new eyes and experience each response as his language for communication with them. This prepares them for our future work together in monitoring and nurturing his development. The second goal is to alert them to my interest in their reactions and interpretations of their baby. If they can accept me as an active observer and participant in their development together, their need for defenses with me is likely to be diminished. In future visits, they will want to tell me about his development. Through this brief viewing of the newborn as he takes in, shuts out, and starts to master his world, we find a shared language, a true touchpoint of opportunity for our future relationship. Later, parents will call me or visit me, saying, "You remember what you showed me that day? Well, now he's doing this! I knew you'd be interested."

A mother I hadn't seen for thirty years once stood up in an audience of 1,500 parents to tell me that I'd seen and played with her baby and she'd never forgotten it. She went on to tell me that I'd made a prediction when he was only two days old. Because he was so feisty, I'd predicted that he would definitely be negative in the second year—and (surprise!) he *had been.* After all those years, she still remembered that someone had joined her in her job of understanding her new baby.

3. Newborn Parents

The newborn baby is not the only one facing a new world; her mother's and father's lives have also changed. These days, doctors and nurses have finally learned that parents need as much care, as much "mothering," as their baby. A new mother and father have made one of the greatest adjustments anyone can make: taking on a mysterious new charge who will be their full responsibility for the next eighteen or so years. As the renowned pediatrician and psychoanalyst D. W. Winnicott wrote: "So here you are with all your eggs in one basket. What are you going to do about it? Enjoy letting other people look after the world while you are producing a new one of its members. Enjoy being turned-in and almost in love with yourself, the baby is so nearly a part of you."

Along with this delight will be a natural anxiety. All parents who care deeply will be anxious. Anxiety serves a vital purpose: calling up energy to help parents meet new responsibility. Anxiety can open them up to the baby and to others who can help them.

If anxiety is overwhelming, however, it can make it harder for new parents to get to know their baby or lead to depression. A depressed new parent is no longer available to respond to the many cues the baby offers. Nearly all new mothers feel "blue" in the first few days after the birth. They have labored hard and have had to come down to earth after the initial euphoria. One of the roles of a supportive professional is to differentiate between this natural letdown and a more deep-seated one. The former can allow the new mother to slow down and recover physically from the stressful labor. It is common, normal, and adaptive. The latter, know as postpartum depression, affects roughly one in ten women and deserves treatment, and fortunately there are many effective ones. Some of the symptoms of postpartum depression—trouble sleeping, poor appetite or an exaggerated one, fatigue, and irritability—are easy to mistake for the expectable drain of the first few weeks after delivery. Feeling sad and discouraged most of the time, or worthless and no good for the baby, or brimming with anger at the baby, are more readily distinguished symptoms, and last, with the others, for two weeks or more. Family members may recognize the problem before the mother does. If you are concerned about this possibility, be sure to talk to your doctor as soon as you can, and ask for a referral to a mental health specialist familiar with this condition.

In the Japanese islands of the Goto Archipelago, where we once studied families for several years, a new mother is expected to stay in bed, wrapped in her quilt, for one month after delivery. Her baby is wrapped up next to her. For one month, grandmothers, aunts, and relatives come in to take care of her, feeding her and helping her to the bathroom. She is expected to do nothing but feed her baby and recover. While her relatives help her, they speak to her in a form of baby talk. In response, she answers them in a high-pitched voice. For one month, she is a child in their eyes. A postpartum recovery period is accepted and treated as normal in this culture. Perhaps the incidence of postpartum depression is lower as a result.

In the United States, in contrast, we expect a new mother to rise swiftly to the demands of her new job as a full-fledged parent. She is expected to "bond" in the delivery room, before she may have fully recovered herself. Instead she needs to be offered the choice—of keeping her baby with her right away, taking a short break to rest first, or holding her baby for the first few minutes and then having a chance to rest. Increasingly, the importance to fathers of early, close contact with their babies is being recognized, but they too need respect for their individual responses rather than pressure in these first precious moments.

Nowadays, a new mother is rarely kept in the hospital long enough even to recover physically. If she has had a cesarean section, she may have only four days of nurturing and recovery. For normal vaginal deliveries without complications, forty-eight hours often represents the outer limit of an admission's length. (In 1996 Congress responded to managed care pressure to shorten hospital stays for labor and delivery by signing into law the Newborns' and Mothers' Health Protection Act. This act prohibits insurance companies from restricting benefits for hospital stays to less than forty-eight hours for a vaginal delivery or less than ninety-six hours after birth by cesarean section. However, many families need more time than this simply to have baby's and mother's medical needs attended to, never mind to begin to adjust to this life-transforming event sufficiently to be ready for discharge.) Implicit in this early discharge is the message that a new mother should be ready to handle her own recovery and attachment to the new baby, whether she has support or not.

Since new parents can no longer always depend on an extended family and their own parents for help as earlier generations did, a father may be his wife's only support. (A single mother without family support may need to fall back on professional help—if it is available and she can afford it.) But a father has his own new adjustment to master. If he has taken his role seriously and is ready to back up the family adjustment to the new baby, a new father today can strive to be more deeply involved than fathers of previous generations. But, with this opportunity comes a heavy responsibility. Fathers who have had limited early nurturing from their own fathers, as is all too often the case, may be anxious and overwhelmed. A professional who recognizes this can be a major source of support. In my own work, I make an effort to "touch base" with each new father, both in the hospital and at home over the phone in the first week.

Bonding

The pediatricians Marshall Klaus and John Kennell were the first to describe the bonding that takes place between parents and newborn and to emphasize the importance of the first few days. They also pointed out how the needs of new parents were neglected in modern hospitals. As a way of enhancing the new parents' closeness to the baby, they recommended a period in the delivery room during which each parent could touch, hold, and communicate with the newborn. They recommended that the brand-new baby be placed skin-to-skin on the mother's chest and then allowed to suckle at her breast. The father was encouraged to hold and examine his new baby. Now fathers, too, are often invited to hold their new baby against their bare skin. Their research indicated that this could be a sensitive time both for channeling all the eagerness that parents had generated in pregnancy and for allowing them to become attached to the real baby. Later research from Drs. Klaus

and Kennell, and Phyllis Klaus, demonstrated that the presence of a *doula* (an encouraging woman who assists the mother throughout labor and at birth) can significantly reduce the length and complications of labor and delivery. Such continuous support helps the parents have the best possible birth experience and be ready to nurture and reach out to their infant (see Klaus, Kennell, and Klaus in *Further Reading*).

Certain childbirth educators, however, took the implications of the bonding research too literally. Some went so far as to place a sign on the closed door of the parents' hospital room: "Do not disturb—Bonding in process." This interpretation misses both the variety of approaches among individuals and cultures and the long-term nature of the bonding process. It also places a burden on parents that can unnecessarily make them feel that they've failed, before they've even begun. In my research in other parts of the world, I have found that women don't all want the new baby with them immediately. Some seek to recover their own energy for an interval after hard labor. Then, they are ready to receive the new baby. This makes me skeptical of any routine practice of giving the baby to the mother "to bond" right away. I like to give parents a choice, plus the chance to recover and feel eager and hungry to be with their new baby.

If parents are overwhelmed, it is important for a supportive person to be available to them as they get to know the baby. This should be on their own timing. The individual choices of each parent must be respected, if we want to make the best of the initial introduction to the new family member.

Instances in which the baby's condition demands that she be whisked away to the intensive care nursery, and in which there is no opportunity for the parents to greet the baby immediately, have demonstrated that attachment is a long-term process, not a single, magical moment. The opportunity for bonding at birth may be compared to falling in love—staying in love takes a long time and demands hard work. When the first greeting must be postponed, parents can still become fully attached to their baby. It is very important that expectant parents and those who assist them in childbirth know not only that each family has its own timetable but also that strong, long-term attachment is the goal.

Discovering the Real Baby

When I examine the newborn and share her behavior with her parents we get to know their baby together. I like to remind them of the baby they dreamed of and of their predictions during our prenatal visit. Since they are now trying to fit that image to the real baby, it serves us both to be reminded of the adjustment they are making. If, for instance, they've dreamt of a quiet, gentle baby and this one is vigorous, impulsive, and difficult to quiet, the new parents have a lot of work ahead. If they can be conscious of the adjustment, it is liable to be easier. Their feelings of disappointment can give way to the challenge of understanding this particular baby. If we discuss how they feel, they can see me as an ally.

"She has your nose." "He has my father's eyes." "Her voice sounds just like Aunt Hattie's when she's mad." Such comments represent attempts to make the baby into a familiar person and to identify the kind of person she will be. The psychiatrist Bertrand Cramer, in the book we wrote together, *The Earliest Relationship,* speaks of how the parents must reconcile the real baby with an imaginary one that represents important experiences from their own past. Their attempts to label or characterize her are part of the work of getting to know this stranger. Like theatrical directors, they cast the baby into many roles—"little empress," "whiner," "out to conquer the world," "angel," and so on—as they reach into their own family history in trying to understand her. If the baby is miscast, adjustment will be much harder and the parents may need help.

Examining the Baby

As parents examine their new baby, first gingerly, then inch by inch, every detail catches their attention. They often worry about the shape of her head, which may be a little pointed and lumpy. The head must mold for labor and delivery. It can become elongated and shrink in diameter as much as an inch. However, it will round itself out in two or three days. This doesn't hurt the brain. The only kind of lump that will last a bit longer is a big, soft, blood-filled swelling on one side or the other. This is called a cephalohematoma, and it will be reabsorbed in three to four months. Even this kind of swelling does not reflect an injury to the brain, which is cushioned. The soft spot in the top of the head, called the *fontanel,* allows the skull to mold for delivery. If the head gets a bang, the skull will give. It's an important protection.

Bruises do not mean the baby is damaged. If one side of her face droops and doesn't move when she wrinkles up her expression, this could be due to facial paralysis, which is sometimes seen after forceps are used during delivery. (Forceps and/or vacuum extraction are used in 10–15 percent of vaginal deliveries.) This condition is likely to be temporary and usually goes away in a few weeks. Bruises and swelling also go away quickly.

A baby's eyes may be swollen or irritated from the antibiotic ophthalmic drops or ointment that many hospitals give to all babies to prevent infection in a few. In addition, most institutions administer Vitamin K, injected into the baby's buttocks, to prevent bleeding during the first three months, when newborns' clotting mechanisms have not yet full developed and adequate amounts of Vitamin K may not otherwise be absorbed. A shot is also given in the first twenty-four hours to prevent Hepatitis B. Poor baby. The new world is not all that welcoming. She needs the nurturing of her new parents to balance all these insults.

Parents are often upset by all this and the needle sticks done for blood tests to screen for various disorders. While the tests seem a dreadful attack on tiny, tender feet, they are necessary. The baby's feet will heal miraculously. These tests are done to identify jaundice as well as a series of congenital disorders—including hypothyroidism and phenylketonuria (PKU), a metabolic disorder that affects a baby's brain unless it's treated as soon as possible. (In the United States, all newborns are required to be screened for both diseases.) Thyroid difficulties can be handled, too, but we need to start early. Sticking babies' heels for blood to identify these and other genetic or congenital diseases is an important preventive measure, although very few babies test positive for any of them. Many states also require newborn hearing tests before discharge from the hospital.

Many newborn babies begin to get slightly yellow (jaundiced) by the second or third day. Roughly 50–60 percent of healthy newborns and 80 percent of premature infants look a little yellow during the first week, especially between days 3 and 5. This kind of "normal" jaundice can be caused by the breakdown of fetal blood cells after birth. The result is an increased amount of the byproduct bilirubin, which the newborn's immature liver metabolizes only very slowly. This substance gives the skin a yellowish tinge when it reaches a certain blood level. Jaundice that follows this pattern, with blood bilirubin below the typical threshold (12.7 to 12.9 mg/dl), and that disappears by day 10 should not be cause for alarm.

A vital task for new parents is to learn to identify the different cries of the newborn. Any cry on her part is interpreted as a call for help. Parents automatically feel that they must respond and must find the problem that is making the baby cry. It will take time for them to learn how to interpret the cries, however. There are at least six different cries: those communicating pain, hunger, discomfort, fatigue, boredom, and tension discharge. As we encounter them in our exam, I attempt to describe them—their tone, their quality, their duration and intensity. I also try to help parents observe any self-calming efforts the baby makes, for all of these observations can be used later as they learn how to respond to her cries. When they can begin to see the baby's own efforts to calm herself and can differentiate between different cries, they will be able to better understand their role.

Research shows that parents can tell their own baby's cry from another newborn's by the third day. By the tenth to fourteenth day, they can differentiate among cries. The rapidity with which they learn can be enhanced if a caregiver shares this information with them. Instead of a frantic effort to stop all crying, they need to learn to differentiate the cries so they can learn the more realistic goal of helping the baby calm herself and regain control.

Each family needs to work out its own routine for changing, feeding, burping, cuddling, carrying, and rocking the baby or crooning to her. They will gradually learn what works and when the baby needs to be given a period to calm herself and settle down. Learning to parent is a long-term process. We all make mistakes. From the start, I try to emphasize to parents that learning to parent results from learning from one's mistakes. You learn a lot more from mistakes than from successes.

Early Care

Feeding There are two kinds of sucking: (1) nonnutritive sucking, which a baby uses to keep herself comforted and under control, and (2) nutritive sucking, which she uses for feeding. You can feel the difference by inserting a clean finger into her mouth. The first type uses the front of the tongue and a kind of licking motion. In the second, as we described earlier, the end of the tongue starts lapping, the back of the tongue begins to milk the finger, and finally there is a real pull from the back of the throat. All three components start independently, then become coordinated into an effective sucking motion. Parents can feel these differences for themselves. When the first kind of sucking is being used by the baby, she can be alert and talked to. Parents can use these times to talk to her and to play with her. A baby's day should be more complex than just sleeping and feeding.

Regarding feeding, new parents often ask me, "How do I know when she's had enough?" A baby will start out with a short burst of constant sucking. Very quickly, she resorts to a burst-pause pattern. A burst of sucks will be followed by a pause: suck-suck-suck-pause. Psychologist Kenneth Kaye and I studied the pauses to try to understand their significance, for we were aware that babies tended to look around and to listen in these periods. In a pause, a mother often will jiggle her baby, then look down at her to urge her on to more sucking or touch her baby's cheeks as she speaks to her. Fifty percent of the pauses are accompanied by a maternal response, and fifty percent go unnoticed. We asked mothers why they jiggled or touched or talked. The answers were along these lines: "To get her back to eating. She seems to be dreaming or to have forgotten about eating, and I want her to get full." In our study, the baby's pauses when the mother didn't respond were significantly shorter than those when she did. In other words, the baby seemed to prolong her pauses to capture social stimuli. We point to this burst-pause pattern in babies to help emphasize the importance of playing with and talking to a baby at feeding time.

As we talk about the opportunities for play, I like to point out that diapering and bathing can also be important times for communication. Talking to the baby and kissing her stomach are irresistible accompaniments to diapering. Parents can make it a fun time! Many babies hate to be undressed for a bath. If this is the case, parents can swaddle her in a cloth diaper after she is undressed in order to keep her feeling safe. They can then lower her into the warm tub, holding her head up with one hand. While her body is submerged, the diaper can be taken off. She will become active, but not upset, when she's submerged in warm water. While she's kicking and scrabbling, the parents can talk to her and play actively with her. New parents may need permission to feel free enough to play and encouragement to see that play with a baby is just as important to her as the more sober forms of care.

"How will I know when to feed her?" Parents wonder whether to follow a schedule or to go entirely by the baby's cues about when she is hungry. Here's the advice I offer them. Crying is the last sign of hunger. Watch for the earlier ones: The baby who is ready to feed will be in an alert state, exhibit more physical activity than at other times, or start rooting and mouthing, nuzzling at the chest, or bobbing her head as if searching for the breast or bottle. At first, also feed her when she cries. You'll learn which cry means hunger and which ones indicate other things by her response to your attempts to feed her. If she's really hungry, it certainly will be hard to miss. She'll keep on fussing and squirming until you feed her. When you first take her home, follow her cues to feed her whenever you think she wants it. Wake her after four hours to try to feed her, though, if she doesn't awaken herself. That way, you'll begin to work toward a schedule. During the first two to four days, you'll end up feeding her at least eight to ten times every twenty-four hours. Later, in a week or two, you'll know her cues better and you can begin to push her to wait a bit for each feeding. In about two or three weeks, she should be able to wait two to three hours, but she should also be eating at least six times a day. If she is nursing, she'll spend ten to fifteen minutes at each breast every two to three hours for the first few months.

Breast-feeding mothers always wonder whether the baby is getting enough milk. If the baby seems satisfied after a feeding, that's the most important sign. Does she wait for a few hours for the next feeding? Her urine should be clear or light yellow, not dark. Is she urinating several times a day—one wet diaper every eight hours at two days old, four to six wet diapers a day at three and four days old, and six to eight wet diapers a day thereafter? Also, she should regain her birth weight in the first ten to fourteen days of feeding. All babies lose a portion (5 to 10 percent) of their birth weight in the first few days—sometimes as much as a pound—while they wait for the mother's milk to come in. Breast milk may not really come in until day four or five. Meanwhile, the babies' own stores of extra tissue, which they have laid down at the end of pregnancy, protect them. Colostrum precedes breast milk by two to four days and is very valuable—rich in protein and antibodies against infection.

A baby's bowel movements are rather alarming at first. Known as meconium, they are black and sticky. Meconium is made of stored up and ingested cell-breakdown products from nine months in the uterus. By the third day, the stools change to greenish and are mucousy. By the fourth or fifth day, they may begin to be yellow and mushy. This is the first sign that the baby is beginning to get milk. Bowel movements can happen with every feeding or only once a day in a newborn, though several times a day is typical. With a breast-feeding baby, they are not smelly. Often, they are a gaudy yellow or green. (For more information about breast- and bottle-feeding, see Children's Hospital Boston in *Further Reading* and "Feeding Problems.")

Choking and Spitting Up When a baby spits up or gags, you may worry that she is choking. It's very hard for newborns to choke, because their breathing reflexes are good at keeping the airway clear. If your baby is able to breathe and coughs to try to clear her airway, stay with her to watch her through it without disturbing her. If her airway is completely blocked, your baby will need your help to stop choking. She will be gasping for breath, unable to breathe or make sounds, unable to clear her airway by gagging or coughing, or turning blue. Call 911 for an ambulance immediately or call out for someone else to. Then, support your baby's head and neck carefully as you turn her face down, her jaw supported by your hand, with her belly over your forearm. Position her head lower than her body. Then use the heel of your hand to smack her firmly between her shoulder blades up to five times. If that does not clear her trachea so that she can breathe, carefully turn her on her back, supporting her head and neck with your hand, her back with your arm, with her head lower than her body. Then, placing two or three of your fingers over the center of her chest, just below her nipples (but not at the very lower tip of her breast bone), give her five chest thrusts. If she still is unable to breathe, continue to alternate five back blows with five chest thrusts. If she does not start breathing and becomes unconscious, call again for emergency help. But stay with your baby so that you can carefully check for breathing, administer rescue breaths if she is not, and then try additional maneuvers to clear her airway.

You—indeed, all parents—should have a first aid guide such as is found in *The Children's Hospital Guide to Your Child's Health and Development* (see *Further Reading*), which contains additional important details on how to handle infant choking. You should also have emergency numbers by each phone. Then, in an emergency, you won't have to think; you can just react.

If the baby spits up after each feeding, it's probably because she's been taking it down too fast. If you can hear a gulp with each swallow, it has air in it. Prop her gently after a gulping feeding before you "bubble" her—that is, prop her up at a thirty-degree angle for twenty minutes, letting gravity push the milk down and the air bubble up. Then, when you sit her up, the bubble will come up without bringing milk with it.

Nothing in parenting is as rewarding as a big, wet burp after a feeding. To burp a baby, put her up on your shoulder. Pat her gently on the back as you rock and croon to her. She may not have a bubble at each feeding if she doesn't gulp a lot of air as she feeds. But if she's a gulper, she will have bubbles. Every gulp carries air down. But bubbles won't hurt her, and she can always pass them on through to the other end if you miss them. It's not very likely that they'll cause her stomach pain. If you have tried for five to ten minutes and she won't bring up her burp, leave her propped up on her back at a thirty-degree angle; then she'll probably bring it up herself.

The first hiccups can seem like a cataclysm to a new parent. Relax. They'll go away. You can always give the baby something to suck on—the breast, or if a bottle is being used, water or sugar water (one teaspoonful of sugar for eight ounces of water). But they'll go anyway. Hiccups can often be a sign of too much stimulation, so don't add to it.

Although I try never to issue categorical rules to a parent, there is one question to which I give a very firm answer. If parents ask whether to leave a baby with a propped bottle, my answer is *absolutely not.* Every baby deserves to be held for a feeding. Communication at feeding time is as important as the food.

Sleep Mercifully for parents, much of a newborn's life is spent asleep. Since 1992 the American Academy of Pediatrics has recommended that babies be placed on their backs for sleeping. This is because sleeping on the stomach (called "the prone position") is believed to contribute to the risk of sudden infant death syndrome (SIDS). SIDS, the sudden unexplained death of an infant one year of age or younger, is rare, now occurring in less than 1 in every 1,000 births, in part owing to the success of the "Back-to-Sleep" campaign. Still, it is the leading cause of death for children between one and twelve months of age in the United States. The causes are still unclear, although there is evidence that the risk of SIDS is higher if the mother smoked during pregnancy or the infant is exposed to cigarette smoke after the birth. Loose bedclothes, pillows, and saggy, too-soft mattresses that can smother an infant or cut down on available fresh air are also a major concern. Preterm and low-birth-weight babies are also at higher risk for SIDS. The incidence of SIDS peaks in the second and third months. It can be a challenge to get a baby to sleep on her back, but a parent may be able to help her find a cozy, curled-up posture, so that she can settle with her hand in her mouth. An active baby who is restless can be swaddled from the waist down.

"Should I use a pacifier?" Some babies absolutely need one to help them calm down. They are babies who can't or won't find their thumbs. But the advantage of a thumb is that it is always there. A young infant can find it and use it whenever she wants. Most babies need a self-comforting pattern. If they're active or easily aroused, they certainly need a way to fall apart and to relax. I'm always relieved to see a baby who can comfort herself. She'll be an easier baby to parent.

It's important for parents to learn the signs of overstimulation. When a baby is extremely overstimulated, her eyes may seem to float, her arms and hands may go limp, her face may frown, or she may avert her gaze. Spit-ups and bowel movements can be a sign of stress. They can come at unexpected times, along with whimpering, high-pitched cries. These responses are signs that the baby needs time out to recover and reorganize. If you do too much to try to help her, you might just add to the overload. When you've tried everything and it doesn't work, you may need to step back and just watch her. From her behavior, she'll tell you what she needs.

The Baby as the Teacher

As I said before, learning to parent a child is learning from mistakes as well as successes. As you try things out, I tell new parents, let the baby tell you whether you are right or not. When you're on the right track, her face will be placid and content, her body will be relaxed, and her responses will be organized and predictable. When you're on the wrong track, she'll be disorganized and unreachable. She will avert her face from yours. She'll thrash around and be unable to get calm. Her color will change to either very red or slightly blue. Her limbs will stiffen out, and her cry may be piercing and breathless. You may not know what to do, so try one thing at a time, as calmly as you can, including leaving the baby alone to reorganize, as we just said. Over a surprisingly short time, you will learn what her behaviors are trying to tell you. You'll also find that you feel more competent and less clumsy as you handle her.

Many new mothers have said to me, "I wish I could stay here in the hospital where I know my baby is safe." Everyone feels that way. But think of all the klutzes over the centuries who have made it with a new baby. I assure each new mother that she will learn what to do, with her baby's help. Her nurse or pediatrician can help, too, but her best teacher will be the baby, whose special language—behavior—can be observed and trusted.

Starting Out with Premature Babies

When the baby is born early or is stressed by intrauterine conditions that deplete her, each parent feels responsible. Mothers feel they could have done something differently. Whether it's rational or not, the mother feels she has endangered her baby. A concerned father will feel responsible in his own way or may even blame his wife. With this sense of responsibility comes depression. Parents may feel angry and helpless: Why me? What could I have done differently? A rational answer does not help; such feelings go too deep.

The birth of an extremely premature baby, or one who is at risk or handicapped in some way, will elicit three predictable defenses:

Denial—Parents may deny that the problem matters, while sensing how fragile this defense is. Denial tends to distort the reality in one way or another, portraying the situation as too rosy or too grim. This helps parents keep going but eventually needs readjusting. Without a realistic assessment, parents cannot see what they must learn to deal with the problem and how they can help their fragile baby.

Projection—Parents may believe that someone is at fault, imagining that this person caused the problem or made it worse in some way. Doctors, nurses, or others in charge become targets of this defense. Their assistance becomes suspect, and relationships are endangered.

Detachment—Parents may pull away from a baby who is at risk, not because they don't care, but because it is too painful to care deeply and to feel so helpless (see "Prematurity").

These grief reactions and defenses are natural and even adaptive. They must be accepted. Those who care for parents and newborns should understand that such defenses are necessary ones and need not be destructive if they are understood. A caring professional can see them as a part of parents' attempts to recover and to relate to a baby who does not fit the one of their dreams.

After delivery, all babies go through a period of recovery as well. A premature baby, or one who has been stressed in the uterus, will behave in a way that shows her physical fragility. As her autonomic (respiratory and cardiovascular) system recovers from the shock of having to take over prematurely, and as her neurological system matures outside the protection of the womb, a baby will be very vulnerable to auditory, visual, and tactile stimuli. Every touch, noise, or even change in light will be reflected in a change in her color, breathing, and cardiac control. Her motor behavior will reflect her immaturity either in weak muscle tone and few spontaneous movements, or in uncoordinated, jerky movements, which come at unpredictable times and occur after any stimulation. These movements are upsetting to the baby's fragile system. Her state control is poor, and although she tries to stay asleep to avoid overwhelming stimuli, she may shift from sleep to brief awake states within very short periods. In an awake state, she is more often crying than quietly alert and may avoid being looked at or talked to or touched. She may give back nothing but negative responses. For fearful parents, hungry to communicate, such behavior in their baby increases their anxiety about whether she is damaged and whether she will be able to recover. It also makes it more difficult for them to begin to feel attached.

Parents need patient support as the baby recovers. If they can stay with her in the newborn intensive care unit (NICU), they can learn over time how to handle her and will be ready for the job of caring for her when she is discharged. Doctors and nurses can help by demonstrating the baby's behavior and responses to them before discharge. Such a baby can tolerate only stimuli that are at a very low level. She can be held *or* rocked *or* looked at, but only one of these at a time, and very gently. If you respect this low threshold for taking in information, a recovering baby can gradually take more and more.

Over time, each system—motor, autonomic, state, and attention—will begin to show sturdier responses. As the baby becomes less fragile, she can begin to pay attention to auditory and visual stimuli, but still at a low level and for short periods. When she begins to fix on the red ball or her parents' faces, or to turn to their voices or toward a rattle, you can see what a great challenge this is to her nervous system. Her movements will become jerkier or her extremities limp. She may turn away from the voice or rattle instead of toward it. Her eyes may begin to float in her head, her face may become slack, her color may drain, and her respirations may increase. Hiccups, yawns, spit-ups, or bowel movements can all be signs of stress and overload. Parents may need to understand these symptoms, too, in order not to overreact.

By decreasing the stimulation in our preemie nursery, my colleagues and I have attempted to respect the fragile nervous systems of these babies. Heidi Als, a psychologist who has designed a system of "developmental care" for premature infants in neonatal intensive care units, reduced light and sounds and encouraged more sensitive handling in some premature infant nurseries both in the United States and in other countries. As a result, immature, fragile babies have begun to thrive. They have recovered sooner, have gained weight more quickly, and have needed less oxygen and less incubator time. Also, they have been discharged home earlier, in less fragile shape, and have been less likely to require readmission. Dr. Als even demonstrated that attention to these special needs has helped prevent or decrease the severity of intraventricular hemorrhages—a serious but all-too-common brain injury in preemies that can lead to long-term problems with cognitive functioning. Unfortunately, many NICUs still do not respect the principles of developmental care. Yet when parents are included in this process of carefully adapting the NICU to create a "second womb" for the "born too soon baby," they have been able to respect their babies' special needs after discharge. Parents who continue to provide a low-key environment at home will help their babies thrive.

As premature babies or those who are born on time but are small for their gestational age (known as SGA babies, or intrauterine growth restricted babies) mature, their states begin to last longer. They become able not only to pay attention longer but also to suck and eat more effectively. They can be handled and played with for longer and longer periods. However, catching up to a full-term baby's behavior may take longer than parents expect. If parents constantly compare their baby's progress to that of a full-term baby, they will only feel more worried and discouraged. If, instead, they can carefully attend to their own baby's individual behavioral responses, they can fix on appropriate goals. When the NBAS, the assessment described earlier, is done together with parents, the particular capacities of these babies to see, hear, and pay attention are evident, along with their weaknesses. Their need for special handling or early intervention can then be explained in a helpful manner.

A baby with sensory deficits can benefit from very early remedial programs, learning to substitute other senses for compromised ones, while protected from overstimulation. Blind babies, for example, are hypersensitive to touch and sound, so one needs to reduce one's voice and to handle them more gently and slowly. A blind baby can learn to utilize auditory and tactile cues to make up for her blindness *if* these cues are given to her at her own speed. If they are offered one by one as quiet, slow, nonintrusive stimuli, it is possible to watch the baby's behavior to sort out which ones she is able to utilize, and when. Parents of a baby with any type of impairment or developmental delay deserve to have a trained professional who can help them identify the baby's positive responses, teach them ways to help her learn control, and point out the signs of having overloaded her threshold (see "Delays in Development and Developmental Disabilities").

Over the years, I have been impressed with the remarkable ability of babies to recover from insults such as prematurity, and I can be optimistic as I work with the parents of such a baby. Often, redundant nerve pathways in the brain appear to be "recruited" to compensate for compromised ones, and nerve cells may make new connections to bypass damaged cells. The resilience of the very young brain is gathering the recognition it deserves.

There are two pitfalls that parents can learn to avoid as they adjust to a fragile baby. First, anxiety and disappointment can lead a parent to hover excessively. Even the most delicate, stressed baby can achieve more by learning to achieve each step by herself. It is difficult not to continue to hover long after a fragile baby actually needs protection. Letting her have enough space and time to learn each step by herself is difficult but pays off as her sense of autonomy and self-competence develops.

The other pitfall is one we have already mentioned. Although all new parents compare their baby to every other baby, the parents of one who is delayed are even more likely to want the baby to measure up to others. "When will she catch up and be like other babies her age?" parents will ask me. "What age should she be? I'm so scared she'll be slow. Whenever she doesn't make each step on time, I'm afraid she's got brain damage." These questions are an honest reflection of the fears that go with parents' adjustment to a delayed or disabled baby.

The baby's individual responses and her own temperament are the best antidote to such fears. At each visit, parents should ask the doctor to explain the baby's progress and level of development. Even when the months of prematurity and the weeks in the hospital are subtracted, each new step can take twice as long, for it may cost her nervous system that much more to organize itself in order to accomplish each step. For example, the fussy period at the end of the day can start later and continue later, and smiling and vocal responses can take longer to appear in a fragile baby after a difficult recovery. When parents know that this is likely to be true, they can keep their anxiety from interfering with the job they have of helping the baby recover. Patience, an optimistic, sensitive approach, and attention to signs of the baby's resilience are the goals. These are difficult to achieve, and parents deserve all the help professionals can offer. In each chapter in Part 1 of this book, the age levels mentioned must be adjusted for premature babies or those with developmental delays, and, in any case, should not be taken as rigid yardsticks (see "Prematurity").

4. Two To Three Weeks

When parents bring their baby for the two- or three-week visit, they are both likely to be exhausted. Because hospital stays for labor and delivery are generally too short, the first pediatric visit should occur before the baby is three weeks old. Ideally, a home visit should be scheduled in the first ten days to check for problems such as dehydration, hyperbilirubinemia, and drug withdrawal in the baby and postpartum depression in the mother, problems that won't show up during the hospital stay but that shouldn't wait for a three-week visit. This earlier visit is also a time for the doctor to help with feeding challenges—for example, to check that the breast-feeding baby is latching on properly. I would also like to see pediatricians, nurse practitioners, and other professionals who examine the baby in the early days trained to use the NBAS to assess the newborn's behavior. A baby's poor performance on the NBAS will prompt them to look for the common problems of this period, and a mother's responses to her baby's behavior can help them assess for postpartum depression. This is another opportunity to share the baby's behavior with parents and to alert them again to his potential and individuality. The new parents will then feel respected, cared for, and closer to the provider.

The American Academy of Pediatrics recommends that all breast-feeding newborns be seen by a pediatrician or other qualified professional between the third and fifth days after birth and again at two or three weeks to check into possible health concerns and provide any support and assistance needed to be sure that breast-feeding will be a success. (Many countries have adopted home visits during this period as a standard of preventive care.) New parents need comfort and an understanding listener as they embark on this overwhelming new role. Sometimes, a grandparent, another relative, or a nanny comes with them to this first office visit with the baby. I watch to see who carries the baby. If the grandparent or nanny does, I wonder how much the new parents have relied on the more experienced caregiver and how much actual experience they have had with their newborn. I am also looking for evidence of support systems for these new parents.

Many new mothers will be in the midst of "postpartum blues." They may suddenly break into tears for no apparent reason, or they may report they are struggling with anxiety and sleeplessness. Up to 80 percent of new mothers feel this way, but fortunately, postpartum blues are short-lived—they're usually gone within ten days—and without lasting consequence. Such a slowed-down and fragile period can accompany the physical recovery from labor and delivery and the rebalancing of hormones. But it can also be part of learning a challenging new role. A mother who is feeling "blue" is usually working hard at becoming a parent. Often she looks bedraggled, while her baby is carefully dressed in delicate, impractical little outfits and pastel receiving blankets. A new mother will clutch her baby tightly, as if she is afraid she may trip or drop the precious bundle. If she continues to feel dejected, inadequate, or unable to love her new baby for more than two weeks, or if depressed feelings interfere with caring for the baby, then a mother should seek a referral from her pediatrician to a mental health specialist for an evaluation for postpartum depression (see *Useful Addresses and Web Sites*).

A new father often hovers protectively in the immediate background. After taking the mother's coat, he may help her get settled by offering to hold the baby for her. If she gives her baby up momentarily, the father will look down hungrily, longing for the baby to wake up and look back at him. From his handling of the baby, I can tell how much he has been participating in the care. Mothers who dare not share the baby's handling will sit down awkwardly rather than handing over the baby. Every gesture of new parents reveals where they are in making this major adjustment.

As we talk, a new mother will look down at the bundle in her lap after each sentence. If the baby begins to move, she is likely to look at me anxiously, as if to say, "What do I do now?" If the baby cries, I can expect the new father to jump to help. Both will begin to try to comfort the baby, adjusting from one position to another, offering a pacifier—if they've decided to use one—looking at me somewhat beseechingly for help. A mother's last resort is to try to breast-feed. I may have to suggest it. Although women are less inhibited today than when I began my practice, the new situation of being in my office and of being under my scrutiny can be daunting. But as she puts the baby to breast, a mother will often look relieved. Some fathers will take the fussy baby to comfort him and try to spare their wives, demonstrating a shared relationship with this baby.

I have come to expect this tenuous, rather childlike behavior when new parents come into my office. Rather than a sign of incompetence, it represents their ability to accept me in a nurturing "grandfather" role and to let down their defenses. All new parents need a supportive figure who can sort out their questions and concerns. I am grateful for their trust, and I try to indicate this in my voice and comments.

By three weeks, most parents have done an enormous amount of work in adjusting to the new baby. Many phone calls have been made between parent and physician or nurse practitioner. Although the mother and father are just beginning to feel in charge of their lives again, this new adjustment is physically and emotionally overwhelming. Often, the higher the elation of parents after birth, the lower the slump after they return home. The reality of being responsible is awesome to thoughtful parents. "Postpartum blues" can be seen as a way to conserve energy after delivery. I have always urged new parents to conserve their resources in every possible way. Visits from outsiders should be limited to a few helpful, supportive people, excluding, for the time being, all the well-wishers who consume time and energy. If this is awkward, parents can say that the baby's doctor asked them not to have visitors for two weeks. At first, a new baby relies on immunity transferred from his mother before birth and through her breast milk. But until his immune system is fully active, a newborn is vulnerable to germs from visitors. A period as free of outside pressure as possible provides new parents with the space to become a family.

In this first visit, I try very hard to include the father, urging the parents to make the appointment at a time when he can come in. Early in the visit I ask him what his impressions are and what he has noticed about his baby. After he's opened up once, I know he'll communicate throughout the interview. Fathers are eager to be included. Even though they may seem to be remote and defensive at first, I find that they are quickly drawn in when I ask them to take part in the game described in chapter 2, where I ask the mother, and then the father, to talk to their baby on one side while I talk to him on the other. This is a magical way to involve fathers—every father is thrilled when the baby turns to follow his voice, even if the baby has been encouraged by a tip of the head.

By about four weeks, new babies will have learned special behavioral patterns for each parent. For a mother, the baby's extremities, movements, and facial behaviors are smooth and rhythmic in anticipation of their low-keyed, rhythmic interaction. With the father, the baby's facial features all go up, the extremities tense and waiting, as if the new baby had already learned that his father plays with him. When I see that a three-week-old baby starts to show this recognition, I describe it for parents so that they can observe and enjoy it, too. These different responses to each parent are an exciting sign of early cognitive development.

Fathers who can take time from work not only learn to diaper, feed, and play with the baby but also help their wives undergo an enormous shift of focus toward caring for a new, dependent individual. If gatekeeping by a new mother or a grandmother makes the father feel shut out at this time, the likelihood of his feeling involved later may be significantly reduced. More and more fathers are taking advantage of parental leave to support their wives, to get to know their babies, and to discover themselves as fathers. The first weeks can be a critical time for fathers to begin to establish their invaluable roles. In

fact, fathers who are present during pregnancy and involved with their newborn in the first weeks experience hormone changes—decreased testosterone and increased prolactin—that reinforce their nurturing activities.

While I'm talking to parents, learning about them and their adjustment, I observe the baby's temperament. A baby is already a unique individual. His temperament determines how he sleeps, how difficult he is to soothe, how intense his movements can become, how he tries to comfort himself, and how alert he becomes as I handle him through the exam. All of these observations can be shared with the parents from the first so that they know I am seeing the same baby that they are living with. Once parents sense this, they feel much more confident and relaxed as they ask for information and support.

Jaundice

At this visit the doctor should also check for jaundice. When the baby's skin has a yellowish pallor, and there is a yellowish tint to his nail beds and the whites of his eyes, a blood test should be ordered to measure the level of bilirubin, a red-blood-cell breakdown product that causes the yellowish appearance. The blood level will determine whether phototherapy will be needed and may indicate the need to consider a broader range of possible causes for the jaundice. I worry less when the baby's skin alone is a little yellow. About 30 percent of breast-fed babies develop prolonged elevated bilirubin blood levels. Surprisingly, though, bilirubin levels are more likely to drop with more frequent nursing, so it is important not to stop breast-feeding. Only a few, about 1 out of 200 breast-fed babies, go on to develop what is sometimes called "true breast-milk jaundice," which peaks at ten to fifteen days and normalizes anytime from the third week to the third month. It is thought to occur when a mother's breast milk happens to contain an enzyme that increases absorption of bilirubin in the baby's intestine. If the bilirubin level begins to climb above a certain level, the pediatrician will recommend that breast-feeding be stopped for forty-eight hours. (In the meantime, mothers should use a breast pump to ensure that their milk production continues.) As a result, the bilirubin level will rapidly drop. Though it may climb again when nursing is resumed, it usually will not reach such high levels. At this visit, a jaundiced baby should also be checked for infection (especially urinary tract infections) and other possible causes of jaundice.

Some causes of jaundice can lead to dangerously high bilirubin levels, and the doctor will need to look for these as well. These include a mother-baby blood incompatibility that should be routinely checked for during a prenatal visit, or an enzyme deficiency (of Glucose-6-Phosphate Dehydrogenase, or G6PD), which is fairly common, especially in individuals of Mediterranean, Middle Eastern, Southeast Asian, and African American descent. Bilirubin levels may be high for many other reasons too. If, for any of these reasons, the bilirubin concentration in the blood begins to get above a certain level (the baby's bilirubin blood level changes from day to day during the first weeks), then it becomes necessary to intervene. Bilirubin lights will help to break it down. These lights are used as a form of phototherapy. The baby's eyes must be covered, and he must be kept undressed. A newborn hates all of this. While he is under the lights, he will be jumpy and jittery and hard to feed. This behavior will pass in time, and it does not represent any brain damage. Since jaundice and brain damage are often equated by parents, I want to reassure them.

Feeding

Parents usually see feeding as their most important responsibility. The more intense this feeling of responsibility, the less likely parents are to recognize the baby's contribution. At this first visit I try to elicit or point out the behavior around feeding time that gives us insight into a child's particular temperament and the importance of the intensity of the baby's participation. I try to stress cues from the baby that parents can use to enhance the development of the baby's autonomy in the feeding situation.

On our map of touchpoints, which identifies those times in a child's life when certain issues are almost bound to arise, feeding questions are inevitable at two or three weeks. Once the subject is opened, I can expect a deluge of questions: how often to nurse, how to know when a baby is hungry, or how long to feed at one time, as well as questions about burping, spitting up, or bowel movements, and about the father's attempts to give the baby a bottle—especially if the baby is breast-feeding. At first, formula feeding may seem easier than breast-feeding because each parent knows how much milk the baby has taken in when there is a bottle.

Often parents will call, greatly concerned because the baby "spits up the whole feeding." I explain that, after a gulping, noisy feeding, they can expect a big bubble and a gush of milk to follow. A feeding that goes down like an elevator comes up like one. As we said earlier, learning how to "bubble" the baby is one of the major achievements of the first weeks (see chapter 5 for "Spitters"). Often, small practical suggestions from an experienced mother or a pediatrician bring reassuring success. After we deal with such practical questions, parents will often move on to deeper concerns. For breast-feeding mothers, the primary concern will be, Is he getting enough? We discuss the ways they can tell:

Does the baby seem satisfied after a feeding?Does the baby sleep one to two hours between feedings? Does the baby urinate often? (Wet diapers six to eight times a day mean the baby is getting enough fluid.) How many bowel movements does the baby have? (I warn parents that the pattern for bowel movements may change drastically in the next weeks. A baby on the breast may have eight or ten a day at first, and then may change to a pattern of once a week. If a weekly b.m. is soft and curdy, then the baby is not constipated. Breast milk can be completely digested, and with little residue. Many babies have this pattern when they are on breast milk alone, but the pattern will change when they start solids or if formula is used to supplement or replace the breast milk.) Has the birth weight been gained back? (As mentioned before, babies lose stored-up fluid right after delivery. They usually lose 5–10 percent and can lose as much as 20 percent of their body weight in the first four or five days. After that, breast milk or formula can be expected to rehydrate them. Most babies are discharged from the hospital at less than their birth weight. The transition to home is stressful, and a new mother's milk may not come in until as late as the fifth day. Hence, the possibility of gaining weight may not even arise until the second week. By the third week, babies should be gaining their weight back. Every mother and father is relieved to see that the baby is gaining.)

At this visit, it is important for the pediatrician or nurse practitioner to check for dehydration. A baby who has not taken in enough fluid will have sunken eyes, dry skin and mouth, and may be more irritable or lethargic than a well-hydrated baby. (See also *Feeding Your Child—The Brazelton Way* in *Further Reading.*)

Communication

Our discussion of feeding leads into the most important point of all: Getting the baby fed is only half of the job. Learning to communicate with the baby —touching, holding, rocking, talking, and following the baby's bids for interaction and for a break—are as important as getting him fed. Often at this stage both the new mother and father are likely to be too caught up in the mechanics of learning how to feed. They aren't yet able to hear me talk about the communication that goes with feeding a baby. But I bring it up, as I do at each subsequent visit.

Meanwhile, there is a good opportunity to watch the way parents communicate with the baby right in my office. I observe the patterns parents and baby have learned. Does the baby brighten when they look down to talk to him? Have they learned how to hold the baby and where to place him in relation to their faces so they can hold his interest? Many parents have already discovered the rewards of helping their baby pay attention and how to prolong that attention, and as a result, the parents and the baby often gaze into each other's eyes. In the first few weeks, they have already learned a special, low-keyed rhythm of speech and use of facial expressions to attract and keep their baby's interest.

All these little clues reveal how much time this new family has spent in learning about each other. Many anxious new parents devote their first weeks to feeding and sleeping, with no time for communication. If I see evidence of this, I look for an opportunity to model play with the baby. I take him in my hands, hold him out in front of me, and with gentle rocking, bring him to an alert state. Then we communicate in slow, gentle cooing. The baby's responses capture the parents' attention, and they take in the rhythms, the soft voice, and the slight rocking needed to alert a small baby. If a baby is intense and overreacts, I swaddle him and contain his arms before I try to produce an alert state.

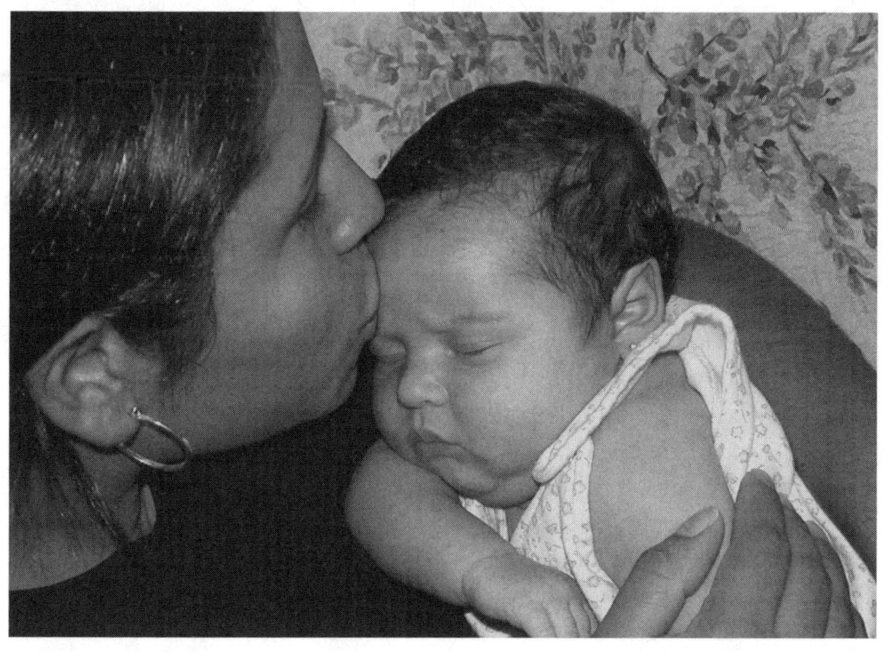

Touching, holding, rocking, talking are as important as getting the baby fed.

If the baby is fed in my office, I try to point out the burst-pause rhythm. As mentioned earlier, a baby starts sucking initially with regular sucks. After thirty seconds or more, he will fall into a different pattern—a burst of sucks followed by a pause. It is helpful for parents to know that when they reward pauses with a smile, a touch, or another social signal the baby prolongs the pauses, as if he actually wants social communication—as well as the feeding. Just food is not enough!

Sleeping and Waking

The next most important task for a baby at this time, one that also challenges parents, is to gain control of his states of consciousness. Readers will recognize these states from the description of fetal behavior presented in chapter 1 and from those pointed out in the discussion of newborn assessment in chapter 2.

Non-REM (Rapid Eye Movement) or Quiet Sleep In this protected state, the infant can shut out disturbing stimuli from the environment around him. He breathes deeply, regularly, and heavily. His eyes are tightly shut, and he is motionless. If he moves at all, his movements are slight, short-lived, and jerky. The self-protective nature of this state is reflected in the infant's curled-up, economical posture, with the hands up by his mouth, all of his limbs in flexion—closing out the world.

REM or Active Sleep In this state, breathing is shallower and irregular. From time to time, the infant sucks, with or without a finger in his mouth. He periodically moves in a writhing way. He may startle once or twice. In this state, he is more vulnerable to outside influences. When roused, he will either awaken sleepily and fussily or struggle to sink into deep sleep.

Indeterminate State This short-lived state is one that occurs frequently as the infant rouses or returns to sleep. In this state he squirms and moves jerkily. His eyes open dully and close again sleepily. He may whimper or cry out, but without focus. He will often try to curl up into a comfortable position, but startling, jerky movements interfere. He looks disorganized, and his frowning face shows the uncomfortable attempts he makes to reach a more organized state—either of deep sleep or of an alert state.

Wide-Awake, Alert State The baby's bright face and shining eyes demonstrate his open receptivity. His movements are contained. If he moves, he moves smoothly and can even achieve a goal, such as bringing his hand to his mouth or holding one hand with the other. His breathing fits itself to the stimulus. With an exciting stimulus, his breathing is deep. For a negative one, it is shallow and rapid. One can see his responsiveness on his face and in his entire body as he attends to an interesting noise or a familiar face. His face, his breathing, and his body's posture all convey interest and attention—or else a desire to withdraw and turn away from an overwhelming stimulus. Parents look for, and learn to help him prolong, this wonderful alert state, for this is a wonderful time for them to communicate with him. An attentive parent soon learns the baby's signals for "I've had enough" when he's tired or for "I want attention" when he's feeling overlooked.

Fussy, Alert State This state often follows the alert state. The baby's movements become jerky and his respirations irregular. He turns away from stimuli, fussing or whimpering from time to time. He makes ineffective attempts to control himself. As he thrashes around, his face reflects his feelings of ineffectuality. In this state he cannot control his movements, his autonomic system (heart rate, respiratory rate, and so on), or his ability to take in stimuli from around him. Helping him to calm down is rewarding for a parent, but he may go into an uncontrolled crying state. Then, parents feel they have been ineffective also.

Crying Many different kinds of crying can be demonstrated: (1) a piercing, painful-sounding cry; (2) a demanding, urgent cry; (3) a bored, hollow cry; and (4) a rhythmic, but not urgent cry that occurs when a baby is tired or overloaded with too many stimuli. His movements are thrashing, yet somewhat organized, in spite of his constant activity. He may quiet briefly as if to listen. He is likely to quiet when picked up, rocked, or fed. This state demands parents' attention, and they learn which comforting maneuvers settle the crying. It serves many purposes.

The way a baby moves in and out of his states of consciousness becomes predictable to parents. His style of moving from one to another is one of the best indicators of his temperament. If he is active and intense, he will move in and out quickly. If he is laid back, he will move slowly in and out of the six states. By now, parents are likely to know that when he is in an intermediate, fussy state, he will begin to cry if they do certain things or will quiet if they do others. His states and the way he cycles through them every three to four hours are their best window into an understanding of their baby. The new parents' first job is to learn their baby's most important language—the signs of each state of consciousness and his way of shifting from one to another.

If they understand this language, parents can gently encourage a baby to organize the states into cycles of behavior. A predictable pattern is now possible because the baby's nervous system has matured and because the parents know more about him. Research has also demonstrated a new stage of predictability in heart rate responses to visual and auditory stimuli in babies this age. At this point, the baby's heart beats faster in response to a negative stimulus and more slowly in response to a positive one. These physiological changes are associated with a spurt in development. By three weeks, the baby begins to be able to wait longer between feedings. He is ready to pay more and more attention to his parents, and this attention will lead to cooing and smiling.

At first, feeding the baby whenever he wakes is the most appropriate response. In this way, parents can learn at which times the baby is hungry, which feedings are successful, and which are not. Often these less successful feedings are times when the baby is not ready. Starting in the third or fourth week, feedings can be postponed for a bit of play. New parents often ask, "How do I know when to stop and play?" The only way to find out is to try. It won't hurt the baby to wait a bit. He will certainly show you when he is hungry, with whimpers and rooting about on your chest. The baby will gradually learn that playful interaction can be as exciting as feedings. Once parents are confident that a baby is getting enough food, they can begin to stretch out a baby's alert states between nursing and sleeping. A mother has more and richer milk after a two- to three-hour stretch than after hourly feedings, and her breasts are likely to develop a better let-down pattern if there's an interval between feedings.

The goal over the next few months is to lengthen the baby's waking moments to three or four hours between feedings and a long sleep at night. Certain new babies reverse day and night. They are up all night and sleep during the day. In order to change this pattern, parents can try to keep the baby awake at the end of each cycle of light sleep during the day. They can then awaken the baby in the evening for a real play period and gradually introduce the middle-of-the-night feeding earlier and earlier. Over time, the baby will start to stay awake longer each evening, learn to sleep longer stretches at night, and learn to awaken in the day.

The adjustment of the new baby's cycles of sleep and waking is the parents' first attempt to fit him into his new world and to bring his rhythms into harmony with theirs. This process, as all experienced parents know, takes years, and because we raise individuals and not clones, it is, fortunately, never complete.

Looking Ahead

The Fussy Period Between three and twelve weeks of age, most babies will develop a fussy period toward the end of the day. Because this phase may arise before my next visit with the family, and because it can be one of the most upsetting hurdles parents face, I make sure to raise the subject during the visit we have at two to three weeks. The chance to anticipate this trying behavior, and to understand its value for the infant, will spare parents some unnecessary panic and anxiety. If they can understand the infant's need to fuss at the end of each day between three and twelve weeks of age, they won't have to feel so responsible for the fussing.

In the past, many of us in pediatrics called this inconsolable, fussy period "colic," and we joined parents in their efforts to stop it each day. Back then, we tried sedatives or medications such as antispasmodics, and we urged mothers to carry their babies around, to nurse them constantly, and so on. All of these things helped temporarily, but they didn't get rid of the daily fussing and crying. Curious about this, I planned a study in which I asked eighty mothers to collect data for me on when and how their babies fussed. All but a few of these normal babies with healthy parents did about the same thing. They had a predictable fussy period that began at the end of each day. When they fussed, it was a kind of cyclical crying, not at all like the cry of pain or hunger. When these parents picked them up or nursed them, the babies would stop, but they'd start in again after they were put down. If they were carried a lot, this reduced the quantity of crying but didn't stop it. Just before the period began, these babies were jumpy: One could predict when it was about to begin. After it was over, parents reported that their babies slept better and longer and more effectively.

Whenever a certain behavior is so predictable and widespread, we can assume that it is adaptive and look for the purpose it serves. I began to wonder if this fussing served an organizing purpose. An immature nervous system can take in and utilize stimuli throughout the day but will become overloaded. As the day proceeds, the increasingly overloaded nervous system begins to cycle in shorter and shorter sleep and feeding periods. Finally, it blows off steam in the form of an active, fussy period. After this is over, the nervous system can reorganize for another twenty-four hours. It's almost clocklike in its predictability.

After I have explained this, mothers often ask, "But how can I stand back and let him cry?" That is not what I recommend. Instead, I give them the following advice. Go to the baby. Try out all the maneuvers you know to find out whether he needs anything. Pick him up and carry him. Feed him, cuddle him, change him. Give him warm water to help get a bubble up. But don't do too much. Once you've reassured yourself that he is not wet, in pain, hungry, or sick, either use soothing techniques or let him be. The normal one to two hours of fussing can easily be prolonged into a four- to six-hour ordeal if parents get too anxious and barrage the already overloaded nervous system with too much handling and stimulation.

At this point in my explanation, many parents ask for an explicit routine. As one father put it, "I'm sure my wife will feel he's hungry and worry that she hasn't given him enough milk." Of course he's right; she will. That's the reason I suggest feeding him first. But if he doesn't really eat well, if he just nibbles off and on, parents can be pretty sure it's not hunger. I suggest that after they have tried all their maneuvers, they give the baby ten or fifteen minutes to "let off steam." After that, they should pick him up to give him warm water and to bubble him; he'll have gulped down air as he cried. Then they need to let him have another cycle of fussing, after which they can repeat the same maneuver. This routine rarely needs to be repeated more than three or four times. After it's over, the baby will probably seem better organized—sleeping, eating, and staying alert in more regular rhythms until the next day's fussy period.

This is the extent of our discussion of the fussy period at this time, for it will not yet seem real to parents. By discussing the likelihood of the baby's developing this regular fuss period every day, and by giving parents an understanding of it, I hope to prepare them. When he does develop this rhythmic pattern at the end of each day, they will be less likely to overreact and to overload him. After introducing this preventive approach, I found that babies in my practice cried for one to one and a half hours rather than the three-hour stretch I used to hear about. Such results make the discussion an important opportunity for this kind of anticipatory guidance.

What about babies who cry more and more? Shouldn't they be taken seriously? Absolutely. If parents find that this fussy period increases in length and intensity despite their restraint and low-keyed efforts, I would want to hear about it. I would want to search for other reasons for this crying—such as a mild allergy or a reflux of acid from the stomach into the esophagus, which can cause pain. There are other reasons for crying that I need to search for when it is intense and unrelenting.

Thumb Sucking and Pacifiers The two- or three-week visit is none too early for parents to sort out their feelings about thumb sucking and pacifiers. I often ask parents whether the baby gets his thumb in his mouth yet. Can he comfort himself? Occasionally a mother will quickly reply: "I don't let him. I don't want a thumb sucker. I've been taking his thumb out of his mouth. If he needs anything to suck on, he can have me as often as he wants. Otherwise, I'll give him a pacifier." Or a father might remark: "I'd rather he'd suck his thumb than be wheeled around with his mouth plugged up." Sometimes parents will disagree on this issue and will ask me which is better.

Before outlining the pros and cons, I try to hear what the parents themselves feel about thumb sucking and pacifiers. Some will remember dreadful childhood battles. "My mother did everything to stop her, but my sister would sneak off to hide just so she could suck her thumb. She sucked it until she was seven or eight years old." I might ask, "Is there a reason why your mother felt so strongly?" Sometimes parents see a thumb as dirty; others worry that a pacifier will ruin a child's teeth.

Some children who suck a thumb or pacifier will develop an orthodontic problem, but the risk is lower before permanent teeth start growing in. There also seems to be less risk with a pacifier than with the thumb (because a pacifier is usually given up sooner), and with the thumb than with finger-sucking (because thumb sucking exerts less force on the teeth.) Sometimes the teeth straighten out on their own after the sucking stops. Many children with these habits do not end up needing their teeth straightened, while often children who do need braces later in childhood have a genetic tendency for misaligned teeth, even if they never sucked a thumb or pacifier. In my experience, dentists don't usually begin to worry about thumb sucking until a child is five years old. Children who are withdrawn and who suck most of the time, or children who go on sucking intensely after age five or six, are more at risk. But the problems of such children are in the area of socialization rather than in the area of sucking. Meanwhile, the importance of such self-comforting mechanisms for the child needs to be a first consideration. They won't be given up unless others (a soft blanket to stroke, a tune to hum) are urged along to take their place.

To give parents perspective on this issue, I explain that thumb sucking is a healthy, self-comforting pattern. Fetuses suck their thumbs. As noted in chapter 2, a newborn is equipped with the hand-to-mouth, or Babkin, reflex. When he's upset or trying to settle down, he will resort to this as a way of controlling himself. The pattern seems to be built in. Babies who make use of it are easier to live with. Giving babies pacifiers as they fall asleep has been found in some studies to reduce the risk of SIDS. If parents ask about the relative merits of thumbs versus pacifiers, I point out the obvious: A thumb is always available. After saying this, however, I turn the issue back to the parents. Preferences and feelings on thumbs and pacifiers have deep roots in family history and culture. "But won't he grow up sucking on his thumb? It will be easier to take the pacifier away," some mothers and fathers will say.

Very few people go to college sucking their thumbs or pacifiers. Parents who interfere with this self-soothing activity, and, as a result, reinforce it as a habit, may be more likely to have children who continue on as late as kindergarten or the early grades. If you want to set a stubborn pattern in a child, interrupt it at a time when he needs solace. He'll only hold on to it harder. This is true of many other "habits" that would be transient unless adults tried to stop them. This is why I suggest to parents that they evaluate their own feelings about thumb sucking as early as possible. A parent who objects to a child using his thumb is bound to let him know it sooner or later. Parents who are bothered to see a child sucking his thumb should consider a pacifier. It's a stressful world for small children. They are likely to seek some sort of self-comforting as their way of managing the stresses. I see this as a very healthy sign of competence, not as a dirty or shameful habit.

One mother in my practice put into words the real issue underlying the struggle over thumbs and pacifiers: "I feel that if only I could do everything for him and do it right, he wouldn't need such a crutch." A child's own self-comforting pattern calls up feelings of inadequacy in parents—maybe even jealousy. For this reason, they see the habit as dirty and embarrassing. One father, after hearing his wife and me go through all this discussion, looked over at his baby who had started to fuss. The baby thrashed a bit, whimpered, then turned his head to one side, pulled his thumb up to his mouth, and settled down. "Well," said his father, "I think he's decided it for us."

This father's wise observation is the answer to a perennial question from new parents: "How do I know when I'm being a good parent and when I'm not?" The only sure way is to watch the baby. Only the baby—not the doctor or a book—can tell you when you're on the right track. Parents, who can team up with professionals to anticipate these times, can think about their choices and make decisions that are right for them and their baby.

5. Six to Eight Weeks

AT THE NEXT OFFICE VISIT, SIX TO EIGHT WEEKS AFTER A BABY'S BIRTH, the mother often comes alone. When the father accompanies her, I feel he and I are off to a good start, and I take this as evidence of how much he wants to participate in each milestone with his baby. Later, parents who are both very involved may alternate visits. By now, the mother, who may still be on leave from her work, may look a bit less tired. She may have dressed up for this visit, looking forward to the occasion, a chance to get out of the house. Since we probably have been in touch several times by phone, she may greet me as if we were old friends. Generally, the first thing she may do is try to show me how her baby is learning to smile and to vocalize. Rarely will the baby cooperate, but her efforts make me know that they are enjoying each other. If she gives the baby to the father to hold as she concentrates on her questions with me, I learn something about the way they are sorting out their roles. If, on the other hand, the mother hovers over her baby or the father dominates the question period, I wonder how much they are sharing, and I may need to reach out to each of them to hear their concerns. If the mother is pale, exhausted, and jumpy, I must be alert to the possibility that the very common postpartum blues are deepening into depression.

Postpartum depression often begins in the first weeks and months of delivery. I've been concerned that short hospital stays of just twenty-four to forty-eight hours leave many new mothers feeling overwhelmed and with no one to turn to—and that this may increase the risk of prolonging the shorter "blues" into postpartum depression. Postpartum blues last for only a few days, whereas postpartum depression, affecting about 10 percent of new mothers, lasts for a minimum of two weeks. At greater risk are older or younger mothers, as well as those with unsupportive partners, previous mental illness or physical disease, or thyroid problems. An irritable, difficult baby also appears to increase the risk of depression in a new mother. Some women keep their feelings hidden, but visible symptoms include fatigue, insomnia, loss of appetite (all easily confused with recovery from labor and delivery and adjustment to a new baby), persistent anxiety, irritability, emotional instability with sudden crying, and, most seriously, indifference to the new baby. Sometimes a mother may appear overly concerned about the infant's well-being, fearful that she or someone else will harm her baby.

Any of these symptoms can be terrifying—both to the new mother and to those around her. Yet postpartum depression is likely to go unrecognized and untreated. Mothers are bound to feel ashamed of feeling miserable at a time when they are expected to be so happy. Even when the symptoms are recognized, the stigma attached to mental illness and widespread lack of access to services prevents many women from seeking help. If untreated, the depression can linger for months or even years, with serious consequences for mother and child. Without early healthcare visits, it's easy for doctors and nurses to miss postpartum depression. Since we know how to detect and effectively treat these disorders, our healthcare system could do a better job of supporting new parents and setting up early opportunities, such as a home visit, for detection and prevention.

At the six- to eight-week visit, my goals are simple. First, I want to assess the baby's development. Is she normal neurologically? Has she been gaining weight as expected? Is her behavior normal? Does she react by smiling and vocalizing? Does she move her arms and legs vigorously? If she is placed on her belly, will she elevate her head and free her airway? When pulled to sit, does she hold her head up? Are the times between feedings spreading out? Does she have a fussy period at the end of the day, or is she crying a lot at other times?

I am also eager to hear the parents' concerns. If they need help with feedings, we can concentrate on that. Do they understand the concept of states and the way these states cycle during the day and night? Can they tell the difference between their baby's various cries? Do they feel more confident about handling these, or is the crying too much for them?

Together with the parents, I watch again for signs of the baby's temperament. Is the baby active or quiet? Is she easily overloaded and hypersensitive? If so, have they learned how to help her calm down? How to handle her without overloading her? We share these observations as I undress the baby and examine her. Parents often find it easier to voice their worries and their questions when I'm commenting on the baby's behavior during the course of the actual checkup, rather than when we are sitting still, face-to-face.

Feeding

Most parents still worry about whether their baby is getting enough to eat. After I have ascertained that the baby is gaining weight appropriately (about a half pound a week), I can assure her parents that she is well fed. Her body should be filling out, and she should be stretching out the intervals between feedings. If the baby is being breast-fed every two to three hours, fifteen to twenty minutes at each breast is more than enough for sucking and for adequate milk. Even a few minutes on each side will stimulate milk production. If a baby is formula-fed, four or five ounces roughly six to eight times a day is the goal. About thirty ounces of breast milk or formula a day should be plenty. More frequent feedings may be needed for babies still taking smaller amounts at each feeding. Babies who spit up large amounts may do better with smaller, more frequent feeds.

Many babies spit up small amounts of milk during and after feedings. The undigested liquid just seems to bubble up without causing any distress to the infant. But vomiting is different—usually it involves larger amounts, and it is more forceful. When a baby vomits large amounts of milk after most feedings, accompanied by painful crying, *gastroesophageal reflux* (GER) is another possibility. A baby with GER may also cough or choke after feedings. If the sphincter between the esophagus and the stomach isn't strong enough yet to keep milk down, the milk will back up into the feeding tube, along with stomach acid that causes the pain. Your doctor can recommend effective treatments for this condition until your baby outgrows it. This usually occurs by nine months, when babies spend so much more time upright. In the meantime it will help to elevate the baby's head during feedings, before burping, and for thirty minutes afterward.

A rare condition, *pyloric stenosis,* often first shows up between the ages of three and six weeks. A baby with pyloric stenosis—a narrowing at the end of the stomach that prevents its contents from emptying into the small intestine—vomits large amounts after each feeding. The milk may seem to shoot out of her mouth and across the room—"projectile vomiting." This problem needs immediate attention since it seriously disrupts a baby's intake and weight gain, but it can be readily corrected with a tried and true surgical procedure.

Another cause for vomiting (though not projectile vomiting) is sensitivity to milk protein. Vomiting large amounts, uncomfortably, after each bottle, along with frequent mucousy bowel movements between feedings, or a dry, eczematous face rash, can be an early indication of intolerance to a formula. If the baby shows any of these symptoms, the parents should check first with their physician before making any changes. Allergies to cow milk protein occur in 0.5–7 percent of infants under six months of age. In addition to vomiting, sensitivity to milk protein can cause diarrhea, bloody stools, and other symptoms of an allergic reaction. Breast-fed babies are not prey to these sensitivities (though they may occasionally be sensitive to certain foods—especially citrus fruits, berries, nuts, and shellfish, among others—that their mothers eat). Early food allergies may be associated with asthma later on, and breast-fed babies may be less likely to develop asthma. It is important to identify a milk allergy as early as possible. Eczema can be avoided if milk is eliminated early. There are formulas made from soybean products that do not contain milk yet are just as nutritious. They do not challenge a milk sensitivity, and they are safe for milk-sensitive infants, though a few babies are allergic to soy-based formulas. If parents can avoid feeding the allergic baby milk, she will outgrow her tendency to react to it. As she gets older, the danger of allergic eczema and intolerance is decreased.

Before solid foods are started at four to five months, it is important to recognize and take care of any sensitivity to milk. Otherwise, the chances of other foods setting off allergic reactions are increased. An allergic child is rarely intolerant or sensitive to one food product alone. Milk and other allergens (allergy-triggering foods or other substances) are more potent if given together. Avoiding allergies is an important goal, especially for families that have this genetic tendency. Breast-feeding mothers who are allergic to certain foods should avoid these, for their own sake, and also because the baby may have inherited a predisposition to these allergies. (See also "Allergies and Asthma.")

By six to eight weeks, feedings should have become expectable and more routine. Breast-feedings should now be easy and pleasurable. If the father feeds the baby with a bottle, a routine for this can also be established that is not, at this point, likely to interfere with breast-milk production. A mother can pump her milk and keep it refrigerated (for up to twenty-four to forty-eight hours) for a father to give. Or he can use one bottle of formula a day, which shouldn't reduce a mother's milk and will give him a real sense of participation.

If the baby is a regular spitter, the parents and I have no doubt discussed this over the phone already. I estimate that 15 percent of normally thriving babies in my practice spit up repeatedly. They spit up small amounts after most feedings and always bring milk up with a bubble, and they spit up whenever they are handled or become upset. As long as these babies are gaining weight, do not appear to be in pain right after feedings, and are content between feedings, this kind of spitting up is not a serious concern. I try to reassure parents that it's common and that they don't need to worry. Slowed-down feedings with the baby held in a semi-upright position can help. Nursing mothers tell me that their babies spit up less when they themselves lie down to feed their babies. After a feeding, a spitter should be propped at a thirty-degree angle, and handling should be avoided for twenty to thirty minutes. That will enlist gravity to hold most of the milk down. Then, the caregiver can bring up a bubble gently if it's still there. These maneuvers tend to reduce the spitting up, but they may not eliminate it. Formula comes up with a pungent odor, but breast milk doesn't smell. When I walk into a house that has that characteristic odor, I can tell right away that there is a formula-fed baby living there who tends to spit up. Baking soda sprinkled on the spit-up will help to counteract the smell. When parents know that the baby is healthy and gaining weight, a sour lapel may not seem like the end of the world.

Breast milk or formula is all that a baby needs at this age. However, according to the American Academy of Pediatrics, all babies should start receiving 200 IU of Vitamin D per day starting in the first two months of life and until the baby is drinking at least a pint a day of fortified formula or milk (fortified cow's milk is not recommended until at least twelve months of age) to ensure adequate calcium absorption and prevent rickets. Vitamin D supplement droplets can be given daily to breast-fed babies, while formulas ought to be fortified with Vitamin D. Solids are not needed before five to six months and probably are not yet digested. An infant's swallowing mechanism isn't mature before that either: She just sucks food down, as if nature didn't mean for her to get solids too early. Milk is the perfect food for babies. Sensitization to other foods can occur at this age and not show up as allergies until later. I don't recommend solid foods at this age for all of these reasons.

A breast-fed baby may not have a bowel movement each day. As mentioned earlier, many babies who are getting adequate feedings and are gaining weight will digest breast milk so completely that they have only one bowel movement every three to eight days. This never happens with formula-fed babies, who usually have one or more b.m.'s a day. Breast-fed babies may change abruptly from a pattern of one after every feeding to one a week. I've had two in my practice whose pattern was one every tenth day. In between, the babies are happy. Toward the end of their cycle (for I do see it as theirs), they strain and act like the stool is bothering them. If it is their normal pattern, the movement will be soft and *not* constipated. Parents, of course, tend to get anxious. They feel this is constipation and rush to use suppositories or to manipulate the baby rectally to produce regular stools. This is completely unnecessary and interferes with a normal rhythm. A constipated baby is uncomfortable and has hard, large, difficult movements. Those of breast-fed babies are soft, not hard, and often have greenish, bile-stained mucus in them. Although the baby may cry out as she passes them, she is not constipated. Breast milk is a perfect milk and can be burned up almost completely. Parents who know this in advance are saved from interfering with the baby's normal pattern.

Formula-fed babies may have b.m.'s every other day, but they are not likely to postpone their stools. Formula is never as completely digested. If a formula-fed baby has hard stools or more than five or six green, mucousy, watery stools, parents should check with their physician. (See also *Feeding Your Child—The Brazelton Way* in *Further Reading.*)

Crying

A baby's cries should be clear to most parents by now. Cries of boredom, pain, discomfort, hunger, fatigue, and letting off steam are all distinctly different from each other in most babies. New parents learn to tell them apart by trying out all the comforting maneuvers: feeding, changing, cuddling, swaddling, and so on. By finding out what works, they then know what to try the next time. But they shouldn't be surprised when the method that worked last time won't help. Learning to parent is a process of trial and error.

As we saw in chapter 4, a regular fussy period, usually at the end of the day, is both common and adaptive in children of this age. It helps the baby let off steam so that she can adjust to a four-hour cycle of sleep and awake states. Gradually, the baby will learn more mature ways of self-quieting, such as listening to voices, watching light, shadows, and color, or purposefully using her hand-to-mouth reflex to suck on a finger and soothe herself.

The way parents learn to handle normal, fussy crying in their baby can be a particularly important touchpoint—a trying time through which they grow as parents and adjust to a stage in the baby's development. It is also a time for a physician to support this growth. Parents who can understand the different cues and what works to soothe most cries—as well as what won't work—may not be as frantic over their apparent failure when the regular fussy crying continues at the end of each day. The studies I have done on average babies indicate that this fussy end-of-the-day crying peaks at eight weeks, decreases gradually over the next few weeks, and is usually gone by twelve weeks.

Parents want to know whether they can spoil a baby by rushing to her every time she cries. They ask, "If we carry her around during this fussy period, or if we feed her a lot, are we spoiling her?" I reassure them that this is not spoiling. In fact, I don't believe "spoiling" is possible until much later in the first year. Parents should try out whatever helps, up to the point where everything they do is just adding to the fussiness. Then, it's time to slow down. They should either carry the baby very quietly and calmly or put her down for brief periods of fussing. Five to ten minutes at a time will help her get it over with. After such a time, they can pick her up to calm and even to burp her, then put her down again.

In my experience, a "spoiled child" is an anxious or driven child. You don't make a child spoiled by attending to her needs. Hovering over her all the time and attending to her with anxiety or anger might lead to an anxious, whiny child. Interfering with a child's early efforts to settle herself may make her dependent on yours. But picking her up to play with her or trying things out to satisfy her will not. Parents and babies learn about each other this way. Mothers and fathers may learn different things about the same baby. A different style of response from each parent can be enriching for the baby (see "Crying and Colic"). (See also *Calming Your Fussy Baby—The Brazelton Way* in *Further Reading.*)

Sleeping and Waking

The baby's pattern of sleeping and feeding should be more and more predictable. As we saw, she should be stretching out the time between feedings until there is at least a three-hour break between them. Parents may now be able to plan the baby's day, and their own, around these more regular feeding times. Depending on birth weight and other factors, babies of two months have longer and longer stretches asleep each night: In my experience, bigger babies seem more likely to sleep longer, while smaller ones, perhaps less mature, seem to need to eat more often. I urge parents of a baby this age to wake the baby and start her day when they are ready. At night, parents can get the baby up before they go to bed to feed her one last time. A schedule helps everyone adjust to the baby. It doesn't need to be rigid, and it certainly should follow her demands, but she's ready to fit in by now. She is more likely to adjust to her parents' environment if they expect her to.

In addition to prolonging the intervals between feedings, which will occur as the nervous and digestive systems mature, the baby continues to perfect her own patterns of self-comforting. Thumb sucking, rooting around in bed, and rocking the head are among the ways a baby calms herself. After feeding the baby in their arms, then rocking and soothing her, parents can lay the baby down in her crib on her back when she's quiet but not asleep so that she can learn to put herself to sleep. They can sit beside her to croon and to pat her gently. If she has a difficult transition from their arms to the bed (as highly active babies do), it seems even more critical to "teach her" early how to console herself at night. (She may also need to be contained by being swaddled from the waist down and settled on her back.) As she scrabbles to find her pattern of self-comforting, parents can gently help her discover her thumb or a pacifier or a position in bed that she can seek each time she rouses. As we said in chapter 4, these self-comforting patterns may worry some parents, but they are important new skills for the baby. By encouraging them, parents will be helping her build on independent strengths for the future. As mentioned earlier, positioning a baby to sleep on her back will reduce her risk of SIDS (see "Sleep Problems").

Communication

Of the baby's many powerful ways of reaching her parents, perhaps none other is as effective as her smile. In these early weeks, parents will have learned what they must do to produce one, and the baby is learning what an extraordinary and reliable response this gentle signal can bring. Parents learn to cuddle the baby, contain her arms, rock her, hold her at a thirty-degree angle, and talk gently to her, with infinite variations for each loving couple. But too great a response to a baby's smile from an eager parent can be as much of a disincentive as too little. You can turn off her smile by overreacting too noisily to it!

By now a baby can watch a parent's face for long periods. As she watches, she will get more and more interested until she breaks into a broad smile. Smiling back is likely to prolong the smile. As she wriggles with glee, she may make a brief cooing sound. If the parent imitates her sound, she will stop moving, and a surprised look will come over her face. She may work hard to

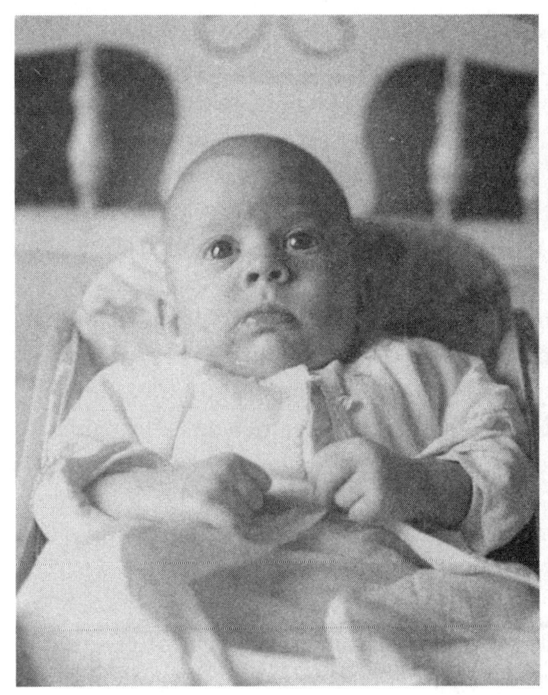

coo again. Unable to do so, she may give up in frustration. Such frustration is evidence to me that she knows what she has done, that she recognizes the adult's imitation, and that she wants to repeat it. She disintegrates when she can't live up to her own expectation.

At our office visit, I watch carefully to see whether parents and baby smile and communicate with each other. Most parents will want to talk about this enchanting new dialogue. Some others even report that all other activities pale beside this new delight. "My problem," said one, "is that I can hardly do anything but look at her and play with her every minute she's awake." Some, especially parents who have very little time at home from work, will get a baby up just before bedtime or before they leave in the morning to play with her. Many parents also report that the baby sleeps better after such a play period. As parents and I talk together during a checkup, I take this opportunity to point out how the baby is trying to intercept their attention. When she manages to engage them, her face lights up, her shoulders rise, and she may even squeal with pleasure. She knows *she* has done it!

New parents, who want to be sure to do everything "right," sometimes ask if they can "overdo" play. "She is so delicious when she smiles and gurgles. I keep her at it until she breaks down and starts to cry. Am I pushing her too hard?" they may ask. The only advice I need to give is, "No! Have fun." This is such a great time for learning about communication. The baby can take care of herself and let you know she's had enough by falling apart. Then, she can even come back for more. Some babies will reflect overload with a kind of small shudder or with hiccups. These, too, are nothing to worry about. Babies reach a point where they can't go on. They seem to wish they could do more, but they can't. Frustration is a powerful force for learning, but babies need help handling it at this age.

Some parents of a two-month-old will ask, "Has she learned to cry for attention already?" Certainly she has. Babies develop an expectancy when parents respond readily. Parents can see this as a welcome sign of learning and early attachment. Who wouldn't yearn for another person who comes to make you giggle, who sings, rocks, cuddles, and smiles—one who is already passionately in love with you?

Temperament

During this second office visit, the baby's characteristic ways of reacting to handling will be more apparent. I try to enlist the parents in watching the baby's activity with me: the way she responds to touch, to sounds, to being undressed, and so on. By this age, quiet babies can be distinguished from more intense, driving babies. A certain temperament has revealed itself by now. Each of these kinds of babies, especially the extremes, demands a particular adjustment from parents. In my book *Infants and Mothers,* I discuss these adjustments and the marked individual differences between babies over the period of the first year.

As the parents adapt themselves to their particular baby, observations about her intensity, her threshold for utilizing versus shutting out stimuli, and her motor style, competence, and ways of self-soothing can be helpful to them. If I watch carefully and speak about the baby's language—which is her behavior—to the parents, they will more readily share their questions about her and about themselves as parents. As we play with the baby together, deeper concerns often surface.

For example, a hypersensitive baby poses a tough challenge to parents and can arouse painful doubts about their ability to nurture. A baby who responds to playful attempts to elicit a smile or to cuddling with frantic activity and crying can be terribly frustrating, even to experienced parents. When parents try to play with a hypersensitive baby, she may arch away, avert her face, spit up, or have a bowel movement. In every system of her tiny body, she is saying, "I'm overloaded." With such a baby, parents must learn subtle techniques of containing, swaddling, and gently playing in quiet, less stimulating surroundings. A hypersensitive baby can be approached through one modality at a time—*either* speaking softly *or* looking in her face *or* rocking her gently—but only one. As she begins to assimilate each modality and to respond warily, another modality can gradually be added, until finally all three are presented together and she is able to respond to them. Learning to take in and combine all three modalities—sight, sound, and movement—is a big achievement for such a vulnerable infant.

Sometimes I can help by asking the parents to watch as I handle the baby, respecting her very low threshold for taking in and utilizing stimuli. I begin by simply holding her, not looking at her face or talking to her. Whenever I move even slightly, she will probably startle and stiffen all over again. I must wait until she is relaxed, *then* look down at her. She will stiffen briefly. When she begins to relax again, I can talk quietly to her in a crooning, soothing way, until she gradually relaxes to look up at me. Perhaps, as I talk *and* look *and* rock her gently, she will begin to smile or to coo gently. If this is successful, I suggest that parents run through the same slow steps, with me or at home. I encourage them not to add any other stimulus until the baby tells them that she is ready. When her body stiffens, then relaxes, that tells them she's processing information and reminds them how hard it is for her not to get overloaded. With only one new stimulus at a time, parents can gradually teach a baby to take in her world *without* shutting it out.

While discussing ways to connect with a hypersensitive baby, I also try to explain to the parents that the concern and eagerness to nurture, which show what devoted parents they are, can be the very qualities that overloaded such a baby. If they can recognize her fragility and respect it, adapting their deep desire to reach and play with her, a new rapport can gradually build between them (see also "Hypersensitivity and Hyperactivity").

A less hypersensitive, but quiet, watchful baby can also frighten parents. Her cries and grimaces are more subtle, and it is harder to know what she needs. She frowns at you whenever you try to reach out for her. If you talk too loud, she turns away as if you were not anyone she wanted to listen to. Every attempt to reach her seems to end in failure. This can make an eager new parent feel rejected.

When talking with parents of such a baby, I give the following advice. Approach your baby slowly and without talking. Look away from her face as you hold her under her buttocks and contain her arms and legs. Gently touch her legs and let her grasp your fingers with her hand. When she relaxes her grasp, then you can dare to look her in the face. If she stiffens and averts her head, you have gone too fast. Wait and try again. When she'll let you look at her, wait until she's relaxed again. Then, start cooing softly to her. If she brightens and tries to coo back to you, you can start a rhythm between you—of your cooing and of her cooing, back and forth—until she overloads to turn away. Don't feel rejected. Realize, instead, that she is a very sensitive baby who needs to be introduced to one thing at a time. When she can take one, add another very gently. Over time, she'll learn how to handle stimuli without withdrawing. Then, she'll be so rewarding—quiet, observant, even grateful for your respect for her.

Jerome Kagan has shown that temperament seems to emerge very early, and that a very sensitive baby may become a shy child. Parents who respect their child's temperament are better able to help her thrive than those who try—unsuccessfully, of course—to change it.

Motor Skills

At six to eight weeks, most babies have begun to control their reflexes to a limited extent. Instead of startles, which have interfered earlier with attempts to move, a baby can now control her limbs. She can lie in bed on her back, cycling her arms and legs. If you touch her hand with an object she's interested in, the touched hand may jerk out toward the object. Long before she can reliably reach for an object, the ingredients that make up a reach are there. She is now successful in turning her head to a preferred side and inserting her fist to quiet herself. This control over her movements has taken two months, and parents can see her practice as she lies in bed in the morning.

When I pull a baby this age to sit by her extended arms, her head lags only briefly. She can now maintain it in a sitting position for a minute or longer. When placed face down, she can pick her head up off the bed to look around and free her airway. In a standing position, her walk reflex is still present, but it's harder to elicit than it was at birth. Parents can watch as the reflexes that were present at birth gradually go underground and more voluntary behavior develops.

Cognitive Skills

Being human, parents experience great excitement at the first signs of intelligent learning in their babies. By six to eight weeks, babies have already developed all kinds of expectancies. For instance, when you rock a baby gently to bring her up to a thirty-degree angle, she knows that this is a position for interaction. She alerts predictably. As I examine a baby, I like to see when she produces smiles and vocalizations. I want to observe her ability, by eight weeks of age, to differentiate between her mother, her father, and a stranger.

In our laboratory at Children's Hospital in Boston, we have watched babies on videotape for three-minute stretches. By observing a baby's fingers, toes, hands, feet, and facial behavior, we can actually tell to whom she is reacting. In front of her mother, her movements are smooth and cyclical. Her hands, feet, fingers, and toes extend toward the mother and withdraw at a rate of four times a minute, in smooth cycles. Her face brightens softly. As the mother looks, the baby looks away gently at intervals of four times a minute. With her father, every part of her body reacts differently. Her body gets tense and jerky. Her face brightens, her eyebrows go up, her mouth opens in a grin, and her fingers, toes, arms, and legs jerk out toward her father as she expects a playful interaction from him. With me as a stranger, she will brighten at first. Then, she will turn away or will look at me as if she recognized me as a stranger, in the same hooked, fixed stare that she saves for objects. In this way, observed carefully, a six- to eight-week-old baby can be seen to differentiate between the three of us. I like to point out these subtle differences in behavior to new parents so they can learn to watch their babies.

At this age, too, objects become more fascinating. A mobile becomes a source of great pleasure, and she will watch it for longer and longer periods, even trying to stay awake to do so. At this age, babies also watch their hands, turning them over and over in front of their eyes. This way they learn hand-eye coordination, which will help when reaching begins at about four months. She will then quickly learn to reach a target accurately, having practiced all this time. By four to five months, when a baby reaches successfully, she will be able to keep her hand in peripheral vision to make it work accurately for her.

Immunizations

At the two-month visit, there must be immunizations: Current recommendations for this age include the second Hepatitis B shot (HepB #2), which may be given any time during the baby's second or third month (the first dose is given at birth), Diphtheria, Tetanus, and Pertussis (DTaP), Hemophilus Influenza (Hib), Polio (IPV), and Pneumococcus (PCV). (For updates to this schedule and other information on immunizations, check the Web site of the Centers for Disease Control and Prevention [CDC] at www.cdc.gov; for a printable chart of recommendations as of January 2006, see www.cdc.gov/nip/recs/child-schedule.htm#printable. This site includes catch-up schedules for children who have delayed immunizations.) The recommendations need to be attended to from this date on in order to be assured that your baby is as protected as she can be. I recommend that you hold the baby close for the injection and be ready to comfort her afterward—either by rocking, dancing around the room, or giving her something soothing to suck. Reactions from shots are always frightening. Fever and swelling around the injection site are uncommon and aren't necessarily serious, but should be discussed with her doctor or nurse. Concern that the mercury-containing preservative thimerosal used in vaccines might have caused autism has led to its removal. It remains to be seen whether the rising incidence of autism in recent years will level off as a result. Though mercury is a known neurotoxin, vaccines themselves have not been proven to cause autism as of this writing, and they are critical in protecting children from epidemic outbreaks of other serious diseases, many of them permanently disabling or life-threatening. New research may bring new understanding of vaccine risks and benefits, so be sure to ask your doctor for the latest information.

Looking Ahead

Back to work? "I have to think about going back to my job. My leave will be up in four weeks. I can hardly stand it. They have offered to let me stay out another month, but I can't afford more time off without pay. How will I be able to leave my baby? Who can I trust to leave her with?" Before this visit is over, I will hear this question in one form or another. The timing of the parents' return to work raises many important issues. If they plan to leave the baby with another caregiver, we need to address their feelings about separation, as well as our concern about the care that the baby will receive. If the father is to share the care, they will want to discuss this arrangement. If there is to be a secondary caregiver at home, I should, ideally, meet this person as well.

Depending upon the parents' circumstances, I am likely at this visit to encourage at least four months at home for the mother. Four months gives her time to get through the fussy three-month period and enjoy a month of pleasure, with the baby smiling and gurgling at her. If she must share all these new steps with a substitute, it is awfully hard on her. Sometimes, parents who had well-laid plans set in motion for day care or a nanny/caregiver at home will find their feelings changed. "I just can't bring myself to think about it," said one mother. "Every time I think about leaving the baby, my mind goes blank and I feel overwhelmed." Parents must weigh these strong and important feelings against their need for two salaries or pressures from employers. It is one of the toughest of all decisions. When a family faces this first major separation, it is a touchpoint that makes them vulnerable, open to the support I can offer as I deepen my relationship with them.

If parents feel that they both must work full-time, I then encourage them to take time to look for the right caregiver. They need someone they like and can trust, and they should always watch this possible caregiver for their child with other babies to see how he or she interacts with them. It is important for them to consider how they will feel if this person takes care of their baby and shares her with them. I remind parents that the more loving, attentive, and skillful a caregiver is, the more reassured and the more jealous they will be. I urge them to get someone they can be jealous of. But they should also try to find someone who cares about them and their adjustment. Parents must be able to participate in decisions about their baby, whoever is caring for her. In my book *Working and Caring* (see *Further Reading*), I go into each of these issues in depth.

In child care, the ratio of babies to adults is absolutely critical—it should not be more than three babies to one adult. High-quality care is expensive, but it's essential to the baby and to parents' peace of mind. Equally important is the caregiver's ability to understand and respond to each baby as an individual. A good childcare center, though, also nurtures parents. I wouldn't recommend any center where a parent does not feel welcome—at all times. The best caregivers are hard to find and may require parents to reserve a spot months in advance (see Part 3, "Childcare Choices").

Sometimes parents ask, "How long would you recommend I stay at home if I had a real choice?" If this choice appears possible, I suggest one year. By the second year, a baby can handle playmates, so a group situation is not so stressful. Before that, the optimal solution is for one or both parents to work only part-time, so that one parent is available to the baby for a large part of each day. I see this opportunity as one that is almost as important to the parents' development as it is to the baby's. (See Greenspan, *The Four-Thirds Solution*, in *Further Reading.*)

If a family just can't afford this option, I still try to help them work things out. If a mother can figure out how to keep nursing, by pumping her breasts at work and perhaps nursing at lunch, both she and the baby will benefit. It's wonderful for a mother to be able to put the baby to breast when she gets home from work. (See Huggins in *Further Reading* and *Useful Addresses and Web Sites* for help with pumping milk at work.)

For mothers or fathers who plan to stay at home for a time, I nevertheless encourage them to respect their need for time to themselves. After the huge changes of new parenthood, they need to re-cement their relationship with some time together. This may be a very good time to think about hiring a sitter occasionally in order to get some time away from the baby. A short time will do. It is vital that parents find a sitter they can trust.

The parents' difficulty in separating may be the most significant hurdle in leaving a new baby. The baby may miss them, but parents will surely feel lost without the baby already. Parents need the baby more than she may appear to need them. Caring new parents need to prepare for these feelings, for they are common. A short time away can be a real help in mastering these feelings of loss. When they first leave, many mothers prefer, when possible, to return for each feeding. If necessary, however, a mother can pump her milk beforehand to leave it with the sitter.

Sometimes, a mother will ask me: "Will she know me if I go back to work and have to leave her?" I assure her that the baby will. She'll show this by the special movements and rhythms they have learned together. A mother can watch for these so that she won't feel so separated.

At this six- to eight-week visit, parents often ask whether they can take their baby with them when they go out or to their offices. I assure them that they can and mention that the only problem with crowds of people is that many of them will have infections that the baby could pick up. It is a good idea not to let unknown or runny-nosed people hold her or lean over her to play games. Everyone wants to hold a small baby. When we'd travel with one of ours, all the dear old ladies (and some gents) would try to hold her, and some would eventually sneeze in the baby's face. I'd have to say to these well-meaning invaders, "I'm sorry, but I must protect you. My baby is under surveillance for a serious infection." No one wanted to hold her then.

6. Four Months

Over many years of practice, I remember looking forward especially to the four-month visit. Parents and baby are now "an item." Bonds of affection are weaving them tightly into a family. Even brand-new parents are likely to be more self-confident by now. Either parent may carry the baby, tossing him about with new nonchalance, like a package. When they sit down, they place the baby out in front of them to coo and gurgle over him. If he is sleepy, they wake him to perform. They watch other people to check whether they are noticing and admiring this remarkable offspring of theirs. Innocent bystanders in the waiting room are regaled with his latest achievements. It's likely that friends and coworkers find them a touch boring.

Once in the office, both parents will tickle him and coo in high-pitched voices—anything to elicit one of his adorable responses for me to admire. When I must undress him, they hover over me to be sure I'm handling him properly. When I give him his vaccinations, they wince and grab him away from me. (As of January 2006, the Centers for Disease Control and Prevention recommends the second dose of the following immunizations at four months: Diphtheria, Tetanus, and Pertussis [DTaP], Hemophilus Influenza [Hib], Polio [IPV], and Pneumococcus [PCV].) The baby's parents *know* him now and are at a peak of their love affair with him. All this is very good news to me, and I enjoy observing him as he reacts with them. He will have even more clearly different behaviors with each of them than at the last visit—smooth with his mother, jerky and playful with his father. He will grin and coo to me across my desk but will break down into wails if I come too close, or if I lean over him to examine him. My office and I are strange to him. This represents the earliest signs of stranger awareness—which will only peak at seven or eight months, and comes at a period when the baby is making a real spurt in cognitive development. Already, he is sizing me up for comparison with the familiar figures of his world—parents, siblings, sitter.

The passionate new feelings of parenthood may be overwhelming to some parents. "I can't talk or think about anything but my baby. My friends who don't have kids are sick of me. When I walk around with her, all I want to do is show her off. Is there something wrong with me?" I can reassure parents that this storm of feelings is called "falling in love." Parents are so in love with their baby that they feel he is a part of them. Every achievement he makes feels like it's their own. With this pride goes the wonder of watching their child master a new task for the first time. Watching him learn is awe-inspiring. Of course they are wrapped up in that baby! Everyone who has ever had a baby knows the feeling. From a pediatrician's point of view, it is the best thing that could happen. These deep attachments will become the anchor for a secure childhood.

So much else has happened as well. In just four months the family has reorganized itself. By now, each member knows his or her role. The difficult adjustment to understanding the baby as an individual has been mastered. The fussy periods at the end of the day are being replaced by a period of intense communication. This formerly dreaded time becomes the most exciting period of play. If crying or "colic" is still an issue, we'll need to look into the underlying reasons (gastroesophageal reflux, milk protein allergies, lactose intolerance, self-regulating difficulties, among other possibilities). Be sure to check with your pediatrician: The squeaky wheel gets the oil.

After sharing the parents' exuberant delight in their baby, I may hear concerns expressed in the areas of feeding and sleeping. The baby's development will create choices for parents in the way they choose to handle feedings and sleep cycles. I use this touchpoint to help parents understand the baby's side of the issues that will arise. If they can understand his developmental needs, they can make choices that can help prevent problems in feeding and sleeping.

In the feeding area, easy routines will be upset by competing interests—the baby will want to look around and listen. He will not stay at the breast or bottle. He may even become difficult to feed. Parents may worry whether he's

getting enough. But if they can see this brief period (one to two weeks) as an exciting cognitive burst of interest in the environment that competes with feeding, they won't confuse it with failings on their part.

In the sleep area, it is now critical to set up rituals that will help the baby learn to get to sleep on his own in the first place and to sleep through an eight- or twelve-hour stretch without waking. At this stage, the central nervous system has matured enough to allow a longer period of sleep. Helping parents understand the baby's sleep cycles will prepare them to nudge him toward an independent sleep pattern. As we will see, these new feeding and sleep issues are touchpoints that parents and physician can address before they arise, and prevent problem behavior from setting in.

Feeding

The now-predictable schedule makes a new kind of "normal" life possible again for parents. No longer does the baby need to choose his own feeding times. He can be awakened in the morning to fit the family schedule. Then, parents can plan the other feedings every three to four hours, with morning and afternoon naps between them. Usually, six breast or bottle feedings a day are needed at this age. The last feeding can be set by parents, who may find it helpful to wake the baby up to be fed just before their own bedtime to prolong the baby's nighttime sleep. If the baby has already established a fairly regular schedule, a parent will recognize when there is a new change occurring. If he is irregular, it is harder for them to figure him out. For this reason, I encourage parents to press the baby toward some sort of steady schedule. If he is gaining weight and thriving on his formula or breast-feeding, they can be sure it suits him.

A mother who is working outside the home can pump her breasts a few times while at work each day to bring breast milk home to her baby. She'll find that having a picture of her baby with her will help. Every employer ought to offer nursing mothers ample time to pump milk (fifteen to thirty minutes each session), as well as a quiet, comfortable, and private place to use for this purpose—and a refrigerator to store the milk in. Employers will find that breast-feeding mothers miss fewer days at work than those who feed their babies formula, since breast-fed babies are better protected against illness. A mother can leave the person caring for her baby with her milk from the day before. (Breast milk stays fresh for twenty-four to forty-eight hours if refrigerated. Frozen breast milk can be refrigerated for twenty-four hours after thawing, and then, if unused, must be discarded. Many women find it helpful to freeze small amounts in separate plastic bottles or milk bags. These should be labeled with the date so that they are used within three months.) She and the baby can enjoy three good feedings—in the morning before she leaves, in the evening when she returns, and one more before his bedtime. It is important to her milk supply to waken him for this third feeding at the end of a working day. So is a healthy daily diet for the nursing mother of at least 1,800 calories, or 500 calories more per day than before pregnancy, with plenty of fruits, vegetables, whole grain breads and cereals, enough dairy products to respond to increased calcium needs, and plenty of protein. Breast-feeding mothers should certainly pay attention to their diets and supplement them with vitamins and iron. It is wonderful for both mother and baby if she can come home to gather him up for an intimate breast-feeding. That's "quality time"! (See *Further Reading* and *Useful Addresses and Web Sites* for more information on breast-feeding.)

It's always amazing to me that the breast can adjust to a baby's increasing demands. The breast as an adaptable organ is unparalleled. Not only does the amount of breast milk adjust to a baby's needs, but so do the relative proportions of fats and proteins! However, after four or five months, I also check to see whether a breast-fed baby will need iron supplements, which partly depends on the mother's diet and whether the baby is ready for iron-containing solids such as pureed meat in another month or so. As he grows over these first few months, he will have more than doubled his birth weight and will have grown four to five inches. After feedings have settled to a regular, predictable every three- or four-hour pattern during the day, there will still be off-days when the baby wants to eat every two hours. These represent growth spurts when his needs are temporarily out of proportion to the balance that the breasts have achieved. By eating more often, he stimulates them to respond with richer milk and more of it.

As the baby's brain develops, a spurt in his awareness of his surroundings that occurs at four and a half to five months will interfere with smooth feedings. At this age, the baby's eyes are better able to focus at further distances. Suddenly, parents find that the baby is fascinated by the shadow of the plant on the wall, the light through the window, everything except the close-up breast or bottle. The baby is suddenly aware of sights and sounds in a brand new way. As each irresistible new noise or sight distracts him, his interest in feeding fades. He pulls the breast around with him as he looks in every direction. Each new stimulus demands his attention. For example, babies at this age become excited about new toys, literally panting with anticipation when they see something new. This new development predictably interferes with the child's feeding and sleeping and will bother and frustrate parents if they have not been prepared. I try to make this touchpoint an opportunity to help parents see this change as normal and exciting, a positive sign of growth that they can plan for and take pride in. The baby's new visual distractibility can be cut down during feedings simply by dimming the lights. Or, each feeding can become a time for new kinds of play and communication. The baby's first attempts at reaching will make each feeding a lively game.

(In another couple of months, when you've started him on solids, he'll want to help with the spoon! He will need to smear the food over his face and in his hair, and if you are holding him, he'll smear it over you! That kind of exploration is as satisfying for him as being fed. Although it will make feeding more difficult, it is another sign of growth.)

At this point, many breast-feeding mothers tell me that they think their baby is "ready to wean." They may even start to wonder if he's ready to start solids. When I remind them that they wanted to breast-feed through the first year, they reply, "I did, but he doesn't want it anymore. Whenever I start to feed him, he pulls away and won't stay at the breast. Every sound or motion distracts him. He just won't take enough at any one feeding. I think I'm losing my milk." The nursing mother is running headlong into this same new developmental spurt—in visual acuity and cognitive awareness.

Mothers who have been savoring the warm, uninterrupted intimacy of breast-feeding often feel deserted at this time. The baby's new independence and focus away from her feel like a desertion. Until now, it has been possible for the mother to think of herself and her baby as a single unit. No longer. In fact, psychoanalysts such as Margaret Mahler have spoken of babies beginning to "hatch" at this time, or of a "psychological birth" several months later than the physiological one. If mothers do not recognize what is happening, they can become sad and frustrated. They may feel as though they are losing the wonderful love affair they've developed. They may have trouble accepting the separation as a spurt in the baby's autonomy. Some even become pregnant again to fill the perceived emptiness.

When mothers seem to me to be experiencing such feelings, I can point out that the baby isn't losing interest in her breast. He just has a whole new set of competing interests. They are *temporarily* more important than the familiar experience of breast-feeding. This spurt of interest in the world lasts one or two weeks. Then, babies will return to the breast with renewed vigor. There is no reason to give up in the meantime. Instead, the mother can adapt to this new development by letting the baby look around and explore, and can even give him a toy to handle while nursing. During this time, daytime feedings may not stimulate the milk supply sufficiently. The baby may be too excited to eat properly in the day. Morning and evening, the feedings should take place in a quiet, dark room where there are few distractions. That will keep the breast milk coming through this period. Soon babies will start preferring solids, because the situation for feeding them is more complex and they can be more involved while being fed. Nursing at the breast may be too passive at this time—babies this age are anything but passive! The quiet, cooperative little infant has become a whirlwind of activity. It is more and more exciting to take in and learn about a whole new world.

Feedings are no longer simple events for parents. The distractions can be a real threat to the instinct that all mothers have. They feel they must get food into the baby. If parents can understand what is behind the baby's distraction and refusals at feeding time, they need not feel they are failing. Supporting the child's excitement in learning is also a vital part of parenting. Understanding this important developmental step—the cognitive burst of the four-month touchpoint—can help parents avoid invitations to struggle or to force-feed, and prevent serious eating problems later on.

Later, when solids are started, some babies will wait for them and demand less milk. That first spoonful of rice cereal can seem like a life-changing step away from the complete, idyllic union of a breast-feeding mother and her baby. "I really feel sad that he needs anything but me," said one mother. "It's been so delicious to have him completely dependent on me." With feelings like these, many mothers find it easier to nurse first, and then try the spooned-in solids.

Other mothers have quite a different set of feelings: "I can't wait to start solids. All my friends are starting, and their babies are way ahead of mine." When I ask what a mother means by "ahead," she might reply, "Well, they weigh more, and they must be familiar with more different tastes. They've already learned not to gag on the spoon." My answer to this is that solids-too-soon can put extra fat on babies, and fat babies are not healthier. (See recommendation of the American Academy of Pediatrics discussed later in this chapter.) In addition, she should not worry about the gagging; this is a normal part of learning to master use of the spoon, but is also a reason not to rush. The real question for parents is whether they want to raise their baby with a competitive, keeping-up-with-the-Joneses attitude. I try to raise this issue while respecting the understandable desire of parents for their baby to be "the best," the most perfect of all. This natural part of caring fuels all the strenuous adjustments a parent must make. But when parents seem too driven, lacking in any humor over this competition, I need to point out the price for the baby of too much pressure.

Sleep

By four months, many babies no longer need a late-night feeding, and others are able to sleep from a late-night feeding to an early morning one. A baby's nervous system has now matured enough for him to begin his night with non-REM rather than REM sleep, and to spend more time in non-REM sleep, which now or soon will include the deeper sleep of Stages III and IV. A four-month-old is able to sleep for a twelve-hour stretch with only occasional, brief awakenings at night. An eight-hour stretch of sleep means that the baby must get himself back down into deep sleep at least twice. In order to sleep through twelve hours, he must be able to settle again at least three times. If he is to sleep independently, he must learn patterns for self-comforting each time. For all these reasons, the period from four to five months is a crucial time for parents to decide about their role in helping the baby learn to sleep. For a baby to sleep through the night, he must be ready to cycle between deep and light sleep several times. As I help parents to see the implications of this I am taking advantage of this early opportunity to prevent sleep problems later, and to extend their understanding of the ways parents can rely on their pediatricians.

Sleep experts have found that all of us cycle between "quiet" (or non-REM) sleep and "active" (or REM, for rapid eye movement) sleep, coming up to the REM state roughly every ninety minutes. Every three to four hours we come into an even more active state, closer to waking. As a baby comes up into light or "active" sleep, he is likely to cry out, to become disorganized, and to thrash around in bed. Since a baby should sleep on his back, he is likely to startle, throw out his arms and legs, become upset, and cry. If he's already rolling over, he may have discovered that lying on his stomach tends to provide more containment for this disorganized activity. Back sleeping is particularly important in the first six months. However, aside from starting the baby out to sleep on his back, there's little that a parent can do to keep him in that position all night once he's learned to roll over. (Keeping sheets, pillows, and blankets out of his crib, and making sure the crib has a firm mattress, will help to reduce the risk of SIDS.) As he cries and moves around, the baby may get more upset. If he has a pattern of self-comforting, such as finding his thumb, or if he can get himself into a comfortable "nesting" position, he will settle down again. Some babies scrabble their way into the corner, apparently seeking the pressure on the top of their heads that they had in the womb. An active, intense baby has a more difficult time settling himself down. Thrashing around, more and more upset, he shoots up to a wide awake and alert state. Then he wants to be held and comforted. He hasn't yet learned to quiet himself. Parents of such a baby will feel compelled to dive in and offer the baby the comfort he needs to calm down.

Most babies can settle themselves over these ninety-minute cycles. But a baby's sleep is more likely to be disrupted when these three- to four-hour cycles end more abruptly, with arousal to a wide-awake state. Some cry out as if in pain or fear. They aren't awake, but they may awaken themselves by their own thrashing, uncontrolled behavior. Parents find these periods very difficult. They feel they must go in to help the baby settle. Feedings at 10:00 P.M., 2:00 A.M., and 6:00 A.M. are predictably based on these arousal periods, though babies may or may not still need a feeding at one of these times. However, if parents rush in, they will become part of the baby's arousal pattern and will then have to be there to help him settle himself every three to four hours. If they pick him up each time to feed, change, and settle him, he will become dependent on their ministrations and will not learn to quiet himself back into deep sleep. Understanding these patterns and the effect of their response on the baby will help parents stay out of a cycle that the baby can learn to handle on his own.

At this important touchpoint—when parents begin to express their distress over the nightly wakings, and their babies' sleep patterns are maturing—I must first make clear the difference between helping a baby learn to settle down and leaving him to "cry it out." I don't think any baby *ever* needs to "cry it out" over anything. Being left to cry it out doesn't teach a baby anything except that his parents can desert him when he needs them. The task for parents is to learn not to jump at the first whimper, but instead to develop a supportive bedtime ritual that balances the baby's need for their soothing with his growing ability to settle himself. When a baby is put to bed in the evening, parents can sing to him or feed him and croon to him in a way that's different from what they do during daytime feedings—softer and slower. Then, the baby can be put to bed before he's completely asleep, while the parent sits there and pats him calmly but firmly. If he has a pacifier or a "lovey" (a favorite blanket or stuffed animal that he strokes and cuddles to soothe himself), this can be used to help him. A baby who is always allowed to fall asleep at the breast is not learning to get himself to sleep. He's learning to use his mother for that purpose. As a result, every four hours at night, when he comes up to light sleep, he needs her as part of his pattern.

Sleep problems are often a combination of the baby's struggle to learn to sleep on his own and parents' difficulty in taking a step back to turn this task over to him (see "Sleep Problems"). Many parents are reluctant to leave a child to be independent at night. I can understand that. But parents who find it hard to leave a baby until morning will make themselves part of his self-consoling pattern when he wakes through the night. This can set a pattern that is likely to last into the future.

Working parents in particular may find it difficult to separate from the child at night, because they have been away all day. A warm, intimate ritual in the evening and time to cuddle in the morning before work can help them deal with this feeling. But many working mothers find they need their babies at night. We discuss their issues and the risk that separation will grow more and more difficult for the baby later on. But the decision to help the child learn to sleep through must be their choice, and I will support them—either way.

Many parents have reasons to feel compelled to respond to fussing at night. Single parents, who may be lonely themselves, may find it particularly difficult to let their child work out his own pattern of settling himself. Parents who have felt deserted by their own parents will want to avoid repeating this pattern and may find it impossible to leave a baby to learn his own means of self-comforting. Parents who work full-time and are conflicted about the limited time they have for the baby, or who have had difficulty in separations and in developing independence in their own past, may not be able to acknowledge the baby's readiness for independence at night.

More and more families in this country believe strongly that the whole family should sleep together in a "family bed." For most of human history, all over the world, co-sleeping has been the way most families have spent their nights. But if new parents are considering keeping the baby in their bed, they will want to understand that such a decision can affect the family for many years ahead. An open discussion of this issue between parents and their physician can prevent unanticipated crises later on. Such concerns are a predictable part of the four-month touchpoint, when independent sleep becomes more of a possibility for the baby. If a child can be helped to learn to sleep through the night at this age, it needn't become a "problem" later on. Parents will want the child out of their bed sooner or later, but this will prove more difficult once the child has become dependent on their warmth and the rhythms of their breathing and heartbeat to settle back to sleep. Then, parents may become punitive as the child, understandably, resists sleeping alone later on. Anticipating these issues can prevent such conflicts later. (See "Sleep Problems" on co-sleeping and SIDS concerns.)

Once a baby is allowed to sleep in his parents' bed, he cannot be evicted whenever the parents feel that they want their bed to themselves without consequences for the child. The transition will take time and may be much more difficult than giving the baby his own crib from the first. In my conversation with parents on this topic, I also help them anticipate predictable times when they may want to have their bed to themselves again—for example, as sexual feelings re-intensify once labor and delivery and the new baby's arrival recede into the past. Better to move a child to his own bed well before this occurs, or as early as possible in the next pregnancy, than to impose this major change at a time when there will be so many other ways in which the baby will feel that he is losing you.

In some cultures, parents and children sleep together because of lack of space. In Japan, the traditional arrangement is called *kawa,* or "river." The mother is one bank, the father another, and the children in the middle are the river. In families where this tradition is still practiced, the father moves out of the bed when there is more than one child, if there's room for him to move out. The mother continues to sleep with the children until they are five or six years of age. Then, the grandmother may even take over! In parts of Africa and southern Mexico, a mother and father have traditionally slept with the baby between them until the next pregnancy. Then, the child would be put out of the bed to make room for the next baby. This seems like a double whammy for the child to me.

In cultures where there is a choice, it is not necessary and does not seem fair to push a child out abruptly later. So, the decision should be made in advance, with full awareness of the changing pros and cons of co-sleeping as the child grows. Parents must examine their own biases and consider the long-term consequences of their decision before they make up their minds. If they do decide to co-sleep, they will want to watch the child for autonomy issues in other areas of his development.

Teething

Most babies begin to get primary teeth after the age of four months, usually at six to nine months. There is an old-fashioned saying that babies should have a tooth for every month from six months on. This is not to be depended upon. The timing of teething is genetic, and late-teething parents are likely to have late-teething children. None of my children even began to get teeth until they were nearly a year old. Neither did I, my mother said. There is no known disadvantage to late teething. Children should, though, have all of their "baby teeth" by two or three years of age.

Permanent teeth begin to form in the gums in infancy. Allowing milk and milk sugars to remain in the baby's mouth for long periods (four to eight hours) can cause "baby bottle teeth" and cavities, which in turn can even affect permanent teeth. Parents should not leave their baby with a bottle of milk in his bed!

Teething becomes a catchall to explain every upset at this age. Every time a baby whimpers or squirms, "it's his teeth." By blaming everything on teeth, parents are likely to miss other reasons for the baby's behavior. Frustration at not being able to do what he wants to do is one reason. He may want to reach or to move or to pay attention. Boredom and other forms of discomfort are other reasons for "teething" complaints.

As they come in, teeth bother babies because they are like a foreign body in the gum. They probably feel like a splinter in a finger. The tooth causes swelling around it. When the baby sucks, there is more pressure on the already swollen gum. So he squirms, whimpers, and refuses to suck. Whether a child is teething should be easy to determine: If he is, he will cry out when you press on his lower front gums. If parents can rub out the initial swelling before they offer him the chance to suck, he can suck with less pain. To do this, parents should wash their finger and rub the swollen gums before each feeding. After the first cry, he'll love the massage. Pain around the lower front teeth, the incisors, is more likely to interfere with feedings. After the first two teeth come in, the baby is used to the dull ache of other teeth as they break through. Teething pains probably don't last more than a few weeks. All of a sudden there is a clink against a cup or spoon. A ridge of tiny white dots has cut through the gum, and it's done! But the timing varies from one baby to another.

Communication

At four months, a baby's cooing and babbling become irresistible. A parent may reply, "If only I knew what you were saying!" But often it seems that we do. By now, parents have also had plenty of time to practice "motherese," that soft, gentle, high-pitched baby talk that says to their baby: "Now I'm talking only to you." Some parents are uncomfortable with this way of talking or fear that their baby will not learn to speak properly as a result. But "motherese" is an economical form of communication that clearly indicates when it's time to pay attention. This way a baby can save precious energy and tune out when adults are talking with each other about adult matters.

In the fifth month, babies begin to play games with their new achievements. They learn to cry more deliberately, to wait to see whether anyone is coming, then to cry out a second time. This is a big step toward mastering the cognitive processes needed to understand causality: It means the baby is beginning to realize that when he does something, something predictable happens.

Parents tend to blame this kind of exploratory, communicative crying on teething, on fatigue, or on "being spoiled." Each of these may certainly play a role. If parents think their baby's teeth are the reason he's complaining, they can test it out, as we just suggested. If it's fatigue, the baby can be soothed to rest. He may have to cry a bit before he can relax. If nothing works, maybe his parents have become *too* available and need to let him know that he can try to entertain himself briefly. Parents may even feel he is learning to be manipulative, but what is manipulation for a baby if not doing whatever he can do to get what he needs or wants? They can try safely hanging up interesting things for him to look at or reach for, but nothing will interest him as much as they do! At this age, it is too soon to worry about spoiling, and more important to encourage a baby to keep working on his efforts to communicate, and, from time to time, to satisfy himself.

With the development of this new, more precise ability to communicate, an exciting new dialogue has begun! Coughing, sneezing, gagging, and squealing can all become purposeful behaviors now. Gradually, the baby learns to master them, to produce them at will. Later, with his experiments, he will learn that "da-da-da-da" calls up his father's face. When he whiningly says "mum-mum-mum-mum," his mother comes running. Soon after, he will learn how to master these vocal games and how to use them to draw in the people around him. The ante is raised.

Parents may wonder, "How do I know when he really needs me or just wants more attention?" It may not be clear at first. But when it happens over and over, there will be signs. Does he cry out, then wait to see whether he gets a response? Does he show in his facial behavior that he's "learned" to get

a response? He may even look self-satisfied afterward. This marks a very important achievement—the baby has learned not only to expect responses but to produce them. For the parents, too, this will be a turning point. Instead of automatically responding to the baby's cries and signals, parents must pull back to figure out when it is important to the baby's learning for them to get involved, and when the baby needs a chance to manage with a more minimal response from them that means "You're okay on your own right now." At the point where they feel manipulated, they must make a decision. Much of the time, this new dialogue will bring a deeper relationship and new pleasures; nevertheless, parents will need to adapt to this new balance between the baby's ability to communicate and his need to handle boredom, frustration, and a whole range of urges on his own (self-regulation).

Learning

Motor and cognitive learning are inseparable at this age. The efforts of a four- to five-month-old baby are spent in trying to learn to sit, to use his hands to balance while sitting, to reach, to put objects into his mouth, and to transfer them from one hand to the other. These activities open up new worlds to explore. Whenever a parent pulls a baby up to sit by pulling on his arms, he will strain to get himself up. By five months, he'll work so hard that he'll come up on stiff legs into a standing position. Standing, he'll look up at an adult as if for approval. Already he is in a hurry to get upright.

Babies at this age can't wait to get going. Some fuss and fuss until a parent sits them up in a chair or lap. But frustration is a powerful force for learning. Parents can show a baby how to pull himself into a sitting position, but it will take a long, frustrating month or so for him to learn to do it. Parents can do what they can to help, but they mustn't feel that they *have* to go to the baby all the time.

If parents get a chair or a swing, the back should be tilted so that the baby is not too upright. He can strain his back if he is slumped forward in it for too long. The motorized swings do soothe some babies and reduce their frustration, but I don't think they are necessary.

Learning to transfer objects from one hand to another is a great step toward playing with them. A baby at four months should be trying to play with and handle objects. By five months, he usually can hand an object back and forth. I'd tie several handy objects on a safe string (too short to get caught up in or strangled by and carefully secured) across his crib, as a cradle gym. They should be available to him for handling and exploring. Mouthing, touching, and fingering them all become his way of finding out everything he can about objects.

I am always thrilled when a baby explores my face as I hold him at this age. This is such a tender gesture, and it demonstrates a keen sense of exploration in him. This learning will eventually lead to a sense of "person permanence"—the awareness that people are real and continue to exist even when out of sight.

Rolling over is an unpredictable milestone for many babies. Many normal babies never roll over. They are contented on their backs or stomachs and don't care whether they turn or not. Fat babies have too much to move and are likely to be inactive. The first time that a baby turns over may be a reflex response. When babies happen to writhe and turn themselves over, the suddenness is coupled with a strange new posture. This frightens them and they cry out. A parent rushes to find them in the new position. But they are overwhelmed, and they may not try it again for weeks.

Parents who hear that other babies are already rolling over wonder whether they should teach their baby this skill. I do not recommend it. This motor milestone is the least reliable one. There is no particular time that is appropriate for a baby to be rolling over. It's much too individual. When a parent asks about this, I take the opportunity to discuss the reasons for not comparing one baby with another. Comparisons and competition can put parents under pressure, leading them to push the baby to "catch up." It is much more important to get on his wavelength and value him for what he can do and wants to do. When parents value a baby, he'll value himself. Of course, it is very hard not to compare, and that is one way to learn what to expect. But babies know when parents are not happy with them.

When a baby spends all the time on his back, parents wonder how he'll learn to crawl. I assure them that he'll learn to crawl when he's ready, probably at seven or eight months. If he's on his belly, he can already begin to try to crawl, and he will strengthen his back. Because babies are put to sleep on their backs, it is important to help them spend time on their bellies while they are awake: They need "tummy time." Some parents have misunderstood the "Back-to-Sleep" campaign and kept their babies off their bellies when awake too. The result has been weakened backs, shoulders, and arms. This can easily be avoided by placing a baby of this age on his belly whenever he's awake and parents can be nearby to keep an eye on him. If the baby seems frustrated, parents can get down on the floor at his level and make life interesting down there with little games and toys to watch. But this is not necessary for him to learn to crawl. He will learn eventually and will have learned to do this *himself.*

Looking Ahead

Feeding The exploratory behavior we have spoken about will increase in the next few weeks, so I give parents the following suggestions. The baby will want to hold his own bottle. Hand it to him with the bottom first. Watch him look at it quizzically, then realize that he can turn it around to get the nipple in his mouth. He will have learned something about fulfilling his own expectancy. But you should always sit and hold him when he's eating. Feeding time is about much more than food. Communication with the baby is also essential. Some experts report that the necessary fluids for digestion (hydrochloric acid in the stomach and duodenal juices in the small intestine) are not secreted unless a baby has a pleasant time at a feeding. (There are a number of syndromes sometimes referred to together as "failure to thrive" in which a baby may refuse food or fail to grow, and in some cases this may occur when the baby is not in a nurturing relationship with his environment. Often, though, the tension in the relationship arises from some physical problem in the baby that makes him very difficult to nurture—for example, trouble swallowing, severe gastroesophageal reflux, hypersensitivity of the tongue and mouth, and so on). At this age, a baby will pause during a feeding for you to talk to him, to look at him, and to cuddle him. Then he'll resume his sucking with a pleased look on his face.

At five or six months, when periods of demanding more and more feedings continue for a week or more, it will be time to consider solid food. Around this time, most babies begin to need a supplement to milk feedings. The American Academy of Pediatrics considers six months a good age to start solids. In some cultures, solid feedings are started earlier, often in the hope that this will push babies to stretch out their nighttime sleep. However, the baby's sucking apparatus is not well suited to the voluntary act of swallowing until at least after four months, and early introduction of foods other than breast milk can predispose to allergies.

If you are bottle-feeding, twenty to twenty-four ounces of formula are adequate for this period. Breast milk or formula will still be more important than solids for the first year, so if the baby is harder to nurse or feed with a bottle after solids are introduced, cut back on them to be sure he gets his milk. You can nurse or give him his bottle in a dark, quiet room for a few days until he gets over his initial excitement about everything around him. That way, he'll get the milk he needs to grow and gain. A baby won't gain weight unless he's getting an adequate amount of milk.

Sleep If a baby has established a going-to-sleep pattern, parents can expect him to continue to stretch out the amount of time he can sleep without fully waking up at night. He will still come up to light sleep, scrabble around in bed, cry out, and then find his pattern to get back down. These patterns for self-comforting and for getting himself to sleep will become even more important to the baby over the next two months. On a day when a baby has been overstimulated or exposed to many strange events, he is likely to awaken all over again at night. He may need several nights of comforting in order to resume his former pattern of sleeping through.

Making Time for Play The continuing burst of cognitive awareness will affect every part of the baby's day. Not only feeding time but diapering and bath time will become new challenges for parents, and chances for exploration for him. He'll want to turn one way, then the other, scrabbling around in your slippery hands. This means additional vigilance from parents. A wriggly, slippery baby needs every bit of your attention. It is vital *never* to leave a baby alone on the changing or bath table. *Always* keep one hand on a part of him. At some point, when he's sitting, you can bathe him sitting in a little tub or in the sink *if* you have your hot water heater turned down below 120 degrees. Serious burns can occur when a baby turns on the hot water spigot accidentally. One easy way to bathe a baby is to take him into the tub with you.

Parents wonder how vigorously to clean a baby's genitals. My advice is: Don't be too vigorous—it isn't necessary. For a little girl, a small amount of secretions from her vagina are normal. When you immerse her in a bath, she'll get clean once a day. *Never* use bubble bath or detergents with a little girl. They can irritate the mucous membranes of her vagina. Then bacteria can lead to infection. In both sexes, bubble baths and detergents can cause sensitivity rashes and dry out the skin. They should be prohibited for babies. For baby boys, there is no need to retract the foreskin, and it should never be forced back.

Don't be too fussy about cleanliness. Bath time can be a lovely, amusing time to get close to your baby (but never leave a baby unattended in the bathtub). If you're out working all day, try to fit the bath in when you have time at home for fun. Diapering can be an additional time for games and communication. If necessary, get up early so you can have a leisurely time with the baby in the morning before you leave. Plan to have another as soon as you walk in at the end of the day. Your baby will fall apart and fuss at you when you arrive. He has missed you and saved up his protest all day. But after this period of disintegration, you can have a lovely reconciling time together. Rock him and sing to him. Let him "talk" to you about how awful his day was without you.

Motor Skills In the next two months, the baby will be learning many new and exciting skills. When pulling him up to stand, you can see the excitement on his face. A five-month-old baby *loves* to stand up. He looks around for your approval. Even when he is crying, when you stand him, he gets excited and stops. His long-term goal, after all, is to get on his feet and become upright.

He will try to master sitting in the next two months. At first, he'll sit with a rounded back and a tripod made from his arms. At six months, he'll sit with a stronger back, but he'll still use his arms to balance himself. He can't and won't let go to reach for an object while he's sitting.

When he's not trying to sit on his own, or after he's learned to sit without the support of his arms, reaching, transferring objects, and mouthing them to explore them will continue as vital parts of learning. He'll only need a few brightly colored, nontoxic blocks or rings at a time to keep himself busy. The baby will also play with one hand by fingering it with the other.

On his stomach, or when he collapses from sitting, he'll be likely to get the concept of moving around. He will conceive of creeping on his belly. He will first learn by pushing himself backward, *away* from his goal. He will cry out with frustration. It is difficult for a parent to watch this frustration. A hand held firmly against the bottom of the baby's feet may help him learn he can push himself forward. In any case, he'll learn from his frustration. I can't emphasize enough that nothing is as powerful as frustration to push a baby to learn—as long as it's not too much to handle for him. Sometimes a task may need to be broken down into smaller, more manageable steps so that the frustration won't be overwhelming. Watch him try a new task, get frustrated, but then finally succeed. He will be so thrilled with himself when *he* finally achieves it! He has done it *himself.* When parents are patient and can understand the drive and the intensity in the baby's attempt to learn all these new achievements, they are paving the way to become allies in his development and not sabotaging his inner drive. If they come to me with worries about the baby's frustration, I can help them see this as an important touchpoint, another opportunity for me to enter the family system and deepen my relationship with each member.

Stranger Awareness The new burst of awareness in sights and sounds can affect a five- or six-month-old baby's readiness to accept strangers. Before this, he may have been happy as he was handed from one person to another. Parents of four- or five-month-olds proudly tell me that their baby likes everyone and will enter a crowded room without a whimper. This is likely to change soon. I see a new recognition of strangers in my office at a four- or five-month visit. Across my desk from me, a baby this age gurgles and goos, smiling invitingly as his parents talk to me. If I let myself be seduced and take him up out of his mother's or father's lap, or if I look him in the face when one of them puts him on my examining table, I know he will start crying. He will cry relentlessly throughout the entire exam. If, on the other hand, I look past his face and talk softly past him, and if I can get a parent to hover over him while I examine him, I can do an entire exam without upsetting him. I can even give him his shots without having him shriek for long if I urge parents to hold him tightly on their shoulder, then quickly shift him and distract him with something to look at. His new fascination with visual exploration is so powerful that it makes him disregard unpleasant sensations.

A stranger presents a baby with too many new, unfamiliar stimuli. At this age, he wants to be able to study each one. At this time, grandparents or sitters can cause real upset if they rush at him too quickly or look him in the face when they first meet him. He needs time and space to take in and become accustomed to each new sight and sound. This new sensory awareness and the motor achievements of reaching and handling accompany and fuel each other. He can not only take in his surroundings but he can now also reach out and feel them—two new areas of exploration. No wonder life is so exciting and overwhelming!

The new awareness that leads to stranger anxiety also leads to an increase in the baby's ability to protest separations. More than ever, he needs a stable caregiver. If one parent is at home, the baby will still protest an evening babysitter, and if both parents work away from home, any changes in child care or live-in caregiving will upset the baby.

This change can come as a surprise to parents. "Now he cries every time I leave him with someone else. He never used to mind it," said one mother. This is one of those bursts of development when babies become increasingly sensitive to change and appear to be suddenly much more dependent. The acute phase of this sensitivity may last only a week or two, but the need for a steady caregiver will remain.

Often this new dependency coincides with a mother's return to work or with a new caregiver's arrival. If the changes can be made carefully and gradually, the whole family will benefit. The parents will want to leave the baby with someone he knows and is used to. If possible, the parents should let the baby get used to a new caregiver while they are still nearby. They must know they can rely on the caregiver to understand this new fear of strangers and not to get angry about it. The baby's reaction to strangers is not easy on anyone—and even family members, especially grandparents, are vulnerable to being perceived as strangers. Leaving the baby with a new person for short, gradually lengthening times will ease the transition.

Parents who must return to work often have deep fears that their babies might be damaged by the separation. I can say with conviction that, as long as they find a really nurturing, caring person for him, the baby can adjust without permanent trauma. It will not be the same as having one parent all day, but that can lead to conflict for the baby and parent, too. In the chapter on "Childcare Choices" in Part 3, I describe the qualities to look for in a caregiver at home or in center- or family-based child care. Babies do seem to be able to take in and adjust to more than two people. This has long been clear to parents in cultures where extended families or even whole villages raise a child.

When parents can save some of their own energy for the end of the day and take advantage of this intense reunion, the separation will seem less painful. Sometimes, I encourage parents to sit and rock and sing to the baby when they get home—to talk to him, ask him about his day, and tell him how much they missed him. When parents wonder whether the baby can understand, I explain that he certainly will glean the spirit of it, and they both will be starting a ritual for all the years to come.

7. Six to Seven Months

As a six- or seven-month-old baby sails into my office on a parent's arm, I can see that she already participates in being carried. She clings actively. If I come to meet them in the waiting room, she expects to be picked up by a parent and holds up her plump arms to her mother or father, who says, "Come on. We're going in to see the doctor." At this age, most still welcome me at first, grinning as I play with them, though stranger anxiety is more likely now than at four months, when the earliest signs may first emerge. If they resist at first, babies this age will soon perform and chortle with glee if I avoid making eye contact until they begin to stare intently into my eyes. Still, if a baby looks wary as I come up to her, I ask her mother to hold her. I examine her in her mother's lap. Usually, this visit is a cheerful one, until I must give immunizations: At six months, the third doses of the Diphtheria, Tetanus, and Pertussis (DTaP), Hemophilus Influenza (Hib), and Pneumococcus (PCV) vaccines are recommended as of this writing by the CDC. Another dose of the Hepatitis B and Polio vaccines may also be given (either now or sometime before eighteen months of age).

Beforehand, I can point out to a confident mother each milestone in development. The baby literally overflows with self-importance at this age. She shows off for me across the desk as I talk to her. She hides her face, turning to look back at me. She giggles and squeals in an attempt to attract my attention. If she can't break into my conversation, she will even bounce up in front of her parent or put her hands over his or her mouth in an attempt to interfere. She wants both of us to focus on *her*!

At six and seven months, babies look around as if they owned the world. It is a picture-book age. A baby can sit up now, chortling and playing with one toy after another, with a triumphant look. A baby this age will pick up a toy, examine it carefully, mouth it, turn it over and over, then drop it over the table edge. She then looks up expectantly, making some peremptory sound. The parent stoops dutifully to pick it up. If this retrieval game goes on for a while and a parent says, "Don't drop that, I won't pick it up," the baby will look up, sizing up her parent's determination. She may give up her game and recognize that her parent is indeed involved with me, or she may try a few more games—calling "da," "ma," then laughing out loud. If her attempts to compete with me fail, she may give up gracefully and start to play alone with the toys on the table in front of her.

By this age, a baby's personality seems to be predictable—for her parents and for everyone else around her. The tendencies and signs of temperament—a child's style of dealing with her world—that we saw at six weeks are now fully expressed. I like to share my observations about a baby's temperament with parents at this point so that we both can better understand what is normal for this particular child. By this time, I know parents will leap in to correct me if I'm off track, and I welcome their deeply held beliefs about who their child is becoming.

There are several attributes that are incorporated into the concept of temperament. These elements set a constellation of expectancies for how she will cope with new and old events and how she will deal with stress, and they give her parents a frame in which they will work to understand her. Temperament is an important concept for parents, for they can judge a child's reactions within this expectancy. They know when she is her "usual self" and when she's not. When she's not, they can evaluate her for illness or a reaction to stress, and they can begin to recognize transitions just before a spurt in her development. When she deviates from her usual self, a parent must decide which of these events is taking place. If it's a spurt in her development, they may want to understand that spurt before making decisions.

The nine elements we watch for in assessing temperament were pointed out years ago by Stella Chess and Alexander Thomas and have been refined and elaborated since by William Carey, Jerome Kagan, and others (see *Further Reading*). In brief, they are:

Activity Level
Distractibility
Persistence
Approach-Withdrawal—How does she handle new and stressful situations?
Intensity
Adaptability—How does she deal with transitions?
Regularity—How predictable is she in sleep and in her rhythms during the day?
Sensory Threshold—Is she hyper- or hyposensitive to stimuli around her? Is she easily overstimulated?
Mood—Is she primarily positive or negative in her reactions?

With qualities such as these as a base, a small child can be understood, as can the challenge she poses—for herself and for those around her. My first book, *Infants and Mothers,* attempts to map the progress of three different babies—active, quiet, and moderate—as they and their parents progress through the first year. After the first half of the first year has passed, parents and the baby's other caregivers would do well to discuss a baby's emerging personality and to try to understand each other's ways of thinking about her as they prepare for the many decisions ahead.

Motor Skills

Sitting alone is a major milestone, and the actual age at which it is reached will vary from one baby to another. As we saw earlier, at five months, or thereabouts, a baby first learns to sit up by leaning forward propped on both arms—in a tripod fashion. In this position she is immobilized and unable to change her posture, except by toppling over. By the age of six months, give or take a few weeks in either direction, she begins to straighten her back and to manage the backward-forward balance. But her arms are still propping her on each side. If she tries to pick up one arm, she will topple to that side. Sitting alone is still very precarious. The baby depends on her steady arms to maintain balance. She still cannot get herself into the sitting posture.

By about seven months, a baby no longer needs both arms as props and can briefly maintain a straight back. She still keeps her arms ready in case she needs to steady herself, or else she will fall to one side. She can dare to play a bit with toys in front of her, but if she falls, she knows she cannot get herself back up to sit. She still plays gingerly and attempts to maintain her exciting new posture. By eight months, or soon after, she will be assured of freedom in a sitting position. A baby that age can twist around and can lean forward or to one side. She has mastered sitting and is free to experiment with it. Even if she falls, she can probably struggle up again.

Experienced parents can tell how long a child has been sitting by the complexity of her body behavior as she sits. If she is immobilized, she is still a recent achiever. If she can rotate and lean to each side, she's been sitting for at least a month. At the point where she can get into sitting from a flat position, she is demonstrating a familiarity with handling her body in sitting and crawling that speaks of at least a two-month achievement.

Small motor achievements are developing in parallel with this progress in sitting. As a child becomes adept in handling her body, her hands become freer, more exciting to her, and more available for learning. At six months, her fingers still act in a package. When she grasps an object, she literally rakes it into her palm. By seven months, her dexterity is increasing. As she transfers an object from one hand to another, she begins to explore it with her fingers. In the process, she is gradually separating her forefinger and thumb for more skilled activity. By eight months, she will be able to use thumb and forefinger in a pincer grasp to pick up small objects. As she explores this new achievement, she picks up every small bit she can find. Fuzz on the floor, a dropped aspirin tablet, a small piece of dog food—all become exciting to her. She carries everything to her mouth for further exploration. Lead paint chips and small, sharp objects are hazards now. This is a time for careful cleanup of a baby's entire environment, with no dangerous bits left around.

The pincer grasp, the separation of the thumb and forefinger for skilled behavior, while shared to some degree with the great apes, develops early in human infants and makes possible great developmental strides. "The hands," said Maria Montessori, "are the instruments of human intelligence." Speech and our skill in manual dexterity mark us for complex achievements. No wonder a baby is so excited by this skill. She practices it all day long.

Soon she begins to explore her world with her fingers. Putting a forefinger into every orifice, including electrical outlets, she finds marvelous new uses for her separated fingers. The thumb and forefinger are used to explore the faces of her beloved adults, to explore every possible hole or hidden area. They have become powerful extensions of her eyes and her mouth. Before this, only her mouth was used to evaluate the world of objects and people. Now, she can extend this exploration with her hands. As she explores her world in these new ways, she now can point to the exciting objects in it to engage adults around her, and she discovers a new way to communicate. As

The baby begins to explore her world and the faces of her parents with her fingers.

joint attention emerges, she becomes aware that as she points she is sharing her excitement about her world with someone else who is interested too!

By this time, nearly all babies show a reliable preference for one hand or the other, although their preference may change more than once over the next several years until they settle on a preferred hand for writing. They have probably been demonstrating a pattern in the months before, but by now they suck on the currently less dominant hand in order to free up the one preferred at this point for exploratory behavior. At the seven-month spurt in small motor achievements, the preferred hand can be easily determined (unless there is mixed dominance, when no preference will be established). If an adult offers a toy in the midline, a baby's currently preferred hand will come forward first. The two major fingers of the dominant hand will be utilized most for exploration. We unconsciously push a baby to be right-handed. When we hand an object to a baby, we almost invariably hand it to her right side. If she is left-handed, she must reach across her midline to grasp it. The earlier left-handedness is welcomed, the better.

Curiously, a child begins to lose interest in her feet at this time, for the baby spends less of the day on her back watching her toes. As she learns to stand, her feet will actually become even less agile, less like fingers. By eight or nine months, her exploration of her hands begins to pay off even more. Watch her as she reaches for an object. She shapes her hands to match the shape of the object she is reaching for.

Learning to crawl offers another thrust toward independence. By seven months, most babies start to creep on their bellies. Toppling from sitting, or rolling over from the back, a baby of this age shows her determination to get going. She learns to get herself onto her belly so that she can practice moving forward in this position. *Creeping* is the name for wriggling along on one's stomach. At eight months, as a baby achieves forward creeping, she will begin to add to it. She is likely to get up on all four extremities, rocking backward and forward, to flop on her face and body at the end. Although this may hurt, very few babies cry out when they have brought it on themselves. The urge to achieve is too powerful and counterbalances any discomfort.

As the baby first attempts to coordinate her legs and arms, she recaptures the reflex swimming behaviors seen in the first few months. She begins to crawl backward like a crab. Finally she will figure out how to go forward, propelling herself on her hands and knees, mastering the art of crawling. Each child who crawls has a distinctive way of doing so, but many children never crawl. There is a myth that unless a child crawls, she'll never be coordinated and will have learning problems later. This is groundless. I have seen many children who never crawled but who walked and learned in perfectly normal sequence. Many children go from sitting to standing to walking, never creeping or crawling. Crawling is not a necessary milestone.

When a baby does begin to crawl—but backward—her parents can see the consternation in her face as she gets further and further away from her desired goal. Her frustration mounts. She may scream out as her newly coordinating legs and arms do not take her in the direction she means to go. As we mentioned earlier, a parent can place a firm hand against her feet. She will press herself forward against this hand. The surprise and joy that she feels may well fuel her to learn how to adapt her movements and repeat the forward motion on her own. But she is likely to have a month or so of repeated frustration. Parents can comfort and support, but they needn't try to spare the child these tortured efforts as she begins to learn a new skill. She'll also be learning to master her frustration so that she can learn from her mistakes—a lifelong lesson!

As mentioned earlier, parents at this stage need to protect a child from her own inquisitiveness. Well before this age, all parents should inspect their houses for potential dangers to an exploring, ingenious child. They should look for uncovered electrical outlets, stairs that need gates, and poisons or medicines in or out of cupboards. Windows must have window guards. Babies find everything. The next months will be made up of unexpected surprises, and parents must be prepared for them. Parents should keep ipecac in their medicine cabinet (safely out of reach, along with all other potentially toxic substances) to induce vomiting—if advised to by a physician—in case of an ingestion. They should record next to each phone the phone numbers of the nearest Poison Control Center (the toll-free number nationwide is 1-800-222-1222), the emergency room of the nearest hospital, the pediatrician's emergency number, and the ambulance. Being prepared is important. When an emergency is underway, parents may be too overwhelmed to find these.

Feeding

Swallowing solid, spoon-fed foods is a real transition for a baby. When solids are first introduced, most babies frown, sputter, and drool. They'll push out the spoon and food with their tongue—a reflex that may take a week or so to abate. But parents often take this to mean that the baby doesn't like the new taste, wondering, "Shouldn't I start with something sweet? He doesn't seem to like the taste of rice mush." Of course, the first solid should be fluid and milky, but it probably isn't the taste that is at fault. Learning to swallow, in addition to the familiar act of sucking, is a new challenge for the baby, requiring a new kind of muscle coordination. Any new achievement takes time. I would expect a baby to fuss over solid foods for the first week. At first, parents can forget about how much gets in and see this as a time for the baby to practice swallowing. Their job is to teach him patiently and slowly. Of course, he needs to be propped in an upright position; otherwise, he might breathe the food in. But his hands will get into the food. He will bat away the spoon and use his fingers to help suck the food down. Hands are an important part of exploration at this age, so I would never constrain them—I'd wear a raincoat and let him explore instead.

A baby this age will continue to spew out solids at times. Parents sometimes feel as if the baby is teasing them by doing this. He is not. A strong reaction will only reinforce it. Often, he's already full and really doesn't want the solids. It's a good idea to stop feeding him when he does that. If the baby makes a big mess, cover yourself and feed him in a washable chair, but don't restrain his hands. Let him play with feedings in his own way. He must have time to make the transition from sucking. Also, he's still perfecting his reach and wants to participate by touching his food. If you interfere, you may set up resistances in him about feeding that will make him negative and hard to feed in the future.

In many cultures, babies are introduced to whatever foods are served at the family table, and I respect these traditions. It is important for feeding times to be relaxed and natural. Still, I recommend that parents introduce one new solid at a time. An interval of a week between each solid food helps as a way to find out whether the baby is allergic to any of them. If he is started on solids before six months, his intolerance, usually appearing in the form of a rash, stomach upset, or diarrhea, may not show up as soon as a new food is introduced. By six months, he is more likely to demonstrate his sensitivity within a few days after a new food is added. This makes allergic reactions much easier to monitor by six months. Parents can avert allergies to foods by starting solids carefully and systematically. If a baby responds to a new food with a rash or other signs of sensitivity within the first week, it can simply be eliminated—right away. When this is done promptly, it is sometimes possible to reintroduce the same food at twelve or twenty-four months of age, though the pediatrician should be consulted first in order to rule out the possibility of a more serious repeat reaction. Responding quickly to sensitivities by withholding the offending food, and avoiding those that are known to be especially likely to cause allergies (for example, wheat, eggs, and peanuts), can decrease the long-term risk of allergies (see "Allergies and Asthma").

It is a good idea when introducing solids to start with a single-grain cereal in the evening. Rice is often best, and later, barley or oats. Wheat should be avoided. Mixed cereals are risky, for they present several challenges all at once, and their effects can't be sorted out if the baby does show signs of sensitivity. Parents should use cereal alone for the first two weeks until the baby has learned to swallow. If it is given before his milk, he is more likely to accept it, and in the evening, some parents think it may help him sleep longer at night. Next, a cooked and strained fruit (apple or pear, not citrus or strawberries, which are more likely to set off an allergy) can be given in the morning, and a week later, a cooked and strained vegetable (peas, spinach, green beans, or carrots) at noon. Finally, pureed beef or chicken at noon can be started a week later. Parents need to read labels to be sure each food is pure, containing no other ingredients. If the baby breaks out with a rash after any of these foods, parents should stop giving it and then wait for the rash to clear before trying a different new food after that. Organic baby foods, now widely available, offer extra assurance that no additives or pesticide residues are present.

When new foods are introduced, such as peas or carrots, they can be seen right away, bright green or orange, in the baby's stool. Parents needn't worry. These foods are not completely digested at first, as the intestines must get used to each new one.

At six months, a typical feeding schedule might be as follows:

7:00 A.M. Milk feeding.
8:30 A.M. Fruit, cooked and strained.
12:00 P.M. Meat, vegetables, and milk.
3:00 P.M. Juice or water. Most of the calories in juice come from sugar, and juice can be a major cause of tooth decay and excess weight gain. Dilute and limit it to no more than three or four ounces or less per day.
5:00 P.M. Cereal (and cooked and strained fruit).
6:30 P.M. Milk feeding.
10:30 P.M. Fourth milk feeding.

By separating out solid food meals at first for the morning and afternoons, the baby can get accustomed to four milk feedings. When he is used to them, the solid and milk feedings can be combined.

When you do start solids, your baby will want to hold one spoon while you feed him from another. Expect him to drop the spoon, look down for it, then look up at you to pick it up. He is learning about object permanence. When you start feeding him from a cup, let him help you. The play and experimentation that accompany a feeding are to be enjoyed and encouraged.

The new motor skills of sitting and exploring, and of the fascinating pincer grasp, are major touchpoints of development affecting all aspects of a child's life. In particular, they change the feeding scene radically. A parent who can allow these skills to enhance the child's sense of her own independence in the feeding area will ward off many problems. Learning to play with a cup and to handle it herself is one exciting goal for the baby. Although she certainly isn't ready to gulp very much from a glass or cup, she will want to try. When a parent is drinking from a glass, he can hold the glass for her and offer her a sip. Imitation is always a force for learning. If she wants to try to master the cup, the parent can let her have an empty one to play with, while feeding her from another. A Sippie cup of her own will offer the child even more chances for independent experimentation. As she gets into a practicing phase, she can try her cup in the bathtub. She can drink and pour bathwater and have a great time sloshing about, all the while learning to master the cup—until you add the soap. She may insist on carrying her Sippie cup around with her all day, but this will be just as bad for teeth as allowing her to keep her bottle with her at all times—unless it is empty or contains only water.

A seven-month-old will want to use her new dexterity to explore and master everything that goes into her mouth. Even if parents fill both the baby's hands—a Sippie cup in one hand and a piece of zwieback in the other—she will drop her things to grab the spoon parents are struggling to feed her with. Or she'll get diverted to play with her toast or her own spoon. Parents need to respect this. Feeding is just not as important now as exploration. Parents who forge on with the usual boring routine may be successful, but they are likely to set off resistance. It's just not worth it. I tell parents that they can expect their baby to explore in her own way for a little while, and that letting feedings go during this time is okay. She'll come back to a rounded diet with renewed interest when she's mastered her new skills. This is an arena where a parent's goals and the baby's may conflict. It is also an arena in which she will always win. Parents can step back and enjoy her new skills. For now, her burst of learning will supersede everything else. Fortunately, a child's food needs during this period can be met if she has three good breast-milk or formula feedings (morning, noon, and night—twenty-four to thirty-two ounces a day, depending on the baby's size, should be enough). Since her stomach still only holds a small amount, and her increased activity level requires more fuel, snacks—safe finger foods (Cheerios, soft bits of cooked hamburger, cheese, or fruit, such as bananas)—between these milk feedings can also help. If necessary, she can be given one more milk feeding at 10:30 P.M. before her parents go to bed.

Although solid foods will become a major part of most babies' feeding schedule at six to seven months, they are still not as important as breast milk and Vitamin D drops (and possibly iron supplements) or formula fortified with iron and Vitamin D. If the baby is refusing solids during this spurt, I would cut back to focus on fortified cereal or pureed meat for its iron. Parents can offer them at whatever feeding she will accept them. Two or three teaspoons of solids in addition to the milk feedings will tide a baby over for a twenty-four-hour period at this time. Feeding her a "rounded diet" is often a parental goal, but it isn't as important as avoiding food conflicts now to prevent more serious ones later.

The new pincer grasp, of course, leads to splendid new fun at feeding. A parent can to offer one or two soft bits of food at the beginning of each feeding. As these go down, she can be offered another. She won't be able to chew for a long time, but she can gum up soft bits. Little bite-sized bits of banana, of cooked potato or vegetable, soft parts of toast, even bits of soft hamburger will do.

As the bits get eaten, explored, fingered, dropped, smeared, or otherwise demolished, two more can be put in front of her. If too many bits are offered, she'll just mash them or sweep them over the side of her feeding table. Parents should be prepared for some bits to be extruded back at them or drooled down the side of her chin. The goal is to enhance this new adventure. She may be so intent and excited that she'll let someone feed her regular sloppy food while she is trying to master the lumps on her tray. But she may resist being fed at all. Parents shouldn't struggle with her; otherwise, they'll compound the resistance. This intense stage of exploration is likely to last only a week or so; she wants to be in control.

Sleep

Prior to this stage the baby may have been sleeping eight to twelve hours a night. But now the excitement and frustration of learning new skills, such as sitting, creeping, crawling, and the new fine motor tasks, carry over into the night. Her naps may be disrupted, too, as she practices her new skills in bed. She may be harder and harder to put down. This new disruption is frustrating to parents, who have just begun to enjoy some quiet evenings. Like other touchpoints, this change is a step back that precedes a big stride forward. I try to help parents by offering the following suggestions.

Renew your bedtime ritual to let your baby know how important that is to her and to you. She still needs two naps or two quiet breaks in the day—mid-morning and mid-afternoon. So, whether she sleeps or not, she should be put into her crib in her room at these times. If necessary, you can sit quietly by, not responding, calmly telling her to settle down to rest. Pat her quietly and rhythmically, but without looking at or responding to her. She may not like it, but she'll soon learn that you mean business—that this is the nap and bedtime ritual and not a game.

If you are away all day, be sure her daytime caregiver gives her an afternoon nap that is long enough for her to be ready to enjoy her time with you in the evening, but early enough so that it won't interfere with bedtime. At the point where she begins to get too excited or shows signs of disintegrating, remember that she needs to go to bed. It's awfully easy to forget that she needs to go down at a certain point unless she has a regular time for bed that you all prepare for and stick to. Your firmness and your regular routine will help her. If you are still ambivalent, your baby will sense that and push you. Then she'll build up with more and more frantic excitement and then disintegrate into tears, desperately unable to give up. Once in the bedroom, you may have to try rocking and soothing her, but with the firm conviction that she is going to bed.

Sometimes babies this age become active again at around 2:00 and 6:00 A.M. They cry out pitifully but don't really seem awake. Sometimes, they're up on their arms and knees, rocking away, not even awake, though they may appear to be. Parents wonder whether to wake the baby, feed her, and then put her back down. Since this is the light sleep that occurs roughly every four hours, I advise parents not to get her up. Nor should they rouse the baby or take her out of her crib. In fact, I wouldn't reinforce this behavior in any way. At most, I'd help the baby get herself back down by soothing, patting, and softly crooning, or by offering her a pacifier or her lovey. Even if she comes to full waking with a parent there, I'd try to do as little as possible but encourage her to find her own pattern for returning to deep sleep. Parents who get her up at this stage may have to be part of her sleep pattern for a long time to come.

Parents who have been away all day have the hardest time with this night waking. It is really more their problem than the baby's, and one I can surely understand. But parents with heavy work schedules also need sleep, and eventually the night waking will wear down the whole family.

Communication

At seven to eight months, a baby not only uses syllables with a consonant and a vowel ("da," "ma," "ba"), but she practices them. She will trill and use them in scales in the morning while she lies in her bed. She will try them over and over, using them to call adoring adults to her. Rarely will she assign the proper syllable to the proper person. Babies this age are learning to understand the word "no," and the look on a parent's face that goes with it, but they do not respond to it.

All the bursts in motor and cognitive development make games and play more fun for parents. Each parent should feel free to play with the baby in an active way that suits his or her own temperament. Many mothers at this stage will warn fathers that "they're too rough." Some fathers may say, "You're too soft with her. You give up too easily. Can't you see she's asking for more?" Parents should respect these differences and use them. In this way, a baby learns that each parent is a separate and distinct individual. There is no need for each parent to treat her alike.

Learning

In her play, the baby will be working on her new cognitive skills and expanding them. If a parent hides a toy under a cloth as the baby watches, and then pulls the cloth off, the baby will gleefully greet it with an "ooh" and "aah." She is likely to seem surprised and delighted that the toy is still there. Wait more than a second or two before removing the cloth, and a child this age is likely to seem oblivious. A sense of object permanence—knowing the object hasn't disappeared forever just because it is out of sight—is developing, and she wants to explore its facets. As she learns to creep or to crawl, she sees things from a series of vantage points and must begin to understand what these changing perspectives might mean. (This may be how babies learn that they can point to things that other people can see from different positions in the same room.) She struggles to reach a coveted object. If she does, she explores it and then begins to lose interest in it, shoving it just out of reach. Then, as she strives once again to get to it, its value to her is newly heightened.

Mirrors have been an interest for a month or more. As she looks at herself, she seems to try to get a response from her image. She may even reach out to try to touch herself in the mirror. When she gets a response, she may even startle with surprise. At about seven to eight months, if her parents come up from behind her, she may first try to react to them in the mirror—as if they were inside of it. Eventually, she will turn around to see where the familiar people really are. As she learns to decode the reversals of mirrors, she is learning about space and spatial relationships.

Stranger awareness accompanies the bursts in cognitive development, which continue dramatically. She hunts for lost toys and will lift a cloth or a box to find them. She experiments with person permanence by playing peek-a-boo games. She is imitative in games involving facial expressions and sputtering and other sounds. In the next two months her cognitive development will be thrilling to watch and enjoy. Parents shouldn't get too caught up in her frustrations. She can master them—and she will.

In this period of rapid learning about clues from those around her, a baby will wait at the end of the day for a noise that lets her know a parent is coming home. Her sensitivity will need to be respected in many ways. Exposing her to noises that are too loud or changes that are too abrupt, or even leaving her in a familiar environment or with someone who has been familiar before, will likely bring out the fragility that accompanies this period of rapid learning. All the baby's energy is going into mastery and exploration of these new cognitive capacities.

Person permanence is beginning to follow the same course as object per-

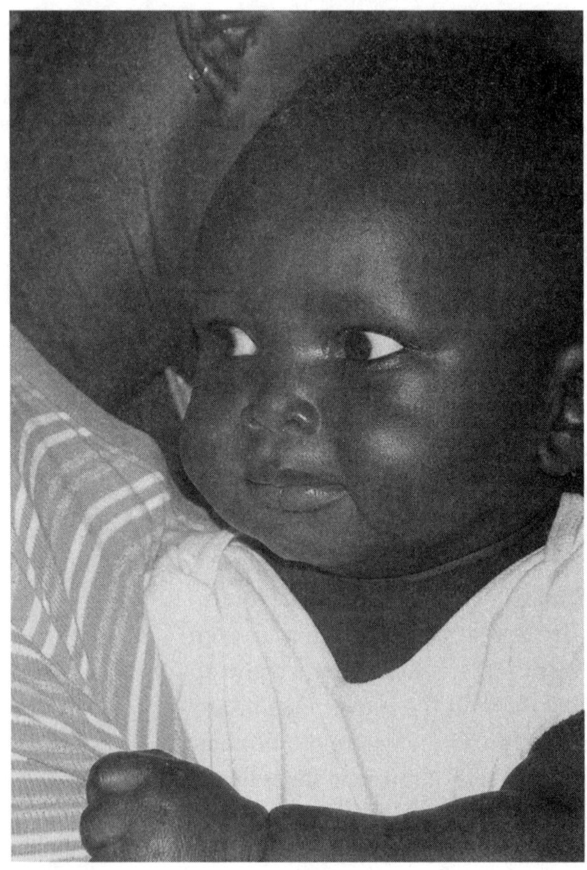

Stranger awareness accompanies bursts in cognitive development.

manence. What does this mean? Separations will be more upsetting as she begins to realize that when important people are out of sight, they are still somewhere, but not with her. Different faces will also be disturbing as she becomes increasingly aware that they are similar to her parents' faces in some ways, but not quite the same. Warn grandparents that they'll do well to wait until she's looked them over and begun to lose her initial wariness before they pick her up. Parents who want to avoid a traumatic episode would do well not to let strangers or extended family members rush up to the baby to hold her. Expect necessary separations, such as those with other caregivers or at child care, to be painful and noisy. Always let her know when you're leaving, and be sure she's in caring hands. When you return, let her know you've missed her. Reduce any unnecessary separations and changes to a minimum for a while.

Parents can play peek-a-boo and other games that play out this anxiety about separations and leaving. Go around the corner and come back. Let her explore your face, your clothes. Play mirror games with her. And have important strangers enter her life—slowly, following her lead, and at her pace—so that she can learn about them. You don't need to overprotect her. But you do need to realize that she's in a major and demanding spurt in her development—a touchpoint in these cognitive and social areas.

Looking Ahead

Feeding Challenges will continue to arise from the child's need to explore and to be in control. These will intensify. When she refuses to be fed, be ready with finger food or a breadstick or zwieback to let her play with. Don't hover over her. Move around the kitchen, tending to your business. If you concentrate on her, she'll tend to provoke and tease you by dropping food or by refusing it. Try the spoon. Let her play with it while you feed her from another one. She may accept all you offer her while she's distracted. But she may not. If not, quit. Once again, don't try to control her play or feed her when she's refusing. It's not worth it.

If she doesn't eat, will she get hungry later? If you haven't created a feud, she probably will, but her desire for mastery is almost an instinctive urge at this time.

Sleeping and New Motor Skills Before a baby crawls or tries to pull up to stand, or as she learns about strangers, she may awaken during the night all over again. Fall back on the routines you've used before to help her get herself back down to sleep.

During the day, when she's frustrated with a new task she's learning, help her learn how to comfort herself—for example, by offering her the same special toy or soft blanket each time. If she has learned to suck on her fingers or a pacifier, help her find them when she's upset or is falling apart. When she settles, tell her how well she's done.

But don't push her into new motor skills that she may not be ready for. Walkers, for example, can divert a baby from attempting to crawl. The thrill of standing and learning to walk is likely to take over. (A child who crawls less and spends much time in a walker will also have fewer opportunities to push up with her arms from the floor and strengthen her shoulder and back muscles.) She may rely on the walker to overcome her frustration at not yet being able to walk, rather than learning to handle it. Overdependence on a walker may delay these milestones. And of course, walkers can lead babies into dangerous situations, such as a flight of stairs, that they are not prepared to handle. (Stairs need to be closed off with safety gates at this age, walker or not.)

Safety This is the period when a playpen may help, because it means you know where she is and what she has access to when you can't watch her. If you don't use one, be sure you have a safe room in the house for her. Her newfound mobility and the need to satisfy her inquisitive cognitive burst will lead her into any available trouble. Be prepared!

Spoiling At this visit, many parents again express worries about spoiling a child. If they are worried about giving a baby of eight or nine months too much love and attention, that is a needless worry. It is possible, though, to take over too often for a child of this age at times when she is frustrated but ready to learn to calm herself, or bored and able to motivate herself. My concept of a spoiled child is one without limits, anxiously searching for them. In the coming months, you'll see behavior that is clearly a bid for such limits. When a child first crawls up to the TV set and looks around to be *sure* you are watching, this is what is going on. You can remove her and/or distract her. But make the limits clear from the start. Discipline is a parental responsibility: Providing small children with firm limits that they can then incorporate for themselves takes years to achieve, however, so don't get frustrated when it takes time and repetition to teach these limits to your child.

8. Nine Months

A NINE-MONTH-OLD BABY RARELY SPENDS THE VISIT AT MY OFFICE IN HIS mother's or father's lap. He is just as eager as his parents are to have him slip to the floor or heave himself up to standing at a chair or table to show off these amazing accomplishments. Most of the questions at this visit will have something to do with his motor development. With a baby so driven to move around, everything—feeding, sleeping, diapering—will be different. New issues of safety, discipline, and anxiety pop up daily as the baby wriggles, rolls, crawls, creeps, pulls, and topples his way from dawn to dusk.

The new dramas and conflicts bring a rebalancing of the family routine and lead parents to reach out for support. The motor spurt and the regression in sleep and feeding that usually occur make this period another important touchpoint, a critical moment in a family's development when they are especially vulnerable, and they are more ready than ever for me to reach out to support them.

One or the other of the parents of this nine-month-old powerhouse will arrive ready to burst. "Well, how are you?" I ask, waiting for the opening blast. "Awful," says the mother. "Oh?" "Yes, Alexander has totally fallen apart. He's either charging around, bawling, or sucking his thumb and glaring at me. He refuses the food I try to feed him. He just won't eat for me, and if you want the whole works, I'm not getting any sleep. He keeps going all day and all night. He wakes up at least once or twice every night. He's a wreck, and so am I!"

After listening carefully, and empathizing with their side of it, I hope to help the parents appreciate their child's side of all this. Perhaps, I suggest, he is difficult and disorganized because he's working on new skills. As he does, feeding and sleep, in particular, are likely to become difficult.

Motor Skills

Learning to stand begins at this point. Given anything to grab—any chair or table will do—a baby will begin to pull himself up. Legs wide apart, body arched forward, he'll grunt and strain against gravity. He'll teeter as he clutches the table edge. When he gets there, he'll stand for long periods, locking his knees, and then bouncing up and down. In my office, if I try to interrupt him by offering him a toy, or by picking him up to examine him, he'll fix me with a withering look that says, "Leave me alone. Can't you see I'm busy?" If he starts to fuss with frustration on my table, he will stop almost immediately if I support him to stand in an upright position. Once up, he will grin with pleasure. His goal is obvious, and his focused intent is so strong that he vehemently protests any interference.

Babies at this age will stand as long as they can, then they will cry, but in frustration rather than in pain. Upright, they discover a whole new world to explore, but they can't yet reach out for it since they so desperately need both hands to balance themselves. If they fall, they wail. The fall doesn't hurt, but the thrill of standing is gone and that's what hurts.

Thank goodness for flexible skulls and the soft spot on babies' skulls. Obviously, nature meant their heads to be cushioned for falls. For the first two years, a baby's skull is pliable and gives with such a blow. The brain isn't bruised by the inevitable tumbles of this age, as it can be when adults fall or hit their heads. Nature has prepared for the motor learning that must go on now. The soft spot (or fontanel) doesn't close, and the bones of the skull don't cement, until after babies have achieved a safer balance and are walking well, at about eighteen months.

Despite this protection, parents must be watchful. If a baby doesn't cry right away after falling, or is knocked unconscious, or seems irritable or lethargic for more than a few minutes after a fall, it could be the sign of a concussion. I'd be sure that you have a rug under your baby at the places where he practices standing, and that you push away nearby objects and furniture that are sharp or hard and might hurt him when he falls. You'll need to stand nearby to catch him when he tries to balance on a chair or stroller, or anything else that is likely to tip over on him when he pulls up on it. A baby can probably take a knock on the head from a wooden floor, but not a concrete one. Parents can't and don't need to protect a baby at this age from every small stumble. After a few falls, a baby begins to learn how to fold in the middle. By poking out his bottom, he gradually learns to balance and to let himself down slowly, with a sedate plop.

Movement is the ultimate goal. When standing and clinging, a baby is pretty well immobilized. But he's already yearning to go forward. Given an upturned chair or a stroller, he will learn very quickly how to push it forward as he hangs on. Early American antique chairs are flattened on their back surfaces where Pilgrim toddlers pushed them ahead as they learned to walk. The drive to be upright and to get going is built into the human infant. Parents often ask at this visit whether to buy the baby shoes. I don't recommend it. If he's barefoot, the toes grip the ground and help him learn to balance. In shoes, he'll slip and teeter more. Socks without shoes are even more slippery.

A baby this age can often get from his belly into a sitting position and then pull on up to standing. What a complex set of motor skills he has mastered in only nine months! All this has given him a sense of being in control of his body and of achieving what he wants to achieve. Now he can take in the world from a standing position! He is bound to work at such a plum all day and all night. He will have it as a goal as soon as he awakens in the morning, and he'll relive it at night, his unconscious pressing him into action during every light sleep cycle. No wonder he may appear to be "falling apart."

As he stands, holding on, he finds all kinds of ways to test his new trick. If music comes on, he tries to dance to it. Everyone around gushes with approval. Dancing is fun! Next, he might try to walk sideways along furniture. That works, too! He can get from one place to another. Now, the forbidden objects on tables become accessible. The world is no longer flat. He has added a third dimension.

Early Discipline

The world of parents has changed, too. Instead of simply applauding every new trick, they must decide about "no's." Should they remove newly accessible objects, or should they forbid certain things and try to restrict the scope of the baby's new excitement? Stoves, lamps, washing machines, TVs, computers, and stray cell phones have become fair game. Houseplants, the leaves

of which may be toxic, are so attractive all of a sudden. How can a parent decide when to remove temptation and when to discipline? In my experience, the fewer the conflicts, the better. The most important issues, and the immutable ones, such as not touching the stove, are better learned if they aren't diluted by too many piddling ones. So, I would remove the attractions that are easy to move and block off the dangerous, large ones with a chair or furniture, leaving very few for conflict.

Although a parent can divert the baby's attention at this age, his determination to be in charge of himself will soon be deepening. Distraction works only for unimportant issues and can too easily turn into a game. Now is the time to prepare for the strident self-assertion of the second year, for everyone's sake. Parents ask me how early discipline begins. The first time the baby crawls to the TV or to the radiator and *looks around* to be sure you're watching, he is asking for discipline. He demonstrates his awareness of the forbidden and his need for limits. It is now time for parents to recognize the baby's bid for their participation in learning how to stop himself (see "Discipline"). This is the first touchpoint in learning when and how to discipline. Parents must decide how to face it and start practicing. It's a long road!

Another heart-stopping surprise in store for parents of nine-month-old babies is to find them halfway up the stairs. Unless they can be there all the time to watch and help the baby, they need to get a gate for each end of the stairs. Later, they can teach him how to go up and down, but it's too early for that now.

The bathtub is another scene of joy and danger. The first and vital rule is: *Never* leave a baby alone in the tub, even for a moment. He could fall down and breathe in water. It would frighten him at best, but could drown him at worst. If a child will be anywhere near a swimming pool, now is the time to be sure it's either covered safely or completely fenced in. As a pediatrician, I've seen too many children with brain damage from nearly drowning in pools not to feel adamant on this point.

As for the rest of the house or apartment, the surest thing is to baby-proof it. If parents can't do the entire home, they should do one or two rooms and make sure that is where the baby stays.

Sleep

As we said earlier, a baby who is learning to get up to standing will practice at night, too. When put to bed, a baby will stand up in the crib as soon as the parent leaves the room. If you put him down, up he comes again—and he will keep on doing this many times. At every light-sleep phase, his new motor goal is likely to emerge. Researchers have recently suggested that there may be a good reason why babies start waking up more often at night between the ages of about nine and thirteen months, precisely when they are learning to stand and getting ready to walk. As it turns out, babies this age spend more time in light sleep than at other ages. No wonder they are more likely to keep waking up at night. But they may need to devote this added time to light sleep because during this sleep phase their developing brains may be laying down the "wiring" the complex sequence of motor memories they will need to call up as they learn to put one foot in front of the other to take their first step! This new burst in a baby's brain development becomes another important touchpoint. In this visit I emphasize the decisions parents must make to reinforce sleep as *the baby's* issue.

Here's what I tell parents to help them overcome the resulting temporary sleep disturbance: Each time you go back to his crib, put your baby down firmly and tuck him in tightly. After the second or third episode of standing, gently lay him down in his sleep position. Sing to him quietly without looking at him so he knows it's not a time for communication. Stay there holding him down, patting him and soothing him to sleep. As he quiets, do less and less. Soften your voice, and pat more slowly. He'll fight and struggle and screech. But don't fight back. That's too exciting. Be firmer than he is. He certainly will need his lovey to help him down, but he won't accept it gracefully. He needs to know for certain that you mean it's time for bed.

Sometimes a mother will say to me, "But he gets absolutely desperate! I *have* to help him get down. He gets stuck at the side of the crib and can't get down. He's frightened." When I ask whether the baby can get himself down when he stands up on furniture during the day, she usually replies, "Oh, yes! He's great during the day. He can let himself down very gently." This is my cue to suggest that the baby probably doesn't completely forget at night. Why not go in and give him a little shove to see whether he won't fold in the middle? A reminder like this, with a few soothing words, may be all it takes. After a few nights, he'll know he can do it for himself. If he calls out for help, parents can call back to say they're there. But it is the baby's job to let himself down and curl up to go to sleep.

An occasional parent will wonder whether to strap a baby in bed to prevent this. I don't like the idea of straps or harnesses at all. In addition to the possible psychological damage, I would worry about the risk of the baby accidentally strangling himself. A little patient teaching will result in learning patterns that will be important to the child for years. This touchpoint is an opportunity for parents to learn how to help him toward independence—in this case, at night. A bedtime ritual assumes new importance at this time. I'd suggest that you nurse or use the bottle as part of the routine in putting him down to sleep. Feed him in your arms, rocking and singing to quiet him. But don't put him to sleep in your arms. Put him into his crib while he's still awake. Do not leave him in bed with milk in a bottle, however, as we said earlier, to avoid damaging his baby teeth. Give him a blanket or a toy to cuddle as a lovey. Sit by him and pat him down, but don't get too involved. If you try to leave before he's asleep, he may rouse and not let you. So at first you may need to stay until he's asleep. Over time, do less and less, so that he can begin to take over. Your goal is for him to develop his own pattern for getting himself to sleep. It may take time, but it's worth it.

For some babies, self-comforting takes the form of rocking—and an increase in this rocking behavior may accompany the approach of an important touchpoint such as learning to walk. The baby will rock vigorously, often making the crib bang on the wall. He may seem to enjoy the noise. Since this rocking calms the baby down, I wouldn't stop it. The loud noise (or destruction to the wall) can be handled by putting the casters at the base of the crib posts in rubber coasters that don't move. Then, the baby can rock and squeak to his heart's content, but his bed won't move. Of course, the screws on the crib will need tightening from time to time.

Usually, after the child starts to walk and has become successful with large motor achievements, he'll be less frustrated at night, and the rocking will slow down. But some children rock at night as part of a pattern of relaxation for a few years. Children with autism and mental retardation are more likely to engage in vigorous, prolonged rocking, but these conditions would be accompanied by other signs as well. By itself, rocking isn't a sign of anything serious, unless it starts for the first time after eighteen months, lasts beyond three years of age, goes on for more than about fifteen minutes when it occurs, or is particularly vigorous. Sometimes such rocking is a child's signal that he feels alone and needs to call for attention, or that he is under too much stress. Introducing a special toy or blanket to cuddle may replace the rocking usually seen at this age, but if it doesn't, I wouldn't worry. He needs his own pattern if he's to be independent at night, and for some babies, this is what it takes.

Each new spurt in development sets off a new challenge and a new chance for learning to get to sleep. Each time it should get easier, especially if parents are determined. As the child gets older and more sophisticated, he'll try more and more interesting ways to divert them from the task of putting him to sleep in the first place. But he is also learning more elaborate and effective self-comforting techniques, and he's learning new limits for himself.

Often parents will tell me that their baby seems to get "higher and higher" at night. I suggest that he's telling them something. He *needs* to crash. Few children can crash on their own. Most need a push from their parents. At the point where he's had enough and is getting less and less organized, that's a sure sign that he needs someone to calm him and put him down. When both parents are away at work all day, it may be difficult for them to be firm and leave the child at night. If they watch for the time when the baby usually needs to give up, and they make bedtime into a cozy, regular routine, everyone in the family will learn to rely on it. The caregiver should avoid having the child nap too late in the afternoon.

Feeding

Mealtime is not exempt from the tyranny of the new motor prowess. "He won't let me feed him anymore," a mother will announce. "He refuses almost everything I offer him. He just bounces up and down in his chair." As usual, the best policy is not to fight but to join. I offer parents the following tips.

Enlist the baby's fingers and curiosity. The more feeding he can do for himself now, the better. While you're busy nearby, leave a variety of important foods—including protein (for example, soft bits of cheese and meat), cereal, fruit, and vegetables—in front of him, but not all at once! If you do, they'll all end up on the floor or all over him—or you. Instead, give him a few soft bits at a time and stay out of the feeding. He'll love to make his own choices and do all his own feeding. He may let you feed him soft foods while he's involved in feeding himself with both hands; but then again, he may not. By now, he needs to do most of it himself.

Instead of struggling with him to keep a cup of liquid upright, let him have his own Sippie cup. Since he will usually turn it upside down, put only a sip in it at a time. He'll be excited about drinking by himself, if he can. Babies enjoy these cups as a transition to real ones because they can take them over and handle them on their own.

While mastering a spoon is not likely to happen until well into the second year, learning to imitate with one, or clank and clatter, is fun for babies of nine and ten months. Again, let him have his own, or even one for each hand, to keep him busy while you wield yours.

All the new fascination with everything but the breast and bottle make parents think of weaning. Bottles seem taken for granted now, like personal property—treasured at times, absently dragged around or discarded at others. Some parents worry that if they wait too long, the baby will become too resistant to giving up the breast or bottle. I don't agree. When a baby shows signs of wanting to give them up, parents should by all means follow him. But there's no real reason that I know of, otherwise, to wean at a certain time. Certainly, there isn't a critical time when weaning is easier, a moment that won't ever happen again. There are many points in a baby's development when he'll be more interested in learning about other things than about being fed by bottle or breast. Food will also take second place many times. And as a background to all these forays into independence, it may be critical to hang on to the lovely, warm, secure ritual of breast or bottle feedings. All the self-feeding of solids is independent. Why not let him regress for milk—and be sure he's getting enough that way? Apart from nursing or bottle-feeding, meals for a nine-month-old baby cannot be long and leisurely. When he starts bouncing up and down and stops eating, he's saying he's bored. Parents need to put him down out of the feeding chair right away and not keep pursuing him with more food. Also, he shouldn't be fed between meals except for regular morning and afternoon snacks. By letting him wait until the next feeding time, you'll teach him the mealtime routine.

When parents ask about weaning a baby, my advice is: Start with eliminating the breast-feeding in the middle of the day. Save night and early morning for last. Be sure he gets enough milk from the cup (roughly sixteen ounces per day, depending on his weight) as you wean from the breast, for once you start weaning, your own milk will decrease, and you won't be able to depend on it. (A larger baby shouldn't need more than thirty-six ounces total a day of combined breast milk and cow's milk.) If you want to keep the nursing routine at night and in the morning for the sake of closeness, don't hesitate. It's such a nice way to start and to end the day. (For detailed advice from experienced mothers on weaning, see Huggins in *Further Reading.* See also *Useful Addresses and Web Sites.*)

Learning

New motor independence brings the need for learning about danger. For instance, soon after he learns to crawl, a baby learns that he can endanger himself by crawling over the edge of a surface. The eminent child-development researchers James Sorce, Robert Emde, Joseph Campos, Mary Klinnert, and their colleagues tested this developing ability to use visual information to assess danger with a fascinating experiment. At eight months, when a child has just begun to crawl, he blithely proceeds across a piece of Plexiglass suspended over a checkerboard pattern, even beyond the point where the checkerboard pattern drops several feet below the Plexiglass. After a month or so of learning from one hard knock after another, any experienced crawler freezes at the sight of the drop. To test the concept of "social referencing," the researchers raised the checkerboard drop so that it appeared only a single foot deep, creating an ambiguous situation. They demonstrated that when a baby needs information about an ambiguous situation, he knows that he can count on his parents' facial expressions, the nonverbal information they automatically provide, to make his decision. He uses cues from his parents to "reference" their approval or disapproval. As he crawls across the transparent plastic surface with the one-foot deep visual "cliff" below, he stops at the edge. Although he could keep crawling safely, he takes note of the drop-off of the pattern below and stops himself on the plastic surface. If his mother is stationed at the other end, giving him facial clues, he watches for them. If she smiles at him, he keeps crawling across. If she frowns and looks warningly, he stops and won't keep going. This experiment dramatizes a baby's capacity to use his parents to help him make important judgments. He takes in all sorts of cues from them—facial behavior and gestures, as well as speech—to help him recognize attitudes and their meaning for him. The direct applications of these new abilities to discipline are obvious: Parents now must not only say "No!" like they mean it, but they must look like they do too.

Peek-a-boo and other repetitive games—such as gently banging foreheads, or rhythmically nuzzling noses over and over—are a baby's way to begin to develop and test expectancies. If you play at touching a baby's forehead with yours, over and over, saying, "Ahhh—boommm!" each time, he'll close his eyes in expectation of each bang. Then, if you change the rhythm slightly, he'll close his eyes on time, expecting you to come close again. When you don't, he'll look up at you and giggle. He's developed an expectancy and loves the violation of it. This is one of the earliest forms of humor, but any slapstick comedy still relies on it.

Understanding of object permanence ("The object is still there even though I can't see it") is expanding to understanding of person permanence ("If Mommy and Daddy go into another room, they'll still exist"). Peek-a-boo and games that involve hiding an object or a person explore this concept. By playing with these repetitions over and over, the baby learns mastery. He learns he can control them and produce them. He needn't be frightened of giving something up, because it will return. He learns this with objects that are neutral. Peek-a-boo and hiding games are more exciting than games with objects because they involve people. The development of trust in one's own environment is intimately tied to mastering object and person permanence. A baby will test rhythms in these games as well, breaking the rhythm to laugh. If you break the rhythm, he looks at you, grinning and waiting. This involves a sense of timing. These games prepare the way for communication, for speaking and sharing the rhythm of conversation later on.

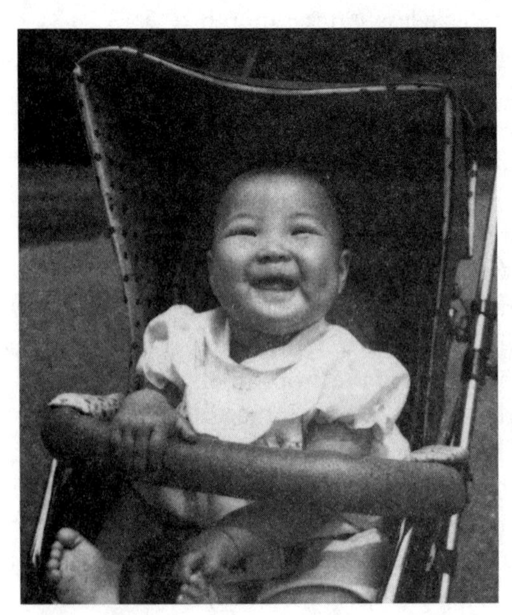

Showing-off games—clapping, "so big," "bye-bye," and so on—all provide the baby a chance to play with adults. The excitement of these games comes from the child's ability to participate and even direct them, and from adult approval. These are grandparents' games! They tap his newfound skills in imitation—one of the most powerful learning modes a baby of this age has at his disposal.

The baby will try out lots of new sounds, like

"ga-ga," "ma-ma," "ba-ba," and "bye-bye," but they may not yet attach to specific meanings. Speech sounds are explored. In bed, he can trill, use inflections, or try out a new sound or syllable over and over. He uses them to call his parents to him. Crying out is not his only ploy now. He can enlarge on it by using gestures and syllables as he begins to try to manipulate his parents.

Causality is a new concept for a nine-month-old and is just surfacing. How do things work? What makes a toy truck go? At this age, exploration includes such efforts as pushing on a truck to make the wheels turn. The child may push it ahead of himself to go after it. This is already an example of testing out his space and mastering it. But, at some point, he will turn the truck over to examine its wheels. It is as if he wants to know how the truck goes—just when he's learning how to make himself go. He won't yet, though, imitate its sound, as if that too could help make it go. That will come later, about midway into the second year, when he is able to make the connection between a toy and the real thing, between a symbol and the thing it stands for. Symbolic play will then become his way of learning that words, too, can stand for things, as he prepares to speak.

Expectation of Success or Failure

By nine months, I can tell by a baby's behavior whether he expects to succeed or to fail at the tasks he sets for himself or that others set for him. I have often had to assess babies at Boston's Children's Hospital about whom I knew very little. When I offer a nine-month-old a task on an infant-assessment scale (for example, the Denver Developmental Screening Test), I observe his behavior, for that is his language. For instance, I can tell a great deal about a baby by such a simple test as handing him two blocks the same size. The baby who expects to succeed with new tasks will grab them, mouth one, rub it in his hair, and then often drop it to see if an adult will give it back. Finally, after lots of testing and exploring, he will put the two together, stacking them to show that he knows they are the same size. Then, he'll look up at the person examining him with a delighted, proud expression. He expects to be praised.

In contrast, a baby who expects to fail may dutifully take the two blocks. He doesn't do much with them, as though he realizes that no one will care. He brings the two blocks close to each other, showing that he is able to see that they are the same size, but then slides them right past. He gives the observer a dull look, as if to express his sense of failure, or as if to say, "I'm no good. I can't do it." He doesn't expect to be rewarded by his own success. Later on, at twelve months, the same baby might knock down a block that he has piled up on another, as if by accident, and look up with a cowed, hopeless expression. At fifteen months, when such a child trips and falls, he looks up with the same cowed look of failure. He doesn't expect to succeed.

At nine months, I can't necessarily know whether this expectation to fail comes from within the baby, from his environment, or from a mismatch between them. Parents and pediatrician should look at the child and his environment more closely, while trying to avoid the either-or tendency to focus only on the child—or to blame the parents. The child may be showing that he needs more encouragement, or that he has problems in integrating information for learning. He may have a developmental delay that interferes with his ability to take in cues, integrate them, and respond to them. Or he may be hypersensitive and attentionally disordered. A child who can't stay at a task long enough, or one with mild neuro-motor problems, may be saying through his behavior that any task is so difficult that he expects to fail. Such children need a careful evaluation and patient, respectful help. Their disabilities can often be overcome in time if they are understood. One of the most serious impairments for a developmentally delayed child beyond the delay itself is the poor self-esteem, the expectation to fail, that accompanies the delay. When we can identify the disorder early, we can prevent that serious consequence. I always watch a child at this age for evidence of inner excitement or recognition of success as he tackles a problem.

Looking Ahead

Feeding From now on, the baby will continue to need more and more control over feeding. When I stress this with parents, mothers especially will say, "But I *need* to get a rounded diet into him." Parents must remember that, at this age, food is not the main issue. The baby's need to imitate, to explore, to begin to learn to refuse, takes priority. By the end of the first year, he must be able to control the situation. And he will—so it's far better not to set up a struggle with him as that time approaches. I would urge both parents to reconsider any attempts to dominate meals and to instead make it a period of interplay and of learning. When our first child was a year old, her antics, refusals, and explorations at the table nearly gave me an ulcer. We learned to let her feed herself. Then, she could either join us at mealtime or she could play near the table, but not on it. You can't expect manners or a "rounded diet" at this age. It's too important to the child to begin to learn to feed himself. The difficulty for many parents is that food was a source of conflict in their own past. It's hard not to perpetuate that history.

Sleep With a nine-month-old, I tell parents to expect the baby to start awakening at night with each new motor task—standing, cruising, and walking. Learning these is so exciting. As we saw, the excitement, as well as the frustration, carries over into the night, surfacing in light sleep. Be ready to keep reinstituting a comforting but firm pattern, helping the baby to put himself back to sleep at each awakening. You can use the same ritual for any impending separation. Warn him that nap or bedtime is coming. When he protests, comfort him, but let him know you still mean it. In the months to come, if the baby seems able to climb over the crib rail, you'll need to lower the mattress height in the crib, if it's an adjustable one (see also chapter 11).

Toilet Training While there are different approaches to toilet training, one of the causes of problems in this area is pressure on parents from outside to train the baby early. One of the grandparents, for example, may suggest that the time has come. Since the goal, as I see it, is for the child to train himself, there is no reason to start now. If you want training to go smoothly, as the child's own accomplishment, you will need to wait. When the baby is two years old, he'll be ready to start learning to do it for himself.

Some parents, however, are having success in the first year with a technique called "elimination communication." This technique is not unlike the approach to toilet training used in many traditional cultures and is similar to what occurred in the old days, when parents had to wash out diapers by hand. It requires that a parent or regular caregiver be in close physical contact with an infant so that when body movements and sphincters signal that a production is on the way, the adult can quickly bring the baby to the toilet or potty. Some parents who have tried this method are thrilled with how close they feel to their baby and how well they feel they know the baby. When it works, "elimination communication" ends diaper use earlier. So far, we don't know of any negative long-term effects. I worry, though, that when this doesn't go smoothly, parent and child will feel that they have failed, leading to exactly the kind of pressure that I advise against. Also, I am concerned about parents who must work. For them, the pressure to return to this traditional childrearing practice may feel like one more way in which they've let their baby down, or missed out on an important time together. (For more information on "elimination communication," see *Diaper Free!* by Ingrid Bauer listed in *Further Reading.*)

Separation In the next few months, separations will become more difficult. Be sure to prepare the baby whenever you must go away. Remind him that "Mommy and Daddy always come back." Show him, again, how a familiar object, a teddy bear or a doll, still exists even when hidden under a blanket.

At first, leave him with someone he knows, and if you can, for only brief periods. When you return, let him know you're back, and remind him that you had told him you always do come back. Gradually increase the time that you are away. This stage will pass, but it can be pretty horrendous. At this stage of development, he is putting much of his energy into becoming independent and moving away. And yet, as he does, he will become more *dependent.*

All transitions are bigger now, because they are fraught with more implications. When the baby is in child care, morning leavings will be hard. This is a precursor to the baby's growing independence. It's a good time to evaluate how the caregivers are handling the baby. Drop by at unexpected times. See whether he's happy or not. Look to see whether the childcare providers are sensitive to his rhythms—sleep, play, feeding, and so on. Also, when he looks at them, are they sensitive to him, and do they offer respect and a caring nod? If so, it will help with your own separation. If not, it may be time to change.

At the end of the day, continue to save time to feel close to him again, perhaps in a rocking chair. Your anguish at being away from him will convey itself, but it's part of your caring. Recognizing these feelings will bring the two of you closer.

Safety Review your safety precautions periodically. With each new developmental stage, especially these new motor triumphs, you'll need to reevaluate all you've done before. Most children's hospitals and toy stores have safety booklets to remind you of all the traps you might have forgotten. (See also *The Children's Hospital Guide to Your Child's Health and Development* in *Further Reading.*)

9. One Year

GETTING THROUGH THE FIRST YEAR DESERVES A CELEBRATION. EVERY BABY album usually has a photo of a chubby one-year-old about to demolish the cake with its one candle. This birthday may also be worth savoring as the quiet before the storm. All of the baby's behavior is likely to go into a period of disorganization soon, before the next spurt. Just before she walks, the toddler-to-be will start waking every four hours at night. She screams every time a parent walks away from her. Under the surface is a realization that she wants to be the one to walk away. Every task may bring on a burst of angry frustration, as does every confrontation or request. All this turbulence is stirred up by the new goal—walking, and on to independence!

I remember a family, whom we'll call the Lowrys, coming for an appointment with their one-year-old daughter. From inside my office, I knew they'd arrived. When I walked out to the waiting room to greet them, I was met with screeches of protest. "Dana always used to like to come," said the Lowrys sheepishly, "but now every new thing brings on this kind of storm." Once they put her down, the screams subsided. She had seen the fish tank and was off like a rocket. Her father felt he should take off some of her outer clothing. He rushed after her, which made her crawl even faster. He dove at her. She screamed, half gleefully at her success in drawing him in. But as soon as she realized he was about to "do something to her," her screeches of protest resumed. After he'd pulled off her cap and her outer coat, he let her go, and she started out again. This time she pulled herself up at the fish tank. In her excitement, she toppled over backward and hit her head with a thwack. She screamed. The Lowrys zoomed over, sure that she was hurt. As I saw this happen, I could tell by her watchful face and alert eyes that she was not. She was frustrated. I asked her parents, "Do you think she gets fed up with falling when she wants so badly to stand up?" They looked at me. They looked at her. Her father held out his hand for her to pull herself back up on again. She quieted completely, looking pleased with herself.

When she saw I was ready to have her come into my office, she looked me in the face. I was prepared for this and knew that I must look the other way. On the brink of independence, a one-year-old's sensitivity to feeling invaded is peaking. Intruding into her personal space by looking at her is bound to raise self-protective feelings. I looked just past Dana. She gurgled. I thought this was a response, so I said, "Hi, Dana." I felt her stiffen, and she began to whimper again. I knew I'd gone too fast. I moved away. This intrigued her and she started to follow me. By now, I knew we could go into my office without a firestorm.

In my office, when I need to examine a child of this age, one of my goals is to keep her as comfortable, quiet, and still as possible throughout the examination. I've found that it helps to ask a parent to hold her in his or her lap and undress her there, and I do not approach her until I see her begin to relax and play with a toy on the desk next to her. At that point, without looking her in the face, I can come closer and settle cautiously on the floor near her parent's lap. I sit and look beyond her at the parent. The baby will have stiffened as I approached. Meanwhile, I continue to talk to the parent while I offer the child her own lovey—a blanket or doll. If she has none, I bring her a doll from my office to hold. As she accepts it and begins to relax with it, I dare to start the exam. I put my stethoscope on her parent's hand, then on the parent's arm, then on the doll. If she is not too threatened, I dare to put it on her briefly. Then I shift very quickly to the doll or to the parent again. I play this game of approaching her through her parent and the doll with repeated passes until she begins to relax. As she does, I can gradually examine her chest, her heart, and her abdomen. I never let her catch me looking in her face. This takes only an extra minute or two, but it's worth it.

Examining a one-year-old's ears can be a major trauma. I examine the baby doll's ears first and then her parent's ears. Finally, I ask the parent to turn her to one side, holding onto her outer arm. I show her her parent's ear being

A toddler's rapidly increasing sense of independence and the dependence that balances it are different sides of the same coin.

examined. I examine her ear quickly as her parent presses the child's opposite cheek against his or her own to be sure her head stays still. After showing her on the doll again, I get her parent to turn her around. I look at the second ear. Then I show her how to open her mouth wide. I ask her parent to "open wide" and to say "aaah" and stick out his or her tongue. Many toddlers will imitate me and their parents. If imitation fails, I ask the parent to sit the child in his or her lap facing me, then to put one arm under each of the baby's arms, locking the child's head in a full nelson hold. I can then open her mouth quickly with a throat stick, examine it, and get out quickly.

When all this goes as planned, toddlers don't need to protest. They accept my maneuvers and realize that I respect their fear of being invaded. The use of imitation with their mother or father and with the doll captures their interest and diverts their fears. These maneuvers do not add more time to my exam, but they make it more effective. A heartbeat is hard to hear in a screaming child. I have also kept the child happy about coming to see me, so that she'll fuss less about coming the next time. For some parents this can make the difference in whether they'll keep the next appointment. When she is happy, I have a chance to observe the quality of her play and can estimate her developmental progress while her parents and I are conversing. Having watched in the waiting room for motor skills, I already know whether I should suspect motor impairment. Having watched the parent with her, I can appreciate the quality of their relationship. By the time I turn to her physical exam, I know a great deal about her and her parents and how they interact.

At this visit, shots would include the Hepatitis B (HepB) and Polio (IPV) vaccines if they weren't given at six months; the Hemophilus Influenza (Hib), Measles, Mumps, and Rubella (MMR), and Pneumococcus (PCV) vaccines, which can wait until fifteen months; the Varicella vaccine, which can also be given at fifteen or eighteen months; and the first Hepatitis A (HepA) vaccine, which requires two doses, six months apart. If the shots have been taken care of or can wait, it is good to have a visit without shots.

Often, the first question at this visit is about the baby's sudden new "irritability." "Every time we want to do anything, she gives us grief. She needs to make all the decisions. She won't put up with us deciding anything!" If this is the case, I see that feelings of independence are dawning. As the baby enters a whole new phase, the first year looks easy by comparison. When a baby is resistant these first times, parents are taken by surprise. "You mean all one-year-olds are like this? None of our friends have run into this yet. We thought we had created a monster." When parents express concerns about this new turmoil, it is obviously a relief to them that I can place it in the context of the baby's development.

Not all babies become independent suddenly and dramatically. But when they do, I am always glad to see it. This is another touchpoint and parents will come to see the progress it represents. Though it means the simple intimacy of the first year is changing and becoming more complex, the burst of autonomy is normal and healthy. A baby's struggle to express herself and to find out her own limits will go on for many years, reaching different levels at different ages. A baby who is too compliant may have to rebel eventually, and it may well be harder when it happens than it is with more assertive children.

At this touchpoint, parents are bound to take the one-year-old's efforts to assert herself personally. Don't. Often thought of as a period of "negativism," the coming months are full of passionate striving to do everything she can on her own: "All by myself," she will say again and again, once she can speak. The tantrums and stubbornness of this period are a predictable part of the one-year-old's job of learning—about herself and her ability to affect others. She must try out her parents' limits, over and over, to understand their rules—and the consequences of breaking them—and to master her own behavior. She is learning about what she can do with her body and with words and gestures, and about how she can impact her world and how it will respond. Now that she can stand, and perhaps even walk, she must face new physical limitations—not fast enough, not steady enough, too steep. Gravity is a new complication. The future is still beyond her horizons, so of course she won't let go of the present when she's told "we're done now," or "it's time to stop." Transitions are a major challenge. A one-year-old often throws all of her senses and muscles into the moment. This is how she learns, but it makes it so hard to stop and let go.

Tantrums, too, seem designed to overpower, undermine, and humiliate parents. But the world and the adults in it loom large over the hapless one-year-old, who is so often thwarted by the mismatch of her ambitions and her abilities. Inexperience and ineptness confront her with failure and frustration in such rapid succession. Who wouldn't collapse on the floor in a heap of despair every now and then? Especially if, like the one-year-old, one is lacking in other ways of settling down and bucking up.

When this new independence comes, parents inevitably worry about spoiling. An independent one-year-old is not a spoiled child. As we saw earlier, a spoiled child is one who doesn't know when to expect limits. She has not been disciplined and has not learned what her own limits are or when to expect limits from others. How confusing, and frightening! The behavior I call spoiled is her way of asking for limits, which she instinctively knows she needs. Firm handling and limits will help such a child, but they won't do away with the normal turmoil of the second year. When the child has overcome the ambivalence and fears brought by this new independence, she will be more reasonable. The turmoil will subside. But the need for discipline will not go away. We will discuss this in more detail as we look at the months to come.

Motor Skills

Somewhere at the beginning of the second year, occasionally sooner, a baby becomes a toddler. The world opens up—the world of independence. With the urge to walk, a child begins to experience a tumultuous ambivalence. Will I be on my own, and do I really want that? Do I want to walk away, or don't I? Must I do it my parent's way, or can I do it my own way? No other period in a child's life is as fraught with these wrenching questions—not even adolescence, although it is a similar kind of turmoil. The conflict between "Will I or won't I? Do I or don't I?" is so intense that it will not be sorted out for at least a year and a half. At a time when no one else cares, a toddler will lie down to have a rip-roaring temper tantrum over whether to go through a door or not. Temper tantrums will peak somewhere in the second and third years, as part of this struggle. Parents invariably blame themselves. They needn't. A temper tantrum reflects an *inner* struggle. The parents may have triggered it, but their actions are not responsible for the turmoil, nor can they settle it for the toddler.

This surge toward independence and the negativism that accompanies it start with walking. These mark a particularly intense touchpoint, an extraordinary growth spurt for the child and a trying challenge for all parents. When parents understand what lies ahead, many a crisis can be defused. The close interaction between motor achievements and emotional development becomes apparent. Mothers of toddlers immobilized in a cast, for instance, have told me that their babies were compliant and eager to please and be pleased —until the period of immobilization was over. As they got to their feet, the toddlers' concepts of their world changed. No more compliance, no more easy ways to be pleased. By walking, a toddler says, "I can walk away and I can come back. But what will happen if I do? I am in control of my destiny, but what do I want?"

Walking actually does not happen all of a sudden. All through the year, a baby has been practicing and trying out the components of walking. As noted earlier, the walk reflex is present at birth and lasts for the first few months. It incorporates many of the motor skills that will surface again later. As voluntary mobility becomes a possibility in the second half of the first year, the walk reflex goes underground. Creeping and crawling take over. Before it disappears completely, at around five months, if you pull a baby to sit, she will often stiffen her body up to stand, a wide grin on her face acknowledging the built-in excitement of standing. She is learning the control over her trunk muscles that will be necessary in standing. As creeping, crawling, standing, and finally, cruising occur sequentially, the ingredients of the process are mastered one by one. Finally, they are ready to be put together. Cruising along furniture has prepared the pre-toddler for moving her legs as she maintains upright body posture and balance. When she finally feels courageous and dares to let go with both hands, she teeters and collapses. But she keeps trying, undaunted until she finally puts all of her sensory and motor achievements together to walk unsteadily. The new sense of mastery glows on her face. She walks, walks, walks with a grin of ultimate satisfaction. She has done it!

Before this great moment, all of her energy, both day and night, goes into this new step. Seeing someone walk can make her scream. Whenever a parent walks away from her, she cries out in frustration. She falls again and again in her attempt to keep up with a walking sibling. At night, this frustration boils up at each cycle of light sleep. A child this age spends more time in light rather than deep sleep, perhaps so that her brain can lay down the memories of movements she's putting together as she prepares to walk. Of course she'll awaken more often now. She stands at her crib side, crying out in revived desperation every three to four hours, as she remembers her attempts to master this new task. Sleeping through the night becomes impossible for her and for her weary parents.

A baby's struggle to learn a skill as important as walking demands all the family's energy. She might be sitting happily in her high chair when the urge to stand and to walk comes over her. You can see her eyes change suddenly. Her hands, busy with finger feeding, become immobile. Sweeping the left-over food off the tray onto the floor, or her parent's lap, she reaches for the back of her chair and squirms around to free herself of the tray. She stands in her chair, ready to topple. Standing and walking are her first priority. Food and hunger are second.

All of the daily tasks of living are turned into scrimmages. Trying to lay her down to diaper her becomes hopeless. She is sure to flail, kick, and scream even at the thought. A parent must learn to diaper her in a standing posture. Suddenly, just immobilizing her to take off her clothes is more interference than she can tolerate. Having her eyes covered to slip off a shirt or jersey means that she must lose sight of her goal. She is likely to have a tantrum over any restriction on her mobility—visual or motor.

Parents of a child who isn't walking at a year will worry and wonder why she is "delayed." Although I tell them they are lucky to have a few more months of grace before the siege of toddler-hood, they are not reassured. There are many reasons why a year-old child may not be ready to walk. Children who are more low-keyed may simply not be in a hurry to walk. In the United States, the average is twelve to fourteen months. A second or later child may walk later. It takes twice the courage for her to dare to let go if she has older siblings whirling by and endangering her newly found balance. Children who are very heavy also tend to walk later, as they must learn to master their bulk.

In my experience, big children are also more likely to be what I've always called "flop-jointed." A child who has highly extensible joints may be delayed in walking by six months. When a child's knees or elbows can extend beyond a 180-degree angle, it is likely that she has extensible ligaments and more flaccid musculature around each joint. This need not be a defect (though there are rare disorders that can cause severe joint hyperextensibility), but it makes it difficult for the child to start walking, which may occur later than expected. As time goes on, such a child develops extra muscle strength to master these unsteady joints. In my practice, some of these children who took longer to master walking and running grew up to become athletes. It's almost as if the drive toward mastery had pressed them even farther later on.

The agitation that accompanies learning to walk can lead some parents to worry about whether a child is "hyperactive." The drive to become mobile and upright makes her keep going constantly—cruising on furniture, crawling frantically, even rolling to get places. Once she's there, she starts out toward something else. This does not mean that the child is hyperactive. She just wants to learn how to be mobile and on two legs. A child who is not truly hyperactive may seem to be for the next several months, until she has mastered walking. Then, usually by about two years of age, she'll settle down to discover the new things she can do—while sitting—with her hands. Still, young children are meant to be more active since they have so much motor learning to do. Also, according to a recent study, a brain chemical thought to play a role in attention deficit hyperactivity disorder, dopamine, may normally be present up until about age five in levels close to those of older children who do have ADHD. No wonder parents worry.

It is difficult to diagnose a child this age with ADHD. This diagnosis might be considered, though, when a child who persists in being truly unstoppable and distractible flits from one thing to another without being able to learn anything from each experience. Such a child may not be able to stay with any task because she is too easily distracted by every sight and sound, or because her need to move seems driven by a motor. She can't stick to any one task. Each new sound or stimulus takes over. If she is alone and without distraction, she can more readily focus and learn. But if she hears a sound or sees a change, she is at the mercy of her response to it. For instance, even something so simple as a block falling down can make her lose concentration. The sound or the visual image diverts her. Even without a clear diagnosis at this age, such a child can be helped to prolong her attention by reducing the stimulation around her, exposing her to one activity or object at a time and gently encouraging her to renew her interest in some new aspect of it when she becomes distracted. At one year, a truly hyperactive, hypersensitive child may already expect to fail at any complicated task. This sense of failure can pervade everything she does. This is entirely different from the single-minded drive of a child learning to walk (see "Hypersensitivity and Hyperactivity").

Sleep The drive to master standing and walking upsets all the daily rhythms. Two naps, which have been predictable before, become less so. At naptime, a baby may spend all of her time up and down in her crib. I often recommend that a parent still put the baby into her crib for a short time in the morning and afternoon, but not to worry if she doesn't sleep.

As we saw earlier, whenever a child who is learning to walk rouses at night, she will be driven to stand in her crib. In the process, she may awaken herself, but she may not. She may stand and cruise around her crib half in her sleep. But as she does, her frustrated screams wake the household. This phase needn't last too long. As I discussed in chapters 7 and 8, she must keep on learning how to get herself back to sleep. Each new daytime achievement, or the struggle leading up to it, will surface by disrupting the baby's sleep cycles. Parents can help by reacting calmly and firmly and by reinstating all the familiar rituals. They should pat her for a while, then leave. If parents reinforce the child's waking by staying or playing or taking her out of her crib, they are telling her, "If you fight hard enough, I'll give in!" Parents who have chosen to keep the baby in their bed should expect these same cycles of disruption. To avoid a wide-awake family gathering every three to four hours, they will need to firmly insist that the child go back to sleep, refusing to get involved in drawn-out interactions that bring her to a full waking state. Sit beside her, holding and patting her down, but avoid getting excited as she builds up and wants to stand. As she sees your determination, her struggle will subside and she'll begin to settle. This way, you haven't deserted her. You are teaching her to be independent. Over time, it gets easier and easier—for both of you.

Another helpful measure that I have always recommended to encourage a full night's sleep for everyone is for parents to wake the child before they go to bed, at 10:00 or 11:00 P.M. They can cuddle her, even feed her if necessary, and help her down again, saying, "Mummy and Daddy are right here, and we love you. We'll be here when you wake up." For some reason, breaking into her sleep rhythms *before* she wakes can work like magic. The chances of her awakening at 2:00 A.M. will be greatly reduced.

When a twelve-month-old baby wakes in the morning, she is capable of entertaining herself. If parents do not run in at the first peep, they may be treated to chirping monologues and little songs. It can be a cheerful way to start the day and builds the child's self-reliance.

Feeding

Parents who have not yet instituted finger feeding will find that their child is resistant to being fed at this point. At this age, the control of feeding must be the child's. Getting the food in by dubious manipulations is beside the point. Not only should more feeding become finger food (though milk is still a mainstay of a toddler's diet), but parents must not set their sights high for feeding a toddler. A "rounded diet" does not have to be a goal for the second year. By the fourth year, a child may be ready to eat everything and to imitate her parents with table manners, but the second and third years are likely to be full of quirky experimentation.

One week the toddler will eat eggs or meat; another week, no eggs, but any dairy product. Occasionally, she will even explore vegetables. But there is no way to count on this. The more insistent the parent, the less successful the parent will be. Over the course of a month, a baby may well consume a rounded diet. But whether she does or not had better not be a parent's concern. Toddlers are extremely sensitive to adults' reactions to feeding. This is probably a sign of the importance of autonomy in this area. In order to help parents turn the feeding choices over to the child, I have tried to define a minimal daily diet. For the second and third year this can consist of the following, though exact amounts vary from child to child, depending on things like the child's size, activity level, and other factors:

- Sixteen ounces of whole milk or its equivalent in breast milk or follow-up formula, cheese, yogurt, or ice cream. (Skim or 2 percent milk won't supply the particular fats that are needed for brain development in the first two or three years.)
- Three to four ounces of protein (a patty of cooked lean hamburger meat, an egg, beans, or tofu).
- Iron—Meats such as hamburger provide iron. Other sources include chickpeas, lentils, baked beans, spinach, and kale. Iron is better absorbed when food high in Vitamin C, such as cantaloupe, tomatoes, or citrus fruits, are eaten at the same meal. Some cereals are fortified with iron. Iron supplements are important for children who aren't getting enough in their diets.
- Half a slice of whole-grain bread and half a cup of whole-grain cereal or pasta over the course of a day provide energy for a one-year-old's increased activity level. (Whole grains also add fiber, helping to prevent constipation.)
- One ounce of orange juice, or a few small, bite-sized pieces of fruit. Limit juice to no more than six ounces per day since it can cause cavities and fill a baby up before she's eaten what she needs most.
- Try a variety of cooked vegetables and leafy greens. Don't assume your child will hate them, but don't expect her to eat them. Don't push them, and don't make a fuss if she won't eat them. Choose ones that are easy to prepare so that you won't be quite so frustrated when she turns them down.

A multivitamin can cover for uneaten vegetables. If a child isn't getting enough Vitamin D–fortified cow's milk or follow-up formula, Vitamin D supplements should be given too. Parents will want to be sure to talk over these supplements with their pediatrician. They will be relieved to hear how much they can make up for during this predictable time of fussing over food.

When conscientious, idealistic mothers hear this from me, they ask, "You mean, that's all she needs in a twenty-four-hour period?" I reassure them that this will cover the basic nutritional needs during this period when autonomy is so important. When an older child is eating well, vitamins may not be necessary. But, by using them, parents can forget about pushing vegetables. "Not even green vegetables?" mothers will ask. "Not even yellow vegetables?" I find I must stress that vegetables and a rounded diet must wait until this period passes and the whole drama of making choices about food is less charged. Even when I succeed in convincing mothers, their own mothers may still worry.

Feeding is an area in which independence and the negativism it engenders hit a parent at a vulnerable spot. These are what make it another critical touchpoint. Parents feel that feeding a baby is their responsibility. To leave it to her to decide what to eat gives them an empty feeling—a feeling of having neglected their baby. The parents' job is to understand and deal with these feelings. When, as an outsider, I can reassure them and back them up with these minimum dietary expectations, parents are grateful and our relationship deepens once again.

When I talk with parents, here's what I recommend. The moment a child of this age loses interest and starts to tease by smearing or dropping her food, or by getting up to stand in her high chair, put her down immediately. End the solid feedings with a bottle or the breast. After that, let her go. Don't try to prolong the meal for "just a bit more." When her meal is over, it is *over* until the next meal or regular snack time. If she gets hungry, she'll learn to respect mealtime. She'll eventually learn to eat when it's offered. But don't hold your breath. Her hunger at this age is easily submerged in the more exciting game of teasing parents. If you do try to feed her, or if you leave food where she can get it in between meals, you are not only devaluing the importance of mealtime, but putting not-too-subtle pressure on her to eat. And you will invariably lose. These are quick ways to set up feeding problems. Her need to control her intake will supersede hunger and any desire for food.

If she starts to hold food in her mouth, or to spit it out, or to gag or vomit, she is telling you very clearly that she views feedings as a pressured situation.

You are consciously or unconsciously putting her under pressure. Sit back and reevaluate what is going on between the two of you.

During these months, parents sometimes are so concerned about getting milk into a child that they let her walk around all day with a bottle. They are likely to find that the toddler will drink even less milk this way. This devalues milk as a food. The toddler may be using it for comfort or even as a way of provoking parents.

Once this habit starts, it is not easy to stop. A child may beg for a bottle, even have a tantrum to get one to carry. Parents will have to be patient and firm, telling the child that she can have her lovey during the day and that she can have her bottle at mealtimes. Then, they can tie her empty bottle to her doll, a stuffed animal, a blanket, or any other lovey for a period. When she has transferred her attachment, the bottle can be dropped from the lovey, with her permission. Meanwhile, milk shouldn't be put in the bottle. If she doesn't drink enough milk, parents can use yogurt, ice cream, or cheese (one ounce of cheese is equivalent to roughly four ounces of milk). Then, when parents do give her the bottle, they can make it part of an important ritual, holding and loving her while they give it to her.

The interminable smashing and squishing of food that goes on at mealtimes will also get to parents. The toddler does it as a part of exploration, but soon she also realizes a secondary gain—that of teasing her parents. Once this starts, parents might as well give up on the feeding and put her down until the next meal. It is important not to make an issue out of her playing with her food, since this will only fuel her teasing.

Although a child this age will enjoy playing with a spoon, she will usually lose the food that was on it. Not until fifteen or sixteen months will she have real success. Meanwhile, she is learning how to manipulate utensils—valuable play.

If a pacifier has become a habit, now is not the time to take it away. Nor would I talk about it. Any attention parents pay to it will heighten its value as a way to tease them. In the second year, a child deserves to have a crutch she can use to help her soften the struggle of being a toddler. When she loses her pacifier, or drops it over the side of the crib to make her parents come to find it, this is part of the fun of torturing them. Parents can tie it to her wrist with a ribbon during the day or to a lovey she cares about at night, or tie it to her crib with a *short* ribbon, too short to get around her neck. She can then retrieve it for herself, if shown how. If parents do not make a fuss about a pacifier, the toddler won't need to use it for manipulation.

Teething

In the second year, toddlers begin to get molars. Chewing on things that soothe their back gums helps to rub out the swelling in the gums. They chew on everything. This is the time to worry about toddlers eating toxins, such as lead paint, for some children begin at this age to develop "pica," the tendency to eat everything. Lead paint tastes sweet, and small children will eat flakes of it. The danger of having lead paint in your house should be less common now, because no modern paint has lead in it. It's present only in old houses. If you live in a house built before 1978 (when lead in house paint was banned), or if your child regularly spends time in one, have a lead-level blood test done on your child. Most health departments will do them for you where lead is a local problem, but in such areas pediatricians should check lead levels routinely at this age, again at two, and when there are additional reasons to be concerned. It is one more needle, and no one likes to put a young child through this, so your pediatrician should carefully assess the specific risk factors in your child's environment, relying on state and local information on lead in the environment in your area. When warranted, a blood lead level test is well worth the child's temporary distress.

Speech

Signs of learning receptive language are becoming increasingly clear at this age. If you ask a child to get a toy or a diaper, she will show that she knows what you are asking, either by doing what you ask or by showing clearly that she refuses to do it, even though she knows what you mean. One-step requests, rather than more complex ones, work best. Speech itself is also getting more and more exciting. She will stand in bed, one arm aloft, declaiming with the inflections and rhythms of a speechmaker. Very few words are distinguishable, but the base for future language and speech is proceeding. She is listening very carefully to the adults around her all the time, especially when they talk with her, and is already making sense of the patterns and rules they follow to string words together. Usually a few words can be made out, like "doggie," "mama," "babee," and "no." Names get connected with the correct person. Pointing and gesturing are becoming increasingly specific, and a child will use her eyes and facial gestures to explain herself. When she wants to get or keep your attention, she'll use pointing and a word. If her vocalization is not quite clear, parents will always correct her by repeating the word. In this way, they give her the message that they expect her speech to get more and more distinct. She may even say it again, more distinctly this time, right after her parents pronounce it for her. She is eager to learn to speak.

Learning

The testing of object and person permanence still dominates a child's day. She will go around a corner, then call to you to be sure you are still there. If you are out of sight, she may make a noise or try out a forbidden task in order to push you to respond and come to her. All of a sudden, after she's been ominously quiet, the television may start blaring. When you come to her, your presence is her reward. No amount of censure counteracts her delight in drawing you in. Being left during the day or for routine separations at bedtime becomes an intense struggle all over again. She may have been very good at leave-taking until she reached this stage. Now, she protests vigorously and tearfully. She wants control over leave-taking. She will leave you, but she won't let you leave her.

To help a child through this period, I advise parents, always tell her you're leaving before you "disappear." In fact, talk about it a little ahead of time. Before she's into the upset of the actual leaving, prepare her and tell her you'll be back soon. As we said in earlier chapters, if she's having a very tough time, just leave her for fifteen minutes the first time. When you return, remind her that you'd promised her you'd come back. Each time she'll learn to trust you. She'll gradually master her feelings about leave-takings. Meanwhile, protesting is the healthiest thing she can do. If she's with a familiar caregiver who loves her, she knows it and will turn, sobbing, to that person to be comforted. After you are gone, she will soon be fine.

Storage This is a new concept. If you offer a child younger than a year two objects, she will grasp one with each hand. When you offer a third, a younger baby will drop one to take the third. By a year, a toddler will try to figure out how to keep all three. She may put one in her mouth to take the third. Or, she may store one or two under her arm in order to free her hand to grab the third. If the objects are small enough, she will grasp two in one hand. She is learning to solve problems and to plan out what movements she needs to make. She has learned to store.

Block Building A child this age will put one block on top of the other. If it falls, she will show her frustration and will turn to some other game quickly. As she learns to build, she becomes more and more precise.

Imitation Peek-a-boo or gesturing games become more exciting and engaging at this age. A child will imitate parts of a new game even if she can't perform it entirely. This shows that imitation is becoming a source of major interest to her. This is the age when toddlers begin to learn so much from older siblings. They will teach her, and she will work at learning from them. She will imitate hunks of behavior from a sibling that she would never learn from a parent or another adult. Small children are much more intrigued by an older child than they are by an adult!

Causality Before the end of the first year, she will push a windup car along to make it run. Sometime around the first birthday, she will know that you did something to make it run. She may turn it over to look at the underside. But she will hand the toy back to you for you to make it run again.

Fears

Because of the rapid increase in the size of her world, a toddler's personal space suddenly has become even more precious to her. This awareness is coupled with her rapidly increasing sense of independence and the dependence that balances it. The two are different sides of the same coin. A one-year-old baby will let you pick her up, but when she realizes that she's allowed herself to be dependent, she'll squirm to get down. She both wants it and doesn't. Any closeness or approach endangers her sense of personal space and control over her world. If she can look strangers over and digest their features as she clings to her safe parent, she can gradually take them in. The most threatening "stranger" could bc an *almost familiar* one—such as mother's sister or father's brother or a grandparent who visits only rarely. In order to give her the sense of control she needs as she sorts out the subtle or obvious differences, such a visitor must be patient.

Looking Ahead

Self-Assertion The thrust toward independence will be flourishing and growing stronger in the next year. "No" becomes a favorite word. Shaking her head from side to side while saying "no" with a glower will become the toddler's most common behavior. Any request will be met with sullen or unrepressed negativism. Parents need to be prepared. If I can use the one-year visit to alert them to this touchpoint, to the reasons why a compliant infant will turn into a stubborn, resistant toddler, they do not feel so guilty and helpless. Otherwise, they take her negativism personally and try to restrain or control it.

Temper Tantrums These are characteristic in the second year, and each one makes parents feel that it's their fault. As we said earlier, they're not to blame. The intensity and passion that a toddler feels about each and every decision are reflected in her tantrum. You can try, but you can't always keep ahead of these peaks of negativism. Often, a firm, uninvolved approach helps the most, for it says, "I wish I could help you, but I can't. You decide what you want, and I'll either go along with it or I'll say no. Either way, it will help you to make up your own mind." I know it feels cruel to ignore a tumultuous tantrum, but anyone who's tried other interventions knows how trying to help can prolong the turmoil. Walking away until it's over or using time-out will often help.

Parents sometimes ask why toddlers have tantrums in public places. For one thing, they're overloaded by the excitement. They also realize their parents' attention is diverted from them, and they want it back. Also, they know they can embarrass their parents, who are more flustered in public. Parental consternation and attempts to smooth over a tantrum are likely to prolong it. My best recommendations both may seem impossible, but they are effective: (1) Let her know calmly that you can't stay at the store. Gather the child and give up on the shopping. Go back to the car, and let her have it out safely in the car—though you'll have to stay with her there, you'll need to do your best to ignore her. (2) Act as if she's not yours and ignore her. She'll stop very quickly. *Then,* sit down and hug her, saying, "It's terrible being so upset, isn't it?" (For more on temper tantrums, see chapter 10.)

Discipline Even when parents can divert a busy toddler by changing her diaper while she's standing up, or by removing valuable, fragile treasures from her reach, discipline will become necessary. Parents should continue to save it for important things, so that it will be more meaningful when they do use it.

The toddler needs to hunt for something that will get to her parents. As I warn parents, it is easy to predict which times of day she'll be at her worst: at the end of the day when you are both tired, whenever you have an important visitor, when you are on the phone, or whenever you go to the grocery store. This newly aggravating behavior will drive parents to seek solutions. These become more apparent when they realize what is actually going on.

At this age, when a toddler asks for attention, she needs a hug or a short bit of recognition, but not anger. Physical punishment such as hitting or spanking will mean two things to her: one, that you are bigger than she and you can get away with it, and two, that you believe in aggression. In talking with parents, I suggest the following approach. When you can, find a way for time-out or a hug in a rocking chair to break the cycle of buildup. It will help you as well. As you stop her, say, "I'm sorry. I love you, but not what you are doing. I'll have to stop you until you learn to stop yourself."

Discipline is the second most important thing you do for a child. Love comes first, and discipline second. Discipline means teaching, not punishment. The goal is for the child to incorporate her own limits. Each opportunity for discipline becomes a chance for teaching. Hence, after a brief disciplinary maneuver, sit down to comfort and hold her, saying, "You can't do that. I'll have to stop you until you can learn to stop yourself."

Toilet Training If the subtle and not-too-subtle suggestions from friends and relatives to start toilet training have not begun, count yourself lucky. *It is still too soon.* Toward the end of the second year, the toddler may become ready to make the transition to the potty herself. Think what we are asking of a toddler: to feel urine or a bowel movement coming, to hold onto it with pressure, and to stagger to a place that *we've* designated, sit down, and finally produce. Then we ask her to give her productions up for good as we flush them away. Isn't that a lot to ask at a time when a toddler is working so hard on the task of becoming her own person? I am convinced that if you do wait to let her get the idea and choose to conform to it herself, you won't end up with soiling, smearing, wetting, or withholding. If you start too early, you might well have any of those as reactions to your pressure. It's got to be her achievement. Be patient and wait! Parents who have chosen to try the elimination communication method of early training may now need to assess whether this has been successful. If a conflict has developed, I recommend letting the child stay in diapers and waiting until she is ready.

Biting, Hitting, and Scratching These behaviors will soon surface, along with other unpleasant behaviors, in the normal course of development. Though mortifying, they are expectable in this period. They start out as exploratory efforts to communicate with others and test out their reactions. They are also associated with periods of overload when the toddler is out of control. If you lose control, too, you will frighten her and reinforce the behavior. So, expect such things to happen. When they do, gather your child up to contain her, but don't reinforce the behavior with too much of a response. Instead, say as calmly as you can, "I don't like that and neither does anyone else. You just can't do it. I'll stop you each time until you can stop yourself." Knowing that babies everywhere act like this at times will help you say this convincingly.

10. Fifteen Months

Parents of toddlers are on constant alert, watching their whirlwind to be sure he's safe and to divert him before he gets into trouble. Their questions to me and the way their attention is constantly divided show me how their days are spent as they prevent their toddler from destroying himself and his environment. During the appointment, they are in minimal contact with me.

The toddler, too, has divided attention. He keeps one eye on his parents, to be sure they're watching, and one eye on the toys. During all this he maintains a wary sense of what invasive ideas I might have in mind. As I observe him playing, I am concerned not only with his neurological and physical development, but also with how confidently he approaches various tasks. Does he expect to succeed? Does he keep trying? When he succeeds, does he expect approval from those around him? Or does he give up easily? Does he try to divert attention from a task that he knows he can't master? Does he realize he's failing and look to his parents for disapproval? If a toddler is overwhelmed by the strangeness and the threat of my office, it is much harder for him to show me everything he's up to, and harder for me to make a judgment about his behavior and his development. For this reason, I try very hard to encourage him to want to come to see me, so that I can have a more accurate snapshot of his development at each visit and be of value to his parents in helping them foster his well-being. Providing physical exams and immunizations is not enough in a pediatrician-patient relationship.

If the child is now walking, I sometimes ask the parents to come with me into my office and let him follow. This does not always work, but the earlier we respect the toddler's independence the better.

When parents announce to me that their child is going to be frightened by me, I know that the wrong cues have already been given. He will comply dutifully—by screaming whenever I approach him. Of course toddlers dislike being examined and hate the necessary immunizations. Of course they have a memory of both of these from past visits. But parents can underestimate the child's ability to live up to the occasion. If his anxiety is respected, we can work around it. New toys in the office and rewards after the exam are also things a child doesn't forget from one visit to the next. When a toddler can master his anxiety, he will feel an inner sense of success.

As the toddler plays in the office, I can see all his new achievements. To get up from sitting, he will push his buttocks high in the air, balancing on both arms. When his legs are straight, he straightens up, a bit unsteadily. Spreading his legs apart, he regains his balance. If he has just begun to walk, he will hold his arms out to keep steady as he toddles along. A wide-based gait is another sign of having just learned to walk. As he gets more adept, his base will narrow. When he's really secure in walking, he can place his legs together and reach up to take a toy over his head. Earlier, that move would have been sure to unsettle him and destroy his balance. You can date a child's walking by watching for these maneuvers.

The astonishing burst of new cognitive abilities that emerge at fifteen months also comes into play as I try to enlist the toddler's cooperation. When I need to measure his head (a baby's head growth is as important as his linear growth, both for the gradual growth of the brain and for a baseline measurement in case of a head injury), I measure my own head. The toddler will look at my tape measure and laugh at the absurdity of seeing it on my head. Then, he may allow me to measure his. The otoscope goes first into a doll's ears, then mother's or father's, then into the child's ears. To weigh him, I ask a parent to step on the scale without him, then with him, and I subtract the parent's weight. Sometimes this tempts the toddler to step on the scale out of curiosity, sometimes not. With luck, we can complete an entirely satisfactory exam without a whimper.

In any case, I have a chance to observe the toddler under a series of conditions. I see how independently he can relate to me. If he is pushed, he'll rebel. This is appropriate. He shows me that by using a new cognitive acquisition—symbolic play—he can transfer his anxiety about the doctor to a doll and can receive reassurance from watching the procedures with the doll. Before being able to think symbolically—to see how a toy, for example, or even a word, can stand for something real—he would see the doll only as one more object to touch and bang and put in his mouth. Now, at fifteen months, he is able to see that the doll looks a little like and stands for a person. This is a major new step, a necessary precursor to language, to being able to use words to stand for other things. Parents can take pride in this important accomplishment, feel reassured by this sign that he is on his way to speaking, and see how much he can learn from them now that he can play in this new way.

Imitation of his parents is usually strong at this age. So, as I use them as models, I watch to see whether he is willing to imitate them. All of these are burgeoning cognitive processes. Meanwhile, I can assess how much equanimity he can muster in the face of an invasive examination. If he can meet and manage stress, using his parents, a doll, and me to help him, he is already showing us the ways that he is learning to cope. However, being examined is a real intrusion on his sense of personal space, which is so important to him right now. Of course it will be difficult for him, and I want to help him.

I save the immunizations for the end of the visit. At this age the fourth dose of the Diphtheria, Tetanus, and Pertussis (DTaP) vaccine should be given (it can also be given at eighteen months); if not given already at twelve months, the fourth doses of the Hemophilus Influenza (Hib) and Pneumococcus (PCV) vaccines and the first doses of the Measles, Mumps, and Rubella (MMR) and Chicken Pox (Varicella) vaccines may be given. A dose of the Hepatitis A (HepA) vaccine should also be given. The HepA series requires two doses, which must be six months apart, preferably sometime between twelve months and eighteen months of age. Additional vaccinations for Polio (IPV) and Hepatitis B may also be needed, if they were not given at six or twelve months. Yearly flu shots are recommended as well. This is the most complicated part of the immunization schedule; after this visit, rest assured that there will not be so many shots all at once.

Inevitably, the shots will be a big blow and seem like a betrayal. I ask a parent to hold the toddler. I prepare him by telling him about it and by showing the shot with a bear or doll. As tempting as it may be to minimize the fact that it *will* hurt, it is critical to be truthful: "It will hurt, but not for long." I ask a parent to hold and squeeze him just as I give it, and then to dance around

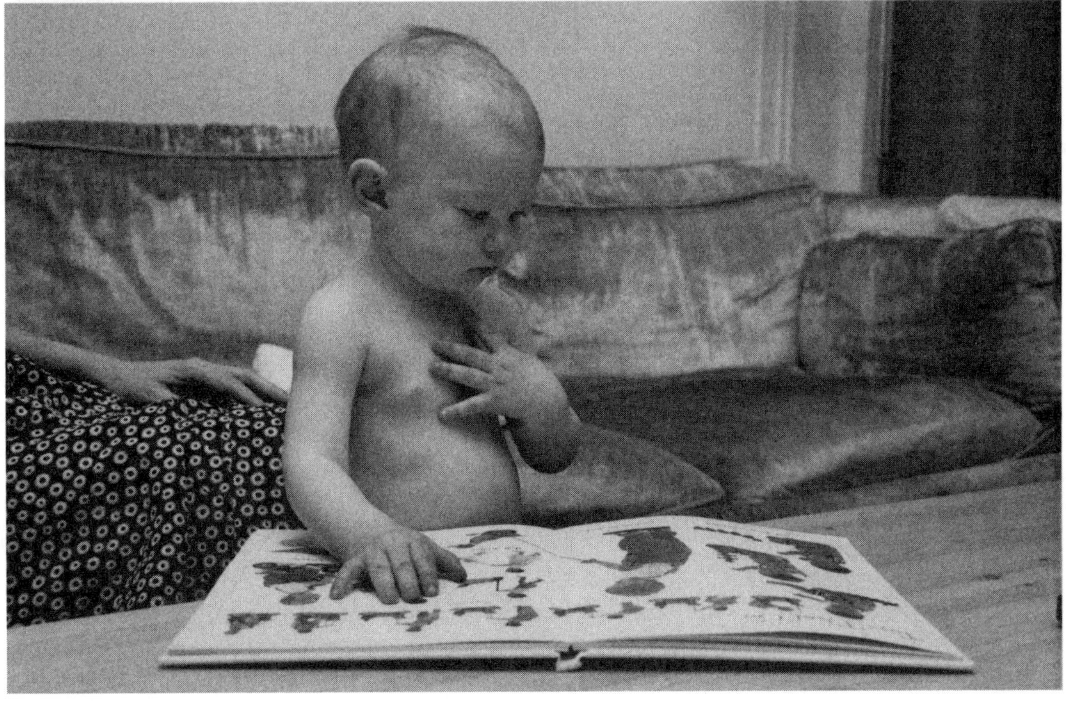

with him as soon as the shot is finished. The dancing as well as the mother's participation can distract him and gives him a chance to recover. Often, it seems to help children master the pain and the fear of being "attacked." After it's over, I offer a little trinket as a reward. Often this is refused. I explain that I know he is angry and I surely understand, but that the shot is to keep him healthy. I want to be his friend *and* his doctor. A doctor is someone who wants to keep children healthy so they can play. A doctor loves them, too. Sometimes my little present is then accepted. But the more important issue is that the parents and I have not ridden roughshod over the child's fears, over his wonderful but fragile new sense of himself as an independent person.

Discipline

Discipline becomes important in the second year. However, it must be seen as a long-term teaching project. Understanding the child's need for learning limits is the most important step for parents, the basis for discipline decisions. What a parent does for discipline at any one time is less important than long-term attitudes and expectations. For this reason, as I said before, I would choose only important issues to confront. The inevitable parental concerns about taming their fiercely independent toddler make this touchpoint another vital time for us to communicate openly.

Many couples, particularly those who have their first child late, don't want to have to change their way of living. They want to teach the child that he can't touch precious objects around the house. While this may be possible to teach, parents will spend a lot of energy and time at it that might better be saved for more important issues. Why not put those keepsakes away for now? Then there will be fewer issues to confront each day. The child will still learn self-discipline and respect for others' rights in all sorts of other ways. Every time parents model thoughtful behavior, he'll be learning from it. But it may not show up immediately.

Parents of a fairly easygoing child sometimes actually ask me how to tell when a child needs discipline. All a parent needs to do is watch and listen to the child. When he touches something forbidden and looks back to be sure you're watching, or when he's building up to more and more provocative behavior, you know he's asking you to step in and say, "Stop, that's enough."

At this age, parents wonder whether to continue or start using a playpen. The answer is probably not, except possibly when it is the only way to ensure a child's safety. A toddler does need a safe place where he can be left to explore. If parents can't set up his room for him to be briefly left there safely on his own, they may have to confine him in a playpen from time to time when they cannot watch over him. But I hope he won't have to be cooped up for too long. It's an insult at this age, a time when experiencing freedom and movement is at a peak. I would certainly rather he had freedom to explore. But letting him be free *does* mean that someone must be on hand all the time.

Temper tantrums have usually made their unwelcome appearance by the time a child is fifteen months old (see chapter 9). They are especially inconvenient and embarrassing to parents when they happen in public. Everyone gathers around, looking at the parents as if they were certified child abusers. In such a situation, parents might turn to the onlookers and suggest that they handle him themselves: "Anybody want to help?" They'll melt away quickly after that.

When distressed parents report the first tantrum to me, they are telling me about a touchpoint—for the child, and for them. This becomes a key opportunity for me to join them in their distress, and, to their relief, to point out that these are an expectable part of a toddler's behavior. A feisty child is almost bound to have them sometime in the second year. As we said before, although parents' behavior or requests may well have triggered the tantrums, they come from the child's own inner turmoil. It's the toddler's basic struggle to master the intensity of his own feelings. Only he can resolve the indecision that is behind them, though he can learn ways to settle himself down from modeling on his parents' unruffled response to his tantrums. After he has learned to handle this struggle, he'll be a stronger and more secure child.

I remind parents of some steps to take. First, remember your options, all directed at leaving it up to the child. Either pick him up to hold him quietly, gather him to carry him to a safe spot where he can work it out himself, or—if he's in a safe place—walk out of sight momentarily. When he can't see you, the tantrum will lose force. Then quickly return to say, "I'm sorry I can't help you more. I'm still here, and I love you, but this tantrum is your job." Giving the child space to resolve his own turmoil is not the same as deserting him. Do it in a way that lets him know you wish you could help. But you and he know that your efforts to help will just prolong the tantrum. Firm limits will reassure him that he will not be dangerously out of control.

Some parents find it hard to leave the scene because they are afraid the child will hurt himself. When he thrashes violently or bangs his head on the ground, it is frightening. However, it is unlikely that he'll hurt himself. If he seems too violent, he can be removed to a rug or a crib. Fortunately, in most cases, he will stop before he hurts himself.

Many years ago, I spent a week in Oregon with some quintuplets. One of them had a rip-roaring temper tantrum. The other four crowded around to try to stop it. Their efforts made him more violent. One tried to hold his arms, another lay down beside him to croon to him and soothe him. Another yelled at him. The fourth threw cold water on him. Nothing worked, so they all gave up. As soon as they did, he stopped crying. He got up quickly and started to play with them, as if nothing had happened. This experience was a vivid demonstration to me that tantrums are a reflection of inner turmoil that only the child can master. Support, but not interference, is the only help. After it's over, parents can find ways to convey that they understand how important this struggle is for him, and how hard it is to handle such strong feelings.

Finding safe, simple ways to teach a child self-control, without getting locked into the child's struggle or descending to his level, is an important goal. Using time-outs—for calming down, not as punishment—works for many parents later in the second year. Firmly holding the child briefly and then putting him in his crib or room are ways of breaking the buildup of teasing behavior before the toddler loses control. When the cycle is broken, parents should make clear that a certain behavior made them act, and then they can offer plenty of hugs.

Fears

With the wonderful surge in independence and the comprehension that exploration brings, a toddler is bound to develop all kinds of fears. For instance, fear of the bathtub is common. At this point, a parent might take him into the tub for a joint bath, being careful not to leave him alone to slide in the tub or to feel precarious about standing in it. Washing his hair will bring on earsplitting screeches, so it needn't be washed often. When it is, the child will need to be supported. You may want to try getting into the tub with him when you wash his hair. You might even let him soap yours before you soap his. Laugh about it together—and be sure to use a shampoo that won't sting his eyes, or yours. The toddler's fear of losing his balance, of being tilted back for a rinse, is worst at this time.

Motor Skills

When the child first learns to walk, he will walk with dogged determination all day long, swayback, stomach jutting out in front, with the wide-based gait we discussed earlier. He will look like a duck with feet splayed out. As he gets familiar with walking and managing his balance, his feet will begin to turn in and become parallel. Only when a toddler has been walking for some time will he be able to do other things when he walks. If he can carry a toy in one arm while he walks, he's had a month of experience. If he can reach above his head or look up when he walks, he's been at it for at least two months. When he can turn and can squat, he's had two to three months' experience.

As mentioned in chapter 8, learning to walk barefoot is ideal. Shoes become necessary as a support later. As a toddler learns to walk, his toes will grip the ground and build up his arches. Shoes are necessary only to protect against cold or sharp surfaces. Walking barefoot is the best exercise for his feet.

Once again, it is important to note that stairs need to be gated at the top and bottom. He will be intrigued with climbing. He needs to learn, but he is not ready to on his own. Carpeted stairs are easier and safer than hard surfaces, but he'll still need someone in attendance.

Feeding

At this visit, my main concern is that the toddler become independent about his own feeding. Does he make choices, and can his parents leave them to him? I reiterate the minimum diet, for I know how difficult it is for his parents (especially his mother) to leave it to him.

Parents often feel that they must at least shovel in some mushy baby food. But a baby this age does not need mushy foods. Everything fed that way could be fed in finger bits or other substitutes. When parents protests that "I can't stand to go to all the trouble of making something special for him, just to have him refuse it," I tell them not to bother. They are reacting to the feeling that their cooking is rejected, but the truth is usually that they feel the need to control what the toddler eats. The solution is to stop cooking for him and respect what he's trying to say: "I want to do it all myself." Parents' hints—like "Look what Daddy went to the trouble to make you" or "Want some of these delicious green beans off Mommy's plate?" or "Look at your big sister; she *loves* her vegetables"—are blatant pressure and are sure to turn the toddler off and lead to feeding problems. If parents aren't tense and don't push, he is likely to eat. They just need to be sure that what they offer him is in line with the minimum discussed earlier: iron-containing meat, egg, or cereal, plus milk, fruit, and vitamins (see chapter 9).

For the few toddlers who won't take milk, yogurt, cheese, or ice cream, other substitutes can be given (though Vitamin D supplements will need to be added if these aren't fortified with it). Whole milk, rather than 2 percent or skim milk, is important for brain development in the first years. When a baby wants to try a real cup but spills most of it, parents can put down a tarpaulin around his chair and let him spill on it, or give the cup to him in the bathtub. They'd best give up on cleanliness for a while, and there is no hurry to get him to give up his Sippie cup. Other, more important things are at stake.

This nondirective approach to feeding is genuinely difficult for many parents, especially mothers. Feeding becomes equated with the maternal instinct. While malnutrition is a terrible world problem, it is not likely to affect most babies who have access to adequate food supplies. When parents cannot handle this critical area of a child's independence, I watch for what psychoanalyst Selma Fraiberg called "ghosts in the nursery." Some mothers have told me dreadful stories about having been force-fed, or left at a table for hours to finish food. I worry that early struggles over food may leave lasting traces, and want to help parents see that they needn't take that risk. The most a parent can do to prevent eating problems later is to step back and leave it to the child. He'll find his own balance and develop a feeling of independence. Any adult knows that the food you choose yourself tastes better.

The cup and spoon can be mastered about this time. If this is made to be fun, the use of these utensils can add to a sense of mastery. Meanwhile, simple finger foods and plenty of milk or follow-up formula are enough.

Sleep

Usually, after walking is achieved, a child is ready to sleep through the night again. The self-comforting bedtime rituals discussed earlier should still be kept up, however. For some children, one nap each day may now be enough, and it should take place early in the afternoon so as not to affect bedtime. If the child wakes in the middle of the night, I have found that waking him at the parents' bedtime may continue to be an effective way of ensuring a good night's sleep for everyone.

Parents who have chosen to co-sleep may be reconsidering this decision now. A child in bed with parents is more likely to rouse at 2:00 A.M. and 5:00 A.M. One possibility is to set up a crib next to the parents' bed as a transition. Parents can then still roll over to pat the child down when he comes up to light sleep. Parents who have had losses in their past, or who have had sleep and separation issues in childhood, will invariably find it difficult to give up the child at bedtime. Then, each peep or whimper becomes a signal for rushing in to offer comfort. Any child who receives this kind of reinforcement will keep fighting for it.

Play

A toddler's main purpose in my office will be to engage me, and his parents, and so he works to distract us from interacting with each other through his play. Going from one toy to another, he is likely to elicit our response by saying, "See? See?" Even though his attention span is still short, I like to be sure that he examines objects with real interest. Can he be enlisted to play with toys at any length, does he flit distractedly from one to another, or does his anxiety about being in my office consume all of his attention?

At this age, the difference between a toddler's enormous energy and normally short attention span, on the one hand, and genuinely diminished attention, on the other, is still often difficult to distinguish, but there are a few things I look for. A hyperactive child often also has a split-second attention span, moving from one toy to another without seeming to derive satisfaction from any of them. He can never allow time for close inspection or any sustained play with toys. His distractibility interferes. Any sound or visual stimulus grabs him. His threshold for taking in any stimulus is low, hampering his ability to selectively focus on useful or interesting information. This distractibility costs him. He moves constantly, in an effort—it often seems to me—to handle this hypersensitivity to his environment. His face may have an indifferent expression or a worried one.

When we can identify a child with a too-short attention span early, I can help parents reduce stimuli around him. At particular times, when he needs to pay attention to a learning task, or eating, this will be critical. If he is hypersensitive to stimulation, as often seems to be the case, he can learn—over time—ways to control himself as he becomes overloaded: taking frequent time-outs (not as punishment but to learn to settle himself), clutching a lovey, or finding active ways to shut down on incoming stimulation. If he is also hyperactive, cutting down on stimulation will still help, as well as careful attention to rhythms and routines for a balance of gross and fine motor activity. If parents do not recognize his problem, they may see him as spoiled or just plain "bad." Their overreaction then adds to his, and the buildup within the family can reach chaotic levels. Parents of such children need support at each visit, and at home, and often a referral for early intervention (see "Hypersensitivity and Hyperactivity").

At this age, most children are able to stack four blocks. They are generally able to find a hidden toy, if you ask them to watch while you hide it under one and then another cloth. We call this "two displacements." This test of object permanence is a delightful game, but also a very telling cognitive task. Symbolic play also starts early in the second year. Does he feed a doll a toy bottle? Does he croon to the doll or carry it in a way that his parents carry him? Does he make a garage out of blocks—a symbolic representation?

When you play a rhythmic game with a toddler—for example, "This is the way the ladies ride"—does he anticipate what is going to happen next? Does he laugh when you hold his hands and clap, then stop? Is he able to recognize a repeated pattern and to react with surprise and delight when this expectancy is suddenly changed?

Causality is beginning to be better understood. The toddler may now try to wind a windup toy himself, rather than hand it back to you when it runs down. Every aspect of play—which, as Montaigne said, is "a child's most serious business"—reveals the toddler's stage of maturity. In it we see the leading edge of learning, of motor skills, and of emotional development.

Speech

The gobbledygook of sounds continues, mostly at night and in the crib. The practicing of words and phrases and inflections shows that a toddler is readying himself for speech. Adults feel compelled to correct his utterances after each mistake. But parents lead children on to the next stage by modeling with their own speech rather than correcting. Most of the time, nouns may seem to be the child's goal, rather than verbs, adjectives, or adverbs—"me," "Mommy," "Papa," "cookie." An occasional "more" and, of course, "no" will also appear. Yet the toddler is already listening carefully to adult language, figuring out how words are strung together, and noticing how actions that involve these nouns are indicated. With their pointing and nodding, of course, they are expressing actions without verbs: "I want" and "Gimme" are already a part of their nonverbal vocabulary. At this age, toddlers begin to show a real frustration in not being able to talk. They gesture very clearly and do understand almost everything you say.

Looking Ahead

The second year is a time for learning all over again how to parent. In the love affair of the first year, the baby's behavior was predictable and usually rewarding. The parents' efforts met an immediate response from the baby. No longer will this be true. From now on, the toddler will make his own choices. "Is he deaf?" a parent will ask. "Or is he hearing me but just doesn't care? What do I have to do to maintain control?" The "terrible twos" can be terrible for parents, but not for babies. The second year is made up of an enormously rapid kind of learning. Many of the times when he's acting rebellious or as if he's not hearing, he is trying hard to sort out his own reactions and must use all his energy to conquer his own feelings. It is a difficult time for parents, for they feel he is just out of control or that he is aiming his negativism at them. The difficult job for parents is to sense when he is working on these inner adjustments, and when he recognizes his rebellious feelings and may need firm discipline. The spurt toward independence carries with it a kind of energy for exploration and for learning about the world that is truly remarkable. Like the first year, learning to parent in the second year is still made up of learning from mistakes. The rewards of the first year have fueled parents as they followed the child for direction. Now, they must find their way at an entirely new level.

An important touchpoint at this age arises out of the child's intense need to try everything out for himself, whether he's ready or not, and the parents' frantic efforts to keep up with him and keep things under control. Confronted with the child's relentless drive, parents wonder who will call the shots. But when parents begin to express their need for control, the child will respond with negativism and resistance. Parents are likely to feel like failures. Constant reorganization to find a new way to handle the resistant child is the story of parenting in the second year. Distraction and diversion become indispensable, but they don't always work. Another critical strategy is to focus on the important things consistently, with reliable firmness, while letting go of the unimportant ones. Parents will also learn to look for opportunities to give the child control—only, of course, for things that he can safely be trusted with—and to stay out of the way on issues that matter only to him. For parents who are not flexible, it can indeed be a terrible year. Faced with a sense of humor, the second year can be a terrific one!

Of course, keeping a sense of humor during this period is easier said than done. "Every time I ask him to do something, he resists," a parent will tell me. Even his posture says "no." "He's either a limp rag or a beast, arched away from me." This negativism arises because every suggestion or request from the parent poses a dilemma for the toddler. "Will I or won't I? Do I or don't I want to do it?" As I advise parents, if you really want him to do something, don't present him with a choice. Telling him not to do it may also work. But if it's important, I'd push on through. If it's not, I'd let it go. The fewer confrontations you have, the better. Then, you'll find the ones that you do have are important learning experiences.

Toilet Training At each visit during this year I reiterate the importance of waiting until the end of the second year to start toilet training. Parents who are in a hurry may say, "But he's already conscious of his bowel movements. He pulls at his pants afterward." Or, "He runs off to hide when he goes in his diapers." These are especially clear signals, and they simply underline that when the time comes, he will want to be in control of his own toilet habits. Be patient. We are waiting for him to feel he can do it himself—and he must be self-motivated, not do it just to please us.

Allergies As we've seen in earlier chapters, the best way to deal with allergies is to prevent them. Many of us have a genetic tendency to develop allergic sensitivities to particular substances, and then to show symptoms later, when exposed to them. Some allergic symptoms—a rash, for example, or sudden, serious difficulty breathing—can be set off by single substances, such as bee stings, latex, shellfish, or peanuts. But allergy-related illnesses like hay fever, asthma, and eczema may be set off by a combination of exposures. It has always seemed to me that many allergic symptoms—including sneezing, wheezing, or a stuffy nose—may require more than one trigger to set them off. It is like piling up wooden block after block until the toy tower finally topples. Up to a certain point, several mild allergens may not bring out such symptoms. But when you add a cat, fur, dust, molds, feather pillows, hair mattresses, and stress, the system cannot take it; and asthmatic wheezing, hay fever, or eczema may result. One trigger may set off the symptoms one time, another one the next. Since an emotional stress or a separation can bring on symptoms of asthma, some parents may fear that their own anxiety or pressure may have contributed to their child's distress. As a result of such guilty feelings, denial may be even more potent in keeping them from acting to get rid of the many possible triggers of recurrences. Denial is likely anyway for diseases whose symptoms come and go, leaving hope that they'll never return.

Early, primary prevention of allergies (preventing sensitization to specific allergens) is an important goal, especially for children who may have inherited a genetic tendency for allergic responses. The best way I know to prevent allergies is to avoid exposure to common allergy-inducing substances during the critical period of sensitization that probably lasts for at least the first six months of life, if not most of the first year. In particular, food allergies can be prevented by holding off on foods such as wheat, eggs, strawberries, peanuts, and others that are likely to cause sensitization and allergies during the first nine months or more. It appears that this can also prevent or diminish the severity of asthma and eczema later on. Secondary prevention is important, too, for if a child who has become sensitized to an allergen can be protected from exposure to it, it has always seemed to me that over time his allergic reactions may become milder and harder to set off. I've found that the older a child grows before his allergy expresses itself, the more exposure to allergens it seems to take to activate his symptoms.

I recommend working very hard in early childhood to prevent an allergic reaction. If a rash shows up, take it seriously. Eliminate any new foods. If the rash continues, change to a hypoallergenic soap for washing the child and a hypoallergenic detergent for his clothes. Eliminate wool in clothes and blankets, and avoid feather pillows, puffs, and mattresses. If a stuffed animal or other toy is the offender, gradually introduce another. If you have forced hot air heat in your house, cover the outlet in his room with eight layers of cheese cloth as a filter. In pollen season, shut the outlet and don't open his window at night. An air purifier also helps.

As a child gets older, let him know what to do about his own allergic condition. Give him a chance to tell you when he needs something for his skin, his wheezes, or his runny nose. When you administer medication for an asthma flare-up, for example, or identify a trigger that can be eliminated, remember to tell him afterward, "See, you knew what to do. And when you did it, it worked."

The most frightening, anxiety-producing aspect of an allergic disorder for a child is the feeling that no one knows what to do about it. To parents, I suggest several things. First, act preventively, as just described. For potentially life-threatening allergic reactions that come on quickly—for example, swelling and severe difficulty breathing after a bee sting—parents will need to learn to give epinephrine shots, and to always be ready with an "EpiPen" (to be packed along on every excursion). If any allergic symptom occurs, call and get help early. Let the child know what you're doing and why. Later, letting him be in control of his own symptoms is the best prevention for the anxiety and feeling of helplessness that sometimes accompany and exacerbate certain allergic manifestations, such as asthma and eczema (see "Allergies and Asthma").

Shifting Attachments A child will almost always treat each parent very differently. He will be the hardest on the parent he can count on most, the mother, if she is the most available. He may treat his father more like someone special, particularly if he's around less often. This different treatment can stir up jealousy. Parents need to realize that this is normal and that it is an important part of testing out strong attachments.

The shifting dynamics in the family will continue in the months to come as the child, who has been everyone's center of attention, strives to become more independent. If he is still being cared for by one parent at home, that parent will often start thinking about going back to work part-time or introducing the child to a play group. It's probably no coincidence that the toddler's independence and the dependence that balances it—shown by following the parent around everywhere he or she goes—drive the parent to think that way. A small play group is a great idea at this age. The toddler will learn so much from his peers in this next year. After he's gotten used to a small group of one or two other children at his own speed, it is easier to think about what kind of child care to choose. The second year is a great time for him to start forming relationships with other children.

Individual Differences The second year seems to highlight differences among toddlers. The quiet, watchful ones become even more observant and sedentary, in contrast to active, intense children who are always moving. The latter hardly sit still long enough to learn to speak or demonstrate their new cognitive skills. They are on the move. Parents are likely to label them hyperactive, for indeed they seem to have short attention spans. For them the need to move is powerful. For the less active, the intensity goes into small motor activity and observation.

Parents can become concerned by these differences. When children are on either end of the spectrum, they need reassurance. So much time is spent comparing one's child with other children. "Why isn't my child walking yet?" "He never seems to move around like other children." Or, "He never stops moving. He can't sit still long enough to look at a book or sit in my lap. All his friends are so cuddly."

Since so many parents engage in these comparisons, I wonder what their purpose can be. I have concluded that parents learn about the processes of development by observing these steps in others. By analyzing the differences between children, a parent can visualize the full spectrum. In my own work, it has been rewarding to see how much can be learned from the very different individualized styles of different babies. What worries me is that so much anxiety about these comparisons can be so draining. Instead of accepting the baby they have, some parents seem to want to press him into the mold of an "ideal" child. If I could do one thing as a pediatrician, I would hope to help parents relish the individuality of their own baby. The danger with comparisons is that they can give a child a sense of inferiority. For example, boy babies are often a little slower to develop than girls but eventually catch up. And yet, parents of boys want them to be quick and active. It seems important to me for parents to focus on their child and take pleasure in that child's developmental style, rather than pressing him to conform to some notion of the "average" baby.

When parents start in on comparisons, I try to celebrate their child by describing how *their own toddler* is learning—his particular quirks, struggles, and triumphs.

11. Eighteen Months

WHEN A TODDLER COMES INTO MY OFFICE, SHE STARTS EXPLORING. PARENTS beam proudly at me, and they melt when I share their appreciation of their child's new stability on her feet and the intensity of her drive to learn about her world. Any single word uttered—except for one—is like a pearl issuing from her lips. They watch me to see if I treasure her language skills too. But as she walks up to my desk or lamp or bookshelf and reaches out, then announces "No!" I get a preview of what her parents' questions will be. Most pressing will be their concern about the toddler's increasing negativism. "She won't listen to me anymore! I don't want to spank her, but sometimes I don't know what else to do. She'll keep on pushing and pushing until I have to do something. Whenever she has a tantrum, she always seems to pick the most embarrassing spot." Mothers will get teary as they speak of the changes in the child. Fathers tend to raise the question of punishment. I know that my biggest job will be to help them understand this continuing surge in independence and the negativism that goes with it. This is central to the toddler touchpoint. Their questions reflect their side of it—their struggle to balance encouragement of her self-assertion with discipline that will teach her to control herself—a long-term project.

Parents will nod in relief when I remind them that all toddlers go through a phase like this. They are learning so much and so quickly. How can they take it all in without a meltdown? But reassurance will only help them for a brief period. Understanding that the purpose of negative behavior is to help a toddler sort out her own independence becomes important. The provocative acts that drive them to discipline her reflect a passionate search for limits. They must find effective ways to discipline in order to teach her these limits. The turmoil that leads to tantrums is a reflection of how passionate she is, and how much she needs help learning to master the intensity of her feelings. If I can help them understand her quest, they may be able to admire and enjoy it.

Today, many parents of toddlers are away all day at work. When they return at night, they dream of a loving reunion. Often, they don't get it. A healthy toddler will save up all her most intense feelings for them. Parents who are at work all day come home to—or pick up at child care—a baby who has been waiting all day to break down. When she sees them, the toddler may let it all go. She lies down on the floor, screaming and kicking, and banging her head on the floor. At the childcare center, if a parent tries to gather her up to dress her to go home, she kicks and screams pitifully. One father told me he nearly dropped his toddler as she disintegrated in his arms. "What's more, I wanted to. I had rushed through work to come for her. I was so anxious to see her. What did I get but a screaming terror who made me hate her. The worst thing was that her teacher looked at me and said, 'She never does that with me.' Boy, did that make me feel awful!"

This teacher may have wanted to reassure him that his child wasn't unhappy at the center. But her remark was an instance of gatekeeping. We have spoken of this unconscious, unspoken competition between two parents (see chapter 1). This goes on as well between caregivers and parents. If the caregiver had said instead, "She's been waiting so eagerly for you. This is the most passion she's demonstrated all day," her father would not have read his child's disintegration as a rejection. Professional caregivers are rarely presented with the same passionate disintegration that parents are greeted with.

Negativism is only one side of the coin; the other is cooperation and caring. In any passionate developmental process, opposite feelings must surface. The toddler must try out both her negative and positive feelings. Without an intensely negative period, a child could be passive and inwardly conflicted. In the second year, a child's intensely conflicted feelings are inevitable and need to be expressed. A parent's role is to recognize them as part of an important process and accept them, but also to help the child learn to contain them. Learning how to exercise self-control and how to live with ambiva-

lent feelings is a long-term process, and these early lessons can be stormy ones. "You seem to love negative children," said one irritated mother when I admired her toddler's negativism. I do—as long as they aren't mine.

Discipline

A toddler needs to explore the limits of tolerance with her various caregivers. Her parents and another caregiver will see different sides of her. For instance, a nanny or a grandmother will say to me that while she's taking care of the toddler, she has found ways to help the toddler calm down when she's worked up. "If I don't, she gets more and more out of control, breaks things, and throws tantrums. She seems miserable. When I give her time out by rocking her, she is so easy. When her parents arrive at the end of the day, she begins to push their buttons. They seem overwhelmed by her. I hate to see her get out of control, but how can I help them?" To answer such a question, I first reassure the caregiver that the child is—little by little—learning about self-discipline from her. Second, I point out that children act differently with different adults. Finally, I would expect the child to act up at the end of the day for her parents. I recommend that the caregiver stay out of the way when the child's parents arrive. Otherwise, the situation becomes a triangle, and no one will win. Just as a child learns a different approach with each parent, so she will from the different nurturing style of another caregiver.

Within the limited hours available to working parents to be with their children, firm discipline can seem impossible. Parents tell me, "We are so glad to see her, but after thirty minutes of her kicking and screaming, we start wishing we were back at work again. On the weekends, it's almost as if she wants to see how far she can push us. She tests us until we are furious and exhausted. I know she's punishing us for being away all week, but we don't have any fun together anymore." The guilt felt by parents fuels this situation. They cannot stand being disciplinarians after being away all day. But discipline is important to the child. A toddler who is testing is sending out very clear messages. She's saying that she needs help in sorting out what she can do and what she can't.

Discipline is not the same as punishment. Discipline means teaching, and it is a long-term process. Every time you need to set a limit, it is an opportunity for teaching: "I have to stop you every time you do this until you can stop yourself." Physical punishment may seem to get the child's attention more quickly and stop the behavior, but this is short-lived and may set up a frightened, resentful relationship between you. It also says "I'm bigger than you and I can overpower you." But what about later, when this is no longer true? When physical punishments seem to the child to imply "I am doing this to you because you are bad," they do not teach her. When you stop the behavior and teach her that it is not acceptable, and that she can learn to act better, she will eventually try to behave—even when you're not there—instead of becoming resentful or simply compliant. The most important argument against physical punishment is that it says, "I don't respect you." Is this what a parent means? Or that the child's behavior does not deserve respect?

If parents can see calm, consistent discipline as a necessary part of loving her, it needn't stir up guilt. I tell parents, save discipline for important things. Then, when a cycle of provocative behavior begins, stop it early. Pick her up to contain her. If that doesn't work, give her a time-out—in her room or her bed or in a chair. This gives her a chance to pull herself together, and it gives you time to collect yourself, calm down, and address her—respectfully and effectively. Let her know you mean it, and that you are expecting her to stop.

Sit down with the child afterward. Try to help her see why you stopped her. Don't wait too long, and don't talk too long when you do. (See also *Discipline — The Brazelton Way* in *Further Reading.*)

If a parent tells me, "She'll never let me do that when she's out of control! She's too upset and so am I," I suggest the following. Decide on your rules ahead of time and plan out your responses. For out-of-control temper tantrums, benign neglect is the best strategy as long as the child is in a place safe enough to be left. For testing a limit, don't wait for more testing. Respond to the first infraction with a clear warning about the rule, and tell her what the consequences are when it is broken. Then, if the testing continues—even just one more time—go to her to stop her, scooping her up and removing her from the scene of the "crime." After she's settled down, remind her of the rule again and of the response she can expect from you when she breaks it. Then, reassure her that you love her. Tell her that you know she can work on her behavior and will get it under control—one day. But don't expect it to stop right away. Repeated misbehavior doesn't mean your efforts aren't working. At this age, consistently repeated responses are necessary for teaching successfully. If you react differently at different times to the same behavior, she'll be confused and will need to test you again. If you are ambivalent, she will know it.

Look for opportunities to reinforce good behavior. Hug her when she is behaving better. Sit down and rock together. She needs to know that you aren't mad at her all the time. Discipline is part of caring and of teaching a child about limits. It takes a long time. No one method is ever magically effective. Spanking may stop the action, but it doesn't teach self-control, and it sends the wrong message, as we've said before. Spanking says that you believe in settling things by force—a lesson you may come to regret later on! Studies have shown that children who receive frequent physical punishments are more likely to be aggressive and anxious.

Feeding

Issues of feeding need to be discussed at every visit. A child this age still needs to explore. At eighteen months she can learn to use a spoon and fork, but at some point, she'll want to regress to fingers. Parents can set out food that she can eat with her fingers or spear with her fork, whichever she chooses.

Mothers who are still breast-feeding will have concerns. "I wanted to finish the first year. Now it's hard for me to give it up. She continues to come and unbutton my shirt. I find it embarrassing but hard not to go along with her." The only reason I'd urge weaning would be if it were interfering with her becoming independent. But if she is autonomous in all other domains, the closeness is all to the good. I've studied cultures where mothers breast-feed the new baby on one breast and the other children up to five years of age on the other. (They won't come after five.) The children do fine, but the mothers look like wrecks. Breast-feeding mothers of toddlers here in the United States often say, "Everyone tells me I should quit." Friends suspect them of just indulging themselves. Why not? A reunion at the breast is so lovely after a working day or after a day of negativism and turmoil.

With toddlers this age, parents also begin to wonder how to wean from the bottle. Many toddlers no longer use it for milk but continue to walk around during the day with it hanging out of their mouths. That use of a bottle bothers me, because—unless it is really empty or only contains water—it is likely to cause tooth decay. Just as when you are weaning a child from the pacifier (as we saw in chapter 9), you can gradually help a toddler make a transition to a blanket or to a doll or other lovey by tying the bottle to one of these (with a string too short to go around the child's neck). Here are the specific steps I recommend to parents. Offer her milk in her bottle in your arms only at meals. When she asks for it between meals, promise her that she can have it before naptime and bedtime, but that you want to give it to her. Make it part of a bedtime ritual. Start with a book, in a rocking chair, then the bottle. In this way, you can bring a child down into a relaxed, sleepy state. Finish with water to wash the milk out of her mouth at night. Never put her in bed with her bottle. She deserves a special time with you. Milk in her mouth through the night will damage her future teeth, as we said earlier. Apart from this damage, she is missing out on an important ritual and a sense of security. She needs you if she still needs a bottle.

Sleep

Middle-of-the-night waking will appear with each new stress, such as a parent's absence, a grandparent's visit, a big day on the town, or a stormy play group. A firm, comforting approach is necessary. To teach the child to be independent at night, parents can fall back on the patterns they have used at other times—encouraging her daytime attempts to be independent and praising her when she's able to comfort herself during the day. Then, the same pattern of expecting her to be independent at night becomes more meaningful.

One nap is all parents can expect in the second year. I recommend feeding a toddler lunch early, then putting her down from 12:00 to 2:00, with no more nap after 2:00 or 2:30 unless she is able to fall asleep at a reasonable bedtime hour even with a longer nap. Many children will find it more and more difficult to get to bed at a reasonable evening time if they nap too late in the afternoon.

Difficulty in getting to bed will increase anyway. I urge parents to redouble their rituals and their determination to *hold the line* at bedtime. The more excited a child gets at bedtime, the harder it is for her to give up. Putting a toddler to bed at this age is not for the fainthearted. The ritual of a rocking chair and a bedtime story certainly helps. A lovey—a blanket or a bear—becomes even more critical at bedtimes. She can fall back on it during the day and at waking periods at night. Parents often feel a bit uncertain about loveys, especially when these are ratty and pathetic-looking. They think that a child with a lovey looks neglected. Actually, the opposite is true in my experience. When I evaluated children at the Children's Hospital in Boston without any knowledge of their background, I was always happy to see one who could comfort herself with a thumb or a lovey. Such a child has already demonstrated her inner strength. She shows that she has been nurtured at home. The ability to self-comfort is enhanced by parents who nurture.

Motor Skills

A toddler's posture frightens parents. Will she always have a potbelly? Her swayback posture, with the potbelly, will continue into the third year. Then, magically, she will straighten up, and her belly will tighten.

At eighteen months to two years, the child spends all day experimenting. Now, she will run everywhere rather than walk, and her excitement as she explores overwhelms whatever limited impulse control she has. Climbing into everything is more and more exciting. But she cannot be relied upon to worry about heights, so parents must protect her. She is probably still too unsteady—and lacking in judgment—to be trusted on stairs, so gates (that she can't open) at the top and bottom are still in order. Whether or not you allow her on the stairs from time to time to practice climbing them (while you are close by to help), make sure they have a rug or padding on them, since she may find a way past all of your carefully closed gates.

If a toddler has been walking for several months, she will start to try to dance, jump, rotate, and test out all of her new motor skills—balancing, twirling, jogging. She will try to walk away from her parents whenever she gets a chance—in a store, on a street, anywhere. Parents will need to have one hand free for her; otherwise, she will take off.

Separation

In the second year, leaving a child can be at its most painful. She is able to protest violently. I have often thought that the degree of protest may be correlated with the strength of her will, and of her confidence to assert herself. In other words, protest is a healthy way to handle separations. Why should she want to be left, when she can now conceive of keeping up with you, and when she herself wants to do the leaving?

I once did a study on the protests that small children made as their mothers left them in the morning. The children whose parents prepared them at home had already begun to adjust to the separation. They were ready by the time they needed to separate. They and their mothers left each other more smoothly—no hanging around, no prolonging the protest. The children who were not prepared at home fell into two groups. Some protested loudly. The others, who withdrew into themselves to mourn, worried us the most. They were not able to deal with their sadness and play with the other children.

To deal with separation, the first step is to prepare the child ahead of time. For example, you might say, "We are going out to do some errands. We'll be home before your snack, and then we'll show you what we bought!" Then, parents should be ready to accept a healthy outburst. Third, they need to promise to return, and upon doing so, remind her that they did. This is the basis of future trust.

Learning and Play

A burst in development is the parents' reward for all of the toddler's stormy behavior. When parents have enough distance to see the rapid learning that accompanies the turmoil, they won't need to consider this the terrible twos. Learning from other children by imitation takes a spurt in the second year. A toddler needs peers. One or two regular playmates are enough. But it is a critical time to get the toddler out of the cocoon of mother-father-child and into the rough-and-tumble world of other children. If she has older siblings, it is less urgent, for she will have the chance to learn from them. This is the time to learn about herself and her relationship to others. She will learn so much from socializing with other children.

One of the most wonderful things I know of is to watch two children of this age playing in close proximity. They play for long periods, side-by-side. It was once thought that at this age children's play was exclusively parallel. It was assumed that they never even looked at each other. But it has been shown that even much younger children, as young as seven months, are already intensely interested in each other, communicating with their faces, hands, even their toes. By the second year, children start picking up and imitating large hunks of play behavior from one another. They seem to absorb play patterns through peripheral vision. Whole sequences of toy play and of communication are copied, even when they do not watch one another. The first child bonks a toy. "No! No! No!" The second child does the same. The first child makes a tower. The second child makes a tower. First child: "No!" She knocks off the blocks. Second child: "No!" and knocks off the blocks. The imperious gestures, the body postures, and the facial attitudes are all similar. Think of the amount and quality of learning that are contained in such close imitation.

Hildy Ross, a psychologist in Canada, paired a two-year-old and a one-year-old in parallel play. Their desire to communicate and to imitate drove them to adapt their individual techniques to each other. The two-year-old dropped back to about a fifteen-month-old level of play. The one-year-old stretched to a fifteen-month-old's level. They wanted so much to communicate with each other. This study showed me how important very young children's relationships can be for learning.

The desire to get to know one another can go astray. Biting, hair pulling, scratching, and hitting all surface and will also be imitated. Often these are aimed at one's "best friend." Horrified parents and teachers overreact and punish the biter or the hitter or hair puller. This overreaction reinforces the pattern rather than eliminating it. Adults may find it a little easier to subdue their initial responses when they recognize that these aggressive behaviors do not start out with clear intent. They occur at times when the child is overwhelmed and loses control. After they've happened, the aggressor is as upset as the recipient. When parents intervene too harshly, guilt sets in. The next time the aggressor is overwhelmed, the pattern repeats itself, and the child is at risk of believing that she is too "bad" to learn to control herself. Adult overreactions reinforce this.

Biting carries the greatest charge. All parents are frightened about this—about their child biting and about her being bitten. What seems to be the most frightening is the loss of control. Parents also worry, "Will it go on forever?" I would recommend trying to comfort both children—the biter and the bitten. The former needs comfort as well as limits because she will be frightened by her loss of control, perhaps even more frightened than the victim was by being attacked. The caregiver needs to sit down with her and say, "No one likes to be bitten. You wouldn't either. Next time you feel that way, remember, I can help you stop before you start." This will have to be repeated over and over. One ingenious mother bought her toddler a rubber dog bone to bite on instead of attacking her friends.

In the past, I have kept lists in my office of young children whose parents were interested in forming play groups or arranging playdates with another child. Two or three who are at similar stages of learning about themselves can learn the most from each other. I've always felt that two biters or two hitters can be put together. If one gets upset, she will bite the other. The recipient will bite back. They'll look at each other as if to say, "That hurt! Why did you do it?" And they'll never do it again. I think that children at this age really do not understand that it hurts. They don't mean to hurt and are frightened afterward. Since the biting is a result of a loss of control, it is too late to stop it at the time. But, over time, they can learn to control it, for they want to. The give-and-take of relationships between toddlers is the best way for them to learn. Adults are likely to interfere with this learning if they overreact.

Mothers of biters wonder if they should bite back. No! That is sinking to the toddler's level and is degrading for her and for her mother. The issue is to teach her calmly that biting is unacceptable and to give her an acceptable substitute, such as a toy to bang or a doll to bite—a way to work it out.

Play remains a child's most powerful way of learning. She can test out many different situations and actions to find which one works for her. It is a child's work, for she's testing herself and her new ideas. Watching her play gives an adult a window into her mind. It is hard to overestimate the importance of play for a small child.

Self-Awareness

In an ingenious and now classic experiment by psychologist Michael Lewis to find out about the child's image of her own body, a child is given a mirror in which to view herself (see Konner in *Further Reading*). After awhile the researcher moves the child away from the mirror and dabs rouge on her nose, without attracting her attention. The researcher then puts her back in front of the mirror to see what happens. It turns out that the child's reaction depends on her age. At one year, children watch themselves carefully, recognizing the strange color on their noses. At fifteen months, they touch the reflection of their own noses in the mirror and try to wipe off the rouge they see in the mirror. They recognize themselves and have an idea that something is different. By eighteen months, they try to wipe the rouge off their own noses. Now, it appears, they are capable of understanding that it is their own image being reflected in the mirror—an astonishing new leap in self-awareness.

A child's reaction to seeing herself in the mirror depends on her age.

Not surprisingly, then, self-exploration at this age becomes heightened. A toddler is intrigued with her eyes, her nose, her mouth. When she gets a chance, she is intrigued with her navel and her genitalia. Little boys at this age are excited by their penises when they are undiapered. Girls begin to poke a finger into their vaginas. These parts of their bodies must be very special to them when they are finally uncovered since they are clothed and out of sight for so much of their experience. No wonder they become areas of heightened focus. Parents needn't try to stop this exploration. These are important parts of children's bodies, and they need to get familiar with them.

Looking Ahead

Toilet Training I advise parents to hold off a bit longer. If "elimination communication" has not been instituted early in the first year, it is certainly too late now. Such physiological conditioning may work for infants since they are more passive and dependent than toddlers. Toddlers, though, will insist on taking such deeply personal functions into their own hands, so they will require emotional and cognitive readiness to make toilet learning their own accomplishment. Although most parents understand the reasons for waiting until a toddler has the concept of what we expect of her and is ready to do it for herself, some will get impatient. "I don't want her going to college in diapers," a parent might say. A very real source of pressure is the requirement of most preschools that children be toilet-trained. Many childcare centers want children trained by two and a half, at the latest. If possible, I'd look for a school that respects the child's need to decide when she is ready to be trained. Children are not magically ready for toilet training at the age of two and a half. And it is critical to leave toilet training to the child. While few parents want to coerce a child, there is a good chance that some of them will push their children into training before they are ready, unless they are aware of their own internal pressures to have the child clean and dry.

At this point, it may help parents to look ahead and know what to watch for. At around two years of age, several developmental steps will begin to come together. When they do, the child will be ready. It will be time to turn the training over to her.

She'll be over the excitement of walking and will be ready to sit down. She will be ready to understand such words and concepts as: "This is your potty seat. Mine is the big one. Someday you'll go on yours like I do on mine." There is a period at about two years of age when children become intent on imitating everything their parents do and want to be like them. They'll try everything. A boy walks like his father, a girl like her mother. Subtly, they are identifying with the important adults around them. They want to wear your clothes. They are even absorbing gestures like adults around them. They can use imitation to capture toilet behavior. At two years of age, most children begin to put things where they belong. They have a concept of orderliness and of where parents put things. This urge to put things away like parents do can be transferred to urine and bowel movements. Negativism comes and goes at around two. Before that, it is always near the surface. To start toilet training when she's negative would mean failure for sure.

All of these developmental mechanisms can help ready a child to conform to society's demands that she be clean and dry all day and all night.

"What other behaviors should I go by?" parents will ask. When a child grunts and pulls at her pants when she's going into her diaper, this shows that she's aware of her productions. When she reaches a relatively tranquil developmental period—not too negative or too feisty—I'd watch to see whether she is interested when you go to the bathroom. Is she becoming tidy? Is she very imitative? Can she follow two or more commands? For example, if you ask her to go to the closet, find your slippers, and bring them to you, can she follow that sequence of three requests? That is a sign that she's acquiring receptive language and can keep two or three sequential commands in her mind.

Given all the pitfalls in toilet training, some parents wonder whether doing nothing is the way to avoid making mistakes. However, a child might not understand what we expect of her if we do nothing at all. It is still necessary to show her the steps, although she must be allowed to refuse if she needs to. Since it is almost impossible for parents to conceive of an eighteen- or twenty-month-old child wanting to cooperate in any way, the best thing to do about toilet training is to put it off until she is ready. But then, she'll need to be shown the steps.

Times to Be Firm with a Toddler In some situations, such as crossing a street, waiting for a toddler to make up her mind is not possible. When these occur, I tell parents, make clear that you are serious, that there is no time for explaining or negotiating. Although introducing a new vegetable is not the moment to insist on having your way, there will be times when your authority must prevail. For instance, parents call me in desperation about giving medicine to a toddler. When the situation is this important, let her know it is not up for negotiation and it's different from other times like mealtimes.

These days, most pediatric medicines are available in some tasty, easy-to-swallow form. But whether a child takes it or not may hinge on what the parent says and the tone of voice that he or she uses. I recommend stating a firm command with the conviction of clear determination: "This is not a time when you have a choice: You must take it, and I must make sure you do."

In a real emergency situation, another way to give medicine is for a second adult to hold the child tilted back in his lap with a full nelson hold—arms up under hers and alongside her head. With her head tilted back so she can't spit it out, you can then pour the medicine in so she either gags on it or swallows. She'll make the right choice. When a child knows you are serious, she will usually give up the struggle quickly.

When children start to climb out of cribs, they need cushions or mats under their cribs. It certainly can happen that a toddler will fall out, but it doesn't happen often. Some cribs have adjustable mattress heights. Lowering the frame that supports the mattress will increase the railing height she'll have to climb, and this should slow her down for awhile. But when she does succeed in climbing out, you may have to put the crib sides down, so that she can climb out without hurting herself. Even though she can leave it when she likes, the crib, with its familiar rails, may help her feel more contained than a new, big girl bed. (Her weight must not exceed the crib's limit.)

A toddler can be virtually fearless.

Even so, her bedroom may now need to act as her crib, and it will need another careful round of childproofing. When she silently sails over the rails, a gate at her door will keep her safe from whatever dangers parents have been unable to remove from the rest of their home. I always hope that this won't happen too early. The beauty of the crib is that it says implicitly: Here is where you belong at night. Once children are in a bed or sleep on the floor, there's no real limit on their roaming. It may help, though, if parents make it clear that once children are put to bed they stay in bed. The expectation that there will be no nocturnal exploration can be established in this way, at least for some children—certainly not for all. The most dangerous thing I know of is to have a child wandering around the house alone. If this happens, parents may need to put a latch on a child's door that she can't open (but that an adult can quickly release if there is a fire), and the whole house will need to be child-proofed—just in case.

The crib is a symbol of the limits that are necessary to protect the child at night. There will be times—for example, when you are traveling—when the crib is not available. In those cases, you will need to make special arrangements. For example, you can bring along a portable crib. Most hotels also have cribs available upon request. I recently had a two-year-old over to visit. She was put down for a nap on the living-room couch. She was told once by her grandparent, and then once by my son, that she was to stay there, but that she could have some music. She stayed right where she was, put her teddy bear over her eyes, and went soundly to sleep.

An eighteen-month-old toddler can be virtually fearless. On the stairs, she steps right out and could easily hurtle through space. Teach her how to climb up and down either by crawling or by stepping while you hold her hand. She'll learn fairly quickly. But a gate is still vital. All the fearless, rambunctious, insatiable energy of a toddler has to be celebrated, but it also must be contained, since there is so little judgment to go with it. Gates, cribs, and firm restraining arms represent security as well as limits.

12. Two Years

THE LONGER THE SPAN BETWEEN VISITS, THE MORE DRAMATIC AND EXCITING it is for me to see the child's strides in development. For the parents, it is rewarding to demonstrate these to me—an interested audience. They will beam when I say, "Isn't he glorious?"

One of the most delightful characteristics of two-year-olds is the way they parade in, mirroring the walk of one of their parents. Of course a toddler remembers all too well what has happened in my office—the shots, the exam, the strangeness. If parents have done their job, we can set the stage for a reconciliation—though there still may be shots to give. If earlier vaccinations have all been given on time, I may be able to put other shots off for now. I always work hard to regain a child's trust at this point. I ask parents to bring the child in for at least four office visits. This is my attempt to help the child overcome the earlier trauma. I want the child to adapt to me again and have a trusting relationship. I explain to parents that I can help him overcome his fear if they will bring him for these short visits, inserted in between my other scheduled ones, and unpaid for, but worth it to me and to them. After I reestablish trust in the child, he will not need to scream at me or resent my attempts to talk to him or examine him on future visits. We can be friends again. These visits generally follow a pattern.

On the first visit, he will first come into my waiting room clinging to his parent, looking angrily or warily at me. As I offer him a toy, all I hope is that he will accept it from me. If his parent reaches for it, I keep holding it. I want him to take the step of accepting it on his own.

At the second visit, I offer him another present, but he has to get off his parent's lap to take it.

At the third visit, he comes across the room to accept it, and I try to look at him for a response.

Finally, at the fourth visit I want him to come around the corner into my office to get the present. I wear my stethoscope so he has to accept me as I am.

By this time, most children are beginning to feel safe again and can separate from their parent's lap in order to accept me. This is a major step for a two-year-old, and it may take even more visits for a particularly wary toddler.

After these quick visits, at the two-year-old visit the child will be able to play in the toy corner with intense concentration while his parents and I talk. If not—if he is too clingy or too frightened to leave his parents—it is time for us to wonder why. I am pleased when parents raise questions like "How much independence should we promote?" "How far shall we let him go?" or "What kind of discipline do we need to use?" If he is "too good" at this age, I do worry.

As the child enters my office, I look for the kind of confidence and security that shows in a child who has developed an expectation to succeed in life. After only a moment, I can see whether these are present. In that brief observation I can tell some of the following things:

Self-confidence—As the child enters my office, he must master memories from previous visits. A secure child will charge over to the play corner of my office as if he owns the place. Coming in ahead of his parents, he is sure that they will follow. He demonstrates in his secure stride that he is ready to overcome memories of shots and intrusive procedures from previous visits. His curiosity about my toys tells of an inquisitive mind, ready to conquer new challenges.

Competence—A two-year-old strides firmly, legs closer together than before, arms at his sides, with upright posture. As he zeroes in on the toys and leans over to pick them up, he uses a firm, coordinated grasp.

Speech—His "hi" or "car" or "no" is vibrant and melodious, not strident. It has an inviting musical sound.

Gender identification—A boy may have already absorbed his father's behavior and a girl, her mother's. This identification is often clear by two years of age and speaks to the power of imitation and early awareness of a child's own gender.

Handedness—A right-handed child is likely to reach for a new toy with his right hand. He might even hold his right hand out to me for a greeting. If he's a lefty, he is likely to use that hand confidently, unless he's already been discouraged from doing so. If he's bimanual, I need to watch for subtle interferences with the development of the dexterity of his left hand, which may become the preferred one for many important activities. (See Wolman in *Further Reading.*)

Play and Development As I talk with his parents, I watch him play. Already his play may reflect his fantasies and his experiences. A toddler's fantasy play reveals his ability to take in, remember, and make meaning—in his own way—of the behavior and events he witnesses. It is evidence not only of cognitive competence but also of a kind of emotional freedom. The fantasy play of a tense, unhappy child will be thin, repetitive, or nonexistent.

Many two-year-olds will play in my office. Many won't. But it is a way to understand each child, so I watch for play at each visit. As I watch, I also learn more about his ability to master the cognitive tasks appropriate for a two-year-old. All of this gives me important clues. For instance, a child might make a square out of blocks, a sort of room. Into the room, he places a girl doll. "Go home," he says as he brings the boy doll up. "Knock, knock! Come in?" He pushes one block aside to let the boy doll enter the room. The two dolls embrace.

In this scene, the child demonstrates his ability to use *symbolic play.* He uses the dolls to imitate the people in his life. A big event for this particular child might be his father's return at night. His new capacity for symbolic play allows him to reenact memories of important events like this. Symbolic play brings out and builds on *imitation.* Through the dolls' behavior, he is already demonstrating his way of seeing gender differences. A child's imitation of conversation and questions that occur in the household demonstrates the importance to him of his parents' behavior. He shows his ability to pick up subtle inflections.

Even a small sample of behavior like this confirms all kinds of accomplishments. When he pushes the block aside to let the male doll in, he demonstrates his motor-planning ability (the sequence of moves that need to be made to accomplish a task) and a sense of *causality* (if you open the door, it will allow you to enter). The child might then bring the windup truck to the "house." Placing the dolls delicately on the truck, he will line them up flat, parallel with the floor, so as not to drop them out. He then winds the key to make the truck run. The level of delicacy with which a child handles toys, his *fine motor competence* as he winds a key, for instance, tells me that that aspect of his neuro-motor system is intact. A child with mild cerebral palsy or other neurological impairment affecting fine motor functioning has clumsy, shaky movements and often overshoots his target. All of this can be observed in a brief period of play.

At the same time, I'm learning about the cost to a child of taking in information from his world, digesting it, and organizing it for action. I can watch a child's play to see how his nervous system accepts, processes, and utilizes information. Is he working to overcome subtle delays in information processing? A child's prolonged attention, his ability to shut out all the other toys, to choose the ones that fit into his symbolic play, is evidence of good control over incoming stimuli. When a child has a hypersensitive nervous system, every new visual or auditory signal distracts him. He darts from one toy to another. If we talk near him, he is distracted by our voices.

Sometimes by two years such a child has learned ways to master auditory distractibility. For instance, his eyes may jerk over to our voices each time we speak. When this happens, he may force his head forward toward the toys to overcome the effect of our voices on his raw nervous system. Although at the mercy of auditory signals, he has learned to master them by redoubling his attention to his task. This kind of "over-focusing" is an effective adjustment, but it comes at a cost: A child who must over-focus resists transitions because he will have trouble letting go of the activity he is concentrating on to start another. Such a child may also master his hypersensitivity with increased motor activity, which both partially overcomes and discharges the effects of this hyper-reactivity. Such a child will need our attention as he enters preschool or kindergarten, and attention deficit hyperactivity disorder (ADHD) may be what we find. Mastering the distractions that occur with a group of children can be hard for him. He may become easily overloaded and fall apart, or else he may zoom into constant action, flitting from one distraction to another. A pediatrician's office may not offer a realistic sampling of a child's behavior, and observation in a group or classroom setting may be necessary. (A busy waiting room may help complete the picture too.)

To watch for signs of hypersensitivity, I clap repeatedly to see whether the child can shut out repeated auditory stimuli. A hypersensitive child will continue to blink with each clap, while one who is not will stop reacting after a few claps. To identify difficulty in organizing visual information, I give him a simple puzzle; a child who is unable to figure out the spatial relationships will soon drop it.

All of these and other observations of sensory, cognitive, language, and motor abilities can be made while the child is playing and I am listening to the parents' concerns. If I observe any problems in these areas, I examine him for minor, often barely perceptible neurological deficits ("soft neurological signs") and/or for processing or attentional deficits. If I am concerned, I refer him for more thorough testing at this age. I am convinced of the value of identifying these difficulties early. Observant parents are often the first to make these observations. Many have told me that they knew quite early that the child was having more difficulty in solving simple tasks than their other children. They observed him (1) frowning as he worked to achieve a task, (2) taking twice as long as he should to repeat a task that he'd already achieved, (3) giving up quickly to go on to a more familiar and practiced routine, and (4) using all kinds of maneuvers to divert an adult's attention if offered a puzzle to solve that he knew he couldn't tackle. All of these observations from parents have made me aware of a child's valiant and resourceful attempts to overcome difficulties in assimilating information and utilizing it, and how vulnerable his self-esteem can become. When I confirm parents' concerns, they are likely to be relieved as we discuss how to help him.

If the difficulties seem mild, I suggest the following things to parents. Try reducing pressure and offering extra support. First, let the child know you can understand that it's hard for him but that he *can* do it. Then, choose times when there aren't other distractions for either of you. Sit down in a quiet, uncluttered place to solve a particular task together. Talk quietly and use only one modality--voice, movement, or visual stimuli. Without putting him under too much pressure, which would just make him turn off, demonstrate the task step by step to him, breaking it up into smaller steps if necessary. Let him try it, fail, try it, fail. Then show him each step again, slowly, one by one. When he masters one step, encourage him, but not too overwhelmingly. After each small step, encourage him to try the next. When he wavers, help him remind himself of the small successes he's already had. If he can achieve small steps one at a time, he can gather the self-confidence to try another. Each one will add to his sense of competence, which may already be battered. Allow him to break away, rest, and come back.

Pacing for such a child is important. If he can learn to pace himself, he'll have learned a great step toward mastery of his nervous system's tendency to become easily overloaded. The hardest job for a parent will be not to hover and overprotect him. Parents need to let him get mildly frustrated so that when he completes a task, it will be *his* achievement, not theirs. He also needs to learn to overcome his frustration and persevere. Pulling back and letting him try are important. It is no easy task to parent such a child. But by giving him a sense of his own capacity for achievement, parents will have begun to prepare him for the future. Needless to say, I'd always choose things he can do well to start and end with (see chapters on "Delays in Development and Developmental Disabilities," "Hypersensitivity and Hyperactivity," and "Self-Image and Self-Esteem").

Getting Used to the Doctor

In the doctor's office, a two-year-old should decide whose lap to sit in or whether he wants to go on the examining table. I allow him to try to pull off his own socks so that he feels in control, and I don't remove his diapers, as I've found it is important to leave on some clothing as a symbol of privacy. With luck, the child will have brought a dirty, bedraggled doll or bear, whose grimy face and tattered body show me how beloved it is. If not, I'll offer a poor substitute he'd already found in my office. I ask, "Can I be Teddy's (or whoever's) doctor?" The child will usually grin. "Teddy Doctor," he might say. I take this as an assent and ask, "Why don't you put the stethoscope on his heart?" I let him use the stethoscope, then the otoscope. "Can you hold Teddy so he won't be worried when I look in his ears?" Holding Teddy tightly to his chest, he may turn one of its ears for me, then the other. After this, it is a snap to examine each of his. "Show Teddy how to open his mouth—*wide.* We won't need to use a throat stick if you can show him how to open it really wide." By the time we've been through all of this, he will usually let me examine Teddy's belly, then his own belly and genitalia. "Teddy's just great! And so are you." The child will glow with pride and, once released from the exam, may almost dance over to my scale for me to measure his weight and height. I hardly need to reward him at the end, so rewarded is he by mastering his own stress. When we can build a firm, respectful relationship through moments like these, it is an important achievement for him and a window into his development for me.

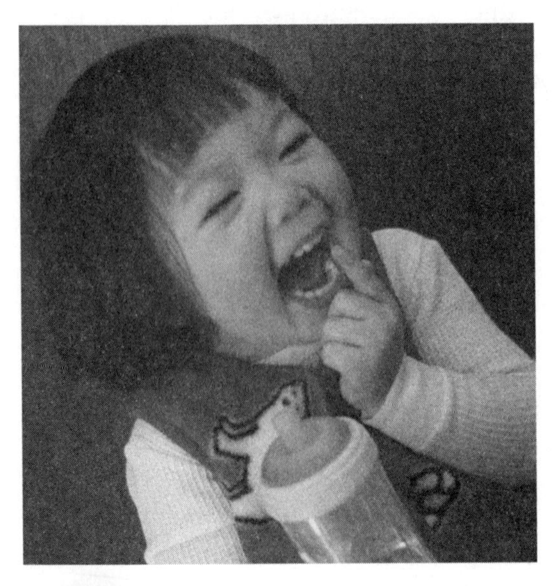

Speech

Though dialogue with parents is perhaps the most critical experience for early language learning, it is by no means the only way speech develops in a toddler. Katherine Nelson, a psychologist at the City University of New York, taped a single child's speech from the age of twenty-one months to three years. These tapes included long monologues when the little girl was alone in her crib. Dr. Nelson and her colleagues, a distinguished group including Jerome Bruner and Daniel Stern, then analyzed the tapes and wrote about their findings in a book called *Narratives from the Crib* (see *References*). One most interesting theory to emerge is that such monologues are not simply practice or play but attempts to make sense of daily experience. There was evidence that this very small child was actually recreating her world for herself. Key experiences, such as being left at nursery school (at thirty-two months), were retold and interpreted: "Her daddy and mommy will stay the whole time but my mommy and daddy don't. They just tell me what's happening and then go right to work, 'cause I don't, 'cause I don't, 'cause I don't cry."

Out of these monologues emerges a meaning to the child's experience and a developing sense of self. This is of course an older two-year-old, who is naturally more accomplished than a child who has just turned two. But speech is so important to a toddler. He will try and try.

A two-year-old will be using verbs to make short sentences and is beginning to use simple adjectives. "Go to store." "Pretty dress." "I *want* that. It's nice." If parents want a two-year-old to say words, they can encourage him by slowly saying, "I think I know what you want, but you must say it to me. Try it. Is it a truck or a house or a doll?" The toddler may well try to imitate the word. So far he probably hasn't identified adverbs such as "quickly," "fast," or "steady," but he's likely to say "up" when he wants to be picked up, and "down" to be put down, and may have understood and given these directions for several months already. If you ask him, "Go get a toy in the other room, bring it in here, and put it on the chair," he will demonstrate his receptive language with clear comprehension and memory of these three steps. The timetable for all this still varies widely.

In a nonspeaking child, a useful diagnostic measure is the use of gestural or nonverbal language. Gestural language is observable in speaking children when they can't quite say what they would like. They will point and act out their wishes in a clearly comprehensible manner. If a child who isn't yet speaking can gesture clearly and use his face and body to express himself, he already comprehends and can use these nonverbal symbols. He isn't likely to be delayed intellectually. It may also be useful to observe how a child uses his mouth for other purposes. If he still drools, or has some trouble swallowing, or seems to have low muscle tone in his lips and tongue, trouble coordinating the muscles of his mouth and throat may delay speech. Though some children will catch up in a few more months, I recommend that a two-year-old who is not yet speaking intelligibly be evaluated by a speech and language pathologist. There is even more reason to do this when the child is already demonstrating his frustration with his inability to express himself by lashing out aggressively.

Speech can be delayed for many reasons. First, hearing deficits should *always* be ruled out in case of any doubt. Parents should ask themselves whether they are hovering and making it too easy for a child, so that he may not need to speak to get what he wants. In addition, a third or fourth child is not likely to speak early, because the older children do everything for him. Parents can watch for the gestural language their child may be using to express himself to them.

If these reasons for a delay have been ruled out, the child should be evaluated for auditory processing disorders. These must be identified by an expert in hearing and learning disorders. Parents need to ask the pediatrician for a referral if difficulties persist. Another possible diagnosis is childhood apraxia of speech, thought by many to be a neurological impairment that results in trouble learning to coordinate and sequence the order of the movements of the muscles involved in speech—lips, tongue, soft palate—to produce intelligible speech. Such children speak late, produce only a few consonant sounds, and leave out more difficult-to-pronounce sounds than other children. As infants, they may not have cooed or babbled, and they may have feeding problems. (See the American Speech-Language-Hearing Association, an important resource for this and other speech and language problems, in *Useful Addresses and Web sites.*)

Children with autism spectrum disorders (autism, Asperger's syndrome, or pervasive developmental disorder [PDD]) will often speak late, and sometimes with specific limitations, and sometimes not at all. In particular, children with these disorders often have trouble understanding the social aspects of language, whether spoken or nonverbal. They may not be able to correctly interpret facial expressions, and they may not even look at people's faces for information (see "Delays in Development and Developmental Disabilities").

Parents are often concerned when a child stutters. Most two- and three-year-olds stutter and stammer when speech is coming in so rapidly. They can't keep up with it. It's like falling over their feet when they're learning to walk. Correcting or saying words for the child only adds to the pressure.

Everyone should give him time and not push or let him feel pushed. Unconsciously, all of us as adults put pressure on a child who's learning to speak. Every time they say something, we say it correctly right after them. We are programmed, one might say, to lead them toward adult speech. If parents can simply relax and enjoy the child's early efforts, given time, this sort of developmental stuttering will disappear. If stuttering persists, accompanied by increasing straining on the child's part despite protection from such pressure, parents should consult a speech and language pathologist. He or she can distinguish developmental stuttering from the far less common stuttering that is more likely to last. For this neurological impairment, early intervention is more effective than waiting it out.

If a child is really delayed in understanding and in expressing himself, he deserves a complete evaluation. A speech therapist is trained to tease out a two-year-old's language strengths and vulnerabilities. Some delays can never be diagnosed precisely, but the good news is that speech therapy can help a great deal. Even if you think your child does not have a serious problem like apraxia or autism, if he is still very difficult to understand by age two, I recommend that you look into getting him evaluated by an expert. School districts should supply speech and language early-intervention programs in the interest of promoting school readiness. Speech therapy at this point can enable a young child to overcome these problems and be ready for the social and learning opportunities of kindergarten and elementary school.

Children exposed to a second language often learn to speak both languages at roughly the same pace as a child who hears and learns only one. Sometimes they may start speaking a little later, and less often, as much as a year later. Though the child will need to use different language sounds to make words, this is rarely a problem, especially if he is exposed to both languages in the first year of life. He will also need to sort out the two languages, but it is remarkable how early children understand with whom each language should be spoken, and how rarely they mix them up. Bringing up a child with two languages is certainly well worth the wait, if there is one, for he will have learned both languages with a part of his brain that scientists now think he will not be able to access for language learning later on. It seems to me that a child who learns two languages from the beginning of life will have a much easier time learning additional ones later—an increasingly important skill in a world where understanding across all kinds of differences has become more important than ever.

Most parents still use some baby talk. Will that hold the child back in learning to speak like an adult? I don't think so. Baby talk says to a child,

"Now I'm speaking to *you,* not to anyone else." But at around this age, baby talk can be given up—if a parent can stand to. That will say, "I'm proud you are growing up and want to speak." Adult speech gives him a chance to model on yours.

Sleep

New language developments may show up in the periods of light sleep when a child is trying to find his way back down. Not really awake, he'll start talking, saying all his new words. He can soothe himself back down to sleep on his own. Parents who have extracted themselves from the child's sleep pattern will now enjoy hearing him talk himself to sleep at night. He'll lie in bed after the bedtime ritual, rehearsing everything he's done during the day. These "crib narratives," mentioned earlier, are sometimes addressed to a doll or stuffed animal. Parents can recognize associations from the child's experiences in the day. Monologues may last for half or three-quarters of an hour. Then, he'll drop off to sleep. All the parents' past efforts to teach a child to get himself to sleep are now really paying off. This gift of autonomy makes possible exciting mastery. By rehearsing his day and interpreting it, he masters the leftover frustration or tension.

Night terrors most commonly begin to appear now, though they may occur in younger children. Distinct from nightmares, they frighten the parents more than they do the child, who is not truly awake during them and will have no memory of them the next morning. Night terrors occur during the transition from deep sleep to light sleep and are characterized by out-of-control screaming and thrashing. The calm presence of a parent to be sure the child doesn't hurt himself is usually enough. Attempts to try to rouse or comfort the child are likely to lead him to become more agitated. Though terrifying, night terrors are not usually serious. When they occur more than a few times in a short period, they may be a sign of a child under stress. In any case, if parents are worried, they deserve to be able to confide in their pediatrician. (See also my book *Sleep—The Brazelton Way* in *Further Reading.*)

Feeding

When I ask parents at the two-year-old visit how feeding is going, the answer is, "He's a slob." The child will drop food off his fork and get frustrated. Then he may smear it around or throw the whole dish on the floor. He wants to be in control of the meal, and he won't let his parents help him. If they comment

If parents can accept a mess while the child is learning to eat like an adult, meals will eventually be a pleasure.

or try to suggest anything, he falls apart. They have to let him eat his way. The child wants to master his utensils so much that failure is a blow. He already may want to do it the way his parents do.

Allowing this independence is very difficult for many parents. It's all parents can do not to urge the child on. The more trouble taken to "fix something special," the more he may balk. He *must* establish the fact that he's in control. The parents' obvious longing for him to eat that "something special" puts him on the alert. The second the parent makes even a helpful suggestion —for instance, that peas are easier to hold on a spoon than on a fork—he falls apart: "No peas!" Parents who persist are asking for feeding problems. If they respect the child for the struggle he's having in learning to eat like an adult, allow him to make his own choices, and accept the mess involved as he learns to use utensils, meals will eventually be a pleasure. Waiting before trying to teach table manners is a must. While this may seem like forever, it will not take more than a year or so for him to be ready to learn.

Toilet Training

As we've said, unless parents have been able to stay home with the baby for most of the first year to work together on "elimination communication," they'll have to wait until their child is at least two. Even then, only the child can decide when the time for toilet training has come. Any pressure parents may feel from grandparents, nursery schools, or helpful friends had better be disregarded. It's *got* to be his achievement, not theirs.

Not until all the signs of readiness spelled out in the last chapter (language, imitation, tidiness, the waning of negativism) are evident should toilet training begin. Probably this will happen sometime after the child's second birthday. When parents and I confer over this important touchpoint, the steps that I recommend are as follows:

First Get him a potty chair that he can take wherever he wants. Call it his and let him get used to it as his. The big one is for you, his parents. The little one is for him to learn with.

Second After a week or so, take him to sit on his toilet, *in his clothes*, while you sit on yours. Read to him or give him a snack to keep him there momentarily. This is just to establish the daily routine of sitting on it. If you take his clothes off, it's too invasive and may frighten him.

Third The next week, ask him if it's all right to take his diapers off so he can sit on his potty once a day. You sit on your potty, he sits on his. Reiterate: "This is what Mommy does every day. This is what Daddy does. This is what Grandma does. Your (doll, bear, etc.) can do it. We go to the potty when we're big like you."

Fourth The third week, take him to his pot with his dirty diaper to undo it, then drop it in. Meanwhile, say something along these lines: "Your potty is where you can go someday to do your b.m. This is what Mommy and Daddy do every day. This is your pot. This is mine." Don't flush his bowel movement away in your toilet while he watches. Parents tell me that their children are fascinated to see it go out of sight. This may be, but the child is also wondering where it goes as it disappears. Children may wonder for years where their b.m.'s have gone. Any child feels it's part of himself. Don't get rid of it until he loses interest and walks away.

Fifth The next step is completely at the discretion of the toddler. In fact, if at any time he resists a step, forget training for a while. You are simply showing him each step so he can take it up for himself. At this time, if he's been interested in the previous steps, you can offer to take his clothes off and let him run around with a bare bottom. If he's ready to try it by himself, offer to put the potty in his room or out in the yard with him. He can go to it himself when he wants to. Then, I'd offer to remind him every hour to try to go, or at the times of day when he is likely to need to use it. If he's ready, he will be able to cooperate on the pot. If he does produce something, leave it there for him to admire. You can congratulate him, but don't overdo it. Too much praise can take away his own excitement about his achievement.

Sixth If he's really ready, you can leave his pants off for longer and longer periods. If he wets or has a b.m. on the floor, don't make a fuss of it. You can put him back in diapers and say, "We'll try again. There's no hurry. Someday you'll do it like Mommy and Daddy and Grandma." You are depending on his desire to imitate and identify with the people who are important to him.

Each step must be at his timing. If he gets worried or resistant, pull back quickly and forget it. Some children begin to care so much that they will have tantrums about whether to go to their pot or not. They will stand in front of the toilet, jumping up and down, saying, "I want to go." The pain in their faces shows the ambivalence underneath their resistance to cooperating. Once they're on the pot, they will hold back. If you push them to try at this time, you are putting on more pressure. The system is already overloaded. Like a temper tantrum, if you enter into it, you reinforce and prolong it. In an area like this, where autonomy is a critical ingredient, the child himself must settle his own internal struggle and make up his own mind. As with a tantrum, you can prolong it but you can't help. The decision is his. He must resolve it, however painfully, before he can make it his achievement. Offer him back his diapers, especially at naptime and nighttime. Try to forget training for a while. He knows now what you are expecting of him, and he must do it when he's ready.

Parents will often say to me, "He's been holding back on his b.m.'s. He stands in front of the potty, screaming as if in pain. I say, 'Johnnie, just try. You know what to do. If you'll just go to the pot, your pain will be all gone.'" This is wrong. The pain is in his head; it is the pain of tortured indecision. The parents' involvement is just fueling this indecision. They must pull out of it and put him back in diapers. If they say that "he acts as if being in diapers is a form of punishment," they may have built up getting trained as too important. All they can do is pull back and leave it to him to let them know when he wants to try again. They can tell him, "The diapers are really to help you go when you want." When either parent asks, "Then, will he go to school in diapers?" that question in itself shows me how antsy they are about his getting trained. To be able to pull out and leave it to him, they will need to reevaluate their own feelings. For those of us who were trained too early or too coercively, it's hard not to reproduce this with our children. But, don't.

When a child begins to hold back on his bowel movements, he is demonstrating a resistance to pressure—either his own or from others. For reasons that may have nothing to do with his parents, he may want to achieve his own training before he is ready. The danger with holding back b.m.'s is that it can quickly lead to constipation. The old myths about constipation poisoning the system are groundless. Children can have a weekly b.m. and be perfectly healthy otherwise. The large intestine will enlarge to adapt. When the pattern changes to a more normal one, the large intestine will adapt again to its normal size. So, it is best to stay out of it and leave his resistance alone.

The trouble with this kind of holding back is that the child's stools are likely to become large and rocky hard. They hurt the anal sphincter when they are eliminated. A fissure in the anus, which may result, is painful. Then, whenever a new b.m. is felt coming on, the memory of a painful one is revived by the fissure. The anal sphincter clamps down to withhold the b.m. A vicious cycle ensues: Withholding for psychological reasons is coupled with reflex withholding at the sphincter level. A cycle of constipation, chronic anal fissures, and even a condition called "megacolon" can result.

When you see this developing, you *must* avoid any pressure. Place the child back in diapers at naptime and nighttime, at a minimum. Tell your child, "You can have your b.m. safely, and I'll see that it won't hurt you." Then, offer him petroleum jelly and place it up in the anus to protect the fissure. Also, obtain an effective bowel softener from the pediatrician. This may have to be used for a long time, until the child *and* the sphincter have forgotten about the painful b.m.'s. He must have soft b.m.'s that cannot repeat the injury to the sphincter. You must be prepared to say, "All this fuss about going to the pot has given you b.m.'s that hurt. Now we're going to see that they won't hurt, and stop all the fussing, so that you can go whenever you want. It's your choice, not ours."

Seventh In learning to urinate at the toilet, a boy should start sitting down. Any boy who learns to stand first won't want to sit down. It's too much fun to stand and spray the back of the toilet (or the wall), to make sounds with the spray, and manipulate his penis. Once the boy has mastered sitting on the pot, his father can take him in to watch the standing up technique.

Some fathers are not sure they can be un-self-conscious doing this. If they can remember that the little boy will be overjoyed to share this with them, they can forget modesty. If the child doesn't want to sit down again after he's learned the excitement of standing and spraying, a father can model that for him, too. Modeling this behavior comes so naturally.

A father must be prepared for his child to want to compare penis size. He may even want to touch. Use this as an opportunity to say, "It's private. Mine is for me to touch and yours is for you to touch." The father can simply say, "Mine is bigger than yours, just as I'm bigger—my feet, my hands, all of me. Someday, you'll grow bigger like me everywhere." When the boy asks about pubic hair, the father can add, "Someday, you'll get hair on your face, your body, and around your penis, just like me." This encourages questions. A father may not feel ready for them, but his answers are more important than anyone else's.

Eighth Night training shouldn't begin until the child is dry at his nap, and until he gives some signal that he wants to stay dry at night. Wait until he's really ready—dry diapers or no urine for at least four to six hours a day. A child will have to be really ready to cooperate at night to make it worthwhile. Unless he wants you to help him, or he controls himself at night spontaneously, I'd hold off on nighttime as a project until he's three years old or older. Many children aren't ready to stay dry at night until four or five.

Girls are often ready to stay dry at night sooner than boys. We don't really know why. A child has to be really ready to wake up and to get up to go at least once or twice a night. Just being able to hold it and control it as in the daytime doesn't mean a child is ready for nighttime training. When the child is old enough, he will get a signal in sleep that allows him to wake up in order to empty his bladder. It doesn't help for you to do it for him by carrying him to the toilet at night. When you've shown him the steps, you've done your job. After that, stay out of it. Children vary as much as a year or more in their readiness to be dry, day or night.

As a society, we are far too concerned about pushing children to be toilet trained early. I don't even like the phrase "toilet training." It really should be "toilet learning." If you have more than one child, you may never need to train any but the first. Children with older siblings often learn from them. You may, however, have to keep the older one from expecting too much. It is amazing how much a younger child learns from the older ones—and it seems to be relatively painless.

Sexuality

Toilet training will increase interest in genitals, in both sexes. Self-exploration and masturbation are also touchpoints of development, and entirely normal at this age. Little boys play with their penises. Little girls find their vaginas and even insert objects into them—all as part of normal exploration. Parents ask, "How much is too much?" If the child withdraws to masturbate when there are other exciting things to do or masturbates to provoke you and others when he's in public, this may be a sign of tension in the child's life. If a child begins to masturbate in public, assure him that it is absolutely okay to investigate and touch himself, but that it is a private sort of thing that he needs to save for a private place. Then, if he's doing a lot of it, look for reasons. Like too much thumb sucking or rocking or head banging, excessive masturbation can be a sign that the child is under too much pressure. These are all normal, healthy patterns for the end of the day or for discharging tension at peak times, but if they persist and occur a great deal, parents should lighten up on any pressure—for example, for compliance with manners at mealtime, toilet training, and so on. As the child gets older, he'll find other, more acceptable ways of releasing tension. Parents will want to talk with their pediatrician about the possibility of sexual abuse if the child has really become preoccupied with masturbation, to the exclusion of his usual interests, or makes sexual gestures that he would have no way of knowing about without inappropriate exposure to adult sexual behavior.

Parents needn't worry when a girl first tries to insert objects into her vagina, for she won't be likely to hurt herself or rupture her hymen. If parents are offended by her explorations, they'd better learn to relax. If she seems particularly involved with masturbation, as we said before, they might look for the cause, but all little girls try to "find out where their peepee is" and why they have a vagina. All little boys explore themselves, too. Sometimes, they cause themselves to have an erection by their masturbation. "Keep cool," I tell parents. If they ask you, give them answers to their questions. Try not to get too longwinded or too complicated. This will only make them wonder why you are so worked up about that part of their bodies.

We all worry about heightening a child's interest in sexuality at this age. I have a doll in my office with a hole in her back. At first, I started to throw her away because it is a distortion of a toddler's expectation. Now I use the doll diagnostically. When I see a toddler looking at it quizzically, I can say, "You wonder why that is there, don't you? You and I know that all of us have holes in other places—in our belly buttons, and in our penis or vagina, and in our bottoms. She's not like us, is she?" A child will look grateful as early as eighteen months. They know already where their anuses and their genitals are. What they are looking for is acceptance of their curiosity and a response to their questions about their belly buttons or genitals, the more obscure parts of their bodies.

Negativism and Aggression

Two-year-olds continue to have violent shifts of mood. Suddenly, they will become angry and out of control. When parents try to help, the child will be likely to bite or kick or bang his head.

Voluntary breath-holding spells can occur during tantrums. These scare parents to death. They wonder whether the child will ever start breathing again. Will he turn blue and damage his brain? Not likely. Once he stops breathing, he'll relax; and even if he becomes unconscious, which is very uncommon, he'll start breathing again. Oxygenation will recover immediately. Breath-holding spells are terrifying, but they aren't likely to hurt the child. Still, parents should discuss breath-holding spells with the pediatrician if they occur more than once. They surely upset parents and even make them hesitant to discipline the child. This is too bad, for he needs discipline just as much as before, and maybe even sooner, but with more firmness and comforting or holding. The most effective response is to hold the child, then put him down in his room, where he's safe. Then parents should walk away, saying, "When you are through with that, I can come back. I don't like this behavior, and I can't seem to help you with it." Afterward, they can comfort him and say, "Someday, you'll learn to control this yourself." (Involuntary breath-holding spells can also occur; they are most common—and most frequent—in the second year. These, too, are usually harmless, but on rare occasions they may cause a child to pass out and even have a seizure. If this occurs, parents should notify the child's doctor.)

A child who is very aggressive in a group, always taking everything away from the others and knocking them down when they try to defend themselves, may not know how to stop. Other parents won't like him or trust him. That's hard on him, for he will know that he's not liked. Parents can talk to such a child *before* he goes into a group and remind him that other children don't like to be pushed around. They should tell him that at the point where he begins to do it, they'll have to leave with him—then, follow through. When parents do leave, they need to let him know that he's got a job to do—to learn to control himself. This child may even need the discipline of being stopped and isolated. This gives him the security of knowing that limits will be imposed on his loss of control. Meanwhile, parents should find a playmate who is just as aggressive. The children will learn from each other about what their aggression means, and they can learn about controls together.

If a child has trouble sharing, I suggest discussing this with him before another child comes to visit. Parents can decide with him which toys he will share, and then they can put the others away. Learning to share is a hard job of childhood. If this is expected of him, he will learn. This is the age to begin.

13. Three Years: Looking Ahead

Just as a child turns three, she and her parents may enjoy a kind of second honeymoon. The toddler's negativism and struggles may begin to resolve miraculously. A two-and-one-half- to three-year-old becomes tranquil and cooperative in ways that make the previous year and a half seem worth it. Parents can't believe this is happening. The renewed tenderness may make them feel carried back to the delicious love affair of the middle of the first year, when all was rosy, but parents feel a new pride in the child's hard-won self-mastery. This tranquil period comes between the trying second year and what can seem at times like a dry run for adolescence between four and six years. (See Brazelton and Sparrow, *Touchpoints Three to Six.*) Relationships between the child and one parent that exclude the other, and a new awareness of aggression, will stir them all up in those years, but when a child is three this can be a blessed time for peaceful readjustment.

If earlier problems persist, this is a good time to try to resolve them. We have a clinic at Children's Hospital in Boston for children with issues that develop over the first three years. With a three-year-old, many parents seem to be able to face common problems that have arisen before, such as difficulties with sleep, tantrums, and eating. Such rapid learning has been going on, for both the parents and the toddler, that there hasn't yet been time or energy to pull back and to face these lingering issues.

Meals

Meals can now become shared family events. By three years of age, a child is ready to eat only at mealtimes and regularly scheduled snacks. Aside from a

morning and afternoon snack, a three-year-old needn't be fed in between meals, and certainly she doesn't need junk food. She needs to look forward to the conversation and the fun of the family being together. Setting her day up so that this can occur is important. Everyone can get up earlier so that breakfast is relatively relaxed, and at the end of the day they can try to make supper together a priority. You can time the afternoon snack to tide her over. Families can emphasize that "at our house, we eat meals together that we all prepare. We all help and we're proud of them."

For a finicky eater, the basic minimum daily diet is not very elaborate (though exact amounts will vary with a child's size and activity level): sixteen ounces of milk, three to four ounces of protein, half a slice of whole-grain bread and a half cup of whole grain cereal or noodles, a few ounces of fruit, and a multivitamin with iron, if the child is not taking in enough in her diet. Again, parents should watch out for the ghosts from their own childhoods, such as memories of parents making them sit at the table for two hours, then angrily putting away what was left to be eaten later. By recognizing the desperation and the humiliation they felt, parents can avoid repeating it. Simple, firm rules for the child and lack of pressure to eat from parents will go a long way toward avoiding problems.

For the Child

Only regularly scheduled mid-morning and mid-afternoon snacks.

No returning to the table after leaving. The child doesn't need to stay, but once she gets down, that's it.

For the Parent

Try to set an example of table manners, but don't nag.

Don't use desserts as bribery.

Don't talk about food or plead with the child to eat.

Don't cook special things for the child alone—you'll be disappointed when she refuses them.

Don't cater to a child's picky tastes—you'll regret it. Just offer her what everyone else will be eating. If she doesn't want it, she'll just have to wait for the next meal.

If food hasn't already become a battleground, a three-year-old will begin to model herself on those around her. She'll eat the things they eat. She'll even pick up a few table manners. If parents can make mealtime a family time with fun and pleasure a central feature, eating will not become a problem. For working families with different schedules, time pressures, and so on, this is not easy. But one or two mealtimes together each day become even more important when a family is stressed.

These pressures are all the more reason to get everyone to help out at mealtimes. Parents shouldn't do it all for the child. Setting the table, preparing simple foods, and cleaning up afterward are wonderful training for a child's future. Though involving the child may still take twice as long as when parents do everything themselves, it is well worth the effort. Don't cajole or beg. Show the child how to do things, encourage her, and expect her to help every day. For a child, a great boost in self-esteem comes from feeling useful and competent: "I'm part of this working family and I help!"

Since many of the child's friends will eat candy bars and drink pop, parents may worry about making her different if they do not supply them. A parent can explain the reasons, point out that "this is the way we are in our family," and encourage her to feel proud. Rather than banning cookies and candies altogether, which will only make them more tantalizing, the child can have one or two every now and then—but don't make these times special occasions, or the importance to the child of these foods will be heightened. If the child goes next door for junk food, parents can try to have a heart-to-heart talk with the neighbor—or other culprits, such as grandparents—explaining their own efforts to help the child develop decent, predictable feeding habits. If they don't get cooperation, they can still make clear to the child why they don't keep any junk food in their house. Provide plenty of healthy snack food. Any substitute caregiver should also know the parents' position.

Toilet Training

A three-year-old may feel as if she had always been trained—at least in the daytime. Any mistake, such as soiling or wetting, will be taken very seriously by her. Any regression in training will occur at an understandable time, such as when a father or mother goes away, or as she adjusts to a new baby. Parents need to help her understand that these are only accidents. Otherwise, she may feel guilty and overwhelmed. She's more likely to forgive herself if her parents let her know that sometimes accidents like these happen when a child is under stress. Repeated failures are likely to occur because of parental pressure or because she's just not ready. (Less commonly, a child who begins to wet again may have a medical problem—for example, a urinary tract infection—so it is worth talking this over with the pediatrician. Some children, affected by a benign, inherited condition called *familial enuresis,* may continue to wet the bed for several years.) Parents shouldn't let her feel inadequate. Diapers should not be used to humiliate her, but as a way of relieving her from the fear of making mistakes. When she begins to get control again, parents can remind her of how much she's achieved, let her know that it has been her achievement, and express their pride in her—without making too big a deal of it.

As soon as she realizes that she's gained control, she's ready for training pants. The beauty of training pants is that she can pull them down easily herself. Don't suggest using "big girl pants" until she's ready. If she wets through them onto the floor, she's likely to feel like a failure, and she may give up and fall back to wetting and soiling again. My advice is to always stay one step behind her. In her eyes, getting ahead of her amounts to pressure.

Toilet training is an important touchpoint for child and parents. The brink of a new achievement takes its toll on them all. A genuine understanding of the cost to the child and her need to follow her own timing in this area can help prevent problems such as bedwetting and constipation. A child will let parents know when she wants to be out of diapers at night. She will start by staying dry at naptime and controlling herself for the first part of the night. She'll demonstrate readiness in the daytime that she can hold on and stay dry even when she needs to urinate. The child's interest in being dry all night is what parents can watch for—and she will lead the way.

At some point, children begin to realize that they want to grow up. They want to be like everyone around them. Most children begin to want to be dry at night between the ages of three and four. Three-year-olds at nursery school pressure each other: "Are you still in diapers at night? Not me. I'm dry!" The other will blush and say, "Me, too," even if she is not. Peer pressure begins early. Adding parental pressure doesn't help.

No matter how often I reassure parents about toilet training, they picture *their* child as staying in diapers forever. No parent feels certain her child will ever really achieve the next step. In such a charged area as bedwetting, unspoken parental anxiety can lead to conflict. Parents care too much—especially when they themselves struggled with bedwetting, which is often the case with familial enuresis. This tends to affect more boys than girls. They may have an immature bladder and immature sleep patterns. At night, this may make it less likely that they will awaken when they need to urinate. These children have a difficult time learning how to hold onto a bladder full of urine throughout an eight-hour period at night. Many of them aren't ready to be dry until they are six or eight years of age and their bladders mature. Many sleep too soundly to wake up. Pressure from family and peers increases their guilt and their conflict about being able to stay dry. Parents need to be reassuring, so that they won't feel so devalued. Certain maneuvers can help them, but I'd only offer suggestions when they ask for help. If a child does ask for help, the parent might say, "Try to hold on a little longer each time after you feel like peeing during the day." That way, the child can consciously "teach" her bladder to hold on longer. But parents need to be careful—even this can be pressure and can be devaluing. It's got to be the child's achievement or the child will feel like a failure.

For parents who are helping a child to stop wetting the bed, I talk with them and suggest the following steps. Once the child has expressed interest, offer to put a pot beside her bed. Even though she may be only a step away from the bathroom, it's still an effort to get out of bed and go there. A special potty can be a symbol that you want to help her. You could let her paint it with nontoxic luminous paint in a design of her own choosing. Then, suggest to her that you'll come to get her up before you go to bed. If she wants to and is ready, she'll wake up when you do go to her. If she won't wake up, taking her to empty her bladder is useless. What you want to do is to teach her how to *rouse herself* at night. When she's ready, she'll recognize the signal of a full bladder in a light-sleep phase. Then, she'll get up and go. She'll even rouse herself to go the first thing in the morning. Be sure you don't take her out of diapers at night until she's ready and can succeed easily. It is likely to undermine her interest in getting dry if she fails on successive nights and wets the bed. At some point, a child begins to care a great deal. Then, it is awful for her to fail.

Another stumbling block on the road to successful toilet training is that of withholding bowel movements. As I mentioned in earlier chapters, it is natural for children to be conflicted about giving up their b.m.'s to the toilet. Why some have more difficulties than others I've never quite understood, but their unconscious conflict had better be respected. The cycle of holding back—creating a large, hard b.m., which then hurts at each defecation—is quickly created. The pain of defecation becomes feared. The conscious fear of pain redoubles the unconscious desire to retain the b.m.

This cycle needs to be broken as soon as it is recognized. Ask your pediatrician to make sure that there is no serious cause for the constipation (for example, celiac disease, hypothyroidism, or Hirschsprung's disease, among other relatively rare diseases) and for help, for example, with a prescription for stool softeners. Parents should follow the suggestions offered in the chapter on "Toilet Training" about giving their child high-fiber foods, and they can use petroleum jelly around the cracked anus. Reassuring the child that this will keep the movement from hurting is important. By talking about the child's fears in simple, reassuring terms, and letting her know that she will master this when she is ready, parents can counteract both conscious and unconscious fears. They should tell her that the petroleum jelly will keep her b.m.'s from hurting, and that the stool softener and special foods will help keep her b.m.'s soft. She can decide to use the potty when she's ready. When a bowel movement is produced, parents should leave it in the toilet until she's lost interest in it, and allow her to flush it when she's ready. She may prefer to go back into diapers to produce a b.m. safely, so parents can offer them to her at naptime and nighttime for this purpose. Once again, boys are more likely to get into this kind of turmoil than are girls, though we do not know why.

Fears and Phobias

The widening world of a three-year-old, and her dawning awareness of just how small she is in comparison to it, will bring new fears and phobias. She may begin to worry about fire engines with loud sirens or dogs that bark, or develop phobias about going to strange places and to the doctor's office. There may be some basis in reality for these fears, and a parent needs to try to help with preparation and understanding, without expecting reassurances to wipe out the fears. Important issues may underlie these fears, and false reassurances can backfire, undermining a child's trust.

A three-year-old is beginning to be aware of aggressive feelings, and these translate into nighttime fears. Fears about what might happen to her crop up. They accompany the new awareness of her own aggressive feelings that will begin to surface. Fears will be acted out, and dreamt about at night. Even if she has already learned to settle herself when she awakens during the night, frightening dreams may begin to crop up at REM cycles. Monsters and witches will threaten and fight in them, and fears of bedtime, of being alone, and of the dark are likely to arise. These dreams will disrupt sleep in the third and fourth years. When there is stress in the child's environment, or when she must make an adjustment to a new situation, fears and disturbing dreams are even more likely to surface at night. The child will need to learn to comfort herself over time, but this can take a while (see "Fears").

As an example of another sort of new fear, a child may worry about all the babies in the neighborhood. She won't go near the house next door because the neighbor has a new baby. Her own baby sister is already nine months old, so her parents are puzzled that she is getting so upset all of a sudden. They thought she'd be "adjusted" by now. However, an older child never completely adjusts to a new baby. At each new stage of the baby's development, the rivalry will surface again. As the baby gets more mobile and more attractive, the older child will have a new surge of rivalry. Underneath her terror of new babies, this three-year-old is likely to be struggling with her own aggressive feelings toward her baby sister. As she feels herself likely to act on them, she must make more and more effort to contain herself. Her effort is costly. Fears, phobias, and nightmares crop up at such times. They represent the cost of controlling unwanted but inevitable feelings.

Parents can talk to a child about the feelings they know she has and prepare her for the surge of fear she'll feel when she hears a fire engine or a barking dog, though she's unlikely to see the connection between the dog's apparent aggression and her own at this age. She also will need to learn how to open up and become aggressive in safe ways. I offer parents the following advice. She can learn by identifying with your ways of expressing aggression. Take her along when you run or play sports. Talk to her about safe ways to handle dangerous feelings. When you are driving and someone cuts in front of you, instead of giving way to road rage, say, "I'm so mad I could have smashed into him. But I didn't." She may not entirely understand you, but she'll be comforted to find that frightening feelings can be discussed. As her aggressive feelings surface, she'll be more likely to put them into words and ask you questions. When she holds back on smacking her baby sister as she passes by, comment on it: "Look at how you controlled yourself!"

Imagination and Fantasy

This is the age when a child's imagination begins to take fire. She will be watching everyone around her in new ways. She'll be learning about them not only by observation but also by imagining whole scenarios about them. She will assimilate this new learning in her imaginary play. Symbolic play (in which she uses toys and dolls to act out events and interactions) has already surfaced in the second year. Now she can use people around her as the inspiration for the imaginary people she makes up.

Eldest and only children develop imaginary friends at this age. The imaginary friend can perform miracles. She can do all of the bad things and experience all of the good things in a three-year-old's dreams. A child will talk about her imaginary friend as if she were real. Parents who are used to being everything for their child may even feel jealous of this beloved companion and worry about the child's lapse from reality. They needn't. Any first child is likely to develop such a fantasy friend. She needs her to rely on. A second or third child rarely is allowed to develop such a friend. The older child prevents this. He may pooh-pooh her imaginary friend or even tease her: "You have a friend, but it's not even a person." In addition, a second child already has a very present companion in the older child. But for the first child, the friend serves so many purposes. The friend can act out all of her imagined experiences.

Adults must respect the private nature of such a fantasy. It is precious. As soon as adults invade this privacy by asking about the friend, they spoil it. The fantasy becomes contaminated by the reality of parents who join her in it. Imaginary friends melt away when adults talk about them. After sharing about the friend, a child may never mention the friend again. Either the fantasy goes underground, or the magic goes out of it. Once, when I asked my grandson what his "friend" looked like, he said scornfully, "Bapa! He's *only* imaginary." As Emerson said, "Respect the child. Trespass not on his solitude."

With all this bubbling imagination, two new attributes appear. A sense of humor is likely to surface, and a child's ability to show empathy for others will become apparent. When a baby cries, she may want to go to it. When another child is hurt, she will watch him carefully to see how he handles it, and she may even show sympathy for his pain. Where do these new personality traits come from? They come from the many sources we've discussed—from the identification with parents and others around her and the way they have nurtured her, and from careful observation of their reactions. They also come from her awareness of increasingly complex feelings—of aggression and a desire to transgress. The richest source of humor, empathy, and compassion is the child's imagination and all of the rich experiences that her fantasies provide for her.

Television

In contrast to the wonderful make-believe and fantasy life of a three-year-old, television can have a deadening effect on a child's play. Young children are exhausted by television. It's a demanding medium—demanding a kind of "hooked" visual and auditory attention. Watch a small child at the end of a program to which she's paid attention. Often, she will be fractious and out of control. Most of us know the feeling of coming out into the street after a daytime movie, jangled, out of synchrony with the world.

Fortunately, most three-year-olds will not sit for too long in front of a TV. They are too excited by their own activities. If they do want to watch all the time, I'd worry. With limited viewing, however, and carefully selected programming, healthy learning from television is certainly possible. Just as children model aggression and violence from TV watching, they can be expected to learn from kindly, caring characters about empathy. They certainly do pick up a great deal. Toddlers will see an *A* in a book and start to sing the song that *Sesame Street* plays for an *A*. This potential makes it even more important that the quality as well as the amount of television watching be monitored by parents. Programs should be carefully chosen for their sensitivity to develop-

mental needs and abilities, and viewed no more than one half hour at a time, no more than twice a day. Ideally, a parent should be participating during at least one of these periods.

A New Sibling

"When is the ideal time for us to have another baby?" a mother will ask. "Ideal for whom?" I generally reply. "Well, I'd like her to want the baby—and to see it as hers." This is wishful thinking. No first child ever wants the invasion of a second child. Parents should decide for themselves when they feel they can handle another. Often, they worry about breaking into the close attachment with the first child. When I hear this, I'm pleased, for parents who can love a child through her second year are really in love with her! Once they feel they can handle another, the first child can handle one, too. Though it will not be easy, in the long run, giving her a sibling is giving her a gift. She will have to learn to share if she has a sibling. An only child may or may not learn to share; a sibling forces the issue.

An older child can identify with her parents and can help with the baby. She may not like the new baby, but she'll learn to accept her as a sibling, and she'll learn so much else in the process (see "Sibling Rivalry").

Peer Relations

From ages two to four, experiences with other children of the same age become more and more important. A child needs these peer experiences. Not only can she learn patterns of behavior from other children, but she can try out her own patterns in safety. All three-year-olds tease each other. They push each other to limits that they dare not test themselves. They make each other angry. They make each other cry. They can't wait to see each other. They hug each other, ferociously locking in each other's arms and legs. They learn from each other safe and dangerous ways to try out their new and complex feelings. Friendships are important, and rivalry is a critical part of friendship. A three-year-old will treat a dear and safe friend as a rival, as a baby to be mothered, as a parent, as every possible partner. Sexual exploration rapidly becomes a part of this learning. Most three-year-olds play some form of "doctor and nurse." This makes for a safe kind of exploration of their bodies.

This exploratory play and this experience with others lead to a surer sense of self. I would worry about a child who doesn't begin to have secure relationships at this age. If other children don't like her, parents should take this seriously. Other children sense it when a child is in trouble, and they keep their distance. An anxious child, or an angry one, or one who has not yet learned to interact with others, threatens the balance they've achieved with their own fears and aggression. If a child is isolated by her peers, there is likely to be a reason.

Sometimes parents can help with early experiences in a group. If a child hasn't had much experience with other children her age, parents can introduce one friend first. They need to find someone who is like her in personality, make a big effort to get them together, then take them on excursions together and let them learn about each other. If a child can make it with one member of a group, she'll learn more about how to handle herself, and the other child will help her enter the group.

If sharing is her problem, parents can explain to her in advance that it can be hard to have to share, and then they can help her with techniques. I'd suggest offering to let her take along one or two precious toys she needn't share and talking with her about being ready to share all the others. When she makes even a small step toward sharing, parents need to give her credit. Learning to share is one of the hardest jobs in life.

The dawning of empathy for others comes when a child voluntarily shares with another. Sure, she's been told over and over, "You must learn to share." But, she suddenly does it without pressure. "Do you want a bite of my cookie?" Then, she watches the face of her friend to see whether this newfound generosity pays off. She knows she needs and wants a friend. This is the first glimmer of a very important human capacity—altruism.

Learning About Gender Identity

A child of three seems to begin to learn how to identify with each parent. She needs to know how they work—how she can be like them and *not* like them. She will focus her passion and completely absorb one parent for awhile, ignoring the other. If you observe a child of this age closely, subtle but identifiable characteristics of one parent can be seen in the child's style of walking, her speech rhythms, her food preferences, and many other areas. But soon, she will turn away completely and act as if that parent no longer existed. The other parent becomes her favorite. She chooses the new favorite for everything, acting as if the former one had no credibility. She ignores that parent and picks up every gesture, every word of the now preferred parent. Why does she need to swing in such a preferential fashion? I think it is economical. In order to absorb each parent so thoroughly, she needs to focus on them one at a time. If she were distracted by attention to both of them, her learning would be less intense and take longer. Episodes of attachment to the parent of the opposite sex have been termed "oedipal" by Freud. When they occur later in adolescence, they are even more intense and passionate. This first "rehearsal" prepares a child—and her parents—for the job of sorting out important aspects of her identity later on.

Needless to say, these shifts in allegiance can be excruciatingly painful for the excluded parent. "She used to wait for me to come home," a father will say to me wistfully. "She was so joyful and so much fun when I arrived. Now, she turns her back on me. As silly as it is, I feel rejected." If parents know what is going on and can be patient during these passionate shifts, they will feel less hurt. Don't give up, I tell them. She'll come back. Just don't let her feel rejected by you. Adopt an attitude of not taking it too personally at the time. At a calm moment, you can say, "I want a time with you all to myself." Read to her at night—alone—or have a special time each weekend in which you and she go off alone. Don't expect too much, and don't force yourself on her. This still can be a time for cementing your relationship while she does the work she needs to do—of learning everything about each of you. All this behavior will last a few months, and then it will change. The parent who then becomes the center of attention can help the other by acknowledging earlier feelings of being turned away.

Sometimes being the favorite can be uncomfortable, too. When a little girl becomes cute and seductive, a father may feel uneasy. Once again, if this is seen as a normal way of trying out her identification with her mother, it can be enjoyed. This flirting may also be used on other men. In this way, a child can tease and hide her intense feelings for her father.

Aggressive Feelings

The more difficult work of this period is that of learning how to handle anger and aggression. This is a long process and is likely to take many forms. With the new horizons open to her, the child will test each parent to the point of a reaction to learn what is and isn't acceptable. A return to previous patterns of temper tantrums may also occur. She may become openly angry and unpredictable. Or, she may become "too good and too compliant." I worry more about the latter. I would rather see a child of this age get angry, tease, and provoke her parents so that she can learn her limits. She is expressing her turmoil openly and learning more, if she receives the discipline she needs, than the child who does not test. This process teaches her how to get herself under control.

Whenever parents realize that they and the child are stuck in a struggle, it's time to reevaluate what's going on. Independence is critical to the child's development of a good self-image. Control is a parental issue. Parents need to respect the child's need for autonomy. But these needn't be in conflict, unless parents are stuck with "ghosts" from their own past—unresolved conflicts from their own childhood. In order to foster a resolution, they often need to face these deeper conflicts of their own.

Wishful Thinking and Facing Reality

Many challenging behaviors, such as lying, stealing, and cheating, will begin to crop up during these next few years. I see these behaviors as a child's effort to reconcile her passionate desires with the realities she cannot change. Children try out lies to see if they could come true, steal when they can't bear not to have something that isn't theirs, and cheat when they can't stand to lose. While children must learn that all of these are unacceptable, parents needn't be alarmed by these predictable behaviors. Setting limits on them and enforcing measured consequences—for example, returning the stolen item to its rightful owner—are critical, but so is forgiveness.

Overreaction, in fact, is more likely to reinforce the pattern. But seeing behavior like this in your child can be alarming, and if you do find yourself overreacting, there are steps you can take to get back on the right path. Here's what I tell parents. Sit down with your child to discuss the problem. Emphasize that you didn't mean to be so harsh. Let her know that *she* isn't "bad," and that she will learn how to control herself as she gets older. Be sure she knows that you think she's great and that you are confident that she'll learn to handle the problem, with help from your limits, over time. Any three-year-old needs to know again and again that you respect and love her just the way she is (see "Lying, Stealing, and Cheating").

Cognitive Development

In the pressured world of families today, many parents of children aged three or younger will wonder when to begin teaching them to read and write. My response: Don't, until she demands it. It's all too easy to overdo teaching letters and numbers. To me, the specific age is not as important as the child's

own desire to learn. Be *sure* the idea of learning these things is coming from her. It's so easy to push early learning on a child who is compliant at this age. But it does more harm than good. In our book *Touchpoints Three to Six* we explain more about early learning.

Although children pressed into early reading may start out ahead of their peers in kindergarten and first grade, in second and third grades, some may begin to slip. Rote learning processes don't generalize to the more complex and abstract learning they will need in later grades. When such children slip from the top of the class, they can lose the adult approval for which they have been performing. They are not stars any longer; adults seem disappointed, and they may feel sad and deserted. Despite evidence that early training of children who are not ready is costly, some parents may still yearn to push their children rather than to encourage their natural curiosity. Books and programs promising ways to "teach your baby to read" continue to proliferate, targeting younger and younger children. Stay away from them. The best way to help your child learn is to help her find the rewards of pursuing her own questions about her world. For this, the safety and support of her most important relationships are critical.

A child learns best who learns for *herself,* not others. Play is her way of learning. When she learns by play, she tries different techniques to find out what works for *her.* When she can't achieve something she is interested in doing, she gets frustrated. Frustration drives her to find out how to do it. When she finally does it, she gets a wonderful feeling: I did it *myself*! This is the most rewarding fuel for future learning that there is. Ambitious parents must learn to watch the child, to stay in the background and let her learn for herself. It's difficult, but necessary. A parent's job in the very early years is to admire and approve, but not to push. As kindergarten and elementary school approach, there will be time to encourage the rigor and discipline needed in later learning.

Choosing a preschool can be done with the same philosophy in mind. Play is the powerful way children learn their most important tasks at this age—how to get along with other children and work in groups, how to handle other adults, and how to learn about themselves as social beings. Much of this is emotional learning: (1) experiencing socialization, (2) learning about aggression, and (3) learning how to identify with everyone around you. Cognitive learning requires emotional learning as its base and will build upon it. Neither one is more important than the other. I'd choose a preschool based on the people who run it and who interact with the children, not for the learning program. If there's pressure to perform rote learning exercises, there may be too little time for children to learn about themselves. Parents should go to school and watch—see firsthand how much time the children have for play and for learning about themselves as people. Learning about oneself and about one's peers is the best learning that can take place in these preschool years. The one thing I'd like for all children to feel about themselves at this age is, I'm important! Everyone likes me! Caring about others is built on a strong self-image.

part two
Challenges to Development

14. Allergies and Asthma

Allergies

ALLERGIES ARE BEST TREATED BY PREVENTION. ALLERGY, ACCORDING TO the American Academy of Allergy, Asthma, and Immunology, is "an acquired potential" for developing allergic reactions. Allergic reactions, the result of the immune system's response to common and otherwise usually harmless triggers in the environment, can include itching, eye watering, sneezing, coughing, wheezing, rashes, and in more serious cases, life-threatening blood pressure drops and swelling that interferes with breathing. Allergic reactions can, in predisposed children, also lead to asthma.

Some children are more likely to react with such allergic symptoms than others. Those who have a family history of asthma, hay fever (allergic rhinitis), or allergy-related eczema or skin rash (atopic dermatitis) may have inherited the tendency to develop allergic reactions. When I know the family history, I can help parents take extra precautions to avoid exposure to the most common allergy triggers in the early years. (Your doctor may also examine your baby's skin and even perform a simple blood test to evaluate the risk for allergies, especially if there is a significant family history of allergies.) There appears to be a critical period—probably at least most of the first year of life—during which a baby who has inherited this vulnerability to developing allergies (also called atopy) is more likely to become sensitized to triggers. Later in life the child will be less likely to become sensitized when exposed to these substances, but if already sensitized, she may respond with an allergic reaction. Children who are exposed too early in life to cigarette smoke, diesel exhaust, or certain solid foods may also be more likely to have allergies later on. The potential for allergic reactions may be reduced in all children by protecting them from early exposure to tobacco smoke and to the solid foods most likely to lead to allergies. These early preventive measures are even more critical to children with a family history of allergy-related illness.

Surprisingly, recent research suggests that rising rates of asthma may be in part related to the lack of exposure to certain triggers, since children from large families, who live with pets, or who spend a lot of time in child care in the first year of life are less likely to develop asthma! Our ever more hygienic environments and our overuse of antibiotics may turn out to be a part of the problem. Our worries about sterilizing our children's environments may not be as necessary or constructive as was once thought. A young child's immune system may need to be exposed to these "experiences" early in life in order to be "trained" not to respond with allergies later on, though this is probably not the case for children with a family history of the allergy-related illnesses.

While it is too soon for anyone to recommend introducing young children to such triggers to prevent later allergic reactions, it is clear that the risk of sensitization can be decreased by avoiding exposure to certain known toxins and allergens in the first year. In addition to tobacco smoke, these include wheat, eggs, soy products, fish, nuts, and peanuts. Once a child has become sensitized, he's at risk for an allergic reaction. Then prevention will mean avoiding further exposure to the triggers he's been exposed to, though sometimes children will eventually outgrow such sensitization.

For children with allergic reactions, simple infections may become prolonged, complex, and hard to overcome. A cold, for example, can hang on for two or three weeks, phasing into the next cold, which in turn adds to congestion left over from the first. Likewise, a simple sore throat may be complicated by congestion, which can add a week onto the infectious period. The tissues swell and make the child snore; the adenoids enlarge and begin to block canals to the middle ear or to the sinuses. Middle-ear infections may need to be treated with antibiotics to reduce the swelling that puts painful pressure on the eardrum.

Treating allergies after they are established is much more difficult than preventing them in the first place or providing treatment in the early stages.

In my practice, I've always made a point of working with parents to identify the child at risk for developing allergies—the child with a family history of allergy-related illnesses, or with early signs of asthma, hay fever, or allergic skin rashes. The only danger of looking for possible allergies is that parents might label a perfectly healthy child as vulnerable. If this can be avoided, however, there is every reason to believe that preventing allergies, or treating them from the beginning, may avert a vicious cycle of allergic symptoms, anxiety about the symptoms, and then more symptoms brought on by anxiety. Avoiding them may be much better than treating them, but when they occur, finding a treatment that works is so reassuring to the child.

There seems to be a threshold for tolerance of allergic stimuli that gradually increases with age, if sensitization can be avoided in the earliest years. I have always thought that this threshold is more likely to be crossed by a combination of allergens than by any one of them alone. Although a child can be quite allergic to one thing—such as cat hair or chocolate or fish—and blossom out with typical allergic symptoms, such as a skin rash or wheezing, after just one exposure, children with asthma or eczema may not react until they've been exposed to several allergic triggers. As mentioned in chapter 10, it is like piling one block on top of another. A child may manage to live with several small allergens (triggers) to which she is mildly sensitive without any symptoms. But when she gets a respiratory infection, or inherits a feather pillow (it turns out that synthetic pillows can harbor allergens too, so these also need to be covered), then the tower of blocks may topple, and she may have a serious flare-up of asthma or eczema.

Some recent research has suggested that not all children react to all of the triggers usually associated with asthma—for example, furry pets (animal dander), dust mites, secondhand smoke, and plant pollen. Instead, it may turn out that each child is particularly sensitive to one or some of these. As a result, parents who diligently struggle to rid their home of most but not all triggers could still have a sick child who is reacting to the one or two allergens that they were unaware of or unable to identify. Parents who suspect this may need to consult a pediatric allergist. Sometimes skin tests can help to identify unsuspected allergens, and it may also turn out that the parents do not have to worry so much about the other substances they have been working so hard to eliminate.

Taking Preventive Steps

Prevention must start early. I urge mothers to breast-feed their infants. Mothers from allergic families, and those of premature or low-birth-weight babies (also at increased risk for allergies) need to know that breast-feeding may help protect their infants from developing allergies later on. I have never seen a baby who was allergic to mother's milk. But I have seen far too many who were sensitive to formula—responding with a congested nose, vomiting, diarrhea, and, worst of all, full-blown eczema. Replacing cow's milk formula with a soy formula will clear symptoms of lactose intolerance (which is not an allergic reaction, and usually results in stomach pain and diarrhea) and milk protein allergies (which can show up as repeated spitting up, vomiting, stomach pain, diarrhea, bloody stools, rash, and even trouble breathing), although it may be a week or more before these symptoms disappear completely. Some babies, though, may even develop allergies to soy formula, and soy is not thought to reduce the risk of developing allergy-related diseases in babies with a family history of these.

A skin rash in an infant under a year old is usually due to the introduction of a new food to which she may be sensitive. The rash usually appears about four or five days after the food has been started. Sensitization to a new food in the first year may make the child vulnerable to developing other allergies and asthma later. In order to avoid this problem, I urge that parents wait as long as possible over the first five months to start any baby food at all. Many parents are eager to start solids earlier in the hope that they will help the baby sleep longer at night. Perhaps they will—though there is no evidence for this—and in the long run, avoidable allergy-related illnesses are bound to lead to far more sleep deprivation! I also assure parents that milk is the mainstay of nutrition for the whole first year. (Breast-fed babies will need Vitamin D supplements by two months of age and by four or five months may need iron supplements as well.)

Most milk protein allergies will begin to show up in these early months, though they may not surface until more allergens—which could be certain additives in prepared foods or grain fillers—are added. When parents do begin to introduce solid foods, I tell them to take the following precautions. When new foods are started, add only one at a time, waiting at least a week or ten days before adding another. Never use mixtures of foods unless you are sure that only one ingredient represents a new challenge. Using mixed cereals and mixed foods, such as fruit mixed with farina or tapioca, is a good way to get into trouble. Read the labels on food jars and buy the purest ones, or, better yet, prepare food yourself. This doesn't have to be a special process before each meal. You can freeze several days' worth of strained fruits or vegetables, for example, in an ice tray and warm up one cube or two at a time.

Eggs and wheat are among the most likely food sensitizers of those introduced in the first year. Wheat is less likely to cause trouble after the baby is six or seven months old. Parents should wait even longer to add egg yolk (ten months) and egg white (twelve months). This represents another instance of a baby's tolerance (or protection from sensitization) rising as her age increases. Fortunately, foods are not likely to remain as very important allergens, and most children outgrow mild allergic tendencies in the second year. When an infant breaks out with a skin rash or with acute gastrointestinal symptoms from a new food, the slow introduction pays off. When you know which food caused the allergic symptom, you can stop it right away. The rash will disappear, and you will have saved the child a lot of distress and discomfort. Sometimes, the shorter the period of time a child is exposed to such triggers or the fewer the number of exposures, the more likely she is to "grow out of" her allergy to it later on. But don't reintroduce a food that has caused an allergy without talking it over with your doctor first.

Some foods, like nuts and shellfish, are more likely to cause serious reactions (for example, severe difficulty breathing) than others, even if a child was only briefly exposed in the first place. Many years of practice convinced me that prevention works. It is worth all the effort you can make to avoid likely triggers in the first year and to eliminate likely suspects as soon as you recognize the signs of an allergic reaction.

Eliminating Triggers

Once a child is sensitized to a trigger, and certainly once she reacts to it with allergic symptoms, it is harder to get rid of the allergy. At that point, I have sometimes found it necessary to eliminate not only the immediate trigger, but also the milder offenders that may build up to make her more vulnerable. If a parent is willing and able to do this, the child may be better able to tolerate the more potent stimulus from time to time. So, with a child who gets hay fever with each cold, or eczema every time she eats wheat or every time she is upset, a preventive approach will seek to eliminate as many of the allergens as possible that she lives with, even though she can live with them most of the time. It is impossible to eliminate every potential trigger, and getting rid of the main trigger is better than eliminating none at all. But the more that can be done within reason, the better.

I would advise cleaning up a child's bed and bedroom first, since she spends a major part of her time there. This is a big job: Feathers, hair mattresses, kapok, wool blankets or puffs, stuffed animals, dolls with real hair,

COMMON ALLERGY TRIGGERS AND HOW TO PROTECT YOUR CHILD FROM THEM

Parents can take steps to eliminate some of the more common allergens for young children who are at risk of developing allergies or who have already shown signs of having them. The following allergens can be controlled to reduce the challenges confronting their already challenged immune systems.

Animal dander If you can't get rid of the family pet, keep it off the furniture and out of the child's bedroom and other rooms where the child spends most of her time. Vacuum at least twice a week. Some dog breeds are supposed to be less likely to cause allergies than others.

Feathers Switch to nonallergenic upholstery stuffing; if you must keep a pet bird, follow the same recommendations as for animal dander.

Stuffed animals, pillows, and mattresses stuffed with feathers, hair, kapok, or other allergenic materials Switch to items stuffed with nonallergenic materials (or cover mattresses with airtight, child-safe plastic materials).

Upholstery, curtains, and rugs Clean or vacuum regularly.

Cockroach droppings In addition to cleaning and vacuuming, consult pesticide firm for child-safe cockroach extermination. Cleaning up cooking areas immediately after use, and frequently drying wet areas in the kitchen and bathrooms, helps reduce cockroaches. Boric acid in small amounts—out of reach of children—under sinks, behind the refrigerator, and so on—is also reported to help. (Child-safe cabinet-locking devices can be used for the cabinet under the sink.)

Pollen Keep windows shut during pollen seasons; air conditioning and air filters can also help.

Molds Follow special clean-up procedures recommended for mold and use dehumidifiers.

Dust Vacuum at least weekly with special HEPA filters to trap small particles. Mop regularly with mild cleaning oil that traps dust.

Flowering plants, dolls with real hair Get rid of them if you can bear to.

Baby oils, powders, lotions, detergents Switch to hypoallergenic brands.

Cigarette smoke This most clear-cut trigger for asthma attacks must at all times be kept out of the air that a child with asthma breathes.

fuzzy animals that can become dust catchers, and flowering plants may need to go. Pets should not be allowed in the child's bedroom. In some cases, families may need to face the sad prospect of finding another caring home for a beloved but allergy-inducing cat or dog. Pillows and mattresses filled with foam rubber or synthetic materials can sometimes also harbor allergens and need to be covered with airtight, child-safe plastic materials. Pure, mild soaps should be used for the baby's bath and clothes. Traces of detergents stay in clothes and can produce skin rashes in sensitive infants. Certain baby oils, powders, and lotions also contain ingredients that can bring out skin rashes. If that should happen, cornstarch and mineral oil are excellent substitutes. If the condition persists, it will be necessary to search for other possible trigger sources, such as rugs and curtains (which are dust catchers). Oil mopping the floor weekly helps to control dust and molds. Air conditioners and air filters are expensive, but they do help protect children from polluted air and airborne allergens that cause infections. During pollen season, windows and doors are best kept shut. Air filters and dehumidifiers can also help. Keeping cigarette smoke out of the house is critical.

Although all of this sounds overwhelming, it must be considered if a child is beginning to get into a vicious cycle with hay fever or asthma. By the time she has had two mild respiratory infections that have led to bouts of bronchitis, or two colds that have ended up in her ears or caused prolonged congestion, I would urge this course of action. If precautions like these have not yet been taken, it certainly would be time now to talk with the child's doctor about other ways to help, including the use of medications.

One of the most important benefits of a consciously preventive approach such as this one is that both parents and child can begin to feel that they have some control over allergic symptoms. By not allowing the symptoms to build up to a major problem, parents may well prevent the development of the psychological component of having allergies.

Asthma

Asthma is a chronic disease of the lungs in which inflammation and hyperreactivity of the airways obstructs the passage of air. It affects at least 5–10 percent of American children. When asthma occurs, it usually starts in the first five years of life. Asthma attacks occur when a flare-up of inflammation, spasm, and increased mucus secretion leads to wheezing and shortness of breath. (Sometimes asthma goes unrecognized when its main symptom is repeated coughing without signs of infection.) An attack can be set off by exercise, cold air, an allergy trigger, emotional stress, or an upper respiratory infection. Avoiding frightening outbreaks of asthma is very important to the future well-being of a child. Today, we have so many effective ways of helping children with these problems that an all-out effort from the beginning pays off. Once an attack begins, children feel increasing anxiety and helplessness if a treatment that works is not found. It is at this point that the child's emotional reactions of fear and worry can take on a life of their own, exacerbating the child's illness.

Eczema, a red, itchy, oozy, scaly rash set off by allergic triggers, often occurs along with asthma. Itching leads to scratching, and scratching aggravates the problem, leading to a self-perpetuating course. The need to scratch can become an automatic response to anxiety or even boredom or frustration and can become a habit all too soon in infants and young children.

SOME COMMON FOOD ALLERGENS

MANY CULTURES INTRODUCE CHILDREN TO NEW FOODS AS THEY APPEAR ON THE family table. I recommend that parents take care to introduce one new food at a time, at intervals of one week or more, so that if signs of an allergic reaction appear, they can quickly identify the offending food and stop giving it to your their child. The following foods are among those that are especially likely to cause allergies:

Eggs Avoid until the end of the first year.

Wheat Avoid until the end of the first year.

Nuts, especially peanuts Avoid until the end of the third year, since nuts are also a choking hazard.

Shellfish Avoid until at least the end of the first year.

Cow's milk protein Best avoided by breast-feeding. Bottle-fed infants who develop a milk protein allergy that is diagnosed by a pediatrician will need to be switched to a soy-based formula.

Many citrus fruits and berries Avoid these until the end of the first year, since they may also be more likely to cause sensitization than other fruits.

Asthma and Anxiety

There is no need to let eczema or asthma cause anxiety in the child. To break the cycle of anxiety and symptoms, I try to alert parents to a reassuring fact: In a family with a tendency toward allergies, the older a child is before she first shows allergic symptoms, the less severe they are likely to be, and the more easily the symptoms can be treated. The child who might have had eczema all over her body, had she developed it in her first year, will, in her second year, have only a mild case in her elbow creases and the backs of the knees.

Although problems such as asthma or eczema can become overlaid with anxiety after a few frightening episodes, I should make clear that I do not think these diseases *begin* because of psychological problems in the child or underlying family difficulties. There is likely to be a genetic predisposition, reinforced by environmental allergens. It is only as these diseases manifest themselves that the sufferer's fears can add on a layer of symptoms and vulnerability to repeat attacks.

Children with asthma are likely to demonstrate their anxiety to parents in a variety of ways. They may worry about being unable to breathe even when they are not sick, or they may shrink from physical activity. They may cling to parents and refuse to go to school. They may even act or feel as if they were having an asthma attack when they are tired, or feel the need to provoke, rebel, or get attention. Parents will inevitably be drawn in to respond to the symptoms as their own anxiety mounts. If they are unable to control the child's symptoms, their guilt, anger, and concern will heighten tensions in the family and in their relationship with the child. In this way, asthma can all too easily become an intensely emotional focus for the whole family.

Asthma can become self-perpetuating. With asthma, when the child wheezes and can't breathe, she soon becomes frightened. Wheezing makes her anxious; anxiety intensifies wheezing. She gets a feeling of helplessness, of being unable to handle the disease or her fear of it. No wonder that asthma becomes "psychosomatic" before very many such cycles have occurred. To counter this, even very young children must be given the clear message that we and they know what to do to prevent asthma and to stop breakthrough asthma attacks.

I learned how important this sense of control is from a little boy whom I'll call Timothy. Tim was a lively little boy, who loved to play ball and tease his friends, and joked with me when he came for routine checkups. But Tim had asthma. When he began to wheeze, his whole appearance and outlook changed. He became beaten-looking and worried, and his eyes took on a haunted look. His face grew pale, and his eyes evaded mine when he came to be examined.

Tim sat on my table with his shoulders hunched, wheezing, his chest pumping away even more dramatically than this fairly severe asthma attack seemed to warrant. "Tim," I said, "you seem worried about yourself." "You'd be, too," he replied, "if no one knew what to do about you—and everything was wrong." In these few words, Tim was telling me a great deal; he felt frightened, discouraged, and helpless. When I gave him a shot of epinephrine to help relieve his wheezing, I told him what I expected to happen. A little later, when it relieved him, I said, "You see, we do know what will work. Now we have to find things that you and your parents can do that will stop your wheezing before you need me."

We discussed the two kinds of medications his parents should give him—long-term "controller" drugs to take every day, and "rescue" ones just for acute attacks. I emphasized that the long-term preventive medications would help him have more symptom-free days and a chance at a normal life, and that with the fast-acting rescue drugs, he would notice relief from an attack soon after taking them. Given the severity of his asthma, I explained to Tim and his parents that he would need to take his controller medication (anti-inflammatory drugs such as inhaled corticosteroids, cromolyn sodium, or leukotriene modifiers) every day to *prevent* airway inflammation and asthma attacks, and that he could rely on his rescue medications (bronchodilators such as albuterol) to *stop* asthma attacks once they started.

Then, I gave him some chores to do on his own behalf—slowly wiping his desk with a clean damp rag (being careful not to stir up dust), staying away from cats, which made him sneeze and itch, turning on an air purifier when he felt he needed it, and feeling free to ask his parents for his rescue medicine when he felt a wheeze beginning. In later checkups, when the suggestions I made had begun to help, we talked about how he was mastering his own wheezing.

One day, Tim came bursting into my office with a cold, wheezing slightly, but cheerily bright and teasing. "Dr. Brazelton, don't use that needle medicine on me. I take my regular medicine every day and I've got my inhaler in my pocket. I'm going to use it after you listen to me. Just hear my chest first, because then I'll show you how I can stop the wheezing *myself!*" I examined him. He then proudly inhaled his own medication and asked to sit in the waiting room for a little while. I called him in thirty minutes later to listen to his clearing chest, and he looked up at me, eyes gleaming, as if to say, "We've got it now, haven't we?"

Tim outgrew his asthma in adolescence, as do many children whose allergies are well enough controlled. He taught me a great deal about the psychological effects on a child when a disease recurs and recurs and none of the adults around know what to do, and also how, with support, a child can begin to feel in control.

Guidelines for Controlling Asthma

Here are a few steps for getting your child's asthma under control:

- You must handle your own panic so as not to convey it to the child. This is the first and perhaps most difficult step.
- Eliminate common allergens (see box earlier in this chapter), and keep cigarette smoke out of the house.
- If respiratory infections last longer than a week or cause wheezing or unusual congestion, ask the doctor whether allergies could be compounding them. If so, a vigorous approach to each upper-respiratory infection should be considered to prevent the more serious symptom buildup. If a child coughs repeatedly without an infection, this may be a sign of asthma—in fact, it is one that is all too often missed.
- Asthmatic wheezing should be treated immediately with cleanup of the allergens in the child's environment, and with medications that work. After the child improves, she can be reminded that the rescue medication worked so that she could breathe easily again. But she and her parents will also need to be reminded that asthma is usually a chronic condition, and that daily medications are critical to cutting down on the frequency and severity of acute attacks. Daily long-term controller medications are prescribed for prevention of persistent asthma in mild, moderate, and severe cases, since they cut down on the inflammation inside the lungs that predisposes them to acute asthma attacks. When daily steroid inhalers are prescribed—a common, effective, and widely accepted practice—parents should discuss their concerns about side effects with their pediatrician, who should monitor closely for these.
- Assuring a child that "we know what to do" will give her a feeling of mastery and will combat the natural panic that is likely to accompany lack of breath and wheezing.
- Consult with your child's doctor about rescue medications, home nebulizers, and spacers that can help a child use inhalers more effectively. It is easier to break the vicious cycle of wheezing and panic if effective treatment is given early.

- If home and office medications aren't working, ask your pediatrician about a referral to an asthma specialist. An allergist may be able to help by giving tests to identify the specific allergens that a child has been sensitized to. Sometimes treatments targeting the immune-system response to these allergens is even offered.
- Be patient, and remember that adolescence can be a real turning point. Many children become allergy-free as the changes of adolescence take place.

15. Bedwetting (Enuresis)

BEDWETTING IS AN UPSETTING PROBLEM. ONE IMPORTANT QUESTION TO ask is: Whose problem is it? At first, it is the parents' problem. As soon as they hear that other children of the same age are dry at night—certainly by three or four years of age—they will start to worry if their child is not. When peer pressure begins, it becomes the child's issue. In a play group of three-year-olds and four-year-olds, competitiveness will soon surface. "I don't wear diapers anymore. Do you?" "No." "Are you dry at night?" "Course I am." Any adult hearing this suspects that at least one of the children is not telling the truth. A child this age (more often a boy) already feels ashamed and under pressure from his peers. By the time a child is five, in our society, everyone concerned will see bedwetting as a problem.

The Child's Readiness

When should parents start worrying about bedwetting? With a child-oriented approach to toilet training, leaving each step in the hands of the child, most children will achieve their own daytime success by three years of age. Is there a predictable timetable for success at night? There are many children who are not "ready" to stay dry when we expect them to. Some children may have immature bladders, leading to difficult night control. There are also children whose sleep patterns are immature. Their arousal patterns in sleep are not well developed enough to alert them to get out of bed to stay dry. These children need to develop on their own schedule, which must be respected. It is also thought that unlike other children, some children who wet their beds may not make increased levels at night of the anti-diuretic hormone (ADH) that limits the amount of urine produced. As a result, it may be more difficult for them to go through the night without urinating. Whatever the cause, peer and parental pressure can add guilt and feelings of inadequacy, but they won't speed up the child's developmental patterns. Parents need to be patient and to wait. Also, they need to help the child understand the reason for his "lack of success." Otherwise, it can lead him to a poor self-image—one of failure. A six-year-old boy once looked at me pleadingly in my office and said, "Will I ever be able to do it?" "Doing it" meant staying dry at night and pleasing those around him. His eyes contained a look of defeat and hopelessness—at six! Bedwetting may not start as an emotional problem, but it can surely become one.

If girls continue to wet the bed at age five, and boys at age six, or if they start to wet the bed after having been dry at night for the previous six months or more ("secondary enuresis"), they deserve a full examination. Their urine should be checked for infection, evidence of diabetes, and other medical causes for new or prolonged bedwetting. This is part of any good checkup if a child is having urinary difficulties. Urinalysis can detect kidney or bladder infections that might contribute to urinary incontinence in both boys and girls. Sometimes, a brief, temporary bout of renewed bedwetting in a child who had previously been able to stay dry through the night can occur when a child is stressed—by a move, a new sibling, or even any new touchpoint that may extract such a price for a new burst in development.

Daytime control seems to be easier for girls (on average, they achieve it 2.46 months earlier than boys), and they are also less likely to wet at night. Some of this may be due to biological differences, but I have often wondered if it might also be due to differences in societal expectations and in subtle sex-linked patterns of behavior, and to expectations little boys have of themselves. By the age of five, a boy is likely to try to hide his "defect." Denial will set in, and he will refuse to share any of his feelings of shame or failure. When I see a bedwetting boy in my office, he is already guarding himself. He will cross his legs when I try to examine his penis. He will blush or get more noisily active when we discuss his toileting. He has already begun to feel vulnerable and guilty. Once the doctor has ruled out medical causes, parents will want to reassure the child that he is okay and then do all they can to lighten up on pressure.

How Parents Can Help

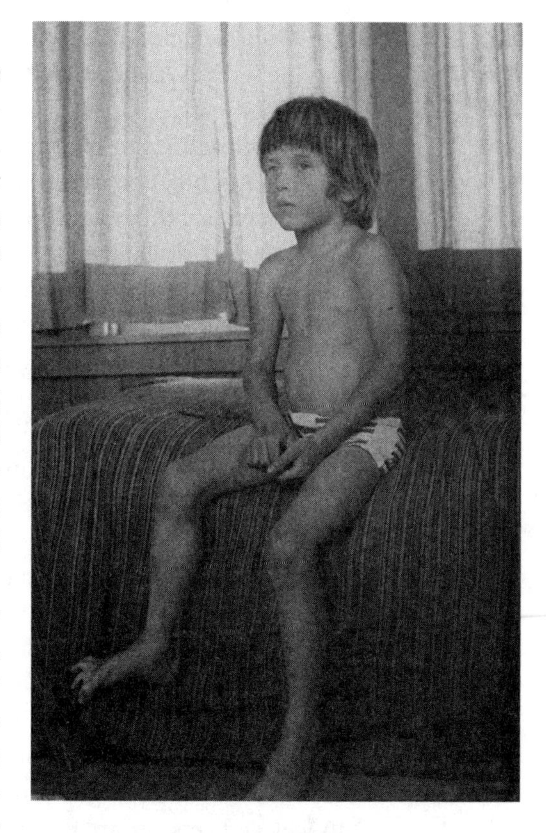

Above all, staying dry at night must become the child's goal, not parents' or society's. Parents must somehow relax the urgency they feel. If this seems impossible, they might consider turning to a counselor or someone who can help figure out how to defuse undue pressure on the child, as well as the parents' own involvement. They may discover that they are driven by their own embarrassing childhood memories of bedwetting, since bedwetting that continues after age five without other medical causes often runs in families (*familial nocturnal enuresis*). This can help parents focus on their task of listening to the child's feelings and supporting his own efforts to stay dry.

If there are issues of poor self-image, of psychological immaturity, or of self-devaluation, they need to be addressed. If the child is under too many pressures from those around him—from school, peers, or family—these need to be lifted as much as possible. A father should reinforce his closeness to his son. A regular weekly excursion together gives the boy a chance to identify with his father and gives his father a chance to understand his son's self-image. Parents shouldn't probe, but they should make themselves available.

When the child is ready for them, here are some other steps I recommend when talking with parents (again, especially with parents who have boys).

- Ask your child to hold on to his urine a bit longer during the day, to help increase bladder control.
- With the child's permission, you can wake him before you go to bed. At that point, he must take control, or it won't work. Don't carry him to the bathroom.
- A special excursion to buy a "nighttime pot" for the child's bedside, one that can be painted with luminous paint, could become a symbol of parental support. Then, you can wake him up to use it. This must be done in a supportive way, without pressure. No matter how close the real toilet is to his bed, this special symbol can be meaningful.

- An alarm clock by the bed to wake him up at 2:00 A.M. could help, *when* he's ready. Before that, it is unnecessary pressure that will work the wrong way.
- Subtle efforts to reassure the child and support him about his masculinity and his success during the day can shore him up for the night. But, if overdone, they can also make him self-conscious.
- When your child wants to talk, you can discuss his feelings, the pressures on him, and the fact that his bladder may need to grow up and it may take a little while for him to learn to wake up in time. If this is a real dialogue, it can be reassuring to him.
- You can help dispel the myth that there is a magical cutoff date of five or six years, after which all children become dry. Societal pressure, coupled with parents' expectations, is too much for a small child to handle.

If bedwetting continues past the age of five for girls and six for boys, or if it interferes with a child's adjustment—his own self-image, his ability to relate to his peers, or his ability to see himself as a successful male—it is time to seek a consultation with a pediatrician skilled in these issues. Once medical causes have been excluded, a child psychiatrist or psychologist might also be called in to help. Helping a child to feel better about himself could strengthen him at an important time in his development. He may also be ready for other strategies—medication, or a pad that senses when he begins to wet and sets off an alarm—if he is interested, and if these are offered as support, not punishment. If he asks for this kind of help, or if he wants to try them, assure him that if they don't work, sooner or later he'll outgrow the problem. Don't let any failures with particular strategies make him more discouraged.

16. Crying and Colic

A CRYING CHILD MAKES ADULTS DISSOLVE. YET, ALL CHILDREN CRY, AND at times, they seem to need to cry. When should you worry, and when should you leave it to the baby?

Before viewing crying in any individual child as a problem, it is important to understand that crying is a universal, adaptive behavior and a baby's most effective form of communication. As we saw in chapters 2, 3, and 4, small infants have at least six types of cries, and each type communicates something different: pain, hunger, fatigue, boredom, discomfort, or the need to let off steam at the end of a stressful day. ("Colic" is a term commonly used to refer to this last kind of crying—unexplained end-of-the-day crying that begins at three weeks, peaks at eight weeks, and usually tapers off by twelve weeks. It had once been thought that this crying was due to a baby's gastrointestinal discomfort. Even though it is now known that this is usually not the case, the word "colic" seems to have stuck.) A new mother can learn to distinguish between these types of cries by three weeks. Studies have shown that even after three days, a mother can tell her baby's cry from another newborn's in the neonatal nursery.

The Language of Crying

An assessment of crying—its rhythm, its timbre, its latency (that is, how long it takes to start up)—and the baby's ability to calm herself and be calmed is an important part of any newborn assessment. The quality of the cry and the ability of the newborn to be soothed give the pediatrician two important windows into the baby's future—a window into her temperamental style, and a window into the "work" the parents must do to comfort her. An intense, active, driving baby is likely to have a short latency to crying and a loud, high-pitched kind of crying that may be difficult to soothe. A quiet and sensitive baby is likely to be slower to get going and to have a lower pitched but insistent wail. She may make repeated attempts to calm herself—by sucking her thumb, looking around, or changing positions. When she finally can't be comforted, her wailing can be insistent and disturbing. These patterns are part of each baby's temperament and style. They seem to be stable in small babies and predict their future temperament with some accuracy. (I describe these individual differences at some length in *Infants and Mothers.*) They also shape the parents' image of the child and influence the adjustment parents must make as they try to get to know her.

Meeting the demands of a newborn's cry is one of the first challenges for new parents. Is she hungry? Is she uncomfortable? Does she need to be changed? Is she tired or bored? Or, could she be in real pain? All of these are questions that mobilize adrenaline and an "alarm reaction" in new parents, forcing them to search for a solution. (An alarm reaction is one that mobilizes instant alertness, increased circulation and blood pressure, and higher oxygen to the brain in the face of a perceived emergency.) Each time their efforts work, they are encouraged by a successful experience. When these don't work, they are likely to try one maneuver after another, often with increasing anxiety and tension. However, I feel that parents learn more from mistakes than from successes. A failure to find an immediate solution may lead new parents to stop, pull back, and wonder "What next?"—and, in the process, to learn to observe the infant. As they do, they learn more and more about her.

Prolonged or Fussy Crying

In my practice, roughly 85 percent of infants between the ages of three and twelve weeks had the irritable, fussy, end-of-the-day crying that is often called "colic," and frequently mistaken as a gastrointestinal disturbance. Occasionally, this crying really is such a symptom, and this possibility needs to be considered by the baby's pediatrician. But only a small percentage of these fussy babies actually have gastroesophageal reflux, milk allergies, or other digestive causes for their crying. For new parents, unexplained, end-of-the-day crying is a severe test of their ability to nurture their baby. As mentioned in chapters 4 and 5, the appearance of this type of crying marks a developmental touchpoint, and I like to prepare the parents for it when their baby is two or three weeks old. Once parents understand how common it is for babies to have these regular, predictable episodes of unexplained, end-of-the-day crying, they can relax, knowing that it is normal and will not last forever. I help the parents to anticipate this phase and see the fussy period as a kind of "letting off steam," a daily reorganizer of the baby's immature central nervous system. By explaining the reasons for this stage from the infant's point of view, I hope to prevent the anguish and overreaction of parents who don't expect such behavior and find they can't alleviate it. If they are not prepared, they are likely to overdo their attempts to quiet her at a time when what may help most is to leave her for short periods to handle her own crying.

When the crying period starts, parents need to decide on an approach to it. They need to be reassured that the baby's emotional and physiological systems will mature in a way that will make the crying period unnecessary by twelve or so weeks of age. Generally, cutting down on stimulation is the best solution. If parents become conflicted and anxious about a baby's crying, they tend to reinforce it—by doing too much. At a time of day when the baby's nervous system is raw, parents' overanxious, hovering ministrations can overload the baby's capacity to take in and utilize their nurturing. More crying can result. The seeds for failure in their interaction are laid down. Constant handling may even interfere with the baby's own patterns of self-comforting and self-consoling.

When the time for this normal irritable fussing has passed, at about twelve weeks, parents may remain too eager or too withdrawn. The baby's cries no longer get an appropriate reaction. The parents either jump too fast, and overstimulate her, or are unresponsive, or handle her ineffectively. Depressed or angry parents quickly convey their feelings to a small baby. More crying and more difficult-to-interpret crying ensues. When this cycle gets locked in, the result can be a frightened, hard-to-reach infant.

If the crying in this period increases and the usual maneuvers of reducing stimulation neither stop it nor soothe it, or if the crying spreads to a longer period than two hours in the evening, it is a sign that there is more diagnostic work to be done. The infant may be hypersensitive and easily overloaded. If this is the case, soothing, low-key maneuvers may work. Parents will discover that a baby like this cries all the more if they look *and* talk *and* rock all

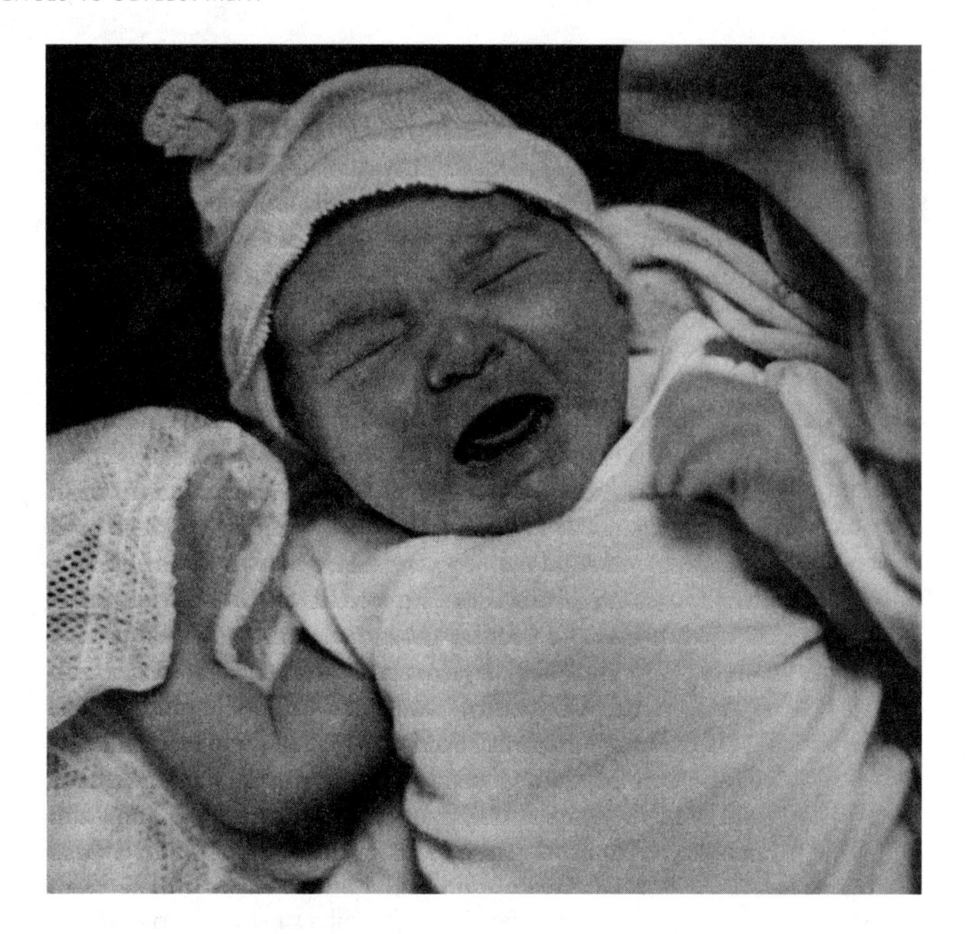

at once. Instead, doing only one of these things at a time is best. If such soothing maneuvers don't shorten the crying, it may be a sign of a medical problem, such as gastroesophageal reflux or milk protein allergy, that deserves your pediatrician's attention.

Other babies may cry as a response to a non-nurturing environment. The inability of these infants to be soothed may reflect parental disorganization or depression. Babies who have severe, prolonged, unexplained crying may have depressed parents who need help to understand and care for an active, intense baby. A pediatrician can evaluate the baby's contribution and, if necessary, seek a counselor or other supports for the overwhelmed parents. Roughly 10 percent of women experience postpartum depression. If serious depression goes unrecognized, it can lead to problems for the mother and the baby (for example, self-destructive patterns, stresses on the marriage, or delayed development in the baby). These are preventable, for postpartum depression can be managed and cured with adequate treatment. I believe that postpartum depression is more common and more devastating in our society than in others because our culture does not adequately nurture and protect new parents.

Parents with an especially hypersensitive baby will need lots of extra support. For hypersensitive infants, inconsolable crying can be set off by many things—any new experience, a transition, or the presence of a stranger. But for some, this will lead to constant disorganized activity. A very hypersensitive baby may also show gaze avoidance or engage in repetitive movements or behaviors, such as head banging, head rolling, or hair pulling, or may pick at her own body or face. She cannot be calmed by ordinary comforting measures. Using a soothing voice, holding her arms to stop her from startling, or even swaddling her, offering her a pacifier, or feeding her will not help. Such babies seem to be crying out for a deeper kind of understanding.

They and their parents need an evaluation by a trained infant observer, a child psychologist or child psychiatrist who specializes in babies. The observer can assess the baby's contribution to the problem and help the parents understand their baby's needs and their own contribution to the situation. In some cases, there may be a neurological basis for intense hypersensitivity, such as disorganization from intrauterine exposures from drugs, tobacco, or other toxins, or stress at birth. In others, new parents may have an instinctive and deep-rooted ambivalence toward their new baby. In many cases, the baby's vulnerabilities and the parents' reinforce each other. If parents can be helped to understand their baby's behavior, and any reasons for it from their own past (their ghosts), they can learn to reach out for the infant. I see such troubles as eminently reparable if parents can seek help at an early stage. (Some children's hospitals have "crying clinics." See Zero to Three in *Useful Addresses and Web Sites.*)

Crying as Part of Development

In later infancy, crying continues to reflect the baby's inner state and calls for attention from parents in very much the same way that we have described for the newborn. As we said earlier, cries of hunger, pain, boredom, fatigue, and discomfort, as well as cries for attention, all have different acoustic characteristics when analyzed with special equipment. For example, a pain cry is absolutely characteristic: a sharp scream, followed by a brief period of apnea (no breathing), followed by repeated, anguished cries, then another sharp, penetrating cry. All other cries map out differently on acoustic spectrographic analysis. A pain cry continues when you pick a baby up. Not so with the other cries. But parents do not need special equipment to analyze their baby's cries; they usually learn to interpret them intuitively in the first few weeks.

As an infant grows, the parents' task is to determine how much each of these different cries demands attention from them, and when and how the infant can "learn" to comfort herself. I am always happy to see a six- to nine-month-old infant who has learned ways to comfort herself—a thumb or a pacifier, a blanket or a teddy bear, or a special behavioral pattern that helps her settle down. When we see such a baby at Children's Hospital in Boston, we know that child has been loved and has developed inner resources to which she can turn when she's lonely or distressed. A baby who has been neglected or ignored will not have learned to depend on her environment or on herself for solace. Such children have a kind of empty hopelessness that comes through in their cries. They make you want to reach out and gather them up. But when you try, they withdraw, turn inward, and are almost impossible to hold because of their physical resistance. Intervention is critical for these babies' capacity to develop emotionally and to develop relationships in the future.

In the regressive periods associated with spurts of development—the touchpoints described in Part 1—crying is part of the usual disorganized behavior. Such crying may also be hard for parents to understand. If they get too frantically involved, they can increase the amount and intensity of it. At some point, it becomes necessary to push a baby to learn to calm herself down. This is when a thumb or a pacifier as a self-comforting pattern can be a major help. This should be "taught" during the day, when she's not too upset to learn it. Then, she can be pushed toward it at other times. Should we encourage such a "crutch"? It seems to me that the answer must be yes. We are living in a stressful time, and even babies need to learn early how to handle their own stresses and those around them.

An anxious, unresourceful child who is often whiny, fussy, and cries a lot may be labeled as spoiled. Though the demanding crying is aimed at getting a response from adults, its very quality seems to carry the message, "You can't satisfy me." A spoiled child is one who has never learned her own limits, who has lived in an overprotective, overloading environment. Because of their own ambivalence or conflicts, parents may try to do everything for such a child. Often, they rush in too soon, before the child can develop any sense of wanting to do something for herself, feeling frustrated, and needing to try again—and before she can enjoy the all-important sense of "I did it *myself*!" This feeling is critical to her future self-image, her sense of her own competence.

Sometimes when a child has been ill or has had a difficult start in life, or the parents have lost a previous child and see him as a miracle—a "Jesus" child—they hover constantly. These children are never allowed to experience frustration, to handle their own minor injuries, to fall down and gather themselves up to get going again. We call this the "vulnerable child" syndrome. Sad-looking and unhappy, they cry a lot. Their crying demands constant attention, as if it were necessary to fill up the space left by their lack of resourcefulness and lack of awareness of their own competence. They test and provoke adults around them, as if seeking constant adult attention to compensate for the helplessness they've come to see in themselves. The reason they seem spoiled to adults is that they are searching so hard for limits and for an image of themselves as competent.

Many of these children need a secure set of limits, learned from parental discipline. From nine months on, and increasingly in the second year, discipline becomes the second most important job of parents. Discipline means teaching, not punishment. The goal is to give the small child a chance to incorporate her own limits. A child with a sense of limits is a secure child. A "spoiled" child tests limits in a search for this security. When a child is provoking or testing or crying for attention over and over, a parent should take her behavior seriously. (See "Discipline" for suggestions and techniques for teaching limits.)

When a child in the second and third years repeats crying, provocative behavior over and over with little evidence of progress, a parent must wonder: Am I reaching her? Does she have a deeper issue that we are not addressing? When possible, I'd look for the issue and help her understand it (for example, a new sibling, a parent away, a new school, a friend who has hurt her, or even depression [see "Depression"]). By the time she has reached the age of three, parents can ask her to help them find a way to stop her before she disintegrates into crying, demanding, and acting out. When she can give any possible solutions, parents must be sure to use them—and then, to give her credit for having taken important responsibility in deciding what would work.

As time goes by, crying should become clearer as a communication from the child's point of view, and parents should understand their role in responding to the needs that such crying expresses. If a toddler or older child cries without meaning or satisfaction, I would worry about this as a symptom of depression and seek counseling. If, however, it is part of a phase that precedes a new development or a new adjustment, I'd see it as appropriate and transitory. One rule for parents—always look below the surface to try to understand a child's crying when there is no obvious reason for it.

17. Delays in Development and Developmental Disabilities

I HAVE ALWAYS FELT THAT PARENTS OF A CHILD WITH A DEVELOPMENTAL disability must take two steps for every leap in development that their child takes; they must let go of expectations of progress at any given time, and they must support the child through his own touchpoints, at his own pace. Many parents of these children have told me over the years that the chronological developmental milestones are not helpful to them, but instead, serve only as an oppressive reminder of the lack of acceptance around them of their child's differences. Through their experiences I have come to see the wisdom of encouraging each child with special needs to chart his course through the touchpoints of development at his own pace.

If you are worried about a delay in your child's development, and if the worry persists, don't wait. Have him evaluated first by a pediatrician and, if necessary, an appropriate specialist—for example, a behavioral-developmental pediatrician, a pediatric neurologist, a speech and language pathologist, an occupational therapist, a child psychiatrist or psychologist, or other child expert, depending on the nature of your concern. As the front line in children's health and well-being, parents should respect their own observations and intuition. If any aspect of your child's development—whether motor, cognitive, emotional, or behavioral—troubles you, call or make an appoint-

ment with your doctor. If the pediatrician or other caregiver, such as the nurse practitioner, says, "It's normal, he'll grow out of it," be sure to ask two questions: "How long will that take?" and "If it turns out later that something was wrong, will any harm have been done in waiting?" If the doctor says that all is well, even though the problem seems to persist, ask for a referral. (For help in obtaining a referral, see American Academy of Child and Adolescent Psychiatry, Zero to Three, and other organizations listed in *Useful Addresses and Web Sites* at the end of this book.)

Assessing Development

Earlier chapters of this book give you a general idea of what to expect at each age. There are various maps of development used to evaluate a child's progress. In the area of general development, one of the first of these was developed by Arnold Gesell and later elaborated upon by others, such as Nancy Bayley, who developed the Bayley Scales of Infant and Toddler Development for the first few years of life. The Denver Developmental Assessment (now revised to include emotional development) is a useful guide for providers and parents.

These and other screening and diagnostic tests have been designed to evaluate a child's development. The knowledge we have recently gained about ways the immature nervous system repairs itself makes it clear that intervention should be started as early as possible if there are signs of delay. Children can recover from many problems of motor, cognitive, or emotional development, or at least make great gains. The earlier these are identified and appropriate ways to support and compensate are found, the better the outcome. It is therefore very important to seek help when you are worried.

Often it is hard for parents to recognize the signs of delay in a child. They may also wish they'd disappear. When they turn to a physician who says, "Don't worry, he'll outgrow it," this isn't necessarily true, and valuable time may be lost. The sooner help for developmental delays is instituted, the better. Without help, anxious parents may either hover or push the child to "catch up." If the child tries to catch up but fails, a sense of despair and hopelessness may then compound the underlying problems. Some of the symptoms that deserve evaluation are described in the following paragraphs.

Hypersensitivity in Small for Gestational Age (SGA) Babies

Some infants are long and skinny at birth. The placentas that nurtured them are small and inadequate, often for completely unaccountable reasons. Many of these babies are hypersensitive to stimulation and easily overloaded, though this difficulty can frequently be diminished by adapting their environment and handling to present them with stimulation levels they can tolerate. These babies are called "small for date" or "small for gestational age" (SGA). They are also said to have experienced "intrauterine growth retardation."

At Children's Hospital in Boston, we have studied many such babies. Although malnutrition, accidents, alcohol, tobacco, drugs, and infections can interfere with placental function in a similar way, the mothers we studied had not suffered from any of these. The infants had nevertheless not stored adequate fat before delivery. Their skin was dry and peeling, their hair was sparse, and their faces were tired, old-looking, and worried. Every stimulus made them startle. Their ability to shut out repeated stimuli was significantly reduced. (See the discussion of habituation in chapter 2.) They could not sleep deeply or pay prolonged attention to interesting stimuli because they were so distractible in either state. They literally shot from an alert or a sleep state into an unreachable crying state, as if crying were the only way they could control their environments. This rapid change in state allowed their parents no time to reach them with touch, voice, or visual stimuli. This, in turn, created anxiety in the parents, whose reaction was to increase their efforts—even more exhausting for them, and perhaps more overstimulating for the infants.

In our research, we looked for ways to interrupt the vicious cycle of hyperreactivity and overanxious parental efforts. When we handled these babies very gently, we were able to help them organize. We learned that we must reduce stimulation to reach them. If we played with them or fed them in a darkened, quiet room, they became available. In a noisy, distracting environment, they averted their gaze and refused to accept any of our attention. If attention was offered during a feeding, they spit up the feeding. They were extremely fussy infants in the three- to twelve-week period. Unreachable, crying for long periods, they seemed to be using crying as a defense against overstimulation.

When the crying periods ended, these babies remained highly sensitive and distractible. At five and again at nine months, they were still at the mercy of every sight and sound. Activity began to replace crying as a way of discharging the pent-up inner turmoil that resulted from too much stimulation. I have long suspected that this might be the origin of hyperactivity for some subgroup of children with ADHD.

An understanding of the underlying hypersensitivity helps parents and caregivers working with hyper-reactive children. By using one low-key stimulus at a time and slowing down at the first frown, or when the baby's quick reaction or state changes, you can gradually calm such a baby and communicate with him. You can pick up such a baby slowly and gently and hold him cuddled until he finally relaxes. Only then can you look down at his face. He may stiffen again, but he'll finally relax. Then, you can croon slowly to him. Again, he may stiffen before relaxing. Finally, you can rock and sing and look at him. At this point, he has "learned" to organize several stimuli at once. Because of their concern, parents usually overdo each attempt to reach these sensitive babies. As a result, both the baby and the parents develop a sense of failure. After we demonstrate the necessity of introducing one stimulus at a time, many parents are able to change their approach. Feeding and other important activities, such as diapering, playing, rocking, and getting the baby to bed, are best done in a protected, quiet, distraction-free environment. Handled carefully, each slowed-down activity gives the baby an opportunity to learn how to manage his raw nervous system.

The challenge for parents is to overcome their natural overconcern, which is compounded by the guilt they feel about "why" their baby is so sensitive. We usually don't have answers. But we do know that, over time, many of these hypersensitive infants can learn to manage better and better, *if* their environment can be understanding and protective. The ultimate goal is a child who expects to succeed and is determined to do so in spite of his difficulties. (See also "Delays in Emotional and Social Development" section below.)

Delays in Motor Development

Either limp or hypertonic (tight or overactive) muscles are of concern in an infant. If a baby doesn't use a limb, or can't lift his head or parts of his body off the bed, I would worry. Do certain muscles seem relentlessly tight? A baby who has tense muscles, but who is able to relax from time to time, is not likely to have a neurological problem. But if the tight muscles interfere with his ability to try out and learn new tasks, he should be checked. For example, a baby who keeps his fingers clenched in a fist, with his thumb stuck awkwardly through them, needs to be evaluated. Does he overshoot as he reaches for objects? Does he have a jerky, uncertain approach as he reaches or attempts to stand? Does this jerkiness and uncertainty increase at times when he's under stress or has a fever? This may indicate a neurological impairment that he can overcome under optimal circumstances but can't manage when stress is added to his nervous system. A child with an imbalance between flexor and extensor muscles will need help in learning motor skills. These are signs that a parent can pick up. Ask your doctor or nurse practitioner to check them. Among the problems not immediately identifiable that can cause motor delays are mild cerebral palsy and other neurological or neuromuscular disorders.

If a pediatrician feels that motor delays exist, he or she will refer the parents to a neurologist, who may recommend therapy. Some of the most effective therapies capture the child's ability to perform and his own motivation, reinforcing his desire to reproduce and improve the desired movements. Effective techniques do not press a child to perform beyond his level of skill. Discouragement or a sense of failure can defeat the process. For this reason, it is critical that professionals help parents to understand this important aspect of any early intervention, so that they and the child can enter into the recovery process. (See "Hypersensitivity and Hyperactivity.")

Delays in Cognitive Development

As we saw in Part 1, cognitive development also follows a fairly predictable map. An awareness of object permanence and of the effects of gravity, for example, shows that the child's mental capacities are growing. A baby's expectations for certain kinds of reactions from important individuals around him are signs that he remembers his experiences and can apply them to new ones. For example, as early as the age of two months, a baby is likely to have different expectations for a father and mother. He probably expects a playful interaction with his father, and a nurturing one from his mother. His own differentiated reactions toward his parents show this expectancy. By five months, his searching inspection of a strange place and his startle to a strange voice tell you of his well-defined expectancies. In the next few months, an understanding of causality begins to appear.

By about fifteen months of age, a baby has learned to think symbolically. When he sees a toy telephone, he holds it to his ear as if it were a real one. But if he still bangs it on the floor, puts it in his mouth, and plays with it in other ways that suggest that he doesn't seem to understand what a toy is used for (what a symbol stands for), then this may be a sign of a cognitive delay often present in children with autism spectrum disorders (such as autism, Asperger's syndrome, or pervasive developmental disorder). It may also indicate that the child will be delayed in learning to speak, since words are symbols and cannot be used effectively until a child understands that symbols stand for something else.

When the appearance of these expectations and abilities is delayed, this may indicate a delay in the baby's comprehension due to an interference in processing information, such as a learning deficit or some other form of disorganization of his nervous system. It could also be due to inadequate experience—with toys or with persons. In a nurturing environment, and in the absence of prematurity or other such conditions, it would be difficult to account for more than a two-month delay in the appearance of any of these expectations and abilities.

It is very important to recognize that a motor delay or disability is not necessarily accompanied by a cognitive delay. For example, even a baby missing limbs or with severe cerebral palsy, without the ability to act on his environment, will still develop a sense of object permanence and causality. When I tested an eight-month-old baby who had two frail arms and stumps for legs, she would look to the ground for a dropped toy. When I used a windup toy to test her sense of causality, she watched it, fascinated. Her head followed its progress across the table. When it stopped, she looked up at me and grunted as if to say, "Make it go." She moved her head and neck forward, looking me in the eye. Her mother said, "That's what she does when she knows what to do but can't do it herself." She had learned about causality strictly from visual observation.

In contrast, a baby of the same age who was in the hospital for failure to thrive (refusing food and failing to gain weight) due to environmental deprivation could not respond to either test. She had no experience with toys she could learn from; nor did she expect to be able to "make one go." With increased nurturing attention in the hospital, she began to take an interest in toys as well as people. Within a ten-day period, she had become teachable. She learned about object permanence in one day. A few days later, she understood the concept of a windup toy. She looked at me first to see whether she could trust me. Then, she handed me the toy to "make it go."

The causes of cognitive delay are too numerous to describe here. They include Down syndrome and other causes of mental retardation, such as fetal alcohol syndrome. Various learning disorders may also first show up in subtle cognitive delays. If parents and pediatrician agree that there is delay, or if parental concern persists, referral should be made to a neurologist, a child psychiatrist, or a child psychologist, depending on the nature of the problem.

Sensory disabilities undiagnosed at birth, such as vision or hearing problems, of course, can also delay cognitive development. Early detection is critical, and early intervention can then help the child compensate. While some simple hearing and vision tests can be done in the pediatrician's office, more subtle problems can be diagnosed only by an ophthalmologist, an audiologist, or an otolaryngologist (see "Speech, Language, and Hearing Problems").

Delays in Emotional and Social Development

A number of conditions can interfere with a baby's emotional development and interpersonal skills. Prematurity or prenatal stress can produce a vulnerable newborn. Hypersensitivity to auditory, visual, tactile, kinesthetic, and oral stimuli can lead an infant to shut out these experiences and, as a result, interfere with the development of attachment to his parents. Such a baby may avert his gaze when a parent attempts to communicate. He may shudder or stiffen when cuddled. When he is picked up to be held, he may either resist or slide through a parent's arms like a sack of meal. If a baby spits up feedings, pushes them away, or has difficulty swallowing, the caregiver will feel rejected and may take it personally. A sense of failure and even anger in a caring adult will discourage warm nurturing and play. Without help, such a relationship can get locked into place and add to any problems of development in the baby.

Some delays are caused by conditions during pregnancy, at birth, or in early infancy. For example, maternal undernutrition, tobacco, drugs, medication given to the mother during childbirth, lack of oxygen, intrauterine deprivation, or intrauterine growth retardation can make a newborn hard to reach. Whatever the cause, these newborns may be at risk for emotional and social delays and may also have motor troubles. For instance, they may be limp and unresponsive when they are fed. They may suck poorly, choke, and tend to spit up. If they respond to social cues, it may be in a very subtle manner. They may not bring their hands to their mouths. When pulled to sit, their heads may lag. No responses are generated that can satisfy an eager, concerned parent. If the reasons for this behavior are not explained, parents can be frightened, fearing permanent damage. It is important for a doctor or nurse to step in to help early and to explain that, over time, most of these babies will improve as their nutrition improves, the medication wears off, and their nervous system has the opportunity to recover. If this does not occur in the first weeks, a neurologist should be consulted. If neurological damage is ruled out, a specialist in behavioral pediatrics or infant psychiatry can be of help.

In assessing a baby who has had a difficult start, we look for certain things from the first that are evidence of an intact nervous system. In addition to assessments of motor development, a newborn's ability to follow a face moving from side to side, or to turn toward the source of a sound, such as a rattle or human voice, should also be carefully examined. Interpersonal skills should continue to develop in the early months. In the first few weeks, babies should learn to pay attention to social cues and to begin to prolong that attention. Smiles and other facial expressions, vocalizations, and body movements toward the caregiver are not only signals of the baby's capacity to interact appropriately, but also needed to fuel the parent-infant interaction. A baby in this age group who does not alert to his mother's voice or who does not show bodily excitement to his father's appearance should be evaluated. Gaze averting, frowning, and a turning away from social cues can be due to a hypersensitive nervous system. They can also be due to an environment that either overloads the baby or reacts inappropriately to him, interfering with the growth of communication.

If a baby seems indifferent to both toys and familiar people, if his emotions seem flat, this is cause for concern. If he also begins to develop repetitive habits—head rocking, eyes floating up in his head, body rocking, hair twirling—or often puts his hands up over his face or ears, this is reason for evaluation. A nonsmiling, nonrelating infant who responds with repetitive, meaningless behavior and with a glazed, flat look in response to social cues could be showing signs of neurological damage or an autism spectrum disorder (see "Autism Spectrum Disorders," below).

In a child of about eight to sixteen months, delayed interest in and play with toys, or delayed interest in people, is a reason to worry. If a child has a flat, apathetic reaction when a toy is offered or a repetitive, meaningless approach to the toy, and little interest when he loses it, his emotional development may be impaired. In this age group, signs of depression or of turning inward—for example, repetitive, meaningless motor behaviors, such as flapping his arms, no differentiation between parents and strangers, a lack of resistance or negativism—are indicators of problems for which parents must seek an evaluation.

A careful evaluation of a baby's behavior and interviews with parents by an interviewer who is sensitive to their fears and concerns can help determine what may be causing the delays. During such an evaluation, parents can be helped to fit their responses to the capacities of the baby.

Autism Spectrum Disorders

The signs we have just been describing—flat emotional tone, repetitive movements, and lack of interest in people—could be symptoms of *autism.* Important hallmarks of these disorders are difficulty making relationships and communicating. A child with autism has difficulty understanding the meaning of facial expressions that other children readily decipher by about nine months. At a year and a half or two, he still can't see that toys can be used to represent real things and will not know how to use them in play as other children his age do. At age two and a half or three, when other children can begin to understand that other people have feelings and thoughts, a child with autism will appear unable to relate to others with this kind of awareness of their emotions.

In addition, an autistic child may avoid physical and social contact, may have difficulty forming attachments, and is likely to be delayed in language development, especially the social conventions of language, as well as in nonverbal communication skills. He may also be hypersensitive to sensory stimuli—sight, sound, touch. Certain sights or sounds may make such a child frantic, while others may not even be noticed. He may engage in repetitive behaviors—swinging or twirling, for example—that offer him the sensory input he seems to crave.

Diagnosis of autism spectrum disorders is not always easy. Yet parents of children later diagnosed with an autism spectrum disorder often say that from the very beginning they knew something was wrong: The baby looked away when they tried to look into his eyes, stiffened and arched his back when they tried to cuddle him, and seemed uninterested or overwhelmed when they tried to engage him in these early communications.

A sensory impairment in hearing (or vision) needs to be ruled out first. A pediatrician trained in developmental disorders, a child psychiatrist, or a pediatric neurologist should evaluate the child. Occupational therapists, speech pathologists, audiologists, and other specialists are also often needed for diagnosis and treatment. The possibility that environmental toxins may be affecting the child's behavior and development also needs to be considered by the child's pediatrician and treatment team. The causes of autism are not yet understood, although important advances have been made. As there are several different schools of treatment, we recommend that parents investigate the references provided in the *Further Reading* and *Useful Addresses and Web Sites* sections at the end of the book. Early identification and treatment are extremely important.

Later Developmental Issues of Concern

Children who develop normally in the motor, cognitive, and emotional areas in the early months can experience emotional troubles at a later time that may then delay their development. In the second and third years, I would worry about a child who is "too good." One who does not develop the expected negativism and tantrums may be burying his drive toward autonomy. A child who stays alone or who cowers in the face of other toddlers may be demonstrating a sense of isolation and passivity that needs attention. If other children shun him, that can be a particularly significant sign. A child with underlying emotional problems may sit in a chair in front of television sucking his thumb, twirling his hair, or fingering his nose or face. He may withdraw from any demanding situation, such as interacting with grandparents, strangers, and other children. He may show poor muscle tone and poor color, and he may eat poorly. A troubled child may have a flat and unresponsive spirit, indifferent to the excitements of his world.

At the other end of the spectrum, toddlers who show extreme emotions, who blow hot and cold, out of proportion to the situation, can also be of concern. If they move from crying to laughing to looking vacant, or if they treat toys and people essentially the same way, they need help. A troubled child may wind up quickly and not respond to gentle, caring ministrations. He seems out of contact with people around him. Giggling, hysterical laughter, weeping, or crying reactions may lead to temper tantrums, alternating with periods of depressed behavior not related to the stimuli that set them off.

If a child seems stuck in such behavior, parents may be frightened and not know where to turn. Friends or a psychologically unsophisticated medical professional may say, "Don't worry. He'll outgrow it." But if these symptoms persist, parents should trust their own judgment and seek a referral to a child psychiatrist. With a proper evaluation, underlying emotional and developmental problems often can be understood, and therapy can be started before the problems become more severe.

18. Depression

All children are sad now and then and go through periods of feeling "depressed." At such times, they need extra comfort and love. If their feelings are due to the usual, inevitable disappointments of childhood, the sadness will be short-lived. But certain signs should alert parents to the need for help.

Identifying Depression

Crying is an active, healthy response to being sad or needy. I am reassured to see a sad child cry. A more seriously depressed child will show several of the following symptoms instead.

Withdrawal—The child is unavailable to others, including parents, siblings, and peers.
A dull, slowed-down look—The child's eyes do not light up, her facial behavior is reduced, and body movements are sparse.
Loss of energy—The child is uncharacteristically tired and inert.
Feelings of hopelessness, worthlessness, and guilt—The child takes little initiative and makes little attempt to express her feelings.

Joylessness—The child no longer seems to enjoy her usual sources of fun.

Changes in eating, sleeping, even bowel or bladder habits—All of these can be affected and disrupted.

Headaches or stomachaches—These may appear before any new event, such as going to school, to a playground, or to a party.

Depressing effect on others—People feel sad around the child. She won't let anyone get close. Often, she's prickly and irritable, easily angered about the least little things.

Change in habits—The child is dirty, her clothes don't match, and her hair is unkempt.

Unless these symptoms are temporary (less than two weeks in duration) and can be understood as reactions to a known disappointment as a depressing event in the child's life, they should be a cause for concern.

As they try to decide whether certain of these symptoms mean serious depression, parents can ask themselves various questions. First, when does the sadness occur? If it occurs only after criticism or unhappy events, it can be seen as appropriate. If it seems to occur without cause and for no particular reason, or is present all the time, I would worry. The child may be saying that her feelings need to be listened to more carefully. When sadness invades what should be joyful experiences, too, then parents should be concerned.

Next, is there a good reason for this sadness—for example, the loss of a dog or a favorite toy, a parent's absence, a new sibling, or the loss of a friend at school? Have there been events—at school, with neighbors, or at home—that could account for feelings of sadness? Perhaps there are several events that have added to each other. A piling up of troubling experiences can set off a depression. But if these events can be identified, and the child's spirits lift as she is encouraged to express the feelings, then she may not truly be depressed. But watch carefully to see if her relief lasts. A normally buoyant, outgoing child can have periods of sadness. Unless these last for at least two weeks, they are likely to represent the normal ups and downs that none of us can be fully protected from.

If, however, the period of sadness or withdrawal is out of proportion to the event and seems to become entrenched, parents should be concerned. Two weeks is a reasonable time to watch and wait. A child who is already quiet, shy, or withdrawn, and who becomes more acutely so, should be taken more seriously. A child with learning disabilities or attentional disorders already has serious reason to be sad and withdrawn and is at greater risk for depression. Her self-image has already been battered. Any new signs of distress should be paid serious attention. A family history of depression lends further weight to these concerns.

Responding to Sadness and Depression

While trying to evaluate the symptoms and deciding whether to seek outside help, parents can respond in certain important ways.

- Take the child seriously. Joking her out of it or trying to make light of her feelings won't work, and it devalues her feelings. Often, if you can recognize and acknowledge a child's sadness without trying to "snap her out of it," you can help her understand it as well.
- Encourage low-key activities that the child enjoys and is bound to succeed at. Do not pressure her, however. Help her self-esteem by recognizing small triumphs and showing that you admire her competence.
- Make clear to the child that you understand she is feeling sad.
- Do not press her to unload deep-seated reasons for her sadness unless they are ones you can handle. If you sense deeper feelings, but feel fearful, you need outside help.
- Help the child feel protected and cared for. Tell her, "I understand how you feel, and we can and will help you. We're here and we love you."

Sadness and depression are a cry for help. While feelings of loss, loneliness, inadequacy, inexpressible anger, and sadness are normal and occur in all children, a parent needs to evaluate whether they are transient ones that the child can handle, or the child feels overwhelmed. If they persist, or if they threaten an already fragile child's tenuous adjustment, the child should be seen by a therapist. Both she and her parents will feel relieved to find someone who can understand her sadness and protect her from the fears and guilt that are compounded by a sense of helplessness. Doctors or nurse practitioners can refer parents to a child psychiatrist or psychologist specializing in therapy with children. Referrals can also be obtained from clinics associated with regional medical centers and medical schools.

When a child's depression is seriously interfering with her usual activities, such as taking care of herself, getting along with family and friends, and learning at school, of if she is depressed enough to be thinking about harming herself, a child psychiatrist may recommend an antidepressant medica-

tion. This step should not be taken lightly. Parents may want to seek a second opinion and refer to the resources listed in *Further Reading* and *Useful Addresses and Web Sites.* Antidepressants may be helpful, but they can have serious side effects, including withdrawal symptoms when they are stopped. Many are not approved by the U.S. Food and Drug Administration for use in children but are nonetheless commonly prescribed for them. In serious cases, a child's suffering and the long-term risks to her mental health may justify the risks, but since no one yet knows how these drugs affect brain development during childhood, they should not be used without careful deliberation. (See Wilens in *Further Reading* and *Useful Addresses and Web Sites* for information about medication.)

19. Discipline

Next to love, discipline is a parent's second most important gift to a child. Yet, while loving a child can seem so simple, disciplining one raises difficult questions. At what age should discipline start? What is "too lenient"? "Too strict"? Does discipline require punishment? These are common concerns, in my experience. While most parents realize how critical it is to set limits, doing it in a consistent, effective way is one of the most difficult jobs for parents. We all want "well-behaved" children but worry about curbing a child's spirit or overwhelming him with too many limits.

Discipline is not the same as punishment. Discipline means "teaching," and the goal is to teach the child self-discipline—over time. It is a long-term goal, and each episode is an opportunity to say, "I must stop you every time until you can stop yourself." Appropriate limits and punishment matched to the child's age and transgression are a means to discipline, not discipline itself.

In recent decades, it seems to me that parents have become even more conflicted about discipline. Yet discipline may be even more important in today's troubled world. When both parents are away at work all day, they hate to be disciplinarians in their precious time at home. But children will save their provocative behavior all day to try it out in a safe, loving environment. Their need to learn limits is just as important when both parents have been away all day as when a parent has been at home.

Some parents are conflicted because they remember having been disciplined too severely themselves. They don't want to repeat painful memories, but they often feel that they have no other model to draw on as they learn to discipline their own children. If they have experienced abuse in their own childhood, they fear the loss of control that led their parents to abuse them. These parents may need help to face their "ghosts" consciously, so that they can avoid repeating their own experience and also meet the child's need for discipline.

Promoting Self-Discipline

Discipline, as we said, means "teaching." To help the child accept the lesson, after disciplining a child (for example, with a temporary withdrawal of a privilege), a parent should sit down with him and assure him: "I love you, but I can't let you do this. Someday you'll learn to stop yourself, and then I won't need to stop you."

Children sense that they need limits and will go to great lengths to compel their parents to set them. At some point toward the end of the second year, the child will make this need known by blatant testing. Whether it is touching forbidden television buttons, dumping food on the floor, or biting, the child will begin exploring what is and is not allowed, with a heady sense of excitement and fear as he ventures forth. Once he is mobile, the outer edge of danger is always at hand.

Without limits, children in the second year begin to act "spoiled." They become anxious, straining to provoke limits from their parents, knowing they can't set them for themselves. From watching such driven children, I have learned the importance of establishing limits, firmly and understandingly. Consistent discipline, saved for important matters, actually helps a child feel secure. It helps the child with his job of learning about himself, about his need for discipline, and eventually, about how to control himself.

Learning limits, one goal of discipline, comes in three stages: (1) trying out the limits by exploration, (2) teasing to evoke from others a clear sense of what is okay and what isn't, and (3) internalizing these previously unknown boundaries. For example, when one of our children began to crawl, the stove, of course, became a desirable destination. Each time she made a beeline for it, we reacted in a dramatic, and to her, satisfactory manner. Knowing already that we'd react, she would look around to be sure we were watching before

she'd reach forward to touch it. If we weren't paying attention, she'd either move away, or she'd make a noise to catch our attention. Until we said the expected "Don't touch," she was in a state of turmoil. If we were tentative at all, she'd begin to reach for the stove to get a reaction from us. If we reacted violently, as we did if we were weary at the end of a long day, she'd dissolve in tears. But, as she sobbed, her eyes scanned our faces, and we could imagine that we saw a kind of relief in those eyes. After a few months, toddling rather than crawling, she'd charge up to the same stove, stop in front of it, say "no" loudly to herself, and teeter away to other exciting ventures. She'd incorporated our limits for herself. In retrospect, we could see that any uncertainty on our part left her uncertain. When we were clear, as we were about serious things, such as the hot stove, she knew it and accepted our limits for her own.

Most issues are not as clear as this, though. Most of the time, children seem to tease about things that really don't matter much to their parents. Parents are caught in indecision: "Is this one worth it? If we ignore this one, will he go on to another? Should I be firm now so that he'll pay attention to me when it's really important?" Because a child senses any indecision, he tends to repeat his behavior or even to accelerate it. In this way you can spend all day saying no to a toddler, and he will spend all day provoking you.

As I tell parents, if you save your discipline for the important issues—for things that really matter—you will be able to be decisive and firm; the child will know it, and your discipline will be effective. Discipline works when you mean it wholeheartedly and when your child senses that it is important for him to respect your decision.

Discipline and Stages of Development

At each stage of development, there are some kinds of behavior that seem too aggressive and out of control, but that are actually predictable events in a child's development. Though the child must be made to understand that these are unacceptable and that limits must be set, if parents or teachers overreact to them in these exploratory phases, they may end up reinforcing them. Children must try out all sorts of aggressive behavior. At certain ages, they bite, pinch, lie, steal, or use unacceptable language. These "probes" may not have bad intentions attached to them when they first show up. When people react vehemently, a child will wonder why. So he'll test the behavior again, as if he needed to see why he got such a reaction the first time. As he tries it out over and over, his anxiety may build up and an unconscious compulsion may get built into it. The behavior that was unimportant at first becomes driven and charged with excitement. Over time, the child no longer has control. The behavior calls up so much anger around him that the cycle for repetition is set. The child and parent get into a rut. To avoid or defuse this situation, there are useful ways of reacting when the exploratory behavior first appears. The following are examples of normal "misbehavior" and ways to teach limits without reinforcing the problem.

Four to Five Months Biting the nipple during breast-feeding is common in a baby this age whose teeth have just emerged and must be tried out. A mother can make clear that she doesn't like it by first inserting her finger into the corner of the baby's mouth to break the seal so that she won't be hurt again, and then pulling the baby away from the nipple. Every time the baby bites you, pull him firmly away in this way, but without too much overreaction. Let the baby bite on your finger instead. Don't expect your baby to understand at first. Fortunately, he'll learn through repetition.

Eight to Ten Months Babies will pull on your hair, scratch you in the eye, or poke you in the face, all without intent to hurt. They are fascinated by hair, eyes, and faces. A parent's reaction adds to the excitement. Let the child know firmly and unexcitedly that it hurts. Let him know you like the exploration, but not the hurting part. If he continues, hold his hands firmly each time until he learns to stop himself. Say, "I don't like it, and I'll hold your hand until you learn not to pull or scratch or poke too hard." Show him that you mean it with your facial expressions, since by this age he now is highly skilled at deciphering your nonverbal behavior. He'll begin to understand if your facial expression and tone match what you say. If necessary, put him down until he's not so excited, then pick him up again to love him and explain your actions.

Twelve to Fourteen Months When your baby walks or runs away from you, looking back to be sure you're coming, he is testing the limits. If there is danger, let him know you can't let him go. If he runs away from you on the street or in a store—when your arms are full of groceries—react firmly: "You cannot do this ever again." Of course he will, but he needs to know where you stand.

Sixteen to Twenty-Four Months Now the child may try out hitting, hair pulling, or scratching other children. He is trying to learn about other children and how to get their attention. Often this is an overreaction to the stress of not knowing the other children or how to handle his own eager desire to get to know them. It usually occurs in a new or a heightened situation. If you or the other parent overreacts, which is easy to do—most new parents are horrified—this will frighten both children. The one who is hurt needs to be comforted, of course, and he may also need to learn to stand up for himself. The hitter will need to be comforted too, for he will be frightened both by his act and by the hurt child's reaction. Pick him up to comfort him and explain that it hurts and the other child didn't like it. Soothe him until he's in control, and then try to give him other ways to approach the child. He will need more experience with other children. It is also important to let him know you will take him out of such a situation if he can't control himself. The less adult involvement, however, the better. If this behavior continues, find another feisty child his own age and size. Put the two of them together and let them learn from each other. Each one may hit. The other child may hit back. Both children will look astonished that it hurt, and they'll think before they try it again.

Eighteen to Thirty Months Temper tantrums and violently negative behavior begin to appear at this age. A natural, important surge of independence comes in the second and third years. The child is trying to separate from you to learn to make his own decisions. Often he is caught in his own indecision at times when it really doesn't matter, *except to him.*

It's not possible to avoid tantrums, so don't try. *Don't* get down on the floor to have one with your child. *Don't* try to shock or distract him out of them. The more involved you are, the longer they will last. It's often wisest simply to make sure he can't hurt himself, then walk out of the room. Soon after you leave, the tantrum or violent behavior is likely to subside. In a while, go back to him, pick him up to contain and love him, and sit down in a rocking chair to soothe him. You want him to know that you care, that you understand, and that tantrums are not something to be ashamed of or punished for. When he's able to listen, try to let him know that you can see how hard it is to be two or three and to be unable to make up one's own mind. But let him know that he *will* learn how and that, meanwhile, it's okay.

Three to Six Years Some children this age will throw or smash things in a fit of anger. At the end of the day, or at some other time when he tends to fall apart, he may lose control. The joy of such an aggressive act is now coupled with the anxiety that occurs at this age when a child realizes what he has done.

First, let him know that he can't do this—that you won't let him if you

can help him in time. Hold him tightly so that his emotions subside and he regains control. Sit down with him in your lap until he's ready to hear you. Then, discuss why you think he needed to do it, why he can't do it, and how badly you know he feels about this kind of destructive, out-of-control behavior. Ask him to let you know what could stop him. If his suggestion works, give him lots of credit. This begins to restore a sense of control to him. You're asking him to begin to realize that he can take control of himself. If he has no ideas of his own, you might need to make a few suggestions—for example, going to his room to cool down, scribbling an angry picture, or pounding some clay on his desk.

Finding Appropriate Discipline

When disciplining a child, thoughtful parents will wonder, "Will I dampen his spirit if I'm too rigid or too punitive?" Loving parents don't want a passive child. If you ask parents whether they want to have an aggressive child or not, most will answer, "No, not aggressive, but I want him to stand up for himself, too." The job, then, is not to stamp out the child's aggressive impulses, but to help him learn to channel them into acceptable behavior.

When parents ask how they can know if they are being too strict, I suggest that they watch for the following:

- A child who is too good or too quiet, or who doesn't dare express negative feelings
- A child who is too sensitive to even mild criticism
- A child who doesn't test you in age-appropriate ways
- A child without a sense of humor or joy in life
- A child who is irritable or anxious most of the time
- A child who shows symptoms of pressure in other areas—feeding, sleeping, or toileting—and who may regress to an earlier kind of behavior, acting like a baby or a much smaller child
- An aggressive child, one who may be modeling his behavior on yours, and who takes out his anger at being too strictly punished on his siblings, peers, or even pets

Any of these symptoms is a signal to parents to let up and confine discipline to important matters.

When asked for specific positive discipline guidelines, I give parents the following advice.

Respect a child's stage of development. In particular, be aware of the kinds of learning he is exploring at each stage.

Fit the discipline to the child's stage of development. For an infant or toddler, try at first to divert him to another activity. If this doesn't work —and it won't very often—you may need to remove him bodily. For a child over two, discipline should always include an explanation (but not an excuse) for his reasons for "acting out"; try to figure out what triggered the child's aggressive behavior and give him a chance to understand it himself.

Discipline must fit the child's temperament. Make use of what you know about your child's temperament and sensitivities. A sensitive child will be devastated by punishment that may be appropriate to an active, wound-up child.

When your child is with other children, try not to hover. Avoid protecting or punishing him in their presence. When you involve yourself in their struggle, you change it from a simple interchange between children to a complicated one, in which at least half of your child's behavior is aimed at you.

Model behaviors for the child. Help him learn controls or ways to deal with a situation by giving him examples. Often the way you help him settle a conflict is more instructive than many, many words. A direct, firm, but loving approach can be the best kind of modeling.

Hold him firmly and seriously so he cannot repeat his action.

Use a time-out, but for a brief period only. After it's over, hug him and explain why it was necessary.

Ask the child's advice about what might help next time. Then try it. If it works, give him credit.

Physical punishment gives the wrong message. Remember what it means to a child to see you lose control and act physically aggressive. It means you believe in using physical aggression to solve problems. Not only is this not respectful, but it only works when he's little.

Watch out for mixed messages. As you say "Don't hit" or "Don't do that," if you are secretly not sure, it may just add to the child's lack of self-control.

Stop and reevaluate whenever discipline doesn't work. Are you reacting too constantly, too ineffectively? Is the child acting out to tell you that he is anxious or out of control, or that he needs more affection?

Pick the child up to love him afterward. This is hard to do, but critical. As you rock him and hold him, tell him that you're sorry that it's so *hard* to learn self-control. He must know that you care for him and respect him in this struggle to learn about himself. "I love you, but I can't let you behave this way. When you learn to stop yourself, I won't have to stop you anymore."

After the discipline is over, help him explain what it's all about. At the time, your own tension will just add to his. But after the episode is over, if you or he can come to understand it, his face will brighten and you'll recognize that you've made a breakthrough in his understanding of himself and of his aggressive feelings.

Remember to reinforce the child when he isn't teasing you. "Look at you. You really are trying to control yourself, aren't you? I'm so proud of you." Every bad time deserves a good one. (See also *Discipline—The Brazelton Way* in *Further Reading.*)

20. Divorce

When parents reach an impasse, they should think about what effect the divorce will have on the children and how they propose to handle this. But they'll also need to face the effects that staying in the marriage will have on their ability to parent and on their children's development. Often, parents will ask me, "Isn't it better for the child if we split than if we stay together and fight?" Not knowing the whole situation, I cannot answer that. An objective family therapist can help if consulted before a break. Split families are not easy for children. Remarried (blended) families are not easy—for children or for adults. But "intact" families in which parents are miserable or at war may be no better, and sometimes are even worse. Adults whose marriages seem to be failing have a major obligation to protect their children as much as they can, whether this means trying to work things out or deciding to divorce. This is a lot to ask of parents who are already overwhelmed with their own feelings. In the aftermath of divorce, it is very hard for parents who may not only be angry, but also frightened, anxious, and grieving the loss of their relationship, to focus on the needs of their children. But there is no other choice.

In the first years after a divorce, a child blames himself for his parents' breakup and dreams of having his two parents to himself again, even though the original family may have been stressed and stressful. While earlier studies of children of divorced parents by psychiatrist Judith Wallerstein showed that children could still be longing for the reconstitution of the original family for as long as fourteen or fifteen years afterward, drawing much-needed attention to the plight of these children, more recent findings are less uniformly dismal.

Psychologist Mavis Hetherington's longitudinal studies of divorce found that by six years after the divorce, 75 percent of children had overcome the strains and sadness of the first years and were functioning normally (see *References*). The remaining 25 percent had major problems that are found in only 10 percent of children in intact families. Dr. Hetherington concluded that divorce is a high-risk situation but does not necessarily always turn out badly for the children. She emphasized that divorce itself may not be more harmful to the development of young children and to parents' ability to raise their children than the fighting that goes on in a bad marriage. While everyone in the family suffers during a divorce, and during the first year or so that follows, the long-term effects of divorce vary depending on a wide range of protective and risk factors, including how parents handle the divorce and how well they recover from its immediate effects to become effective parents again. Over time, it turns out, many other individual characteristics of the child and parents, as well as life events, play a bigger role than a past divorce in a child's well-being and healthy development. As a result, there is no need to label the children of divorce with a self-fulfilling prophecy or to burden their parents with more guilt and anxiety than they may already feel. Instead it may be far more useful for parents to understand the protective factors that they can foster in their children, and what they can do as parents to minimize the factors that put their children at risk.

Parental Responsibility

The most serious harm to children is done by placing them in the middle of parents' animosity—using them as a football. Angry parents all too readily take out their feelings on each other by using the child. That is sure to hurt the child. Her capacity to make solid relationships with other adults in the future is likely to be impaired by this insensitivity on the part of divorcing parents. It seems to me that treating a child this way can make it more likely that divorce will be passed on from one generation to the next. A child who is embroiled in her own parents' strife may grow up expecting marriage to be full of conflict. The job of each divorcing parent is to work against this.

At first, children may continue to wish for the "old family." They will feel deserted by the nonresident parent and will fear desertion by the resident parent, reasoning, "If one can leave me, why won't the other?" Short-term separations become magnified in the child's mind. Every time a parent leaves, the child must wonder, "Will she be gone for good? Will she remember to come back? Who will take care of me?" Or she may wonder, "Why does he leave me? Am I bad, and no one will want me?" Before every separation, parents must prepare a child as carefully as possible. After they return, they must say, "I missed you. Did you miss me? Remember I told you I'd be back at (such and such a time), and here I am. You worry, don't you?" Then, the parent needs to be ready for the child's feelings about being deserted. Every time the child has a chance to air them, the adult has a chance to demonstrate that desertion is not in the nature of all relationships.

The nonresident parent has a parallel responsibility. Visitation should be clear, dependable, and on time. Even a fifteen-minute wait is an eternity for a small child. Visits from the absent parent offer reassurance about what he fears most—desertion. If you are the nonresident parent and must be late, call the child. When you arrive, say how sorry you are to be late. Speak to the child before you speak to your ex-spouse.

A child will fear that the reason the absent parent has gone is because he or she doesn't love her, because she's been "bad." A child takes everything personally. No matter how often she is told that a separation or a divorce is not her fault, she will continue to blame herself. Later, children dare to put their fears into words: "I knew if I'd been a better kid, they'd never have split up." "The timing of their divorce is my fault. I went away to school and left them." "They decided to get a divorce when they caught me smoking." Small children are less able to express it, but they also feel responsible for the split. Both parents must be ready to reiterate over and over and over: "We love you and we never wanted to leave you. We grown-ups couldn't live together, but we both want to be with you. Nothing you do could ever change that for us."

A divorced parent must remember that demonstrating any animosity to the ex-spouse in the child's presence will frighten her. She will take it personally. "If Dad and Mom can fight with each other, they can hate me, too. I must be a perfect child, or I'll be in for it." Any mistake or any deviation in her behavior raises the fear for her that she might be expendable. Parents can help reassure a child that she needn't try to be perfect. She may need constant reassurance about this, for she is likely to regress with the trauma of the divorce. Most children regress in the area of the last achievement. If she has just become dry at night, she may begin to wet all over again. If she has been talk-

ing well before, she may begin to stutter. Her behavior may be either too good or too provocative. A sensitive parent will accept this and discuss it with the child so that she, too, understands it as normal and expectable. The usual limits should apply, however, and are more important than ever. Limits reassure the child that someone is still in control.

Helping the Child to Adjust

After a painful separation, sleep problems are likely to surface. The child may well wish to sleep with the resident parent. The lonely parent is likely to "need" the child. If you're in this situation, think carefully about whether co-sleeping is in the child's best interest, or a comfort you need. A child needs to know that parents will be able to get themselves through this crisis, and that she needn't sacrifice her independence to attend to parents' needs. Parents need to work out their own issues. A child who must fill the needs of a deserted, lonely parent can be hampered in her ability to develop her own identity. The relationships with a parent of the opposite sex can become too intense without the protective presence of the third member of the triangle. A child who lives with one parent is likely to have more difficulty in sorting out her important need to identify with each parent. She can feel the closeness as dangerous in a way that she might not have felt when both parents were present. Also, it may become harder and harder to separate at night as the child gets older. All of this needs to be taken into account before a decision is made about sharing a bed.

Not only are behavior problems likely during a divorce, but the child's physical immunity is likely to reflect his inner tensions. Colds, otitis media, and other illnesses are likely to surface at such a time, adding stress to an already stressed family. They will pass eventually as the family adjusts.

The presence of a sibling can lessen the fear of separation. Sibling relationships can become closer than they were before. Although rivalry will still surface, taking it too seriously can make relationships in the split-up family seem more fragile than they really are. If a child understands that the rivalry is normal, and that everyone is under stress from the divorce, the tension can be lessened. Parents must stay out of the siblings' rivalry and allow them to work it out. It is all too easy for the older sibling to be pushed into the role of the absent parent. This is too much to ask. It is not a time for putting such a burden on a child. She will want to live up to such a role and is likely to push herself. She may well try to play a protective role for the younger children, but this isn't fair. She needs time to heal and recover. She may need to regress, to be nurtured herself.

Grandparents, aunts, uncles, and cousins can become important supports for children during and after a divorce. Not only can they give a child help in understanding the split-up, but they fill her need for reliable, caring people who remain constant in her life. According to Dr. Hetherington's study, involved grandfathers, in particular, can have a protective influence on their grandsons' academic and vocational success by helping them preserve their self-confidence. The grandparents and other extended family members on the absent parent's side remain important, but the positive effects that grandparents can have depend on how much time they are able to regularly spend with the child and on their ability to support the child's parent without intensifying conflicts. Resident parents need to reconcile their own feelings about their in-laws in order to respect the child's need for family.

During a divorce, grandparents are likely to "spoil" the children in the family. They may let down all discipline. The resident parent may feel threatened by the lack of rules at Grandma's. The child will use this: "Grandma gives me what I want. You're mean and you don't realize what I'm going through." For parents in this situation, I point out some common problems and offer the following advice. Since you are feeling pretty raw and deprived yourself, this criticism hits below the belt. You bristle. If these are your in-laws, you will feel even angrier at this undermining of your household rules. If you can, discuss this with your in-laws. Ask them to back you up in your effort to support the child with firm rules and discipline. If relations are too tense for such discussions, simply tell the child, "Grandma does things her way at her house, we do them our way here." Children learn early on to distinguish and accept such differences—unless they are pushed to choose one household's ways over the other's. Nevertheless, discipline becomes even more critical—and even more difficult to carry out—when families break up. Lack of discipline leaves the child in limbo—she must find her own limits at a time when she feels that her house is tumbling down. Respectful discipline ("I'm sorry, but this is *still* the way it is here") becomes a source of security.

If you begin dating, be careful about introducing new people of the opposite sex to your children. Wait until you are pretty sure the child can rely on the relationship. A child of divorce will make new relationships with adults of the same gender as the missing parent all too easily, and she will be deeply disappointed if it doesn't work. When you do form a lasting relationship, point out that "friends" and stepparents are different from parents, but having two of each can be great. Talk about the child's fears of your desertion of her. Tell her that you aren't going to leave her under *any* circumstance.

Find books about divorced families, or introduce your child to other children whose parents have gone through a divorce These days, children of divorce are not a small minority, but it still helps a child going through one to know other children who are adjusting to divorce.

Finally, try not to overprotect the child. Let her make her own adjustment, and from time to time, point out how well she is doing. When a child can master the stress and change, she can take pride in this demonstration of her competence. Your continued love, respect, and discipline can be shown without hovering.

Joint Custody

Judges in divorce cases often do not have enough time or information to decide whether one parent is more appropriate than the other for the major role in the child's custody. In an attempt to be fair to the parents, a judge may divide up the child's week. I have witnessed this too often. It is very difficult for most children of any age to move from one household to another on a half-weekly basis. This deprives them of any permanent territory of their own. I remember a four-year-old who spent half the week with each parent. She stood at the door of her room, guarding it like a watchdog. She had been my friend, and we cared about each other. Because she trusted me, I felt she was secure in saying to me, "You can't come in here. No one can. It's *my* room." I recognized that territory was at a real premium for this child, who was forced to share two households. Parents who intend to share custody should consider moving in and out of the house themselves, leaving the children in their own stable territory. I know this is usually impractical, but at least considering what it might mean gives parents an insight into the disruption a child feels.

While such an arrangement may be too difficult to carry out, at least be sure the child's room in each house is never changed without her permission. If she has to share it, be sure she has her own territory within it. A sign on the door, such as "Michelle's Room," can help. If the child moves back and forth, special toys can go with her. You and your ex-spouse may have to watch to see that these are not left behind.

Share the same routines and rules in each household as much as possible. If some of these are different, don't criticize the other parent's way of doing things. Instead, simply say, "These are the rules in this house." Although two parents can't really treat a child alike, shared expectations help her to sort herself out. Keep siblings together in whatever routine is planned. They need each other. An occasional time alone with a parent, however, is also a comfort. The schedule should be regular and clearly spelled out. A calendar marked with red and green for days in each house can help a child plan her week.

Save negotiation and arguments with the ex-spouse for times when the child is not present. Every switch between households is a wrench for the child. Allow for temporary regressions right after each switch. Talk about them, but don't let up on rules and discipline.

Try not to get angry when the child identifies with the other parent. When she compares you negatively to the other parent, try not to get defensive, but hold your line. When she criticizes the other parent, don't let yourself be drawn in. No matter how angry you may be, when you flare up, you are undermining the child's need for each of you. She also needs the other parent and your acceptance of this need. If the absent parent is indeed absent and unreliable, you can listen to the child's disappointment and sympathize with it without expressing your own: "You miss him so much. You were looking forward to seeing him. It's really hard for you when you don't get to see him." Over time, the child will need to face and accept each parent's limitations, but parents' criticisms of each other won't help.

Stepfamilies

Blending families is not easy. No stepparent should expect their stepchildren to accept them easily or to be grateful to them. They are much more likely to feel that a stepparent is an invader who is taking the resident parent away from them. The needier the child is, the more she will resent the new parent. The Cinderella story of the wicked stepparent is based on long experience. But these conflicts can be aired and dealt with. Crises around discipline, sleep, feeding, and virtually all developmental areas are likely to arise. A smart stepparent will step back to leave it to the resident parent to decide when and where to act.

When it comes to a showdown, stepchildren will make it clear that they do not have to obey, and do not intend to obey, a stepparent. Parent and stepparent must plan a unanimous front before showdowns arise. At one time or another, a stepparent is bound to feel that the spouse, the natural parent, does not offer backing. If the stepparent feels that the natural parent is overprotecting his or her own children, this will make discipline even harder. For all these reasons, couples often notice that they get along better in the few moments they have without the children around. This time alone is very important.

Mark Rosen, in his book *Stepfathering* (see *Further Reading*), offers some excellent guidelines for stepparents, some of which I have adapted in the following list.

- Inborn temperament, which produces individual differences even in small babies (as we saw in Part 1), means that contrasts between step and biological children are not all the result of differences in parenting.
- Every adult reacts differently to every child. The differences between step and biological children are only one source of this difference.
- The behavior of stepchildren continues to evolve, especially after you are married and they are more secure. Often, they store up resentment and it comes out later, after they feel more secure with the stepparent.
- The feelings between you and your spouse will directly influence your relationship with your stepchildren. If your partner doesn't support you and disagrees about your role in his or her children's lives, the chance of a good relationship with them is diminished significantly.
- The other biological parent will always be a presence in the life of a stepfamily. The better the relationship between the ex-spouses, the less stress on the child.
- Expect times of transition—such as visitation with the other parent—to

be difficult. Talk them out beforehand and afterward. Other changes, such as the birth of a new baby, will require even more preparation and patience.

Children who have been loved and supported throughout a divorce and who have been encouraged to make their own adjustments to a newly composed family may develop special strengths. Divorced families have no monopoly on stress and crises. All children need to develop the sense of security, the flexibility, and the independence required in a world full of rapid, constant change.

21. Fears

Fears serve a purpose. They often reflect underlying struggles, and they can raise a child's (or parent's) awareness of those struggles. Fearfulness also leads to stress reactions—with an increase in blood pressure, heart rate, and breathing. This "alarm reaction" may well be what alerts parents to the child's feelings. Parents may also learn more about their child's reaction to particular stresses when fear comes to the surface.

All children go through periods of fear. Fears are usually normal and can accompany common developmental issues. Fears generate support from parents at a time when children need it.

Universal Fears

When do fears usually first appear in a child? Certain fears seem to be built in as reflexes. Fear of falling is seen in new babies in the form of a complicated clasping motion called the Moro reflex, as described in chapter 2. When the baby is uncovered or startled, or when he is quickly lowered, his arms shoot out sideways and then come together as if to clutch anything or anyone close by. A monkey baby uses this reflex to help him cling to his mother as he is carried around. The startled cry that goes with this reflex attracts a parent's attention. Thus, even at birth, a baby is equipped to seek help with his instinctive fear of falling or being unsupported.

Since childhood is beset with predictable periods of fearfulness, it is helpful for parents to understand these fears. Being afraid produces a surge of adrenaline that can lead to rapid learning about how to control the fear. But if the child is overwhelmed by his fearful reaction, this constructive learning will not occur. Parents cannot eradicate a child's fears, but they can help him to take them less seriously and learn from them.

If parents get caught up in a child's fears, they may intensify them without meaning to. This is likely when fears in a child call up unresolved fears in his parents. All parents recognize the scariness of witches, ghosts, or monsters. When a child first awakens screaming, with his tale of the "monster in my room," his parents remember their own childhood fears of monsters. If they overdo the comfort they give him, he senses their anxiety and it adds to his. On the following nights, the "monster" begins to take a more and more realistic shape. As the child's description becomes more vivid, he captures his parents' imagination and they, too, may become increasingly mired in his

fear. By their overreaction, they lend the fear credibility and delay the child's learning to handle the fear for himself. If parents can see that they are overreacting and can recognize that the fears are part of a learning process, they are in a better position to help the child.

Fears inevitably crop up at periods of new and rapid development. As a child grows, his new independence and abilities throw him off balance. Fears reflect this and at the same time call up the energy needed to readjust. As a child learns to handle his new abilities, the fears will subside. Afterward, he proudly senses that he has overcome them. Children say, "I used to be afraid of that. I'm not anymore." When a child has held himself together after mastering a painful shot in my office, I always say to him: "Look what you did! It hurt and you cried out. But then you got yourself together, and you're not crying anymore. You've grown up!" He looks up at me with a real pride in having done it and says, "I'm not even afraid of shots anymore!" He may well be whistling in the dark until the next time, but he feels proud of his achievement. We all do—his parents and I—and he deserves our recognition.

Fears are more pronounced and frequent in some children than in others. The psychologist Jerome Kagan and others have shown that shyness and timidity about new situations are likely to be inborn. In such cases, shy and sensitive parents can have shy and sensitive children. Parents who see these tendencies in their children can avoid compounding them with their own fears. By supporting the child and showing him how they themselves have coped with new and frightening situations, they can do a lot to enhance that child's inner resources.

Stranger Anxiety

Fear of strangers is one of the first clearly recognizable signs of fear in infancy, though it is not always present in infants who have been raised in extended families or by multiple caregivers. The ability to distinguish the differences between strangers and parents is recognizable in a baby's behavior as early as eight weeks of age, as mentioned in earlier chapters. We have filmed small babies from one to six months of age as they reacted with playful adults. Even at one month, we can see differences in the behavior and the attitudes of babies toward their mother, their father, and strangers. They already know their parents' faces, voices, and attitudes and demonstrate this awareness with clear differences in their own responses. The stranger anxiety that surfaces as early as five months, more dramatically at eight months, and again at a year old is not a sudden awareness of the difference between strangers and their parents, but the culmination of a process that has been developing throughout this period. It shows an increase in awareness of the actions of others, and of their own inability to fully predict what will happen with someone new. As we saw in chapter 6, a five- or six-month-old baby must keep his mother directly in sight if he is not to fall apart screaming in the doctor's office. He is watching and listening to the people and objects in his environment with a new level of involvement. A doting grandparent or babysitter of a baby this age would be wise not to rush up to grab him or to look directly in his face without an initial period of "getting acquainted." A wise mother or father will stay well in view in any strange situation at this age.

The spurt in stranger awareness somewhere around the age of eight months can be more all-consuming. The baby will disintegrate unexpectedly in strange places or even when a stranger passing by looks him in the face. Even if he's safe in his mother's arms, he sees this as an invasion. He is becoming more aware of new places and people. This is not a time to leave him with strangers without the chance to learn about them first on his own terms. A parent must hold him close at first, until he's ready to be on his own. After this period of about a month is over, he will still be sensitive to new experiences, but he will have learned how to handle them. Children who are already in some form of child care may have learned to handle certain strangers and strange situations and may be less likely to experience stranger anxiety. But this won't protect them from separation anxiety—the fear of being left by a parent. At some point, these infants may become increasingly upset when their parents leave. They are becoming aware that they can register protest and get something done about it. Also, their new awareness that parents exist even when out of sight (person permanence) may make them struggle more with their absence. As a result, at such times they may need extra preparation and comforting when being left in a childcare situation.

At twelve months, this same awareness of the importance of a baby's "own" familiars and of how he can now crawl or walk away and "leave" them makes his dependency crop up again. Through the second year, as a toddler learns about the new, widening world that has opened up with learning to walk, he will both value and fear his new independence. At the time he's learning to run away from his parents, his dependence on them will be heightened. In my office, he may cling to his parents, noticing what a strange and frightening place it is. When I move up to examine him, he must be seated in a parent's lap. I look just past him, never into his face. With my stethoscope, I listen to a beloved doll or teddy, then to a parent's chest. As we saw in chapter 9, the process can take some time. But the benefit is that in the second year, a child can develop a trust that will last him a lifetime. With children this age, adults who understand and help them overcome their fears of overwhelming new experiences are helping to prepare them to cope with fears that are likely to arise later. Two- and three-year-olds need to learn how to handle themselves in peer groups, for example. Of course, they will be fearful as they walk into a new group of noisy children. I suggest the following steps. First, expect your child to cling to your skirt or trousers. Prepare him ahead of time for what and whom he will meet. Tell him honestly whether you'll stay with him. Tell him how long he can cling to you and how you'll help him get used to the new situation.

If you are taking him to play with other children his own age, let him cling to you until he can begin to identify with one of them. Then he'll slowly sidle up, if that one seems accepting. Try to get him into play with at least one other child before you pull away. After he's made it, get out as soon as you can and leave it to him. If he gets into a battle, stay out of it and let the two children handle it. He'll learn more about himself if he's on his own than if you continue to advise or protect him. Toddlers are ready to learn from each other about handling themselves. Small peer groups help children learn how to handle overwhelming situations—one step at a time. A regular play group of no more than two or three children can be a great help to a child who is shy and fearful. Plunging him too soon into a large group of rowdy and aggressive children may only compound his shyness.

Types of Fears in the Young Child

Between the ages of two and six years, children are more likely to experience and express their fears. As a child learns about his own aggressive feelings, he will become fearful of them—and of aggression in other people and situations. As he learns about his burgeoning feelings of independence and self-assertion, he will need fears to help him master them. His own aggressive feelings start surging to the surface at these ages. They carry with them behavior that the child has worked so hard to control. But now he is more aware of the results of his aggressive behavior—and this knowledge is frightening to a small child who is torn between facing how small he truly is and how badly he wants to be big and powerful. This conflict between his aggressive feelings and his ability to control them may well call up new fears of things in his life: dogs, noises, darkness, heights, and so on.

Fear of Dogs and Other Animals That Bite Two- to six-year-olds may become afraid of anything that they think might bite. (Perhaps this fear of biting animals harkens back to his own biting.) Just as an unknown dog or animal might "bite," so might a new child or an unusual person. For example, a two-year-old riding the streetcar with her mother saw some nuns dressed in long black habits. She'd never seen a nun before. She looked at her mother inquiringly and asked, "Bite baby?"

Fear of Loud Noises Fire engines, ambulances, and doors slamming suddenly call up violent, frightening reactions in a child. He may be reminded of his own sudden loss of control and feel somehow implicated when these sounds are repeated. For the same reason, aggression on television, or even in older children, raises the specter of his own powerfully aggressive feelings. He is frightened by seeing it in others.

Fear of the Dark—of Monsters, Witches, and Ghosts Fears always surface at night. Dreamed-of predators become fearful images projected into the darkness. These occur at a time when the child is going through rapid growth toward independence. As we mentioned, the child is becoming aware of and conflicted by his dependence on his parents. Ghosts, witches, and monsters are adults who retaliate against these longings, pushing the child to fend for himself.

Fear of Heights Fear of jumping off of furniture or out of windows (the Peter Pan fantasies of flying) can arise at this age and linger on. These fears come when a child becomes more aware of the danger of falling from heights and realizes that he must protect himself and control his urges to rush headlong into exciting but dangerous places.

Fear of a Parent's Death Fears about a parent's death contribute to separation anxiety and school refusal, in some children, or to fears of leaving home to go to parties or on a visit. Avoidance of such situations may also, of course, be due to shyness and the natural fear of being overwhelmed by new situations in which a child needs a parent to protect him. But, in a child of around age five or older, it can be due to fears of a parent's death even if his parents are healthy and he's experienced no other losses. This fear could arise from the child's awareness of how much he needs his parents, or from his desire to become independent and grown-up, for example. It could also be due to fear of retaliation for his "bad" wishes. Although these feelings are too deep-seated to bring to a child's awareness, realizing that they are normal ones may help his parents. They may then avoid overreacting to his sudden fear of death—either for himself or for one of them. This is a time when parents can assure a child that they are there to protect him and that they will neither allow him to be endangered nor disappear themselves.

When death comes to someone in the family or to a beloved pet, parents should respect the child's feelings and the fear that will arise. These are times for parents to discuss how they handle their own fears (see "Loss and Grief").

Fear of Strangers and of Being Molested The potential dangers of strangers are on parents' minds so much today that the problem may be as much to protect a child from undue fear as it is to prevent the child from being molested or abducted. A small child should not be put in the position of having to decide whom to trust. It is the parents' job to protect small children as best they can.

While parents must start to teach a five- or six-year-old how to protect himself from strangers, it's all too easy to overdo it. I worry that this generation of children will never dare to make relationships with new people if we frighten them too successfully about strangers. Children this young should not be placed in potentially dangerous situations. When giving the child advice about not letting anyone he does not know touch his body, a parent must carefully balance this with the danger of making him overly sensitive about his body. He certainly needs to be wary of strangers at school or on playgrounds who make him uncomfortable, but that needs to be balanced with a sense that there are people whom he can love and trust wholeheartedly. Perhaps a child's best protection from being overly burdened is the knowledge that he can communicate *any* fears or worries immediately to his parents (or seek help from teachers, when at school), knowing that they will listen and respond.

A child who fears molestation may either be one who has been overwhelmed by efforts of well-meaning adults to teach him to protect himself, or one who is trying to signal that he's already been molested. This is not a typical fear in young children and deserves the attention of a mental health professional with expertise in this area.

Fears of Aggressive Children As a child gets older, peer relationships become increasingly important and complex. The child needs to learn to relate to others from the second year on if he is not to be a lonely, isolated child in school. As mentioned earlier, I suggest the following approaches: Try to let your child learn how to make it into a group through one or two children. If he is shy, let him take his time. Find him a child who is like him, and help them become friends. Then help your child learn a special skill or develop a special interest or talent. If he can perfect himself in a sport or in music or in any area, other children will respect him. When he comes home decimated by having been teased, let him know that you can see how upset he is and that teasing is wrong. Then, you can remind him that everyone, unfortunately, needs to learn to survive being teased. When a child can stand up to the teasing, it's not likely to recur too often. Children also tease others whom they like, but in a playful way. Everyone gets teased.

Fear of Failure All children are afraid of failure. It's a natural state for all of us. This fear can drive us on to success and toward perfection. But it also can be destructive. If a child seems to be overwhelmed by fears of failure, perhaps he needs more basic self-confidence. Let him know you appreciate him the way he is. Perhaps he needs less pressure to perform and more acceptance of who he is. He may need chances to succeed in small ways. I would suggest low-key experiences with children with whom he can compete and learning experiences he can easily and successfully master. If this can be done without increasing pressures on him, encourage his particular talents and skills so that he can "hold his own" in his group. Commend him for small successes, but don't push him to perfection. If he sees himself as successful and as special to his parents, he will begin to gain the necessary self-confidence—slowly and step by step.

Fears of War, Terrorist Attacks, and Disasters—Natural and Manmade Children sense their parents' fears and feelings of helplessness about our increasingly dangerous world. Inevitably, they will have some exposure to images on television and magazine covers of terrorism, military retaliation, torture, and the increasingly frequent natural disasters resulting from unchecked global warming. Small children have no sense of perspective in which to put these fears. The fear of annihilation that we all harbor fits into fears of their own new aggressive feelings and of the retaliation that they fear they deserve. So, they worry and are likely to blame themselves. When adults around them are worried, too, their fantasies get out of control. As adults, we must give small children a sense that others are working to set limits on the world's aggression. As parents we need to convey hopefulness for our society as well as a deep-seated responsibility toward others and toward the earth. Children need to feel safe and to know that adults are involved in counteracting the violence around us as well as the deterioration of our environment.

Ways to Help a Child Deal with Fear

The following advice applies not only to parents but also to all other caring adults who want to help a child handle his fears. First, listen carefully and respect whatever the child tells you about his fear. Help him see that it is natural to be afraid and worry about things. Then, reassure him that what now seems scary and overwhelming can be handled and that as he gets older, he will learn to overcome his fear. Certainly look under the bed or in the closet

for witches and monsters with the child, but don't get too agitated. Let him know you both know they aren't there, but that every child worries about them. You can be accepting of his feelings without conveying that they are real.

Support the child as he struggles to find ways to handle these fears. Let him regress. Let him be dependent, and let him cuddle his "lovey" and be a baby at such a time. He won't want to be a baby for long. Even as you hold him, you'll feel him try to squirm away. Then you can reinforce him for his bravery and for being so "grown up."

Help the child understand the reasons behind his fears—such as the fact that he's trying to learn about new and rather scary situations and feelings. Talk about how he's trying to venture out, to stand up for himself, and to get away from you, and how all this is scary. Use his own terms. Don't get too intellectual or beyond him. It won't help him if you are talking about abstract concepts that he cannot grasp.

Reassure the child that all children have fears at his age. Suggest that he ask his friends how they handle their fears (though they may not admit that they have any). Talk about your own fears at his age, how you learned to overcome them, and the trivial fears you may still struggle with. "I always used to feel funny before going to a party. Even now I stand at the door until I see someone I know or have met and then go talk to them. You'll learn how to do that, too."

Meanwhile, take the child out alone with you each week to do things together. This will open up the possibility of his confiding in you but, even more important, it will give him a chance to identify with you. If he's learning about aggression, he can learn how to be safely aggressive—in the ways that you are. You may not even need to talk about these ways; he can see them for himself.

When he finally conquers his fears, point this out to him so he can learn from his success. Commenting on his achievement will not only take it out of the realm of fear and put it in the realm of conquest, but mark a pattern for him and for you. You can refer back to it when other, new fears or challenges arise.

If a child's fears, or fearfulness in general, begin to invade his lifestyle, if the fears last over a long period (roughly six months or more), or if they affect his capacity to make friends, I would seek professional advice. These fears may be the child's way of crying out to you for help. Ask your doctor or nurse for help in finding a therapist. A clinic connected with the nearest large teaching hospital can give you a referral to a child psychiatrist or psychologist.

22. Feeding Problems

FROM THE VERY MOMENT THAT A MOTHER FIRST CLASPS A NEWBORN TO her breast, she instinctively knows that the loving messages that go with feeding are as important as the food itself to her baby's well-being. She is right. Without these messages, food won't be enough to foster a child's emotional, or even physical, growth. Food is critical to survival, but a baby's ability to use it to grow and thrive also depends on the nurturing communications that parents offer along with a feeding.

The Feeding Experience

While all parents would like their babies to enjoy feeding, parents are likely to bring their own childhood experiences to this critical interaction. Parents' reactions to a feeding challenge are not consciously thought out, but based on old patterns. They may be shocked to hear themselves repeat what they were once told: "You'll sit right there until you eat your vegetables. You'll never grow up unless you eat them." Parents face their own "ghosts" when they run into a feeding problem with their child. They need to recognize that their worries about a child's diet are part of wanting to be a good parent. If they can remember their own experiences with feeding, they are less likely to perpetuate them.

Pushing a child to eat is a sure way to create a problem. For feeding to be a pleasure for a child, by the end of the first year *she* must be given more control—of choices, of refusals, and of when to stop eating. (A parent, though, must be in control of what choices are offered, what is served, and when.)

By its very nature, feeding is an arena in which parents and baby work out the continuing struggle between dependence (being fed) and independence (feeding oneself). No other area of development is as likely to be caught up in this struggle. Independence must win, though, as a family learns to enjoy meals together, it is interdependence that truly triumphs. The way feeding is handled can even influence whether a child grows up with a decent image of herself as a competent, complete person. Her need to express herself in eating becomes every bit as critical to her development as the number of calories she consumes. But this can be hard for a caring parent to see. Ideally, parents should see their job as that of making each feeding a deeply satisfying experience, so that as she grows older, the child can learn that feeding herself reproduces that same pleasure.

The question of whether to breast-feed can be viewed in this light. Breast-feeding can be a close, warm, intimate experience for mother and baby. Since breast milk, as we said in chapter 1, is also adapted to the human infant—nutritionally, digestively, and as a natural protection against infections—every mother should consider it as the first choice. However, if, for whatever reasons, breast-feeding does not feel right to the mother, or if it becomes an unpleasant experience for her or the baby, this should be taken seriously. Her feelings are conveyed to the baby and will affect whether they get off to a good start. A baby held closely and lovingly while bottle-fed (*never* with the bottle propped) will do very well indeed.

Feeding Patterns and Stages of Development

At first, the baby needs to set the schedule (demand feeding). When you, her parents, are still learning to understand her cries, it's better to follow her demands and to learn *gradually* which cries mean she's hungry and which ones mean that she's bored or tired. In the beginning and at later times of crisis, it's always good to fall back on demand feeding. However, once you have a feeling for her needs, it is possible to begin to push her toward a predictable schedule. Everyone in the family will be relieved to count on set times for feeding, sleeping, and playing. By six weeks of age, a full-term baby should be getting more predictable, and feedings should be at roughly three- to four-hour intervals. By twelve weeks, she should be down to five or six feedings a day at predictable times. At twenty weeks, most babies need only four or five feedings, at 7:00 A.M., 11:00 A.M., 3:00 P.M., 7:00 P.M., and 11:00 P.M. or at 7:00 A.M., noon, 5:00 P.M., and 10:00 P.M.; by six or seven months, feedings (milk plus solids) can be given at 7:00 A.M., noon, and 5:00 P.M., plus milk at 7:00 P.M., then, down for the night! If a baby needs help stretching out the feedings, see suggested schedule in chapter 7.

From a nutritional standpoint, babies don't need solid food until six months of age, though breast-fed babies need Vitamin D supplements by two months of age and may also need iron supplements by four or five months. (Both should be present in fortified formulas.) They don't actually learn to swallow solids until after three months. Before that time, they may suck them down, but they don't swallow actively. Many parents are eager to introduce solids in the hope that they will help their babies sleep through the night or stretch out from one feeding to another during the day. They aren't likely to do that. Also, solids introduced too early are more likely to set off allergies than if they are introduced later.

By eight months, a baby will be ready to use her new and exciting pincer grasp—thumb and forefinger. If you give her two or three soft bits of table food when you sit her down—to finger, to pick up, to smear, and finally to put into her mouth—you'll find she is absolutely enthralled. She will work to master these few bits for as much as an hour at a time, so rewarded is she by this sense of mastery over feeding herself. She will even let you feed her mushy foods while she works to master her newfound achievement. In fact, if you don't let her start feeding herself by the end of the first year, you are likely to create a feeding problem in the second year. At a year, she will be shaking her head, clamping her mouth shut, and throwing food at you—telling you in no uncertain terms, "I want to do it all by myself."

By a year, the baby should be competent with finger foods. Soft table bits that she can gum up will go down easily. If they're too lumpy or tough, she could choke on them, so be sure they're sufficiently soft. Sometime after a year of age, she will begin to refuse certain foods—vegetables one month, meat another, eggs another. Once again, she is showing you she needs to feel in control, to be able to decide what she wants to eat. If you can let her *choose and refuse* throughout the second year, you are not likely to have a feeding problem. But it means *you cannot be in control.* She must feed herself. She won't master a fork or spoon for several more months, so she needs to be free to choose from bits of finger food. Feed her what you eat, unless it's not safe for her to swallow. If she doesn't want it and teases you for something else, just say, "Next meal you can have it," and don't push what she doesn't want.

A toddler's meals are full of refusals, of negativism, of teasing to find out the limits. In the feeding area, *of course* she'll always want what you haven't got ready. Don't let it get to you—the kind of food isn't important; it's the game that matters. It will be easier, though, if you set firm limits. You can just say, "This is what we have at this meal. If you want cheese, I'll give it to you at the next meal." She won't want it when you give it to her anyway.

We create unnecessary problems because we feel our responsibility so strongly. *Of course* we are likely to overreact to the responsibility of getting our children fed. A "good mother's" job, we have always believed, is to get food into her baby. But parents find it much easier to relax about these erratic meals if they realize how simple a child's nutritional needs are at this age (see chapter 9). With adequate vitamin supplements, no single vegetable is absolutely indispensable to a young child's health—especially if the cost of such struggles is refusal of other foods too. While vegetables do contain important nutrients, many of these can be supplied by daily vitamins. If such struggles can be avoided, the child's dislike of vegetables is likely to be fairly brief. Picky eaters may need a few years for their taste buds to mature enough to like them, but in the meantime, battles over broccoli will only make vegetables taste worse. Many babies don't like vegetables in the second year. Don't worry if your child doesn't eat a "rounded diet" of green and yellow vegetables. I have seen very few toddlers who will—and I've seen thousands who won't. They have thrived in spite of a diet of *no vegetables* for a year or so. Toddlers who are not forced to eat them may well want to try them at meals when they see the rest of the family eating them!

By four or five, *if* you haven't made food an exciting battleground, a child will begin to try new foods and to approach the famous "well-rounded diet." As for manners, forget them until the child is three or four years old. Before then, she'll begin to learn them from modeling on you, though she won't yet be able to show you what she's learned. She won't learn them by being told "Do this. Do that." However, I'd set firm limits on how much food she can throw or smear around. When a toddler is particularly negative, I'd give her only two bits at a time. When she begins to rub them into the table or to throw them around, stop the feeding. Put her down until the next meal. Also, don't let her graze between meals and daily morning and afternoon snacks if you want her to learn about limits.

Parents who pride themselves on their cooking—and those who have postponed childbearing into their thirties or later—often find it harder when their tasty efforts are rejected. If you can realize, first, that you are taking it as a personal injury and that's why you overreact, the situation can be defused. Unless your child is missing the very few essential foods described in chapter 9, tell her she'll have to wait for another meal. Make clear that she can always refuse what you are offering, but she can't just pick and choose what she wants to have substituted.

Feeding and Independence

Some small children will appear to go on binges—they'll eat nothing but hamburger for two weeks, for instance. This won't hurt a well-nourished child. But going on binges may represent other issues—being negative, being like her friends, or testing you to see whether she can manipulate the family at mealtimes. All of these are familiar, normal reasons for such fads. Don't cater to these binges. Don't jump to make up a substitute. If you do, she'll decide she wants something else from you. If the family is eating something else, say, "That's it. You don't have to eat it, but I'm not making a meal specially for you."

Binges, pickiness, refusals of certain foods, and many other variations in feeding can be entirely normal phases in a child's development. A young child needs to establish independence about feeding. She needs to find her identity in the family, to make her own choices, and to test out the limits of your tolerance. Meals will be a lot more enjoyable if you can recognize and respect this. If you can't, and if (like so many of us) you are a parent who gets anxious about how little your child has eaten, you can expect fireworks at mealtime. Your clever inducements, tasty alternatives, bribes, and diversions may get the meals eaten for awhile. The trouble is, they won't work in the long run and you'll have unnecessary feeding problems. Feeding herself is a precious and exciting activity for a child, and it must be an area for autonomy. Otherwise, feeding will become a battleground, and *the child will win*—one way or another.

However, if your child consistently refuses even the necessary dietary requirements I've outlined over a period of months, this may be a time to seek help. If she is not gaining weight or is falling below the standard weight chart, it certainly is time to seek outside advice from your pediatrician—and from medical specialists, if necessary. Since many physical disorders will affect feeding, the doctor will first want to rule this out. If there is no medical problem, a child psychiatrist or psychologist can evaluate her and help each of you with your role in feeding issues. Don't despair and don't wait too long.

Preventing Obesity

In the United States, children as young as age four or five are more likely than ever to be overweight (over the 85th percentile of the weight-for-length curve) or obese (over the 95th percentile of the curve), putting them at risk for adult obesity, diabetes, high blood pressure, and other serious health problems. They are also more likely to have overweight or obese children, as genetics is one contributing factor. Other factors include poverty, race, and gender: Poor children, African American, Native American, Latino children living in the United States, and girls all appear to be at greater risk.

Parents can help their children avoid obesity right from the first. In the first weeks and months, as parents learn to distinguish their baby's different cries, they can help her begin to distinguish hunger from other kinds of distress. They will recognize the many hunger cues that come before crying—increased hand-to-mouth activity, head bobbing, rooting, and lip smacking, for example—and the cues that go with having had enough—such as gradual slowing of sucking and relaxed muscle tone. As they learn to respect their baby's hunger and satiety cues, so will she.

For older children, there are many more opportunities to encourage healthy eating and activity patterns. Here are a few simple rules:

- No grazing. Three square meals (and maybe a morning and afternoon snack)—and that's it.
- No television at meal times, no eating while watching television, and no television in children's rooms—ever. The total number of hours per day of TV is a strong predictor for obesity, and a TV in a child's bedroom is an additional risk factor.
- Keep junk foods (high-fat, high-sugar foods like fries, chips, soda, candy, donuts, and so on) out of your home. Once your child becomes addicted to their intense tastes, healthy foods are likely to lose out. Don't make an issue of it though, as this will only make junk food more desirable.
- Your child needs physical activity every day. Walk or bike together instead of driving whenever you can. When you can't get out of the house, you can put on some music and dance together. Keep exercise fun, low-key, and without pressure to perform.
- Make mealtimes a fun, relaxed time for being together as a family.

(See also *Feeding—The Brazelton Way* in *Further Reading*.)

23. Habits

As they grow, children explore a wide variety of behaviors. A number of repetitive actions, such as head banging, thumb or finger sucking, and rocking are tried out as ways to ease tension or as self-comforting maneuvers. If these are not fixed as patterns, either by parental attention or because the child has an excessive need for self-comforting behavior, the child will abandon them and try out other behaviors. In this way, a child explores a whole range of habit patterns. A habit can become fixed when too much is made of one particular pattern of behavior, or when a child is not able to explore a range of self-comforting habits to find ones that are more acceptable and more adaptive.

The importance to a child of self-comforting measures, such as sucking a thumb or clutching a beloved doll or blanket, was made clear in Part 1. These are the child's safety valves in a stressful world and should not be seen as problems. Other habits can begin as normal exploration but can become problems if parents overreact or the child is under too much stress. Masturbation and nail biting are examples falling into this category. Tics, though involuntary, may also intensify under stress.

Masturbation

All infants begin to explore themselves by the second year whenever their diapers are removed. A boy can produce an erection by manipulating himself. He looks amazed, then pleased with himself, experiencing a new sensation. A girl inserts her fingers into her vagina, her eyes looking glazed, her body rocking, as she finds out that this part of her body has special feelings. Since this part of the body has been covered up by diapers throughout the first two years, the toddler can become fascinated with the new sensations. He may hide in a corner to explore himself. When he senses parental disapproval, his desire to find out more about this exciting experience is heightened.

Even when parents can tolerate this behavior in the child in private, they worry about whether it will become all-consuming and appear in public. Since such normal behavior was often shrouded in shame and mystery in parents' own childhoods, they find it hard not to worry.

I remember some solemn-faced parents who consulted me in a state of deep concern. Their fifteen-month-old girl would lie down on the floor to rock, using a pillow or her fingers to stimulate herself. Her faraway look and the flush that came over her face as she rocked frightened her parents. They thought she was having a seizure. When I observed her "spells," I realized that they were a kind of masturbation activity. But given their intensity and frequency, the possibility of child abuse had to be considered.

This little girl lived in a busy, exciting household. There were three older children and two grandparents. All of them played with her constantly, teasing her and pressing her to respond. As a balance to this, she retreated into her own world, using masturbatory activity as a technique for withdrawal. I told them that it wasn't necessarily abnormal, but I suggested that they reduce the excitement around her and that they put her in her room alone twice a day for break periods. "Won't she just masturbate in her room?" the parents asked. I replied that she might, but that she needed the opportunity to calm herself in some way and to get out from under all the pressure. The parents of course also wondered what to do when the child began rocking like this in public. I suggested that they see this as a sign that she needed to withdraw from too much stimulation. They should pick her up, hug her, and take her off into a quiet atmosphere. The parents tried these measures, and the symptom "disappeared" within a week.

When parents worry about a child masturbating, the first advice I offer is: Don't emphasize the behavior. Don't show disapproval or try to inhibit it. If it is frequent, look for underlying reasons. Is the child very tense? Is he overstimulated? Has he other ways of self-comforting?

If your child is tense, comfort him by holding him quietly and rocking and soothing him but not while he is masturbating. If the child masturbates in public, take him away from these overwhelming environments. Put him in his room or another quiet place. Don't worry about what he does in his room; in fact, point out that masturbating in private is really okay.

Find out if others around the child are paying too much attention to this habit. Other children or adults in the house may be overreacting and telling the child that it's taboo. Instead of helping him, this serves to fix masturbation as a pattern.

Only if the masturbation is excessive and if the child withdraws from participating in interesting activities would I worry, particularly if he uses such a pattern a great deal. Is it a constant pattern for handling stress and overload? For example, maybe the child should be evaluated for hypersensitivity or some form of autism. Have you had his urine tested for a urinary tract infection? Does a girl have vaginitis? Both girls and boys may have a physical reason for excessive masturbation. Another possibility, especially if excessive masturbation is accompanied by imitation of adult sex acts, is that the child has been exposed to such adult activities or has been sexually abused. If you are worried about any of these possibilities, talk them over with your pediatrician, who can help you sort through these concerns and refer you to the right specialists.

Nail Biting, Thumb Sucking, Hair Twirling, and the Like

Many children go through periods of nail biting or other self-comforting habits. They sit in front of the television, or in their beds at naptime and nighttime, biting furiously on one fingernail or another, or sucking vigorously on a thumb. Parents who watch them feel their blood pressure rising. They cannot refrain from pushing the finger or thumb out of the toddler's mouth. Or they say, "Aren't you hurting yourself?" The child nods silently but continues to search for a free splinter of nail. Parents try valiantly but cannot refrain from a comment: "Remember how you made your finger bleed last time?" The toddler continues to nod silently. By now, he's rocking himself gently, and his eyes are glazed, looking off into the distance. Parents feel shut out, even jealous. They may try again—in vain—not to comment. Finally, in a last effort to stop the behavior and regain contact with the child, the parent will blurt out, "Just stop it then."

The child's eyes come alive. He stops the behavior and looks directly at his parent, as if to ask, "What's the problem?" Automatically, the wet finger starts toward his mouth again. This time he strains to hold himself back. He pushes his hand reluctantly under himself, sitting on it. He is impatient for the episode to end. When his mother leaves the room, he is relieved. He resumes sucking or searching for a ragged edge of fingernail.

By their protests, parents have reinforced his behavior, bringing it from an unconscious regulatory status (used to comfort, soothe, or control himself) to a conscious one, which the child now uses as rebellion against the parent's unwelcome and poorly understood intrusion.

Most habits get set in this way. Most of us have experienced this same form of intrusion from our own parents. When we see this withdrawal behavior in a child, it is difficult indeed not to wish to break through it and make contact. Parents, as well as others around a child, see such behavior as a sign that the child is somehow "deprived." They are likely to feel that only a poorly nurtured, lonely child would keep on in this way. This is not true, though it may be that the child is stressed or anxious. Thumb sucking, nail biting, rocking, and so on are intensely private self-comforting patterns, necessary to most children and many adults at certain times. During predictable stages of a child's development, they tend to reappear. They tend to become entrenched habits when the outside world resents them and tries to intrude.

Tics

A tic is a sudden jerk of a part of the body—often a blink of the eyes, a twitch of the neck, or a shrug of the shoulders—that occurs involuntarily and repeatedly. In a child, tics often appear when he is concentrating or is under tension, and they vanish almost completely when he is asleep. Often, the child is not aware of the tic. If his parents call attention to it, the pattern may increase. Often parents associate the sudden jerks with a seizure. Their reaction can transmit a sense of anxiety to the child, which may exacerbate the problem. Most tics fade away after awhile, often lasting only a few weeks. They can first occur as early as age two and are most common between ages ten and twelve. They may recur when the child is going through a stressful time, such as an adjustment to a new school or a new baby in the family. Since this may be a time when parents are feeling stressed, too, parents are even more likely to reinforce the tics in some way—by calling attention to them or by worrying openly about them. If they continue, look for the underlying tension and try to address that. If the child is going through a period of adjustment, be sure he has plenty of support and affection. But expect him to handle the stress and to learn from it.

Unless tics are associated with other unusual symptoms, interfere with usual activities, or persist and become upsetting to the child, they should be ignored. There are some medical and neurological causes (for example, Tourette's syndrome) for severe tics. (Some medications may also be associated with tics.) Your pediatrician may recommend investigating these if he or she determines that your child's tics are unlikely to be the typical transient tics often seen, especially in boys, in childhood.

24. Hospitalization

While hospitalization is frightening both to children and to their parents, it can also be a positive experience. With the nurturing atmosphere that pervades most children's hospitals these days, a child can grow in self-esteem and maturity by learning to conquer the fears and anxiety of a stay in the hospital. At Children's Hospital in Boston, we have learned to help children gain a sense of mastery from their hospital experience. Studies have shown that such efforts to bolster the child's sense of security and control can succeed. The experience of being away from home, of being sick or hurt, and of being taken care of by adults who are not one's parents will always be a traumatic challenge for a child. A parent's role is to support the child in ways that will help her learn and grow from such an experience. Parents need to be part of any child's experience in the hospital.

Preparing a Child for the Hospital

I draw on many years of experience and observations when I offer parents the following advice. First, prepare *yourself.* Before you can help your child, you must handle your own anxiety about the separation and the coming event. Insist that your doctor answer all of your questions. Share your worst fears with the doctor and with adults you can trust. Ask your doctor or ask at the hospital about the procedures to which your child will be exposed. Arrange to be with her at critical times, such as the day of admission, the day of an operation, or at the time of any painful procedures. Plan to spend at least the first night or so, until she adjusts to being there. Even if you have to fight with the hospital to arrange this, I would advise it. No hospital should expect a child to be without a parent for the initial adjustment or for any of the painful, frightening events she may have to endure. Many now allow parents to room in around the clock, and even some intensive care units have begun to let parents stay overnight with their sick children. The presence of a parent is vital if a child has to face separation from home and painful procedures. But if you can, also plan on taking breaks for yourself, and time with adults who can support you, so that you can handle your feelings before going back to face your child's. You may need time to cry, or pray, before you pull yourself together again.

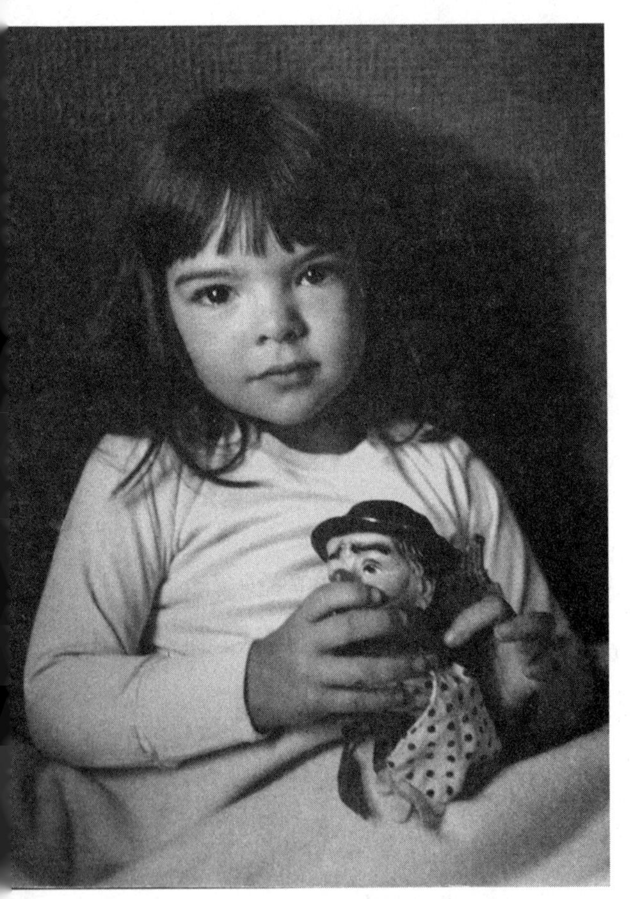

We know from experience that the best way to prepare a child is to be as honest and as complete in the description of what will happen as possible. Prepare the child in advance with clear, simple, straightforward information as much as you can. Don't ever tell a child "it won't hurt," if it will. Depending on the child's age and the situation, you may have to say, "You'll be in a ward where other kids are sick, and where they have bandages and tubes that go into the veins in their arms to give them medicine. You may be frightened, but I'll be with you. After the operation, you'll have tubes in your arm, too, because that's also the way nurses and doctors feed you while you are getting better, and while you don't feel like drinking or eating. You'll have to have needle sticks—maybe some in your finger and some in your arm. They hurt, but not for long." Explain that the nurse or doctor will have to test her blood: "That's the way they tell how sick you are and how to make you better. It doesn't feel good to be pricked in the finger.

I'll hold your other hand if they'll let me and if you squeeze me so tight that it hurts *me,* maybe it won't hurt you so much. See if you can squeeze me that hard! And cry when you want to! It's okay to cry!" Then repeat your words as you and she go through it all.

If your child must have anesthesia, ask the anesthesiologist what method will be used. Warn the child about a face mask, or a needle stick, and tell her that you will be with her as they give it to her. Again, if you have to, fight for that. Assure her that you'll be there as she wakes up (if in fact you are sure you can be) and that you'll help her through the day or two of feeling sick after the operation is over. When she starts feeling better, she can have ice cream and so on. Knowing that you are near and will protect her as much as you can is critical to her sense of security. Most hospitals for children have nurses and child-activities specialists who know about children's reactions to pain and to hospital procedures. Ask them to help you. They are the conscience of the ward and are responsible for making any hospitalization a child- and family-oriented experience.

To prevent problems, many children's hospitals today offer onsite tours, or virtual ones via the Internet, for parents and the children who come in for elective admissions, especially for surgeries that are planned in advance. These tours are important in allaying the fears of parents and children and preparing them for the realities they must face. Staff members take the child through the admissions office, and up to the floor where she will be, and then show her, in the safety of her parents' company, the operating room, the treatment room, her bed, and finally, the playroom. They give her and her parents an overview of what will happen when she comes to be admitted, replacing their fear of the unknown with a sense of mastery. In the studies I mentioned earlier of children's recovery after surgery, we have found that there is a significant difference in how well and how quickly children recover physically if they are prepared for the procedures they will have to endure. The symptoms that we used to see after the child went home—such as bedwetting, fears, night terrors, and regression to babyish behaviors—can be short-lived when a child has been well prepared for a hospitalization. These same studies showed us that children were most willing to listen to the explanations and preparation *if* the parents were present. A child needs to know that her parents understand and approve of what will happen to her. Then, she can trust that the medical procedures are not so dangerous.

But what helps when children cannot be prepared in advance? The majority of hospitalizations are emergency admissions. Some children's museums have special displays for children to see what goes on in a hospital. There may be stethoscopes, doctors' and nurses' gowns, an operating room all set up, a hospital bed with buttons that crank it up and down, and even a laboratory with a microscope to examine the blood that is taken by a needle prick on admission. We think that this is valuable preparation for children whose illnesses may necessitate emergency admissions. I would recommend that parents introduce children to such a display, or read picture books to them about going to the hospital, when they are well, so that if they ever must undergo an emergency hospitalization, they will be prepared.

No one, of course, can predict the events that surround an emergency. This is a time when the child needs a parent the most. If you are there, you can explain every procedure as it comes and support her through it.

In the Hospital

The parent who is present with the child during a hospital stay can explain the necessity for medication, needles, or intravenous feedings or injections; what they will consist of; how painful they will be; and how short-lived the pain may be. Give her a reason for the procedures and explain how they will help. When each procedure is over and she's made it, congratulate her. Point out how tough going through the procedure was, but that she's conquered it!

The fears of mutilation that occur in a child's mind whenever she is ill are important for a parent to consider and to talk about. Be honest and be realistic. Also, illnesses, for a child, seem endless. In the midst of feeling sick, she has no sense of ever having felt differently. She will feel that this illness is permanent. The sense of helplessness that goes with an illness can be both overwhelming and alarming. A child will inevitably feel that her suffering is retribution for something she has done. When a parent says something like, "If only you'd worn your boots," she's convinced her illness was meant to punish her. Her mother's statement serves to confirm what she already believes—that sick children are really bad children.

This sense of responsibility and the inability to be in control reinforce the underlying feeling that she'll never be well again. A fearful resignation can set in and may affect a child's ability to fight the illness and to recover. She'll refuse to take her medicines. She'll act out in negative, willful ways that deserve punishment. She'll almost demonstrate relief when she is punished or reprimanded. If you see this pattern developing, you must sit down with your child to talk it out. Let her talk about her feelings. Let her know that she is not responsible for her illness. Reassure her that you and her physician know how to treat her, and that she will get better. As she begins to cooperate, remind her that she is helping herself. When she does recover, give her a chance to realize that you and she did know what to do, and that now she is better. Most of all, let the child feel a sense of conquest after an illness or hospitalization is over. The child who achieves a sense of mastery over illness will be better prepared for conquering future difficulties.

As mentioned, most children's hospitals have a playroom and a child-activities specialist. Such a specialist is trained in child development and in therapeutic play techniques. Ask that person what kind of play would be appropriate to help your child work out her feelings. The playrooms are usually equipped with dolls that have bandages and splints, and even with pretend intravenous equipment. These are designed to let her "play out" her illness and her fears. In the playroom, a child can feel safe and can meet other children who are going through similar ordeals. There, they can learn about themselves and their illness and get a sense of conquering it themselves.

Whenever possible, give the child a sense of being in some control over her world and her own destiny. Look for the opportunities, however rare, when she can have a choice. Even a child swathed in bandages and immobilized in splints can blow at a mobile, dictate a story for you to write down, or spit in a tin can. Let a child smear finger paints or knock down blocks or do whatever activity she can. If she can feel in control at all, she is no longer completely at the mercy of the painful world of illness.

As we said before, stay overnight the first night, at least. Even if you have to sit in a chair through the night, it is worth it to the child. In the daytime, you can have another family member come in so that you can go home to sleep, but you will have supported the child through that first frightening night. If she's in for a long time, you'd better pace yourself. Plan to leave for certain periods of the day. A break in the day can be a godsend for you, and it can push the child to learn to rely on the nurses, the doctors, and the play specialist. She'll feel more secure when you can feel confidence in them, too.

When you leave, prepare the child for your leaving. Never lie or try to slip out. She must be able to trust you. Tell her when you will return and try to be on time. Before leaving, help her relate to a special nurse or playroom person. Help her to know her doctor and her nurses as people who care about her. Then, while you are gone, she can feel that you approve of your substitute. When you return, remind her of your promise. A child's fear of being deserted is intensified while she is separated from home and in such a strange, threatening place. Each time you return as predicted, she'll feel safer.

Whenever possible, have other members of the family come in to visit. Many hospitals allow siblings to visit. Nothing can cheer up a sick child as much as seeing a brother or sister.

When Your Child Comes Home

When your child returns home, expect a reaction. Most children regress to an earlier stage of development. They usually give up the last developmental achievements they have just made. For instance, a toddler who has been toilet trained for months may start wetting her pants and bed again. Or a four-year-old who has given up fears and nightmares may start seeing monsters in her room at night or wake up screaming. These reactions are normal and even healthy. Not only must you expect them, but you should help your child understand that they are all right and perfectly normal after a stay in the hospital. Helping her understand her reaction is like opening a door for her toward understanding herself. Then, she needn't feel so guilty and embarrassed about this regressive behavior.

Helping a child talk out or play out her reactions to the painful experiences and the separation from home is therapeutic. You might set up a play hospital where her doll or teddy bear can relive the experiences she has had. That allows her to express her fears and anxiety in the safety of home. The terror, the pain, and the fear of a repetition can all surface, but as she plays them out, this time she is in control of what happens. She can be reassured, and assure herself, that she has managed it all successfully. She will have gained a sense of mastery from what might otherwise have left her with lingering fears.

25. Hypersensitivity and Hyperactivity

While all children may seem "hyperactive" to their parents at some time or other (especially after meals!), attention deficit hyperactivity disorder (ADHD) is more than just overflowing energy. A child with this disorder is not only driven by frenetic activity but also struggles with uncontrollable impulsiveness and a short attention span that is often further disrupted by distractibility. These problems interfere with the child's life at home, in school, and with other children and adults.

Identifying Hyperactivity

Hyperactive children are much more likely to be boys than girls, and as a result ADHD is often not identified in affected girls. I have always thought that hyperactivity is probably due to a "raw," hypersensitive nervous system that is at the mercy of every incoming stimulus. The child is not able to shut out unimportant stimuli and thus cannot focus on the more useful, comprehensible ones. Every incoming signal is transmitted without being screened. The discharges of the nervous system into activity are just as uncontrollable, and the brain does not seem to shut down unhelpful impulses.

The hyperactivity of ADHD sometimes does not stand out from high-level activity still within the normal range until the child begins school, where new demands to focus and concentrate are made. A watchful parent or pediatrician may, however, see the signs and symptoms much earlier. In some cases, one of these early signs is hypersensitivity to stimuli. If I clap as such a child plays with toys, he will startle. As I keep clapping, his startles may diminish, but they will continue. A child without this hypersensitivity to stimuli will shut out my clapping by the third or fourth clap. An anxious child may need five or six. A truly hypersensitive child will blink for ten to fifteen claps. A child with ADHD may startle for the first five or six, but has often already learned ways to diminish the impact of repetitive stimuli that he is unable to filter out. He may start to sing, turn his back, or become active in other ways as he attempts to shut out these repetitive noises. After I stop, he will invariably become noisy and active, as if he were trying to discharge the stored-up overload.

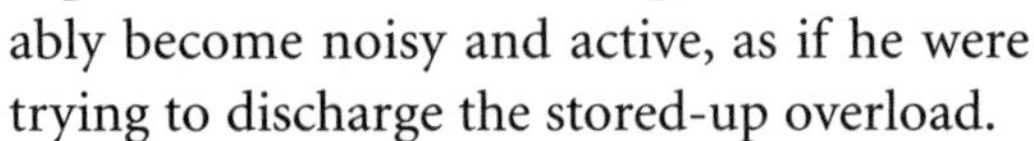

ADHD is likely to include a kind of heedlessness. The child may trip easily or run into furniture, either because of his inability to stop himself long enough to think before he acts (impulsivity), or because he has additional difficulties planning out a successful sequence of movements (motor planning), or both. He may not appear to notice when he hits himself or when he fails at a task. He has become familiar with failure. An indication of this expectation to fail is a child's attempt to cover up or to distract the observer from his failure. He may try to divert your attention to another task. As he fails, he propels himself into a kind of emotional lability. Crying, laughing, and running around the room are all attempts to handle his impulsive recklessness. He cannot control himself.

Because the child cannot shut out unimportant stimuli, his attention span is short. He will start and stop an activity, then become excitable or restless. Although hyperactivity often accompanies ADHD, some children with attentional difficulties are not hyperactive. All this can only be sorted out by professionals who have had long experience with these problems. If parents notice that their child is distractible and at the mercy of stimuli, if he is emotionally labile and can't manage himself, or if his frantic activity seems to be the result of an overloaded nervous system, they should ask their pediatrician for an evaluation as soon as possible. He or she can make referrals to child psychiatrists, pediatric neurologists, psychologists, and occupational therapists as needed. Additional problems may compound these symptoms, since many children with ADHD will also have learning disabilities or even depression. The goal should be to single out the child's strengths as well as his weaknesses and build a treatment plan on these. The child will need to be told, in terms he can understand, why he is being evaluated, and what strengths and vulnerabilities the evaluation uncovers. These can be linked to the troubles he is already aware of and cares about.

Treatment may consist of medication (usually a stimulant), cognitive behavioral therapy, parent counseling to help organize a supportive environment, special education, and in some instances, psychotherapy (for example, as is all too often the case, when a child's self-esteem has already been damaged by the disorder).

Medications for ADHD

If medication is used to treat ADHD, it should always be prescribed and monitored by a physician. The child needs to be included in the decision about medication. Parents should let him know that the medication is to help him achieve what he's trying so hard for: the ability to stop his activity and to pay attention. If it helps, he can take part of the credit. Stimulants have been used to effectively reduce the symptoms of ADHD for several decades, and for many children the resulting increased ability to stop fidgeting, sit still, stay focused, and wait their turn has made a world of difference in their self-esteem and their self-image, and ultimately in their chance for becoming productive citizens. The overuse of these medications in children who do not have ADHD or who have been misdiagnosed with it has drawn the criticism it deserves. It has also called attention to our flawed educational system, which often fails to respect children's rhythms and different learning styles. Some young children need to move around as they are taught in order to learn. Others need intervals of physical activity to balance times of intense focus. With physical education programs slashed in many school districts, very active, though not hyperactive, children can be expected to become wound up, and this makes them harder to distinguish from children who really do need treatment.

Parents' Role

In addition to providing a calm, nonstimulating environment, the parents' role will be to reward each bit of progress. Even the simplest positive behavior, such as sitting still for a brief meal or finishing an easy task, should be praised. Parents need to let the child know how proud they are when he can manage to control his disorganization. Because bringing up a hyperactive child is a long, taxing job, each parent must make some time to relax and recharge. Parents who believe in their child's strengths, and who cooperate in treatment programs with optimism rather than anxiety, will convey this to the child and contribute greatly to his growing self-control.

The most serious potential complication of this disorder can develop from the child's recognition of his own inability to control it. He grows up with an expectation to fail that hampers all his other efforts to learn and to conform. This sense of failure and the poor self-image can be more serious than the disorder itself. A child can learn to manage ADHD, but if he expects to fail, he will develop ways of behaving that set him up for failure.

I've suggested to parents of these children that they make a chart of (1) how the child behaves as he builds up to a peak of discharge, (2) how he behaves at the peak, and (3) how he behaves afterward. Can he then calm down to pay attention? If a child begins to understand his own behavioral patterns, parents may be able to help him cut off the peaks by learning to anticipate them. A young child can learn to fall back on a crutch, such as his thumb or a lovey, as the urge to act builds up, or to go to a rocking chair to quiet himself. Then he may be able to pay attention. When a child can achieve this kind of mastery, he deserves the reward of knowing that he has worked hard to overcome a very upsetting disorder. If he can achieve such a pattern by five or six years, he may be able to master school and the prolonged periods of attention that it will require. This can be a long and demanding process. These children need both a lot of patient encouragement and a sense of themselves as successful! If he can learn bits of self-control, he deserves enormous praise!

ADHD at Later Ages

It was once thought that ADHD was a disorder of childhood that ended with the onset of adolescence or adulthood. But it is now understood that this condition is usually a chronic one. Most children with ADHD continue to have some symptoms in adolescence, though hyperactivity may become less prominent, while difficulty paying attention, staying on task, remembering details, keeping track of one's homework and belongings, and other organizational challenges persist. Many adolescents with persistent ADHD will also have symptoms as adults. Though the diagnosis of ADHD depends on symptoms occurring prior to age seven, some adults may not realize they have this disorder until much later in life. It can interfere with their safety (they have a higher incidence of motor vehicle accidents and substance abuse), their productivity (they have more difficulty maintaining a career path consistent with their potential), and their important relationships. But now that we know that ADHD can continue into adulthood, medication, cognitive-behavioral therapy, and a clear understanding of this disorder for the affected individual and his loved ones offer the hope of overcoming its challenges.

26. Illness

THIS CHAPTER IS NOT A GUIDE TO THE CARE OF SICK CHILDREN, BUT IN keeping with the goal of the book, offers simple first steps to help parents channel their understandable anxiety over a sick child into positive, secure action. In all cases, check with your own doctor.

Children get sick so fast—nearly always in the evening, after doctors' office hours. One moment they are playing energetically; the next moment they're cranky and disorganized. Suddenly, they stagger or lie down. Their eyes glaze over and their color changes to either a fierce red or an ashen gray. Their breathing rate doubles, and they seem to be gasping for breath. Small children whimper inconsolably or won't cry at all. They can't tell you what's wrong. They obviously feel awful. Their collapse is all the more sudden in that while they are playing, they resist giving up. When they finally do, they are so pitiful. All but the most experienced parents will feel a painful surge of anxiety. The first step with a sick child is to pick her up, comfort her, and assure her that you are going to help her feel better. Illness is a time when both children and parents reach out for each other, and children will remember for the rest of their lives the way their parents took care of them when they were sick. Working parents will need to find a way to stay home with a sick child.

PREPARING FOR EMERGENCIES

ALL PARENTS SHOULD MAKE THE FOLLOWING ADVANCE PREPARATIONS:

Have the phone number of the doctor, the emergency room of the hospital, and the Poison Control Center by every phone in the house, and programmed into parents' cell phones. (The national toll-free number for the Poison Control Center is 1-800-222-1222.)

Make everyone who takes care of the child aware of these numbers.

Buy a reliable guide to emergencies, such as *The American Red Cross First Aid Book* or the *Children's Hospital Guide to Your Child's Health and Development*, and read the advice on preparing for emergencies (see *Further Reading* at the end of this book).

Childproof the house: kitchen, bathroom, garage, and yard included.

Preparations such as these enable a parent to be calmer and more effective in an emergency. Anxiety in an emergency is normal. It provides the adrenaline needed to rise to the occasion.

When to See the Doctor

Parents today are often well informed about medical care and are concerned about overtreatment of illness, side effects of medications, and the problems of unnecessary tests. The possibility of nonessential tests being ordered has been compounded by the rise in malpractice suits and the resulting climate in which physicians must work.

When you are trying to decide when to take your child to a physician or to a hospital, these concerns will necessarily come to mind. Using judgment about when to start with home remedies rather than rushing to a doctor's office or hospital can not only save a child from the added anxiety but also give her that extra security of feeling that you, her parents, know what to do.

In any emergency, or with any unexplained change in a child's health, of course, such concerns are irrelevant, and you should call a physician right away. Even for the more common childhood illnesses, there are good reasons to seek medical care. These include treating any persistent infection, forestalling complications after a child has fought the infection long enough, preventing recurrences, and making a child more comfortable when you've tried all you know.

A physician or nurse practitioner can tell whether the child is sick enough to need treatment or further investigation. He or she will assume responsibility and offer a more objective opinion than you can muster. Finally, a physician's very authority can relieve you and the child of feeling responsible for the illness. A small child may feel that an illness is her own fault and that she's been "bad" and deserves it. Sometimes this perception is hard for a parent, the voice of discipline, to counter. Parents, too, have normal guilt feelings that surface when a child falls ill. Through calm explanation, a doctor can exorcise this guilt and offer comfort, as well as medical treatment, to the family.

Fever

Fever is not an illness but usually an indication of the body's effort to fight an infection. Children between six months and three years of age are likely to have high fevers because their bodies' temperature-regulating mechanisms are still immature. Fever is a healthy response of the immune system to infection, both viral and bacterial. Most fevers are caused by viruses rather than bacteria and will not require antibiotics or medical treatment other than fluids and fever-reducing medicines safe for children, such as acetaminophen or ibuprofen. Giving your child a chance to build up her immunity by fighting most of these infections on her own may be the best thing you can do, but you needn't make that decision on your own. If a feverish child is brought to me too soon, I can't always tell where her infection will localize, and I won't know whether she can handle it herself or will need help. Unless she shows certain symptoms (mentioned below), I'd rather see the child after she's fought her own battle for twenty-four hours. At that point, I can make a proper diagnosis and determine whether treatment is necessary. Still, a fever over 100.2 degrees (Fahrenheit) in a baby under six months of age, or 102 degrees or more in a child older than this, should prompt a call to the doctor as soon as possible.

Is her neck stiff? Can you bend it forward onto her chest? The neck of a child with meningitis cannot be bent forward, whereas a child with aches from the flu won't like bending her neck forward but will be able to do it. A really stiff neck needs immediate attention.

Is there interference with her air passage? All children with a fever breathe faster than normal, but if there's a wheezing or a crackle with each intake of breath, she may need medical help.

Does she pull on her ears as if they were painful? Ear infections accompanied by high fever may require medication, so she'll need to be checked soon.

If your feverish child has any of these symptoms, call your physician or nurse practitioner. If not, you can afford to try your own remedies at home first. You can see whether she'll improve on her own for at least twenty-four hours. It's a good sign if she perks up and eats normally after a dose of acetaminophen.

Taking the Child's Temperature Until a child is five or six and can cooperate, mercury-containing oral thermometers can be dangerous. Digital oral thermometers are safer but also must be kept under the tongue. For younger children and infants, pacifier thermometers are a good alternative, but they must not be used as pacifiers except when taking a temperature. Digital and mercury thermometers can be used for axillary temperatures. If you can, hold the child against you with her arm tightly against her chest and enclose the thermometer in her armpit for four to five minutes for a glass thermometer, or for a digital thermometer, until it beeps. This may be hard to do with a wriggler. An axillary temperature will be one degree (Fahrenheit) lower than a rectal temperature, unless an instant underarm thermometer is used. If you take your child's temperature rectally, lay her across your lap on her belly. Insert the tip of the thermometer, greased with petroleum jelly, only one inch into her rectum and hold it tight, using your thumb and forefinger. The rest of your hand should rest on her buttocks, so that your hand and fingers holding the thermometer bounce with her as she wriggles on your lap. In that way, you won't lose the thermometer or break it or hurt her with it. A tympanic (ear) thermometer is another option, but it will not be accurate if not positioned properly to completely cover the ear canal, or if the child has been lying on that ear, or has been outside in the cold.

To tell whether a fever is dangerous, don't go by degree of temperature alone. That is not the most critical factor. A child with a high fever who looks alert and responsive is much less worrisome than a child with a lower fever who is limp and unresponsive. In other words, a major change in her behavior—from playful and energetic to mopey and lethargic—is the most important symptom.

Dehydration The first concern with a fever is dehydration. Get some clear fluids into the child as soon as possible. Dehydration is one of the main reasons children with a fever look so terrible. It must be combated constantly in order to help fight the infection behind the temperature. With infants, dehydration can even be life-threatening. Feed clear fluids in little sips at a time, for a fever is often accompanied by an upset stomach. If the child is nauseated and vomiting, it is even more critical to start to counteract the dehydration. One teaspoon of a sweetened fluid with a bit of salt, such as ginger ale, weak sweetened tea (use sugar rather than honey in infants under a year old), or a mixture of one pint of water, one tablespoon of sugar, and one-half teaspoon of salt—can be spooned in or drunk every five minutes for the first hour. (Formula may be hard to handle right now, but a breast-fed baby should continue nursing, especially if she won't take a bottle.) A tablespoon every five minutes the second hour and an ounce every few minutes the third and fourth hours (about a cup every hour) will counteract both an upset stomach and dehydration. A quart of liquid a day is a goal in fighting dehydration accompanied by a fever, though the exact amount a child needs will depend on how much fluid she has lost, as well as her weight. For example, a healthy 10-pound infant needs about 15 ounces of fluid a day, while a healthy 50-pound child needs about 50; both will need more than this with a fever. An oral rehydration solution made for infants and children (not a "sports drink") can also be used. Your pharmacist or pediatrician can help you find the right one and determine the appropriate amount to give for your child. Then, you can always keep a supply on hand.

If a child continues to feel miserable, acetaminophen (Infants' or Children's Tylenol, but not aspirin, since in certain rare instances it has been associated with a dangerous condition called Reye's syndrome when used for babies or children with fever) can be given to help bring the fever down according to the instructions on the package or the advice of your doctor. If the child still looks sick after twenty-four hours, no matter what her temperature, it is time to call your doctor. If you have been able to bring the child's temperature down by giving her acetaminophen or by putting her in a lukewarm tub, she will feel and act better. If she doesn't, she is telling you that she needs attention from a physician.

Convulsions In a small child, a high fever (above 103 degrees Fahrenheit) can sometimes cause a convulsion (febrile seizure). Convulsions with fever are more likely to occur in children under three or in slightly older children who have a low threshold for them. Seizures are frightening. The child stiffens out, arches, and then her limbs will jerk spasmodically in repeated jerks. She may have trouble breathing and drool. She will have lost consciousness in the process. If this happens to your child, move her to the floor (on a soft mat or pillows if you can) and away from anything she might bang against, but don't restrain her. Be sure to position her on her side, or in a semi-seated position with her head lowered, so that you can keep her airway clear and prevent choking if she should vomit. Contrary to old wives' tales, a child will not swallow her tongue. If this is her first seizure, call her doctor for help right away. Call for emergency help if she has difficulty breathing or is turning blue, or if the seizure lasts for more than twenty minutes (ten minutes for a child already on anticonvulsant medication), or if a second seizure occurs before the child regains consciousness.

To foreshorten a febrile seizure, or to prevent one if a child's temperature is rising rapidly, parents can work to bring the fever down. Fluids and fever-lowering medications like acetaminophen, as mentioned, will help, but they can't be given to a child still drowsy from a febrile seizure and must wait until she is completely awake. But parents can start with a lukewarm sponge bath, taking care to warm the water if the child begins to shiver or if her lips turn blue. Don't use cold water, since a sudden, extreme temperature change can be dangerous in this situation. If she recovers in the tub, you can wait to get to your doctor, unless this is the first febrile seizure she has had. If she does not recover in the tub, get your spouse or a neighbor to call an ambulance, the fire department, or 911, and call your child's doctor to tell him or her to prepare for you at the hospital. In all likelihood, the seizure will be over before you can get there, but if it's a first seizure, it's critical to have the child checked out. A serious illness like meningitis, which can cause both high fevers and seizures, must be considered—and treated right away if it is found.

Sometimes rushing off to the hospital before you bring the fever down may actually prolong the seizure. Once the child is alert and conscious, give her clear fluids and acetaminophen. Be sure to read and follow the directions on the label.

If a child has a fever and has had a febrile seizure once before, I'd recommend starting her on a regular round-the-clock schedule of acetaminophen, not to exceed the total daily allowable amount, and using the dose specified for her age and weight on the label or by her doctor. Every time she starts to seem feverish, you can do this to prevent a sudden rise in her temperature, which is what brings on seizures. Some doctors may also recommend an anticonvulsant, such as diazepam, to be given whenever a child who has had a previous febrile seizure comes down with an illness that is likely to lead to fever. In any case, you will want to discuss with your doctor ways to handle

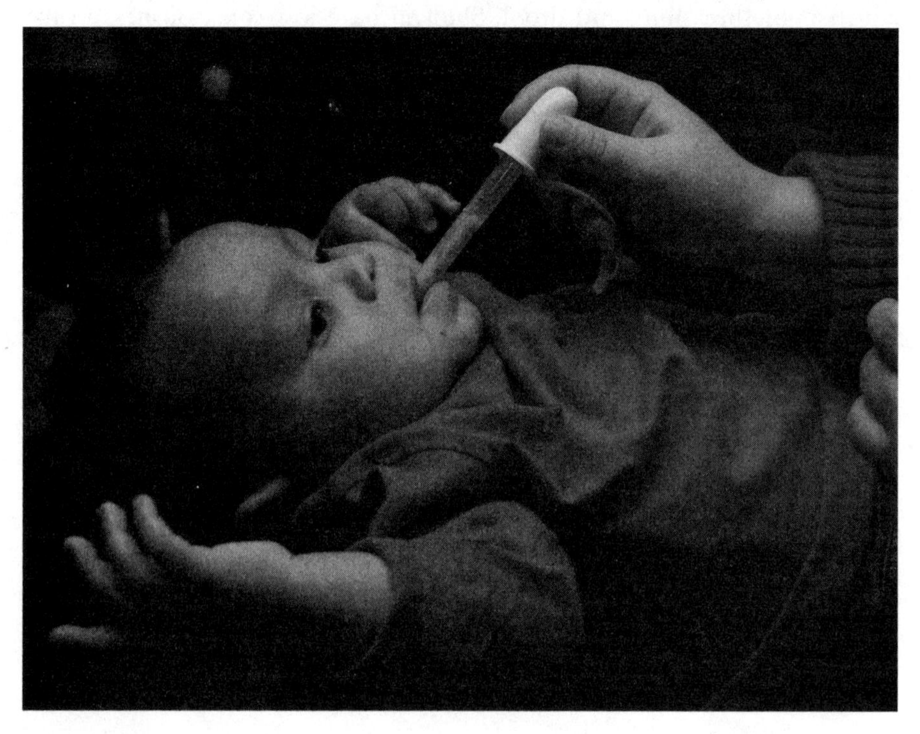

and prevent seizures. Incidentally, a child who has had a high fever without a seizure is much less likely to have one with the next high fever. Seizures without fever will require further investigation by the pediatrician, and often, a pediatric neurologist, to determine the cause and appropriate treatment.

Refusal to Drink

When my daughter was two, I faced just that problem. I knew she was getting dehydrated because she hadn't urinated in eighteen hours, her lips were dry, and her eyes looked sunken. If she would not drink, we were faced with hospitalization to rehydrate her.

I'd told the parents of my patients that if they were determined about something, their child would know it and would cooperate, but I hadn't yet had a two-year-old of my own then. I knew that if I didn't make my daughter drink fluids at home, someone at the hospital would. So, I warned her that if she wouldn't drink the warm, flat ginger ale in her cup, I would hold her nose and pour it down her throat. She refused again, so I forcefully hoisted her into my lap. Again, I assured her firmly that I'd simply have to pour in the drink. At this point, she seemed to understand that I was absolutely serious and would not be budged from my stance. She finally began to drink and was soon rehydrated and cheerful. She didn't seem to bear me a grudge for my brutish behavior. Though I felt that I'd been mean, and hated it, it did keep her out of the hospital! When a child is sick, a parent may feel cruel but must nevertheless be determined to protect their child from the illness rather than from the treatment.

Colds

The common cold is likely to last for a week in older children, two weeks in toddlers and babies, but talk to your doctor if your child seems to be getting worse rather than better after three to five days. These are trying times for families, especially when small children begin child care or preschool and so these illnesses are bound to be more frequent. To make your child more comfortable, encourage plenty of fluids. When necessary, I'd stop food for a day or two and just stress fluids. Using a vaporizer in her room helps to liquefy secretions in her nose and sinuses so they can run out. I do not like nasal suction unless it is absolutely necessary, as the suctioning device is intrusive and causes as much nasal membrane irritation as it relieves.

Prop your child up in bed so that her head is slightly higher than her feet to help reduce nasal congestion. Administer diluted saltwater nose drops (one-half teaspoon salt per eight ounces of boiled water that has been cooled to room temperature), or use a saline nasal spray half diluted with water before meals, so that your child can drink and eat even though her nose is full. But, as we said, when a child has a cold, eating is not a priority; fluids are all she really needs.

It may be necessary to repeat the diluted nose drops every four hours at night to help your child breathe. If the cold isn't visibly better within two or three days of administering home remedies, consult your doctor. (Nasal sprays used for longer than that can cause the nasal tissues to swell.) Common colds do serve one positive purpose: They help raise a child's immunity. But that's small comfort if she gets earaches or other common complications.

Croup

Croup is a particularly frightening ailment to parents and children. The child can't pull air into her lungs without a harsh croaking sound. It has been compared to the bark of a seal. When the child tries to speak, she is hoarse. Not being able to get enough air is alarming to her. As she panics, her airway goes into a greater spasm, making breathing even more difficult. Croup is caused by viruses that can also cause upper respiratory infections, so the swelling and narrowing of the airways seen with croup often appear during or just after a cold. It is common in children under five, and more severe the younger they are.

When parents become frightened, too, this aggravates the problem. Anyone who encounters croup without being prepared for it ends up remembering the episode as one of the most frightening of their child-raising years. Knowing what to do can defuse much of this anxiety. The following steps help in the majority of children.

Put a chair in the bathroom—a rocking chair, if possible, then turn on the hot shower full blast with the door to the bathroom closed to steam up the room quickly.

Sit down near the shower with your child in your arms, rocking and singing to soothe her as the steam slowly makes her breathing easier.

Give your child a lollipop to suck on. It will soothe her throat and help her relax.

Give her sips of liquids unless she is having too much trouble breathing.

Prop up her head, even when she's asleep.

After breathing the steamy air for a half hour, your child should be getting better. If she isn't, you need help. Call your physician immediately. If you can't reach the doctor or his or her emergency back-up, call your local emergency room.

You'll need to call for emergency help if your child is fighting hard to breathe (one sign may be that the muscles of her rib cage and neck move in and out with each breath), or if her lips begin to look blue. Call her doctor right away if she has a high fever, since this, along with severe difficulty breathing, can be a sign of a much less common but more serious illness, epiglottitis. Since this is caused by a bacteria rather than a virus, it usually starts suddenly, unlike croup, which crops up in the course of a cold.

If you must take your child to the hospital in this croupy condition, try to keep her as calm as possible. Being handled by strangers in a strange place will add to her anxiety, so stay close to her. If she is put into a "croup tent" to be sure she gets enough oxygen, get in with her—it won't be so frightening to her if you are there.

If the condition improves at home, set up a "croup tent" around the child's bed or crib. Secure a sheet to the top and two sides of the crib, or to the bedposts, leaving two sides open for air to circulate. Run the steam from a vaporizer in under the sheet. Prop the child on pillows and sit beside her to comfort her; crying can make her airway tighten up again. Stay near her through the night. If you can get her through the night with these techniques, she'll be dramatically better by morning. She may worsen again every night for a while, but she won't get as sick or as frightened on the second or third nights as she did on the first. Most croups (about 98 percent) can be handled at home, without medications, but if the child gets worse and runs a temperature, it's time to see the doctor.

Diarrhea

Dehydration is the primary danger for a child with diarrhea. Up to four loose stools a day won't be likely to dehydrate her, but if they are very watery, or there are more than six a day, she is likely to become dehydrated. Then she'll urinate less often; her mouth, tongue, and lips will appear dry; and her eyes will seem sunken. She may become irritable or drowsy. Push her to drink clear fluids (as described earlier)—broth, sweet tea with a little salt added, or flat ginger ale are best. For a baby, formula may be difficult to digest during a bout of diarrhea, but continue breast-feeding, especially if the baby won't take the bottle. The child's digestive system needs to rest, so give her only foods that can be absorbed easily. But don't withhold the child's usual milk and other dairy products unless your doctor advises you to do so. Once believed to aggravate diarrhea, these foods appear to hasten recovery and help make up for nutritional losses.

A child who has recently been toilet trained may need to return to diapers. Just offer them; don't make a fuss.

Blood and mucus in the stool are danger signs. If you spot any or if severe diarrhea persists for more than twenty-four hours, call your doctor.

Earaches

Most of us remember the misery of earaches in childhood. Very young children can't tell you what's wrong but will finger their ears and cry. Earaches are very common, and the most common cause for them in children under age six is a middle ear infection (otitis media). This kind of earache usually occurs along with a cold or nasal congestion. The tissues in the throat swell, blocking the opening of the eustachian canal in the back of the throat, which leads directly to the middle ear. Pain is the result as fluid and pressure mount. If you suspect an ear infection, you will need to consult the doctor. If you are right, antibiotics may be prescribed. If the throat and nasal passages are also swollen, I have found it helpful to shrink these tissues and relieve the pressure with an antihistamine or decongestant. I also always recommend trying decongestant nose drops diluted in half with water for infants six months and over. Putting one or two drops in each nostril, and then quickly turning the child's head so that the painful ear faces downward, often seemed to help. But never insert anything into the ear. Call the doctor if the pain persists.

When ear infections keep recurring, you need the advice of an ear, nose, and throat specialist (or ENT, also called an otorhinolaryngologist). Your child's hearing should be checked, since chronic fluid in the ears can interfere with hearing and, as a result, learning to speak. Tubes can be surgically placed in the eardrums—a method of treatment that can really help with chronic ear infections.

Nosebleeds

Nosebleeds are frightening and always seem twice as bad as they are. First, try to stop the bleeding by pinching the nose to put pressure on the vessels inside of it for about ten minutes. Place ice on the bridge of the nose. Do not have the child lie down on her back or put her head back. I've found it helpful to wad a bit of toilet paper into a half-inch square and push it firmly up under the upper lip so it presses up on the septum (the dividing wall) of the nose. Once you've stopped the nosebleed, tell your child to try not to blow her nose too soon, or it certainly will start bleeding again. If the bleeding lasts for more than twenty minutes, call your child's doctor. If it lasts more than an hour, the nose may need packing by an expert. Nosebleeds require emergency attention if they result from a blow to the head or nose.

As a preventive for recurring nosebleeds, apply petroleum jelly morning and night inside the nose, along the middle septum. This works when the air, indoors or out, is hot and dry, or when your child is suffering from a cold or allergy. If nosebleeds keep recurring anyway, consult your doctor.

Parents can use preventive approaches to help keep their children safe and healthy. Many accidents, a major cause of serious injury in childhood, can be prevented with careful childproofing at home. As a child grows, new hazards emerge—stairways, detergents under the sink, open windows without safety guards, and so on—and new precautions must be taken. Infections can be reduced with breast-feeding, immunizations (including flu shots), and careful hand washing—especially after changing diapers, in flu season, and for children in group child care. Parents can begin teaching a child to wash her hands, and to cover her mouth and nose when she coughs or sneezes, in the second year, though patient repetition will be needed until these become habits. When a child is sick, a parent's close presence—to offer a cool washcloth for her forehead, a quiet story, or a sip of soothing ginger ale or tea—will never be forgotten, and it can become a model for the child's efforts to nurture others. Remember that the child's immunity will be stimulated by each infection. The ones she can handle without medication give her immunity a real boost. So don't get too discouraged by a burst of illness.

27. Imaginary Friends

Nearly all three- and four-year-olds develop imaginary friends. I'm always delighted when they do, for these are signs of a child's developing imagination, as I've mentioned earlier. A child needs privacy as he dreams with his imaginary friend. This is a part of his world that should not be invaded.

The Importance of Imaginary Friends

Imaginary friends are to be welcomed, as I suggested in chapter 13. From a cognitive standpoint, imagination is a very important sign of a child's efforts to understand increasingly complex aspects of his world that previously simply went over his head. But as imagination surfaces in the third year, a child's ability to keep reality and wishful thinking apart is not yet well developed. The capacity to make up an imaginary world, to construct imaginary people, to bring a beloved doll to life, is a sign of a child's rapidly developing ability to test the limits of his world. An imaginary friend becomes a way to cast out the new devils that now besiege him. Hate, envy, lying, selfishness, uncleanliness, and any other flaw he's learning to feel guilty about can now be ascribed to someone else—an imaginary friend. Or else, he may insist that he is the imaginary friend, as he tries to shed his misdeeds. We can see this as a child's first effort to conform to what everyone expects of him, to search for right and wrong. This search is only a beginning, and it is fragile. The child wants to accomplish it independently. A child must be able to engage in these explorations apart from his parents. Their intrusion diminishes his ability to find out about the world on his own.

From an emotional standpoint, imaginary friends can serve a very important purpose. They give a child a safe way to find out who he wants to be. He can dominate these friends and control them. He can be bad or good safely because of them. Through them, he can identify with children who are overwhelming to him. He can safely "become" another child. He can also identify with each of his parents in the safe guise of these imaginary friends. He can try out being a male or a female. He can try out all sides of his personality. This is one of the ways a four- or five-year-old begins to find his identity.

Concern about a child's withdrawing into loneliness is valid. He should be learning to socialize with peers his own age. But he still needs time to himself. If a child could not give up his imaginary friends for real ones, I would be worried, too. If he withdrew from active participation in school or in play, the imaginary friends could represent a symptom of too much isolation and of a lonely child. But if a child can leave his private world to play with other children, I wouldn't worry.

What effect does TV have on this important process? Undoubtedly, it cuts down on the time a child might devote to exploring his own fantasies. If he is allowed to watch television for too much of the day, he will not have the necessary time or energy to explore the world on his own. Television forces a child into a kind of overwhelmed passivity. Bruno Bettelheim pointed out that fairy tales and other traditional bedtime stories stimulate the self-exploration of aggression and the identity seeking that a child needs at this age. Television, except in small doses, has the opposite effect, imposing an artificial world of violence and unreachable good and evil and dominating the child's own imaginative adventures.

What about a child who uses an imaginary friend to "lie" his way out of a bad situation? This is an extremely common event at these ages. A parent may well wonder whether the child knows the difference between the wish and the reality, for lying at this age so obviously represents wishful thinking (see "Lying, Stealing, and Cheating"). Without confronting him, the parent can point out the child's need to wish for a different outcome. By accepting the wishful thinking but bringing the child back to reality, the parent is help-

ing him learn about his limits within the real world. The message a child needs to hear is, "You don't need to lie. I can love you, even if I don't like what you've done." It also lets a child safely explore an unreal world, because he knows his parent will bring him back to reality.

Responding to Imaginary Friends

At first, this excursion into fantasy is too vulnerable to share with parents. A child's own private language and private friends are precious and must be respected by adults around him. Older siblings, unfortunately, are likely to get wind of these imaginary beings. When they do, they may make fun of them and destroy the freedom to explore fantasy that they offer. A first child has the opportunity to explore and revel in his newly developing imagination. A second or third child is never left alone and is likely to be shoved into reality by older siblings.

Parents, too, may resent imaginary friends. Why is this? I think most parents feel left out and are jealous. Giving up a child is one of the most difficult tasks of parenting. The more intensely he protects his private language and his private friends, the more shut out and jealous his parents are likely to feel. Also, a four-year-old's creative exploration is so new that it frightens first-time parents. They are likely to wonder whether a child really "knows" the difference between reality and the fantasies he is constructing. Will he get lost in unreality? Will he use a "bad" friend to lie his way out of difficulty? Will he prefer this fantasy life and begin to shut out playmates? These are common concerns of parents of children this age.

Should parents get actively involved with the child's fantasies? Should they set the table for the make-believe friends, or should they deny their existence? I would follow the child's requests. Many children ask their parents to stay out of the imaginary friend's world. If parents do not ridicule the child, and if they show respect for his friends, he may want them to accept his friends at the table. Then I would certainly do it. Playing his game with him will not prevent him from knowing the difference between imaginary and "real" friends. Imaginary friends can be a kind of rehearsal for future friendships.

If parents feel they need to cut short the child's imaginary play because he is too involved or too isolated from other children, I would recommend the following steps.

Discuss the issue with him and suggest that you can help him to have more playmates. Let him know that you value his imaginary friends and respect his wonderful fantasies, but you'd like to see that he has "real" friends, too. His real friends will have their own imaginary friends, and maybe they can share them.

Set him up with one or two regular playmates who are his speed—not too overwhelming or too aggressive. Don't push him, but do continue to give him regular opportunities to get to know them. Help him understand his reluctance to join a group and let him know that it's okay to feel this way. Many inexperienced children at this age need to be backed up as they learn to socialize by playing with one child at a time. Pushing such a child makes him feel inadequate and guilty for not pleasing you. When your child does make it, let him know that you recognize how hard it's been and that you're proud of him.

When he hides behind his imaginary friends instead of playing with live ones, don't confront him. He will then use them to withdraw even more. Explain that you understand why he needs them. Tell him you love him and his imaginary friends, and you want him to feel safe enough to play with other children too. You will help him.

Find opportunities for outings or activities that suit your child's interests, and invite the other child and his parent to come along or join in. Choose things that would tend to encourage interaction. For example, if your child likes to poke around in the stream, go to the stream together and let them explore. If he likes to do crafts or simple science experiments, help them to get started with one of these. After a while, they'll start to have their own ideas about what to do together (see Part 3, "Friends").

In short, a child's life is enhanced by imaginary friends. These are a sign of healthy emotional and cognitive development among three- to six-year-olds. Parents need not be concerned unless a child remains isolated. However, they must deal with their own feelings of being left out of their child's world. If they understand the important developmental processes that these wonderful friends are serving, they will be better able to handle their own natural jealousy.

28. Loss and Grief

Learning about loss and grief can be an important experience for a child. It can also be an opportunity for the whole family to share the feelings, the belief systems, and the defenses that are necessary for handling grief.

When major natural or manmade disasters such as hurricanes or terrorist attacks occur, I am often asked by the media to suggest to parents how they might shield their children from the anguish of such tragedies. Of course we wish we could shield children from them. But even young children know when something terrible has happened—from TV and magazine covers that we can and must try to protect them from. When we succeed, they still know—from the stricken expressions on their parents' faces and in their voices. Without our help in trying to make sense of such catastrophes, children are left alone to struggle with the unknown, with the fears and fantasies that fill in the gaps in their understanding.

"Why did that mommy get lost? Where is she now?"
"Why did those people die?"
"Can they ever go home?"

Underneath these questions are the universal fears of children in the face of death: Will my mommy leave me? If she does, will it be because I'm bad? If I let myself get angry with Daddy, will he go away, too? The children watching a disaster on television wonder if their parents would die like that. They wonder if they themselves would die that way and why a figure of authority, like a mother or a father or a president, would allow something so awful to happen. Where does the body go? What is death anyhow? A child's nightmares about death—their own or their parents'—can be triggered by such events.

When such catastrophes occur, I urge that every family sit down together to share with each other the sense of tragedy. Children need to hear that their parents would not leave them. They need to hear from their parents that the deaths they have seen or heard about are not a child's responsibility, and that they did not result from a child's bad deeds or wishes. It is necessary for families to share the grief of the children who lose a parent or sibling. We cannot and should not try to protect our children from a deep, caring identification with others who suffer great loss or from their own grief. Grief is a vital and inevitable part of life. Longing for someone who is temporarily or permanently lost adds an important dimension to a child's ability to care about others.

At such times, we can put into words the beliefs that enable us to face loss and death. We are given the chance to explain our own feelings about death, as well as our convictions about religion, about an afterlife, and about the memories that keep others alive after death. When a close member of the family dies, parents can be so overwhelmed by their own grief that they may not be able to face grieving in their children. Often, children don't begin to show the signs of their own grief until after parents begin to recover, as if they needed to hold back on their own overwhelming feelings until they could feel sure their parents would be okay—and ready to withstand the expression of their own grief.

A Loss in the Family

If a parent or grandparent or aunt or uncle dies, it is important for adults to share their feelings with their children. Trying to shield them from the parents' own feelings of loss or depression can be disastrous. Even very young children know all too well when a parent is depressed or is in a crisis. Attempts to hide the event or the feelings it engenders amount to a desertion for the child. Parents often say to me: "Isn't she too young to learn about

death?" I can assure them that it is better for a child to learn about a death from her own grieving parents than it is to experience a parent's withdrawal without having been given a reason for it. A child's sense of death is more primitive than an adult's. She will tend to equate it with being left alone or deserted. If parents withdraw without sharing the experience they are having, it is confirmation of the child's worst fears: Grandma has died. Now mother is so sad that maybe she will die, too.

When parents can convey their grief, their own questions about mortality, memory, and the meaning of suffering, the child has an opportunity to experience *in safety* the kind of questions that plague all of us. She can share the intense emotions of grief and sadness with her parents. The parents themselves experience the wonderful thing that happens when there is a child around—a child in a bereaved family gives the rest of the family a sense of future and of purpose. When she makes her weeping mother smile, the child can experience a rare sense of power in changing her mother's mood to a positive one, if only briefly. I am constantly struck with the observation that a small child will attempt to comfort a grieving parent.

I remember once making rounds in our hospital and meeting a young mother who told me about the loss of her new baby. As she spoke, she began to sob silently. Her two-year-old was playing quietly in a corner of the room. When he saw his mother's tears, he toddled over to her lap. As he crawled up, he reached to pat her cheek clumsily and to wipe away her tears. His mother looked down at him to smile and to draw him close. He had reminded her that he was there to balance her grief.

Explanations about death can be tailored to the age of the child. I would tell a child as much as you think she can understand. It need not be too frightening. You must prepare her for conversations that she will overhear. You might say, for instance, "Grandpa was getting so old that he wasn't able to do all the things he wanted to do. When someone gets very, very old, their body gets so worn out that it just stops working. It was hard for Grandpa to keep on living when he got that old." A child may ask, "But why did he leave us? I miss him, and I want to play the games we used to play." You can answer honestly: "None of us knows why someone we love has to die and go away. The body just gives out. We all feel terribly sad and lonely. We all worry about where he has gone, whether he's happier and more comfortable now. We want him to be peaceful, but just like you, we hate to have to give him up. What I plan to do is to remember all I can about him. I'd like to talk about all the things we can remember about him, so we can keep him with us that way. Can you remember some things about him to tell me now?"

In talking about death to a child, a parent can listen for indications that she fears her own thoughts or deeds have brought about the loss. Magical thinking is a part of being three, four, five, or six. At these ages a child will need repeated reassurances that acting badly and having angry thoughts don't make people die.

Sooner or later, a child will begin to wonder about her own death: "When will I die? What does dying feel like? Where will I go? Will I be all alone?" All of these questions will present opportunities for observant parents to try to allay some fears and to share their own similar feelings about death and loss. If you have religious feelings about death or an afterlife, this is the time to share them. If you find solace in nature, in myth, or in memory, try to convey this to your children. Children love stories from the past. Talk about what it was like when you were a child and your parents were young and taking care of you. Make your own life as a child come alive for your children. They'll get the point, and it will be a balance to the grief.

The Death of a Pet

When a pet dies, a child will take it as seriously as the loss of a person, and she will need you to, too. Never lie about these serious matters to a child or take them lightly. If you lie—for example, if you say the pet has "gone to sleep"—you will lose her trust. And a parent who is casual about an animal's death is setting an example of callousness about life itself. Tell the child what you can about the animal's life and the animal's death. Encourage the child to unload her grief and her anger at losing a beloved friend. Allow her, and yourself, a period of mourning before you introduce another pet into the family. It is important for the child to have this time to try to face the reality of the loss and to experience the sense of caring that goes with losing a beloved pet. Again, expect her to feel personally responsible for having caused the loss, and explain that she is not to blame. Let her know how the death occurred, whether it was an accident or a natural death.

The Death of Another Child

When another child is sick or dying, children will be vulnerable to deep fears. They will identify with the sick or dying child: "Will I be next? Will the same thing happen to me? Why did her parents let her die? Was it because she was bad and deserved it? I wish I hadn't ever been bad to her. Maybe I made her die."

Although many of these questions may seem irrational, any adult who has experienced a serious loss will recognize that the fears they represent are universal ones. When someone close to us is sick and suffering, we all feel responsible. We all feel as if we deserve retaliation for our misdeeds or our inadequate caring. In explaining the reality of the other child's illness or death, parents can also make clear that they have the same feelings. Trying to deny or hide the reality of the illness or the grief and fears of adults would be a great mistake.

Schools can do a lot to help children deal with their fears about illness and death. One of my patients told me about the way a local school handled the situation of a six-year-old who had an inoperable brain tumor. He had been experiencing frequent headaches and had had to miss school because of them. When he came back to his class one day, he had a convulsion in the schoolroom, which all his schoolmates witnessed. After that, he was too ill to return to school. The teacher realized that witnessing this convulsion and the inevitable deterioration of the ill child had been devastating to her class. She talked to them about the boy's illness and tried to explain it as well as she could. But the sense of loss still invaded the mood of the classroom and left some children inhibited and scared. The teacher called all the parents together to tell them about the sick boy and urged them to share their children's grieving. She warned them about the likelihood of certain feelings and fears: feelings of guilt, of identification with the dying boy, and of sharing the responsibility for his illness. As she talked with the parents, she realized that the children needed a chance to say goodbye. She got up her courage and went to see the boy's parents to request that she bring the children by to see him. The parents were touched and knew what it could mean to their son. They chose a day when he was at his best. All of his schoolmates came to see him. Each one had made a special little present. Each one sat by him, touched him, and gave him a sign of how much they cared about him. He was exhausted but exhilarated after their visit. He went downhill rapidly afterward but talked constantly to his parents about "my friends." The children in his class now felt as if they could talk about him, could remember him as "theirs." They had needed to say goodbye.

After decades of overemphasizing the risk of infection and underestimating the need that children and families have to spend time together when a family member is ill, most children's hospitals now allow all family members to visit with a sick child. Parents are urged to stay with a sick child in the hospital as much as they can (see "Hospitalization"). I remember a terminally ill two-year-old, whom we will call Willie, who was dying of cancer. He'd lost all his hair from radiation and chemotherapy. He was terribly thin, virtually skin and bones. But he had a charming, winning smile. He was a favorite of all the nurses and doctors. His parents were wonderfully attentive, and one day they asked whether they might bring in Willie's two older brothers, four and six. They, and we, were afraid that Willie might not get to go home again, and they told us how devastated the two older boys were.

Willie was sitting in a playpen in the middle of the nurse's station when his parents arrived. His wispy face brightened a bit when his mother came over to pat him on his bald head. His father touched Willie's hands when the tiny boy held them out to him. We could tell that his father was almost afraid to pick him up because he looked so fragile and weak. His mother said, "Will, we have a surprise for you!" Willie's eyes lit up a bit, and his cocked head seemed to be asking what it was. At that moment, the two older brothers came off the elevator and rushed over to this little skeleton of a boy. When Willie saw them, tears began to stream down his cheeks, and he pulled himself up to stand at the side of the playpen and hung over it, both arms extended toward his brothers. He kept repeating, "Oh! Oh! Oh!" as if he couldn't believe they were really there.

The four-year-old reached out to Willie to rub his head and his face. He touched and touched and touched his little brother. Willie fawned and squirmed with each touch, as if he couldn't get enough of this touching. He looked adoringly up at his brother, as if he hadn't seen him for far too long. The other brother pulled a chair over to the playpen to sit down beside Willie. He asked his parents whether he could hold him in his arms. By this time, there were tears in the eyes of every one of us who was watching. The head nurse nodded to the parents. The father picked his son up gently to put him in his brother's lap. The six-year-old began to rock and to croon to Willie as if he were a baby. Willie cuddled up into his brother. He reached up to feel his brother's face with his all-too-delicate hands. He explored his brother's eyes, his hair, his mouth. Eventually, exhausted, he laid his head back on his brother's shoulder.

Such episodes underline the importance of visiting for siblings. All of us could see what his brothers meant to this child and what he meant to them.

We could see how critical it was to any dying child and to the other children in a family to have a chance to reunite and to say goodbye.

At some hospitals, there are programs to help parents and children face and share their grief, either with special family grief counselors or in groups with other parents or siblings. Sometimes these programs are also designed to address the grief of hospital and school personnel who must deal with the loss of a child or of a parent. Such programs institute the open sharing of feelings—on the wards, at home, and in the schools (see *Useful Addresses and Web Sites*).

29. Lying, Stealing, and Cheating

In any period of rapid learning, a child's imagination serves a vital function. Through fantasy, he can explore the ideas he is developing. In fantasy is safety. He won't need to act out his feelings and desires if he can dream them out. Imagination and the use of wishful thinking help a child explore his new world without the dangers of going overboard. He can be a powerful, frightening wolf in his dreams at night. He can roar like a fire engine. He can learn about witches and robbers as he revels in his fears. An active imagination gives him a chance to be a monster, an aggressive animal, and an adored parent—all in one dream or fantasy. Symbolic play—in which a toy animal or a truck or a doll can stand for something else—comes within the child's reach late in the second year of life.

Behaviors in which fantasy and reality meet for a small child are lying, stealing, and cheating. These are normal behaviors in four- and five-year-olds and can be opportunities for parents to teach a child about responsibility to others. That lesson is a lifetime project for all of us.

The main difficulty parents have when these kinds of behaviors first appear is to control their own overreaction based on their memories. They may have been caught at such acts, and shamed and punished. They may have been told of children whose lying, stealing, and cheating got them into serious trouble later on. These painful childhood memories and fears about their child's future make parents react with horror at the first signs of these behaviors. If they can think back to their own past, it becomes easier to understand the child's side.

Lying

All four-year-olds lie. An active imagination is a sign of emotional health at around ages four and five—*even* if it leads to untruths. And it will.

Take a child, whom we will call Alex, who watches his father play with a computer every night. Totally absorbed, the father smiles, frowns, and even laughs out loud as his computer comes up with unexpected results. One morning, when his father leaves for work, Alex steals into his father's study to inspect the computer. Imitating his father, he begins to play with the buttons and keys. All of a sudden, the computer whirs and hums. Although the babysitter doesn't notice, it continues to hum until Alex's parents return that evening. Frightened by the noises that he can't control, Alex hides. His father, upset about his computer's condition, storms into dinner, accusing each member of the family in turn. When he comes to Alex, the frightened little boy blurts out that the babysitter went in there and smashed the computer. By now, Alex wants so much to believe his story that he begins to add details to make it more credible. By the time the sitter arrives to deny her involvement, Alex's father is horrified at the complexity of the lies that Alex has constructed. He punishes Alex harshly. By this time, Alex's wishful thinking has made him believe that his story is true. He feels betrayed and undeserving of his father's anger. As a result, there is little chance that he will learn anything positive from this experience. He has lied in order to protect himself from his father's initial accusation, making a creative attempt to please his father and to erase the damage he has done in trying to identify with his father's devoted attachment to his computer. The angrier his father gets, the further Alex is pushed into his fabrications.

Parents of four- and five-year-olds need to be prepared for such lies. As a child's magical thinking surfaces, a parent can enjoy, if possible, the fanciful results. Overreacting is likely to set them as a pattern, as it may lead the child to believe that he is indeed a liar.

Often parents ask me what to do when their child lies. First, try to understand the circumstances that led to the episode. Trust the child to mean well, and try to understand his reasons—his fantasies and wishful thinking. Help him to understand them, too. Next, don't corner the child or overreact violently. Conscience at this age is just emerging; guilt comes *after* the act and in response to facing disapproval. The long-term goal is to help the child incorporate a conscience—as psychoanalyst Selma Fraiberg said, "to bring the policeman from the outside to the inside." Requirements that are too rigid or punishment that is too severe may end up with one of three results: (1) a conscience that is too rigid and relentless, (2) fierce rebellion that makes a child seem amoral, or (3) compulsive repetition of lying.

When you have overdone your criticism or punishment, or when you are wrong in your accusations, admit it to the child. Use this as an opportunity to discuss how anxious his lying makes you. But assure him that you understand his side of it. Remember that a child's love for his parents is greater than his love for himself. You can all too easily undermine his self-confidence. But be sure he knows the limits on his lying.

You will know that you are making progress when you and your child can discuss each episode and when you can help him understand his own reasons for lying. When he can begin to acknowledge the truth, you can be certain you are on the right track. At a later stage, a child will begin to respect others' feelings and rights.

If, however, lying is repeated again and again, becoming more and more

insidious and less related to reality or understandable, you are probably putting too much pressure on the child. This could be an indication that the child does not feel safe to develop his fantasy world at his own pace. A child who punishes himself and begins to withdraw, who becomes unavailable, or who shows signs of generalized anxiety and self-deprecation, with increasing fears and/or night terrors, may be showing signs of the same basic problem. In such a situation, you must lay off harsh punishments and reevaluate your own reactions. Also evaluate the child's life circumstances and the pressures on him. Let up on any unimportant issues. Admit to the child that you've been reacting too harshly. Sometimes it helps to use dolls or stories to talk and play the issues out with the child.

If you're really worried, seek a professional evaluation for your child. Remember that consistent lying is most likely to be a symptom of a child's inability to accept the limits of his world and the frustration, anxiety, and fearfulness that go with it. These need to be addressed, not suppressed.

Stealing

Small children engage in stealing for at least two reasons. First, everything "belongs" to a two- or three-year-old until someone tells him differently. Hence, if he sees a toy in a toy store or is wheeled by a bag of cookies in a grocery store, the things he sees are his—until he learns that such things belong to others. Learning this takes time. As with lying, a traumatic punishment will only drive the behavior underground, only to come out later in less acceptable ways. Gentle explanations of how to respect possessions, coupled with firm limits, are much more effective than punishment.

A more subtle reason for stealing is the desire to identify with others. As the intense desire of a preschool child to identify with his parents, his siblings, or his schoolmates increases, he may take important things from them. In his own concrete way of thinking, he will believe that having a possession of the other person's amounts to being like the other person. When stealing first appears, it is exploratory and acquisitive rather than a sign of being "bad." If you explode, you are likely to engender fear and repeat stealing in the child. Of course, it frightens a parent when a small child steals, and particularly if he seems to understand what he's done by lying about it. But if you can understand the universality of stealing for children and the motives behind it, you can avoid overreacting and causing this behavior to become fixed as a future pattern. A parent's goal, for stealing as for lying, is to use each episode as an opportunity for teaching, but a child will only be ready to learn if he is not overwhelmed by his guilt. Helping a child understand his reasons for taking others' possessions leaves him available to hear you when you discuss others' rights. Learning to respect others' possessions and territory is a long-term goal. Handled with sensitivity, each episode of stealing can lead in that direction.

First, to prevent more stealing, don't make a huge scene. This will only frighten the child. Try not to label him as a thief as you talk to him, and try not to harp on the incident afterward. It is wise not to confront the child by asking him whether he stole; this may just force him into a lie. Simply make clear that you know where the object came from, asking your child to produce it if necessary, and saying, "You know you can't take something that isn't yours." Then, help the child return the object to its owner and apologize, even if it means going back to the grocery store and suffering the embarrassment of returning the object or paying for it. Let the child work off the cost by doing chores. Be consistent about all this each time.

Preventing stealing involves patient teaching—over and over. Show the child how to ask for what he wants. Have simple rules about sharing with others, such as "You don't take another child's toy without asking her and offering her one of yours." Explain the concept of borrowing and returning a toy: "You may ask whether you can play with it. If they say no, that's it. If they say yes, you must offer to return it." "If we are in a store and you want some cookies, ask me whether you can have them. If I say yes, wait until I've paid for them before you take them." In this way, you are teaching the child respect for others' things, demonstrating the manners he needs when he asks for something, and helping him learn to delay gratification.

It is also important to explain why such rules are necessary—"in order to protect others' toys the way you want to protect yours." Your goal is not to punish but to teach him about others' possessions and about curbing his own wishes for those possessions. Try to understand why he did it, and help him understand himself. Help him see your point of view: You can't allow him to take others' possessions. Then ask him how he plans to handle it, to give part of the responsibility of limits to him. If he can come up with a satisfactory solution, you can give him credit. Finally, and most important, when he succeeds, be sure to let him know you are proud of him.

If stealing continues, look for possible underlying reasons. Is the child guilty and frightened and reacting by a sort of repetition-compulsion? Is he so insecure that he needs others' possessions to make him feel like a whole person? Do others already disapprove of him and label him? Does he feel—perhaps without realizing it—that he is missing something deeply important, for which stealing others' belongings is a misguided compensation? If he repeats his acts of stealing, he may be asking you for therapy. Don't wait until he feels like a failure and the labels stick. Seek outside help—your child's doctor or the child psychiatry department at a teaching hospital can refer you to someone.

Cheating

Other people do not like a child who cheats. But to learn not to cheat, a child must be mature enough to understand rules, in games or at school. He also must mature beyond the easily frustrated, easily discouraged state of three-year-olds. By five to six, a child can learn the concept of open bargaining rather than subversive cheating. Maturity brings with it more logical thinking, and the egocentrism of the three-year-old gives way to an awareness of others. A social conscience is now in the making, but a child also needs to be able to delay gratification, tolerate frustration, and overcome feelings of humiliation in order to stop cheating, even if it means accepting that he will lose. Learning to bargain rather than to cheat takes time.

A parent's job is to further this awareness. Punishment that is inappropriate or too strong will just stunt these developmental processes. A better technique to stop cheating is to handle it gently and openly. You can explain the consequences of cheating in a nonjudgmental way:

"It isn't really fair to her, and she won't like you."
"Would you want him to cheat on you?"
"What is fair for you is fair for everyone else."
"If you win by cheating, she might never want to play with you, or else she'll learn to cheat you back. Do you want that?"

A child's social conscience is modeled on yours and the rest of the family's. Be sure you are giving him a chance to understand your own social values—in his own terms.

30. Manners

In most cultures, teaching manners to a child is an important part of early child rearing. The respectful bow of a Japanese child, the hearty greeting of an African child, and the handshake of a European child are marks of respect and acceptance of the other person.

Manners represent our values, our social styles. We need them throughout life in order to enter and fit into a group. They signal our respect for other people and are essential to gaining the acceptance of others.

Their importance begins early. Two-year-old children learning to play together on a slide will stand in line and may even respect each others' turns. When an aggressive child crowds in, the "line" will decide as a group whether to allow this or to shove her out. By the age of two, a child is already expected by her peers to respect the rules of the game—when they do. Rules, like manners, define the behavior that others expect from us. A child who is either too aggressive or too retiring to follow the rules is labeled undesirable by the other children.

Learning Manners

Children begin learning about rules and manners in infancy, though most parents aren't even conscious that they are teaching these lessons. For example, when a baby bites her mother's nipple, the breast-feeding mother is shocked and reacts with both pain and surprise at her five-month-old's aggressiveness. She pulls back, takes the baby off the breast, and reprimands, "No, you can't do that!" She has just taught her baby the rules of nursing. The baby is beginning to learn respect for the other person while learning these breast-feeding rules, though they will need to be taught over and over again.

Not until a child begins to tease and test limits in the second year do parents recognize their role in "teaching" manners. One of the first real battlegrounds of manners is feeding time, as mentioned in earlier chapters. While learning the rules, a one-year-old must try out all possibilities. She must drop food over the side of her tray, pour out the contents of her cup, mash food into her hair, and refuse one food after another, testing each rule in a search for limits.

During the second year, the opportunity to explore limits and her own autonomy is more important to a child's development than learning the manners we will expect later on. By age four or five, after she has mastered the basic mealtime skills, she'll begin to identify with the adults around her and pick up the manners she sees practiced by her parents and older siblings. On her own, she'll use a napkin to wipe her face, handle a fork and spoon, and ask if she may be excused from the table. Parents can remind a child about saying "please" and "thank you," but should not expect her to make this a habit yet. At this age, children have a strong desire to imitate the actions of those around them. They want to be like them. They already sense how important rituals or manners are in seeking others' approval. However, if directed to "do this" or "don't do that," any vital four-year-old will rebel. Learning how to do things herself has become too important and exciting for her to acquiesce to parental direction. That's why your best chance of teaching acceptable behavior is simply to model it for your child. If you have a three- or four-year-old, I urge you to set an example but not to comment too strongly on your child's progress in learning manners.

Social Rules

As a child begins to learn the everyday rules of mealtime, bedtime, and bath time behavior at around four years old, she is ready to start imitating some of the social manners that parents and older siblings have been modeling all along.

Going to see grandparents can be an excellent opportunity for learning. You can prepare your child with a little story about what will happen when she visits her grandparents' house and what will be expected of her. As you talk to her, help her rehearse the desired behavior. For example: "Grandma and Grandpa will be so glad to see you. Will you be ready to hug them and to let them kiss you? Or will you want to run and hide? Lots of kids your age are shy, but grandparents have waited so long to see you that they can't help wanting to hug and kiss you."

When other people will be present, prepare your child to greet them as well. "Do you remember Mr. Green, who lives next door to Grandma and Grandpa? Well, he's going to be there, too, and I'll bet he holds out his hand for you to shake, like this. Daddy will shake hands with Mr. Green, so you can see how grownups do it. Then maybe you can do it, too."

If and when your child does practice these mannerly behaviors, comment favorably, but don't overdo your praise. You are setting up an expectation, not making a big event of it. If she is unable to live up to your requests, don't nag. Simply let her know that you'd still like her to learn these formalities, and you hope that next time, she can do what "everyone else does." The result of both too much pressure and too much praise is to convey that manners are negotiable. Manners, like mealtime and bedtime routines, should become part of a well-established pattern rather than an issue for negotiation.

When it's time to say goodbye, again let your child know what you expect of her. "You can thank Grandma and Grandpa for the delicious dinner and give them a hug goodbye. Grandma and Grandpa told me they'd noticed how grown up you are!"

If either grandparent has a disability or uses a cane or crutches, you'll have an opportunity to prepare your child to be sensitive to others. You might tell her, "Grandpa has to use crutches now because his legs hurt, but he's a little ashamed that he needs the crutches. Sometimes even adults are ashamed to be different from everyone else. So the best thing that we can do is to be sympathetic and helpful, but not talk too much about Grandpa's crutches. You might ask him how he's feeling and try to notice the times when he needs help. For example, if his crutches fall, you could pick them up and give them to him."

At four and five, a child's awareness of differences is at a peak. She is likely either to be uncomfortable or to overreact. For instance, if she sees a blind person on the street, she might announce loudly, "Look, Mom, she has a cane!" All such situations offer opportunities to teach consideration for others. "Yes," you might say, "she uses a cane because she can't see, and the cane helps her feel the curb and the walls she might run into. Shut your eyes and see how hard it would be to get around by yourself. It's wonderful that

she can do it alone, don't you think?" Once she takes this in, you can add, "She might not like having people pay attention to her cane, or shout out things about it. You can tell me softly." Helping your child find ways to handle her feelings actually comes as a big relief to her. When you model appropriate behavior, you help her to reduce her feelings of anxiety.

Conveying the Pleasure of Manners

Manners make life easier and more pleasant. If you can explain this, instead of presenting them as a chore, you'll get better results. For instance, if you say "excuse me" in the supermarket when you accidentally jostle someone, your child will imitate your behavior. Most people will smile back at this welcome behavior. Children can learn to understand that manners not only make relationships easier but also help them cope with unusual, stressful situations. Manners not only offer a framework for responding to everyday situations; they also help children deal with the unexpected. A child who feels comfortable with routines for the usual events is likely to handle the unusual ones more successfully. When your child does rise to an occasion, be sure to recognize her for it. Saying something like "Everyone admired the way you helped that little boy get up when he tripped and skinned his knee" will make your child feel good about herself.

When a child learns good manners without undue pressure from parents, she is proud of the skills she has mastered. Rather than an artificial structure imposed on her by adults, her manners spring from within. She has control over them and they are hers. Most of all, she will feel empowered in her sense that manners—and the help they give her in winning the esteem and affection of others—will always be available to her.

Rudeness

One common reaction to excess pressure to learn good manners comes out as conscious rudeness. When a child is aware of what is expected, she may act out with overtly rude behavior. This indicates that the child knows what she should do, but she feels more pressure than she can handle and reacts with behavior and language that are sure to get a response.

If your child reacts this way, you might say: "Of course, I'm disappointed. You and I know you know better. Maybe you're feeling like I expect a lot from you. But I do. I want other people to respect and like you. I know how great you are, and I want them to know it. I'm sorry you're feeling this way, but I hope you can be more sensitive to other people next time." At the first sign of resistance, you should avoid adding pressure. At that point, the child may not be able to listen, and this little lecture can be saved for a later time.

If a child is rude all the time, I would worry about her. There is no reason to put up with constant insensitivity to others by the age of four or five. This may be a sign of inner turmoil, or of the irritability often seen in children who are depressed. If it persists and invades all of a child's reactions, a consultation with a child psychologist or psychiatrist might be wise. Rudeness shuts out the world and compounds the child's anxieties.

As we said at the beginning of the chapter, manners reflect the agreements underlying our social interactions. They are less important in themselves than as keys to the larger social realm. A welcoming set of manners is like a passport, allowing freedom and access to people beyond the family. A child who is sensitive to people's feelings and has "nice manners" will find more smiles and new friends than frowns and wary resistance as she sets out to explore the world.

31. Play

PLAY IS A CHILD'S WORK. AS HE PLAYS, HE HAS A CHANCE TO RELIVE HIS experiences, try out questions about his world, and most of all, play out his dreams. In play, he may feel the safety of not being watched or directed, and the freedoms and exhilaration of constructing his own ideas. In play a child can embellish his new developmental achievements, experimenting as he goes. For example, when he has learned to walk, he may pick up a large wooden block that's too heavy for him, drop it, and lean over to try to pick it up again. He may hold it in both hands this time, teetering as he concentrates. Losing his balance, he sits down hard, but still holding onto the block. Now he can turn it over, mouth it, push it to make it go, growling to sound like a car in motion. After a few tries, he runs the block up a chair back, pulls himself up while still holding on to it, and walks uncertainly but successfully with his conquest in hand. What has he learned? (1) To enlarge on the new task of walking. (2) To balance while holding a heavy toy. (3) To turn a wooden block in his imagination into a noisy car. In this one bit of play, we see an athlete, a scientist, and a builder of dreams.

When does play begin? At each diapering, at each feeding, each time he's put to bed, the baby starts to respond to his parents' rhythms, smiles, strokes. By four months, play can become more complicated: A baby can add peek-a-

boo and begin to play with a toy strung over his crib. If he bats it, it will swing around. And then it comes back to his hand. When it moves it makes interesting shadows on the wall. The baby begins to feel that he can have an effect on his world, can try things out. This is a time when play can postpone more primitive requests—such as crying to be fed. The baby learns to fill up his own space with independent play. A parent can begin to push him into a schedule.

Much of play is a series of experiments, testing how the world works. By seven to eight months, when he crawls, he can crawl toward a forbidden television set or lamp. As he advances he looks back to check his parent's watchfulness. He learns that a parent will react by rushing over to pick him up to remove him or to restrain his arms. He is learning to predict and control important adults around him. He tries it again. His mother drops the phone to rush to him. He squeals with delight. What a source of power!

Once a child can walk, all kinds of new experiments are possible. He can walk around the corner and out of sight of his parents. If that doesn't bring them, he may screech, partly afraid he has lost them, partly to get a response. When his parents rush to find him, he has learned more about himself and them.

By fourteen months, one toddler may sit beside another toddler. One of them picks up a block to shake it. Without seeming to look, the other shakes his block in the same rhythm. Their play becomes matching. They try out rhythms, hiding the toy, throwing it, testing the friend by stealing his.

They are starting to explore social skills, communicating without words, joining and not joining a friend. Both toddlers learn what brings an explosion, a smile, more fun. Much of play is based on expectations, playful surprises, and variations. A father may play peek-a-boo but with a variation. He sets up a rhythm of hiding inside his raincoat, then poking his head out. The toddler responds each time with squeals of delight. Then the father violates the rhythm. He doesn't come out. The toddler waits, then looks warily for him. Has he disappeared, or maybe, more important—"Has he deserted me?" When his father drops the raincoat to pick him up and hug him, the toddler squeals in ecstasy. He has learned that disappearances may not last. People can still be there, even when they're out of sight.

By eighteen months, a child will imitate much of the world around him. He takes a teddy bear and the play bottle, and cuddles the bear to moan and rock. He wraps it up in a blanket. He leans over it, crooning and singing. He has taken the step into symbolic play. He acts out what he has experienced in his own nurturing.

At three years, a child can even act out a great variety of grown-up roles. A little girl might put on her mother's jacket like a dress, then saunter down the hall just like her mother, swinging her arms, cooing in trills and words from her mother's favorite song. She *is* her mother. She has incorporated her mother's walk, her gestures, her vocalizations. She has digested her femininity and is trying herself out as a grown-up woman. A boy will do the same with his father or an older brother. Fantasies are thus not an escape from the world, but an exploration of how it works. As children grow older and play more elaborate games, they learn to play according to rules. Even here they

experiment, and they may try to cheat to see what reactions it brings. They also learn to play cooperatively: Building forts, playing hide and seek, or acting out a story all require working together. It is easy to see how a heavy dose of television or video games can usurp some of the learning and joy of free play. It substitutes ready-made fantasies and passive watching for independent, active exploration and free-wheeling imagination. The extra richness and freedom of outdoor play, with its endless discoveries and new sensations, can be a high point of childhood. There the child can step fully into the roles of explorer, experimenter, builder, and dreamer.

Watching a child play after a traumatic experience demonstrates how much value play can have for a child. After a hospitalization, for instance, watch him play out all the many frightening experiences:

- Separation from home and family
- The scary strangeness of a smelly, small, sterile hospital room
- The hovering of strange nurses and doctors
- Being undressed
- Needles and blood taking
- At times, no one to comfort him
- Pain after an operation
- The worried expressions of parents, conveying their own fears

For weeks after he finally gets home, he may dare to act out these experiences with his toys. He puts his dolls and stuffed animals to bed, screams at them, "Shut up, you bad child." He attacks his teddy bear with a butter knife. He sticks his arms with the end of a pencil. He may even say what has been in his mind all this time, "If you hadn't been such a bad boy, I wouldn't have to hurt you like this." Play brings out all these thoughts and feelings and is bound to be therapeutic. A child may have to play out traumatic experiences over and over and over—to heal the frightening memories bit by bit. Play, without adult domination or interference, is the way a child learns about himself and his world.

32. Power Struggles and Emotional Manipulation

"You don't love me! If you did, you'd let me stay up and watch TV. Everyone else's mother and father does. They love them and you don't love me!"

This blatant attempt at manipulation will be familiar to parents. It will be accompanied by a wretched, oppressed expression. The lack of subtlety of such a request indicates that the child knows she hasn't a chance. But it will still hit home, and many parents will react angrily.

Such maneuvers are quite normal within the parent-child relationship, and unless parents overreact, not all that insidious. Both parents and child want their own way. Children are trying out their wings. They attempt to manipulate in order to learn the parents' limits. It is all part of learning to live with each other.

In thinking about emotional manipulation, parents should first remember that they, too, try to influence their children's behavior—with rewards, praise, bribes, and threats. Children soon learn to model themselves on their parents. Even a toddler soon learns that bringing her favorite book over to her parents is more likely to distract them from their conversation than simply asking for attention. Looking sad or nestling next to a parent on the couch is effective, too. No one would attribute an artful or insidious purpose to this behavior.

When visits to the supermarket are marred by temper tantrums, and quieted by promises of a "reward" by the parent if the child will be good for "fifteen minutes only," who is trying to control whom? Does either expect to win? I doubt it. I see this as a kind of language between them. At least it makes the supermarket visit a lot more exciting than it might otherwise be. If there's always the threat of a tantrum, and if the parent is constantly trying out tempting new rewards, the humdrum chores become quite lively. And in the process, each explores the other's limits.

Early Struggles for Power

During research at a childcare center, we observed four-month-old babies and noticed that these babies never became very invested in the caregivers or in play. They smiled and vocalized politely to the caregiver when she talked to them, but they rarely wiggled as they talked. We realized that they were conserving their emotional energy. However, when the mothers (or, in some cases, the fathers) came to get their babies at the end of the work day, each baby looked at her parent hungrily for the first few seconds and immediately started wailing. She would sob uncontrollably until her mother picked her up. When she got into her mother's arms, she'd squirm as if she were uncomfortable and turn her head away when her mother tried to kiss her. Each mother said the same thing: "She's angry that I left her all day." Sensitive and sophisticated caregivers point out to mothers that their babies have saved up their strong feelings all day. Now that they feel safe and loved, they can dare to let these feelings out. They cry and fall apart because they feel secure. During our study, one mother said, "You mean, he's manipulating me by this crying! But he's only four months old. How does he know it bothers me so much?" She looked down at him to chuck him under his chin, saying lovingly, "You bad boy! You're glad to see me!"

When these babies disintegrated in their parents' arms, they could feel the strong emotions they were generating. Babies and small children need to explore the limits of their power: "Can I get away with this—or not? How far can I go? Look how red in the face she gets when I tell her I don't want to wash my hands. Will Daddy get angry *every* time I leave my shoes in the front hall when he comes home? How far can I go?" Such teasing is a way of testing the strength and the importance of each parental expectation.

A child who has been at day care or preschool all day is loaded with exciting events to share, but her overworked parents must rush into the kitchen to prepare dinner. The child will work hard to keep them paying attention to

her. Why not sit down with her first and go to the kitchen after everyone is back together? Take her into to kitchen to help.

Children also manipulate parents into struggles with each other. It's their way of testing who's boss and where to go for indulgence. "Mummy said I could. Why don't you? Why is she so nice and you're so mean?" If the result of this test is an argument between the parents, and the stricter one is not backed up, a lesson has been learned. The child has discovered that her parents would rather fight with each other than back each other's decisions. She realizes that she can often get her own way if she ignites a disagreement. This gives her a sense of dangerous power—heady but frightening. It makes for an anxious, insecure child.

A child tests her powers in almost every part of her day. At mealtime, it takes the form of throwing food on the floor to see whether a parent will pick it up. An older child might say, "I won't eat this hamburger, but if I can have a hot dog, I'll eat it." Parents model this behavior when they say, "You can't have dessert until you've eaten everything on your plate." At bedtime, the glass of water or "I've got to go to the bathroom again" routines are not very subtle, but they serve the purpose of prolonging bedtime. Parents do their share when they say, "I'll let you watch a half hour more of TV if you'll go right to bed this time."

What is accomplished by all these maneuvers? They represent a necessary exploration on the part of both parent and child about the limits of each other's power. When I ask parents why they don't put a stop to the endless bedtime dramas, some will admit that they hate to end the day, to give up the child to sleep. "If I cut her off too soon, she'll go to bed feeling unloved and deserted." I'm not convinced that a child feels unloved or deserted when there are definite, firm limits to the bedtime routine, but I see how the struggle can be a way of softening the separation for both parent and child. Unconsciously, each is dodging the pain of separation, fearful of the future when even greater separations will be necessary. It seems so long ago that my own children called for one more glass of water. I miss it even now.

Responding to Manipulation

Should you, as a parent, allow yourself to be manipulated? It certainly depends on the circumstances and on the importance of the event. There is no reason why you can't enter into the game of being manipulated and share your child's pride when she sees how cleverly she has maneuvered. The ability to get one's way subtly and artfully can be an asset for every child's future.

However, you also want to set the record straight: While you admire her cleverness and want to acknowledge it, you may still not let her do what she wants. Make clear that you see her side of the issue, but help her see the pros and cons of her attempt. Demonstrate your respect for her, but stick by the rules you have set.

In order to encourage cooperation and cut down on a child's need for manipulation, the following suggestions may help:

- Before problems arise, discuss the issues. Openly present the choices and the way you'd like the child to behave. Use times when the child is in control of herself to discuss issues—not when she's in the midst of a struggle.
- Respect her for her capacity to make the choices you offer. Gear them to her age and ability to maintain control and to remember the choice she's made.
- Remember that provocative behavior is the child's way to test parents and learn limits.
- Examine your own tolerance for the child's misbehavior. Perhaps certain activities make you overreact.
- When possible, help her see that your requirements are in everyone's best interest. This gives you both a sense of communicating with each other, and helps prevent power struggles.
- Recognize that escalation of pressure and of manipulations results in escalation of defiance; offer alternatives.
- If you definitely want a child to do something, never ask, "Will you?" Instead, say, "Now it's time."
- Praise her after cooperation is achieved.

When we as parents use manipulation, we risk undermining trust, detracting from the child's ability to live up to the situation. When parents are direct and honest in their expectations for a child, she has the experience of being entrusted and empowered. A child can then make her own choice, and can realize the reward of achievement when she can live up to it. At the same time, parents are modeling for the child an alternative to emotional manipulation.

33. Prematurity

THE BIRTH OF A PREMATURE BABY IS ALWAYS A SHOCK. ALL THE WORK of pregnancy as preparation for labor and for the new baby's arrival is cut short. Neither a premature baby nor his parents are ready. They all face many adjustments.

The incidence of premature births is on the rise. At the same time, our ability to save very small babies has dramatically increased. Infants born after 24 weeks of gestation can now survive with our present medical technology. Medication given just before an anticipated premature birth can help the baby's immature lungs begin to function after birth. Intestinal problems that threaten many premature babies can now often be avoided. Not only are these extremely vulnerable immature infants more often saved at birth, but complications that endangered their future development are under better control as well. And yet, problems such as cerebral palsy, bronchopulmonary dysplasia, or vision or hearing problems are still common.

My colleague Heidelise Als has instituted her Neonatal Individualized Developmental Care Assessment Program (NIDCAP) in many neonatal intensive care units (NICUs) to recreate, as much as possible, the conditions in the womb. In these nurseries, the nurses and doctors protect babies' vulnerable senses (visual, auditory, tactile) by reducing noise levels, by covering isolettes to cut out the constant bright light of nurseries, and by carefully adjusting medical procedures and routine activities, such as cleaning and feeding, to make them as least intrusive as possible. These changes have resulted in significantly more rapid recovery rates, less need for oxygen, more rapid weight gain, and improvements in the babies' ability to respond to their environment as they recover and grow. By respecting the preemie's immature sensory organs' thresholds for taking in and utilizing information, this kind of external environment enhances his ability to recover more successfully.

The next step in assuring these fragile babies an optimal future is to include the parents in their care as soon as possible. Parents who deliver such a fragile, immature baby are bound to grieve and to feel terrified about his future. Giving them the opportunity to be there with him, to witness each advance in his recovery, and to participate in his care as soon as it is safe will give them an important chance to recover as he does—step by step. They can then be ready to understand and care for him at discharge.

Parents' Anxieties

A mother automatically wonders about her own role in a premature birth. Why was I unable to carry him? Was there something defective about me—or him? Did I do too much? Was I eating wrong? What did I do to this baby? Automatically, grieving sets in. The mother blames herself and feels helpless, even angry—at herself, but also at the world. She is likely to project her anger onto her husband and onto the caregivers of her baby. "Why aren't they doing more for him?" is a thinly veiled cover-up for her own feeling of inadequacy.

The high-tech, alarming surroundings of the NICU reinforce parents' image of their baby as fragile. Only when they see the strengths of the baby will parents begin to escape these anxieties. Over the years, many of us who have worked in these nurseries have fought for parent involvement. Concerned parents can be incorporated into the care of a premature baby early on. They can watch his recovery, and their own recovery can parallel his.

In certain premature nurseries in the United States and in other countries, a caregiving approach called "kangaroo care" has also been successful. In this approach, the tiny premature baby is kept directly on a parent's chest, skin to skin, as much as possible. The baby benefits from the warmth of the parent's body and from the heartbeat rhythm so familiar in the womb. The parents benefit from the closeness, the chance to get to know their baby, and the sense that they are helping him from the start. The baby recovers more quickly, gains weight, and is less likely to have complications.

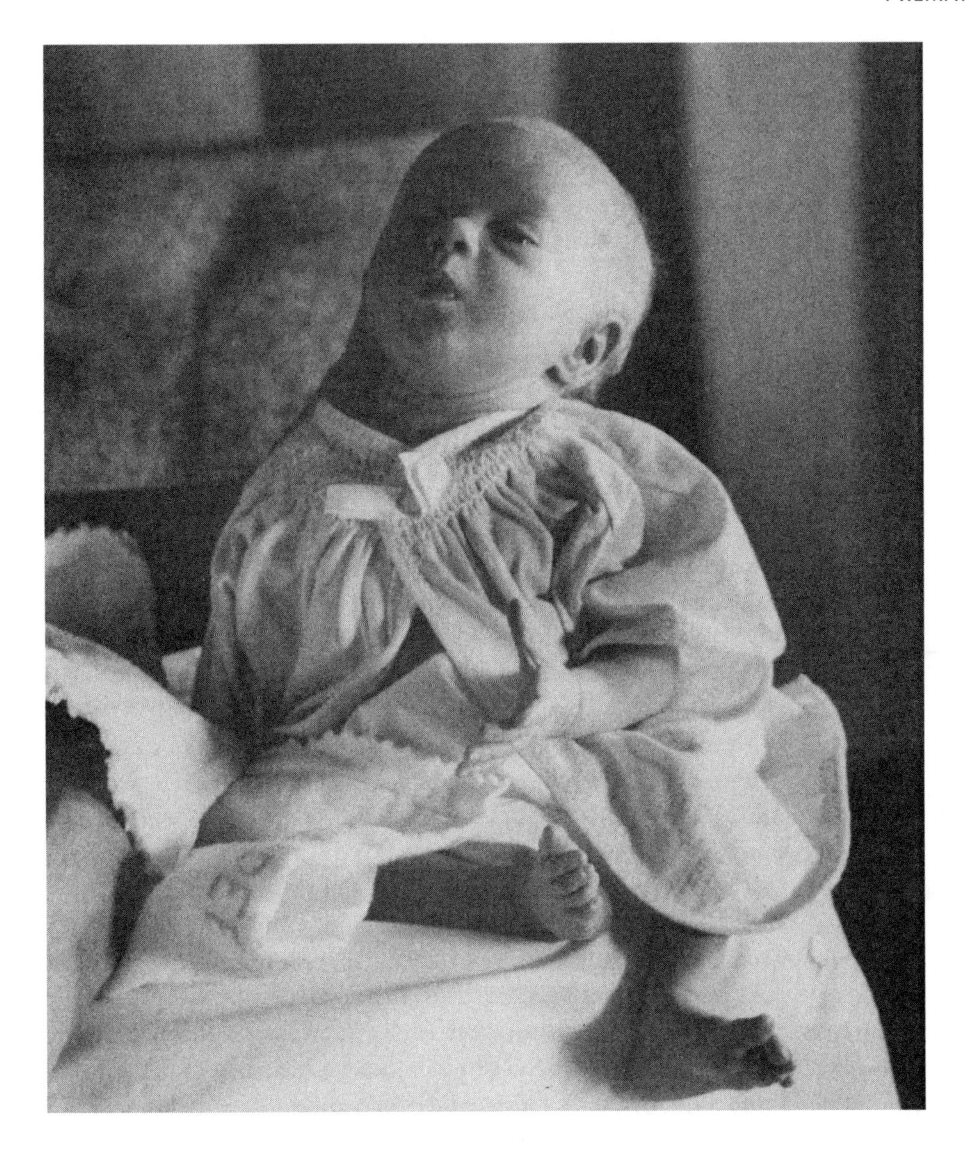

Recovery and Growth

In the quieter atmosphere of a modern NICU like the one just described, with less bright light and other stimuli, the fragile nervous system of a premature baby can organize more quickly and more effectively. He can gradually learn to get his breathing, heart rate, and blood pressure under control. Then he can begin to shut out the world around him when he's worn out, and to be alert to it when he's ready for more. A premature baby who is not overloaded will eventually cycle through the six states observed in all newborns. He will slowly learn to pay attention to positive interpersonal stimuli as he recovers from his early delivery.

Any stressed infant is likely to be hypersensitive to confusing noise and to bright lights as well as rough handling (see "Delays in Development and Developmental Disabilities"). The more attractive the stimulus (such as the human voice and face), the more the baby will overreact. As we said earlier, in order to reach such a baby with information that he can utilize for learning about himself and his world, each stimulus must be reduced in intensity, frequency, and duration. We have found that a premature or stressed infant can take in and respond to only one sensory modality at a time—either touch or voice or face or being picked up—and with very careful adjustment to the baby's responses. When he breathes fast and hard, or when his color changes, he is saying, "I've had enough."

Deep sleep can be a defense for a premature baby. Fussing and crying can be a way of shutting out the world, though one that drains energy. An alert state is vital to his learning, but it may overload him, too. Caregivers must respect this low threshold. As they interact with him, they must watch for cues of exhaustion.

The infant's motor behavior is another way he can signal exhaustion. When his movements become limp or jerky, changing from their previous tone and quality, he needs to rest. These changes are observable and are part of the premature baby's language of communication.

As the infant recovers from the early birth, he will become more and more able to accept a parent handling him, talking to him, and looking him in the face. When he can accept all these at once, he is already recovered and well-organized.

Parents are encouraged to visit the NICU daily and participate in feeding, changing, and cuddling their baby. They gradually overcome their natural fear of handling him. As they see him recover, they learn to identify his strengths and capacities for progress. Little details such as the tiny knit hats seen in some NICUs, names and pictures on the incubators, and toys brought by the parents personalize the tiny being and help parents see the individual child.

Once they learn that the baby may survive, both parents begin to worry about whether he'll be "normal." The inevitable comparisons to a normal full-term baby begin—and may last the rest of his life. Any parent who has been through the trauma of delivering a fragile infant is at risk of classifying that infant as vulnerable for years to come. The danger of hovering and of creating a "vulnerable child syndrome" is great. Parents need help in focusing on the infant's developing capabilities instead of on "what he might have been." This will take time. When parents can concentrate on the baby they have, instead of the one he might have been, all their energy can go into reinforcing his potential growth and development.

If, however, parents are constantly comparing him to their friend's babies, they are bound to find him lacking in some area. This drives them to try to help him compensate. They will watch his every move, lest he fail. Before he can build up the desire to try out a task, and to generate enough energy to try again, and to become frustrated until he succeeds, they rush to help him. Each success becomes theirs, not his. His self-image may remain that of a helpless, inadequate ex-preemie—a vulnerable child.

Parents can be cheered by how much we have learned in recent decades. Even infants with disabilities can profit by the new techniques for early intervention after discharge. There is increasing evidence for resilience in the nervous system of a premature baby since many of the pathways in the immature baby's brain appear to be redundant. In other words, even if there are damaged areas, other areas can often take over the functions of the damaged ones. Early intervention—that is, treatment started in the first months and years, during the most rapid period of brain development—can facilitate this process. It can also help an infant compensate for a neurological impairment, just as a blind baby learns to utilize touch and hearing with increased sensitivity. These techniques must be started as early as possible once the premature infant is stable and able to handle this kind of stimulation. For this reason, all premature infants should be assessed before discharge to judge the need for early intervention. Parents deserve to know how to reach such an infant and how to help him build on his own strengths.

The premature baby is likely to develop at a slower rate than a full-term one because of the cost of organizing his fragile nervous system. To adjust the baby's age for developmental expectations, I always add the number of weeks that the baby was short of full-term birth to the number of weeks a baby has spent in intensive care, and subtract the total from his chronological age. Some studies suggest that while an infant is acutely ill or on intensive support systems, such as a ventilator, brain development slows. All of his energy goes into his physical recovery. After he's well, his brain will begin to make progress and "catch-up" can begin. If parents expect a definite delay in his development, they may be spared the anxiety of wondering when he will ever catch up to his age group. They can help him just where he is and bask in his real progress.

While the majority of premature babies born at over 26–27 weeks gestation grow up with normal abilities, the incidence of learning disabilities and attentional disorders or hyperactivity is higher in premature babies than in healthy full-term ones. These conditions can be watched for. If parents suspect one, they should have an assessment by a qualified infant observer, or, for an older child, a child neuropsychologist. If they can be guided to understand the baby's particular challenges, they can help him master his difficulties. As we said, children can learn to compensate for developmental delays and disabilities. Early recognition of them can help the child progress toward his own potential rather than becoming set in a pattern of frustration (see "Delays in Development and Developmental Disabilities" and "Hypersensitivity and Hyperactivity"). Early intervention programs for these babies are available in all major cities (see *Useful Addresses and Web Sites*), and a parent should seek one as early as possible. They can help bring out a child's strengths, and it is a comfort for the parent to be with other parents who must face similar hurdles.

34. School Readiness

Before a parent even begins to assess a child's readiness for school, several issues need to be addressed. Can she separate from home? Is this the right school for her temperament? Will she be able to get along with other children? Will behavior problems interfere?

All of these questions need to be faced as a child starts preschool, and they will come up again at each transition, including first grade. Although the adjustments at preschool and again at kindergarten levels make an enormous difference to a child's ability to face later challenges, the same kinds of adjustment issues are likely to recur at each transition.

If there is a choice of schools, you should visit each one. Look for a balance between cognitive and social learning. Too much emphasis on cognitive learning at this age may mean that the child's need to grow as a social being is neglected. The physical layout and the degree of adaptation of the rhythms of activity, teaching, and relaxation to individual children reflect the approach of each school. Watch the very active or the very quiet children to see how they are helped to fit in. Above all, assess the teacher's capacity for warmth, patience, and ability to encourage the individuality of each child. Will she be able to like your child? Your own reaction to the teacher may be the most sensitive way to predict this. Her ability to relate to your child may be as critical as her teaching skills in reinforcing your child's belief in her capacity to learn and her courage to take the risk of making mistakes that she can learn from. I would urge you to be sure that your child's emotional development will be fostered so that she can realize her cognitive potential.

Readiness

Parents today are often haunted by the feeling that children must be prepared to compete early, to succeed from the start. Few can resist the urge to prepare their children by teaching them the skills they'll need in school—reading, writing, and arithmetic. If children are not ready, they are likely to feel overwhelmed, and that they've failed before they've even started. Instead, children need to be introduced to concepts in smaller steps, and when they're ready, that prepare them to learn these skills later on. Simply reading to a young child, and modeling interest in learning from books, is a powerful way of preparing a child for later academic demands, even though the cuddling that accompanies "story time" is the most delicious reward. Parents can start early, as programs like "Reach Out and Read" have shown, by helping very young children discover that the print on a page tells a story. This is an example of a "pre-literacy" concept that can motivate a child—without pressure—to want to learn to read. Pressure on children to perform before they are ready seems to me to be cheating the child of opportunities for exploration, for play, and for the learning that comes from experimentation. Failure, followed by frustration or boredom, can set the stage for resistance on the child's part to learn when later chances come along. Too many "precocious" learners burn out later. Most important is the child's own eagerness to learn and her self-concept. She must feel that she herself is in control of her learning.

Psychologist Betty Bardige quoted a study of three-year-olds in which children from poor, underserved, and stressed families had only half as many words and concepts with which to start preschool. Can they catch up? In families where parents talk and read with their children, by the age of three they are already equipped with the words and concepts that will give them a head start in the learning process.

The structure of a school experience requires many things of a child. She must be able to concentrate and pay attention, while tuning out distractions. She must have the physical stamina and patience to sit for long periods, as well as the capacity to fit into the rhythms of rest and activity of the school. A child must have the capacity to understand, remember, and follow two-

and three-part directions, do assigned tasks, manage personal possessions, and handle her own clothing. This is all a necessary part of learning to learn in a group, but it is demanding.

The way a child's learning style and abilities are welcomed may shape her readiness to learn in the future. Fine motor skills such as cutting, drawing, and writing demand considerable neurological maturity as well as the patience, care, and perseverance that come with emotional maturity. It would be a fallacy to think that all children are ready for these challenges at the same time. "Late bloomers" in any area deserve to be identified and have their pace respected. Giving a child who needs it an extra year to mature may be much more critical than timing preschool so that a child arrives in first grade when she is six. The goal should be to build an interest in learning in the child herself. Too many children are pushed because they are bright enough, but not enough attention is paid to their maturity and readiness.

As decisions about preschool, kindergarten, and first grade arise, the following reasons to give children extra time should be considered:

Family patterns of slow development—"late bloomers"
Prematurity or physical problems in early life
Delay in physical size or development
Immature motor development—awkwardness, poor motor skills, such as in catching or throwing a ball, drawing, or cutting
Easy distractibility and short attention span
Difficulty with right-left hand or eye-hand coordination, such as in copying a circle or a diamond
Lagging social development—difficulty taking turns, sharing, or playing. If the child is shunned by children her own age, take it seriously.

Each of these might be a reason to allow a child to mature another year before starting preschool, or to stay in preschool or kindergarten a year longer. However, if any such delays or disabilities continue to interfere with the child's progress, arrange for a careful assessment—neurological and psychological—to identify the underlying problem. While the child may well outgrow the problem, it is important to understand the reasons for the delay and also identify her strengths. There are many programs for children with attention disorders, motor delays, and learning disabilities, and there is no sense in leaving these to mature with time alone when intervention is needed. (See *Useful Addresses and Web Sites* at the end of this book and "Delays in Development and Developmental Disabilities.") Find one that fits your child's difficulty, and be sure it's a positive and exciting one—not one that pushes such a child to "grow up," to "be good," or to "pay attention." Such programs can be punitive, and they fail to reinforce the child positively for her successes. Instilling a sense of failure will surely lead to more failure. Find a program that builds skill while bolstering the child's confidence and also one that focuses on helping you understand your child better.

Preparing a Child

Parents' readiness to separate from a child is as important to a child's school adjustment as being ready herself. Every parent worries, "What will they think of her? Will they see how smart and wonderful she is, or just focus on her difficulties? Will the teacher be kind and encouraging, or will he dampen her spirit?" All of these concerns reflect a natural anxiety on parents' part about sharing their child. These questions cover up the fears of separation and the inevitable competition between parents and teachers. Parents see the child's entry into school (or child care, if this has occurred earlier) as the beginning of the end of their intimacy with her. "Next, she'll be a teenager! Before we know it, she'll be gone." Parents must face their own issues about separation before they can help the child with hers.

Preparing a child in advance for separation and the demands of preschool will make a big difference. Tell her whatever you know about what to expect. Take her to meet her teacher and to see her room beforehand. Be sure she knows one or two of her classmates, if you can. If necessary, woo them ahead of time by taking them together to a park or a zoo (see Part 3, "Friends"). Maybe you and the friend's mother can introduce them to school together the first day. Let the child take something special from home. When you get to school, introduce her to the teacher, to the cubbyhole for her belongings, to some other children, and to the play area. Demonstrate your confidence in the teacher by a complimentary statement such as, "What an exciting day you have planned! We feel very lucky that Georgia can join this class." My mother always took a plate of fried chicken to a new teacher. I was so embarrassed, but in retrospect, it surely softened her toward me.

Tell the child when you are leaving. This is very important. Kiss her goodbye, and don't prolong it. Tell her when you will be back, and *be there on time*! Once you have said goodbye, leave and don't turn around. Compliment the child afterward on how well she has handled it. She's made a big step! Listen to the account of her day. Don't send a child by bus the first few days—until she feels equal to it.

If the teacher reports that the child cries steadily, you may want to introduce her to school more gradually. I can't believe that leaving a child crying all day at school could be a learning experience for her. Plan with the teacher to return after a short while, and stay in school to see whether your presence might anchor the child. Consult with the teacher. Use different techniques to draw the child into activities. Find a pal for your child and woo her. Sometimes, a parent may need to stay in the classroom for as long as a week before a child begins to feel comfortable in the new setting. But of course it is worth it in the long run. You can gradually increase the amount of time you spend away from the classroom.

Many children adjust nicely at first but then show signs of regression at home. Symptoms in apparently unrelated areas, such as sleep, feeding, or temper tantrums, which have long since been handled, may recur. To me, these regressions demonstrate the kind of energy a child is mustering to meet the challenge. When a child has to handle a new situation, she is likely to regress temporarily, as if she were gathering energy for the important adjustment. By regressing, she can return to an earlier stage of development, collect

whatever parental backup she needs, and reorganize herself. Regression often frightens parents, but it needn't unless it lasts too long. The learning that occurs during this period of reorganization is well worth the temporary recurrence of old patterns. Each child is likely to fall back on the developmental issues that she has last conquered. If she's just conquered fears at night, she'll begin to see monsters again. If she has just stopped biting her nails, she is likely to start again. Your role will be to support her in understanding the reason for her regression and to help her understand herself as she strives to cope with the new challenges at school. As she begins to succeed, let her know how proud you are.

Some children will begin to have stomachaches or headaches in the morning before they must leave for school (see "Stomachaches, Headaches, and Stress"). They may beg to be allowed to stay home. If these problems continue, or if the episodes of regression increase, they may be signs of too much pressure. The first step is to talk to the teacher. Find out whether there are stresses at school that you can alleviate. Is the child getting along with her peers? Is she learning? Does she show signs of feeling inadequate?

Don't set yourself against the teacher. Even though a child may complain that she (or he) is too strict, or say, "She's so mean to me," you won't help by agreeing. Let your child know that you and the teacher will both be trying to make life become easier at school.

Talk to the child about her backward slide. Let her know that you understand and that you'll try to help. Explain that staying home would not help her and that you expect her to keep going. Assure her that all children go through periods like this when school is new and scary. It doesn't mean that anything serious is wrong, but that she's facing a new, demanding life and also leaving the safety of home. If you feel that the child is afraid of leaving home, try to understand the underlying issues. Ask her, "Are you afraid that something will happen to me? It won't, for I won't let it." "Do you wonder whether I'm playing with your little brother (or sister) and forgetting about you? I never could. I'm so proud of my big girl. I think of you all the time, but I *expect* you to grow up and be ready to go to school. Your brother will have to learn this, too, and you'll be able to help him."

Since a child's ability to cope with the stress of leaving each morning could well be tied to her physiological status, be sure you know that she's not rundown or anemic. Many children wake up with low blood sugar levels at this time. Low blood sugar can contribute to headaches or stomachaches. I've always thought that anxiety can push the blood sugar level down even further. I recommend that parents leave a glass of orange juice by the child's bedside.

She should drink it as soon as she wakes, before she gets out of bed to move around. If she feels better, she will eat a better breakfast and will then be better able to handle the stress of school and separation from home.

The period of adjusting at school can be stormy. Parents worry that the child's bad behavior will label her in her teacher's mind. They may press her at home to "pay attention and be good in school." This won't help. Instead, remember that each child adjusts at her own rate. Try to make home a welcoming oasis of safety and warmth. Let the child blow off steam at home to balance the school pressure. Don't pressure her to perform in all areas at once—give her space. Back up her self-esteem: The basis for that is laid at home. Then she can have the confidence to model on the examples you set for curiosity about the world, openness to new ideas, and a readiness to take risks and learn from mistakes.

Going off to preschool or kindergarten is a child's first and most important opportunity to learn about adjusting to the outside world. She will be able to learn to participate as part of a group, to read social clues, to conform to grown-up expectations and rules, to learn about social mores of children her own age, and to develop her own style for making and keeping friends. These new skills will serve her in her pursuit of academic achievements that will come in time. What the child learns about handling herself in a group and about embracing new situations will last her forever (see also "Self-Image and Self-Esteem").

35. Self-Image and Self-Esteem

The excitement of mastering a task can be seen in young babies as they roll over, grasp a cracker, or stack blocks. When they achieve a task, watch their faces glow. These experiences provide a base for a sense of one's competence, and of positive self-regard. When parents encourage a baby to learn a task by himself, they set the stage for a good future self-image. As the child struggles and finally triumphs, the light in his eyes begins to glow. This is his recognition of having fought for and achieved a task by himself. Parents' own expectations and past experiences will influence whether they can afford to let a child experiment, get frustrated, learn from his mistakes, and then succeed on his own. Without this balance of independence and encouragement, a child can develop an expectation of passive compliance or failure and become dependent on excessive praise. He needs to fight for himself in order to realize his own competence.

Encouraging a Positive Self-Image

How can you, as a parent, offer both autonomy and support to a baby? What can you do to encourage a child's positive self-image, to build his positive feelings about who he is becoming? Being warm and loving is certainly the

first step. But you also need to model, transmit, and reinforce attitudes most likely to serve him in confronting challenges and solving problems—for example, patience, perseverance, and resourcefulness. Qualities like these are usually picked up by a baby as he identifies with his parents. But in addition to identification, an infant's early efforts to act on his world contribute to his image of himself as competent.

For example, take a toddler who is playing with a simple puzzle. It is essential for a parent to learn when to sit back and watch him rather than rushing in to help as he tries to fit in the pieces, turning them one way then another, dropping them in his frustration. As the baby picks up the pieces to try again, he mouths them, watching the puzzle as if it were an adversary. Finally, he takes the chance. He places the piece on the puzzle board. He turns it and it fits! He looks around triumphantly. At this point, your best move is to say softly, "You just did it—yourself!" You will be reinforcing him as he recognizes his own achievement. From your quiet words he will also learn to be his own cheerleader whenever he begins to feel discouraged. Had you stepped in earlier—to show him, or even to encourage him to keep trying—you would have cut his triumph in half. *He* persisted and *he* did it. It can be very difficult for a parent to sit back and allow a child to experience his own frustration and go through some failure before succeeding. But it may be a critical part of his recognition of success when he does succeed. Frustration can be a positive force for a child's learning—about himself—as long as it doesn't overwhelm him in the process. If a task is too far beyond a child's developmental readiness, a parent may need to step in to break it into smaller steps first before pulling back to let the child try and fail and eventually succeed.

How can parents arrive at this fine line between the challenge of frustration and the discouragement of overwhelming obstacles? This is possible only by watching the child and observing whether he shows curiosity, persistence, and the ability to succeed at a problem, or a look of defeat and inertia. Both too much encouragement and too much pressure defeat a child's own incentive.

Balancing Praise and Criticism

The pressure on a small child to learn to read, write, or perform tasks that may not be appropriate for his age and stage of development is a danger if it overwhelms the child's own sense of competence. It is quite possible to teach a child to read, write, or play an instrument at a surprisingly early age. He gathers in rewards from everyone around him as he performs. But precocity carries a price. His performance may be motivated by a desire to please others rather than by any inner curiosity of his own. If he learns just to please others, he may not get the same sense of having achieved for his own reasons.

A certain amount of praise can reinforce a child's awareness of his own success. But too much, as mentioned before, can become pressure rather than encouragement. Harsh criticism can induce passivity rather than energy to solve problems. How do you know when to criticize and when to praise? Once again, watch the child. If he's becoming irritable, he's probably under too much pressure. If he seems hesitant and fearful of asserting himself, he may need constructive encouragement and less criticism.

An increasing number of studies are showing how strongly children identify with our patterns of behavior. If we are too critical, the child will learn to be critical and will see it as an acceptable way to treat others or himself.

While we cannot change our own styles and outlook just to influence our children, we can learn ways to nurture a child's initiative and boost his self-esteem. In any new task, encourage the child, but don't shape it for him or press him. Praise him gently for his persistence in the face of failure—and when he succeeds. But also help him learn to praise himself. Let him try out several different ways of doing the same thing, and let him fail until he finds one that works. If he gets in a jam or follows a dead-end course, don't rush to help him. Let him discover his predicament, and praise him when he tries again. Let him try every new task in his own bumbling, exploratory fashion. Let him tangle his laces, spill his milk (don't give him much at a time!), knock over the stack of blocks, or break the crayon. All of this, of course, must be within the bounds of safety and respect for others. But never forget the enormous power of frustration to fuel a small child as he searches for mastery and a sense of his own competence.

Boosting Self-Esteem at All Ages

The following is a brief outline of the many opportunities to boost a child's self-esteem through play, feeding, and encounters with other children:

Early Play

1–4 months: Lean over the baby to elicit his smiles and vocalizations. As he smiles, you smile. But wait then for his next smile or vocalization. When he produces one, reinforce it with a *gentle* imitation. As he smiles over and over, watch his face for recognition of his achievement in influencing your response. Don't overwhelm him.

4–6 months: As you lean over him, vocalize gently. Wait for him to try to imitate you. When he does repeat it, let your face express your realization of what he's done.

6–8 months: Play peek-a-boo in a way that will elicit his imitation of your play. Then follow his behavior, don't lead. At one point, violate the rhythm by not opening your hands. Watch his face as he recognizes this violation of his expectation.

8–10 months: As you read a picture book to him, ask "Where is the doggie?" If he can point to it, encourage him. "Where is the Mommy?" He points. You say, "Right." His face glows.

Feeding

5–8 months: Let him hold a spoon or cup when you feed him.

8–10 months: Let him begin to pick up two or three small bits of food to feed himself. Don't worry if he drops them.

10–12 months: Let him imitate you with a few sips in a cup, and let him try using a spoon.

12–16 months: Let him continue to feed himself finger food, hold his own bottle (in your lap), and imitate with a cup.

16 months: Let him use a fork to spear his food. Let him decide whether he wants to eat or not, but don't try out a hundred things to try to please him.

Learning About Other Children

1–2 years: Give him occasions for play with peers. Prepare him ahead of time. Don't leave him until he's ready, but encourage him eventually to stay in a play group without you. Interfere as little as possible in toddlers' play. Even biting, scratching, and hair pulling can be learning opportunities if you can stay out of it. However, don't leave a child over and over again with an overwhelmingly aggressive or passive playmate. He will learn most from more equal relationships. Don't push him to share his toys. Let other children teach him. Set out toys that he can share.

3–5 years: Encourage him to play independently with others. Stay out of their crises. Reward him for his successes in learning about others. Encourage one or two regular buddies, playmates who come regularly, so that he can get to know them well, to understand and rely on them. They'll give him the skills he needs to be competent with other children, and they'll teach him to share and to be considerate of others' feelings. When he can woo and help a friend, he's ready for mastering a group of children, and he will feel proud of himself when he does (see also "Play").

36. Separation

The passionate attachment that sweeps over parents in the first months of the baby's life is intense. The surge of nurturing feelings that are uncovered drive new parents to say, "I've never been in love like this before." Learning to become a nurturer is both the most exhilarating and the most demanding task any young adult will experience. Any separation can be painful.

Underlying any intense attachment is a deep fear of loss. As a parent gives himself to deep caring feelings, the other side of the coin must surface. What if I lose my child? Will she care about losing me for part of the day as much as I do? If I share her, will she love someone else more? The first real separation is bound to bring a grief reaction.

Child Care

"Leaving my baby for someone else to take care of is the hardest thing I've ever had to do. When I look back at her in someone else's arms, I can hardly bear it. It is as if I'm leaving part of myself. I'm not sure I can do it day after day."

This parent is putting into words what so many feel when they put their baby in child care to go back to work. The way this parent expresses her feelings makes clear that the pain of separation is *hers.* Given good care, babies may adapt more quickly than parents (see "Childcare Choices," Part 3). Although they miss their parents and always relate passionately to them at the end of the day, when they are in good care they seem to adjust well. But we all know it may matter to the baby in subtle ways, such as developing regular, reliable patterns of expectation. Adjusting to more than parental care is a challenge for the baby, though it may be an asset in the long run.

When parents turn a baby over to another caregiver, they will feel loneliness, guilt, helplessness, and even anger: Why must I do this? Certain defenses against the intensity of these feelings are common:

Denial—saying that the separation doesn't matter, either to the baby or to yourself

Projection—assigning the role of competent caregiver to the other person and the bad one to yourself, or vice versa—that is, both admiring and resenting the "other" and suspecting her of not taking "perfect" care of your baby

Detachment—attempting to dilute your intense feelings of deep attachment to soften the pain of leaving your baby.

Mothers and fathers are likely to face such reactions after a passionate start with a baby. These reactions are usually unconscious, but they demand energy and can leave parents feeling depressed. I urge parents to recognize these feelings and to allow them to surface. An awareness of the anguish that separations will bring frees a parent to confront this reaction and to master it. Burying such feelings, in contrast, can become debilitating and destructive. Work can suffer and home life can become tense as both parents try to suppress their feelings. Separation and reunion with the baby each day become extremely charged events. "Why does she always turn away when I come to get her? Is she angry with me? Have I lost our closeness? Am I damaging her future?"

Some parents find that discussing these normal, universal feelings with a spouse, other parents, or an understanding teacher can help defuse them. Recognizing the grief of separation and the defenses against it can lead to ways of mastering them without diluting the intensity of the relationship. When working parents tell me how guilty they feel at having to leave their baby, I reassure them that feeling guilty is normal. Of course they will feel that way. Guilt is a powerful, motivating force. It drives people to find solutions for coping with separation. The baby will make it if the parents do. Babies have plenty of love to go around, but they need to know that parents are there for them at the beginning and end of every day.

The baby will learn her own ways of coping if she is in the care of a nurturing person. Her protest when you leave is necessary and healthy. She will then turn to the other person. It is important for her to develop a caring relationship with that person (see sections on stranger awareness and separation in chapters 6 and 8). Together with colleagues, I have observed babies in child care as they learned to cope with separation from their parents. They seemed to cut down on the intensity of their interactions during the day. They played, but perhaps not as vigorously as they would with parents. They napped but didn't seem to sleep as deeply. They stored up their powerful reactions for the reunion at the end of the day. When a baby's parent loomed into sight, the baby would often pointedly turn away, as if to master the intensity of her feelings at the reunion with this all-important person. Then, she was likely to blow. She had saved up her protest, her intense feelings, all day for the one she could trust. No wonder some caregivers may say, "She never does that for me, dear." Parents need to realize that these intense reactions are necessary to a passionate reunion.

When you understand that the pain of separation is healthy, normal, and inevitably a parental issue, you can learn to handle it. Part of the challenge is learning to save your most intense feelings for the reunion with your baby at the end of each day. As we have seen, the baby can do it. So can you. Once you have searched for the best possible care and feel assured that your child is safe and in the hands of someone who can love and nurture her, you will need to trust that person. It's difficult, for your natural competition will surface at each separation and reunion.

Taking certain steps can help a great deal.

Get up early enough to have a few minutes of cuddling and relaxed play with your baby before you take her to child care.

Let her refuse food at breakfast. Let her tease you about getting dressed. A few moments of this will give her a sense of being in control of her day. At child care, she may not dare to express negativism.

As soon as she's old enough, develop a routine of talking to her about leaving, but always add, "I'll be back." This is for you as much as it is for her. You are preparing yourself, and her, for separation.

Work with the childcare provider to develop a separation routine. Take off the child's outer clothing yourself, hug her, turn her over to the caregiver, then say, "Goodbye, I'll see you this afternoon. Ms. ——— will take care of you while I'm gone." Then, once she has begun to interact with the caregiver, say goodbye and go. Don't prolong the parting. It makes it much harder. Be prepared for protest. By leaving, you give her a chance to protest but also to turn toward the activities of the day. Children are remarkably resilient in an environment that respects and cares about them.

Nursery and Preschool

From the child's standpoint, a first separation from home is never easy at any age. But as they grow older, children need peers and play opportunities that you as a parent can no longer provide. Even if a child has siblings, she needs peers her own age. The opportunities to learn about herself in a social situation are great. The pain of an initial separation from you will therefore be balanced by her and *your* awareness of what she will gain in this new setting. The attraction of other children, games, and group activities balances the pain of leaving the safe coziness of home. Again, there are ways you can ease the transition:

Prepare yourself first so that you can then face her feelings.
Read stories to her about separation and about the exciting aspects of play with other children.
Introduce her to at least one other child in the nursery school or play group. Invite this child and her parent to go somewhere with the two of you.
Introduce her to the caregiver or teacher beforehand and see to it that she knows you like that person. Stay with her for awhile for the first week or so—until she's adjusted.
Allow her to regress—dress her in the morning. Let her sit in your lap. Don't put pressure on her to sit still and finish her meals.
Let her take a lovey or a reminder from home each day—even a picture of you.
When you get to the nursery school, take off her outdoor gear. Put it in her cubby with her. Be sure the caregiver or teacher says hello to her.
Hug her and be sure she has a chance to turn to someone else—a child or an adult.
Remind her when you'll return.
Leave—don't linger. But don't run off without saying goodbye.
When you pick her up, hug her and allow her to blow up at you. Hug her until it's over. Then say, "Now we can go home and be a family again. I missed you and I know you missed me. But we'll always have each other at the end of the day."

A child is likely to have a delayed reaction to her first separation from home. Her renewed dependence will probably surprise you. Long after she's made the initial adjustment, she'll regress to a clinging protest about leaving home all over again. Regressive behavior may well reappear, such as soiling, wetting, or increased crying, thumb sucking, dependence on a bottle or a lovey, sleep difficulties, night fears, or bad dreams. All of these are evidence of the stress of learning to handle new feelings. See this regression as normal. Reassure her that she'll be able to give it up when she's feeling in control again. Meanwhile, you'll help her.

When this delayed reaction occurs, you may have to repeat all of the steps to prepare for and handle separation. Talk it over with your child's caregiver or teacher and ask whether you should stay again for a few days to soften the separations. Talk it over with your child, too, so that she understands herself.

You and your spouse should now institute a special time with the child each day and a saved-up special time for the weekend. At such a time, each of you can be with her alone—with a bedtime ritual or some other special activity. Ask her about her life at nursery school. This special time will allow her to identify with each of you more intensely. On the weekend, you should each save at least an hour alone with her. In that hour, you do what *she* wants. Use it as an opportunity to get close to her.

Each year, the first few days of school will be difficult. The rigid routines and the expectations of school close in on the child. Each new school year is a rite of passage, a reminder to a child that she is growing up and must become independent. The hardest thing about these days is likely to be leaving home and old routines. If she has younger siblings at home, she'll wonder, "What will they be doing while I'm gone? Will my parents miss me?" Leaving home can be a thrilling step into the world, but it brings a sense of loss. This sense of loss is bittersweet, carrying with it all the warm security of home that the child is giving up as she makes each step into the world (see also "School Readiness").

Moving

Losing friends and an old neighborhood can surely be a setback for a child. When it is necessary to move, a child should be prepared in advance. She should have a chance to make a new friend in the new neighborhood as soon as possible. Find one or two new acquaintances that you think might be likely to become friends for your child. Take your child and a new friend out together once a week until they feel close to each other. A new child can enter an already closed group more readily through another child. It won't be long before the new friends will take over.

But a child mustn't be expected to give up her old friends. Have a going-away party before you leave. Then, if possible, after the move is made, take her back to see her old friends and the old house. Even if you have to travel to get back there, I'd do it. If the old friends are not too far away, try to have them come over at least once or twice to visit. Encourage your child to talk about the old neighborhood and the old friends. Pull out pictures of them to remind her. Telephone them. Write them for a while. Giving up close relationships in childhood can be painful. But it can also be a time to learn how important friendships are (see "Friends," Part 3).

37. Sibling Rivalry

RIVALRY BETWEEN SIBLINGS IS NORMAL AND INEVITABLE. CHILDREN LEARN about each other and about themselves in rivalry. At the same time, they learn to care about one another. Despite this, parents find it almost impossible to stay out of their children's fights. Why? Many decades ago, the renowned psychoanalyst Erik Erikson pointed out to me that no parent feels entirely adequate to more than one child. When children get into a struggle, an underlying guilt makes parents feel that they must protect one or the other. They quickly make any situation into a triangle. The children's rivalry is fueled by the goal of getting parents involved.

Accepting Rivalry

A parent's feeling of not being capable of loving two children begins when a mother is pregnant with a second child. In my office, when a mother proudly announces her second pregnancy, I often sense this worry. I ask, "How does your older one feel?" The mother will flush and look sad. Some may start to weep. It is so difficult to anticipate bringing home an invader of the love affair that one has created with the first child. Sibling rivalry is intensified by these close feelings of attachment between the parents and the first child. At first,

the older child will aim her anger at her parents, for deserting her. Then, as the baby begins to be mobile and to get into her toys, she will find ways of torturing the baby in order to involve a parent in her rivalry. She will manage somehow. As the baby gets more and more attractive to outsiders (most second children learn early how to win an audience), the older child's face will sag, and her whole body will droop. She may withdraw to sit in her parent's lap, thumb in mouth, watching visitors play gaily with the charming baby.

As we pointed out in the book *Understanding Sibling Rivalry—The Brazelton Way* (see *Further Reading*), learning to live with others in a family is one of the most important experiences that anyone can have. Learning to share is not a skill that is taught very often these days. We as parents may worry too much about protecting a child from her feelings of rivalry. The ideal is to teach a child how to feel responsible for her sibling and for the whole family's wellbeing. Rivalrous feelings needn't be denied in order to accomplish this. Learning responsibility for others comes from learning to share with a sibling, to face rivalrous feelings, and to find the caring ones that accompany them.

To help the older one feel involved, depending on her age, give her tasks to do for the baby: feeding the baby, bringing diapers, helping to hold him and to cuddle him when he's upset. Let her choose the baby's clothes, help get the baby dressed by lying down next to him to talk to him while he's changed, hold the baby for part of the feeding, and help push the carriage.

When you are taking them out together, prepare the older child: "Nearly all strangers love babies. It's not that they don't like you. Come and sit with me when you are feeling lonely, neglected, and jealous." Then, gather her up when everyone fawns over the baby.

If you're at home all day, you will have a special set of worries. Being at home, you feel you should be making it pay for the children, since that is the reason you're at home. Rivalry makes you feel you're being unsuccessful. When the children fight for you, as they will, you feel completely unrewarded.

If you work outside the home, it is critical to plan for your reentry each day. Expect the children to fall apart as you walk in the door and to set up an intensely rivalrous situation. Calmly but firmly, sit down with one on each side to ask about their day. After you've talked with them both, you can start the end-of-the-day chores. Be sure they help. Let them choose which chores they'll do, and thank them for their help. Be sure you have some time with each one at the end of the day.

As we've said earlier, each parent should plan a special time *alone* with each child at the end of the week. Talk about it all week and make sure you keep it reliably special.

Valuing Individuality

Parents often wonder how to treat each child equally. The answer is simple: You can't. Each child has a different personality and needs a different approach. However, it can be exhausting to try to shift gears for each one. It makes a real difference to talk openly—but privately and nonjudgmentally—with each one about their uniqueness. For instance, you might say to one, "You need me to speak softly." To another, "You always need me to speak angrily before you will listen." This eventually gives them insight into themselves.

When they torture you with "You're always nicer to him than you are to me," you can say, "You are very different people—which is great. So I need to treat each of you differently. When I speak loudly to you, it's to make you listen, but that doesn't mean I love you less." If you don't get caught up in feeling guilty about the different feelings you have for each one, they needn't feel it either. Children from large families, or those who are raised with other children nearby, seem to have an easier time in respecting each other's differences.

By valuing each child's individuality yourself and then conveying your awareness of his or her individual strengths, you'll encourage each one. As you make these strengths explicit, the child will be able to understand and value them. Even if you yourself have preferences for certain traits, based on your own experiences, you don't need to pass on negative labels for other traits. If you can understand the basis for your own preferences, you will be less likely to pass them on in any pejorative way.

When parents can stop feeling guilty about shortchanging one child or the other, they will find it easier to stay out of sibling fights. If you are involved in them, you create a triangle that allows each child to manipulate you. They never get a chance to work things out with each other. Leave their fights to them, saying, "You know, I don't know who's right and who's wrong. You'll have to figure it out yourselves." Then leave the room. You'll find that they fight a lot less if you aren't there to tantalize them with the possibility that you might be drawn in to take sides. I have never heard of young siblings really hurting one another when a parent wasn't present or very nearby.

Gender Differences

Although many parents feel strongly about gender differences, few want to stereotype boys and girls. Such differences are indeed complex. Despite the desire of some parents to treat children of either gender in the same way, the child of the opposite sex will have a particular appeal to each parent. You will inevitably treat children differently because of their gender. What you must not do is devalue either one. Just as every little girl needs an admiring father, every boy needs a mother who believes that he's *the* greatest boy of all.

Tattling and Teasing

When tattling occurs, which it will, try never to reward it. Remind the tattler that he would be very upset if someone told on him and that you really don't want to be involved. Since parents need to stay in touch with children's play for safety reasons, staying out of fights and not responding to each wail may be difficult. Keep an ear out for unusual sounds (or an ominous lack of noise), but try to leave children to work out their conflicts on their own as much as possible. If siblings continue to tease each other endlessly, resist taking sides.

If necessary, separate them for a time-out period. Consider inviting friends for each one. A playmate of each age helps enormously. Reward a child when she has been positive in her reactions to her sibling.

Age and Birth Order

A child's age and place in the family will necessarily influence how that child is treated. The oldest child will always be a special child to her parents. This will be a mixed blessing. While she gets a lot of pressure and can suffer from new parents' mistakes, she also gets a privileged relationship. She is likely to be given responsibility for a certain amount of babysitting, caregiving, and housework. This can give her a sense of competence and importance to her parents that will last into adulthood.

A second child may complain that no one loves him, that he is always "second," and on and on. This will be compounded if he is a middle child. If parents can avoid feeling guilty, the child won't feel rewarded by his complaints and will eventually see that he gets his share, too. Many second children become competitive and make up for being second by being successful at competing with the first. Middle children often learn to find value in their roles as go-between or peacemaker. Subsequent children will feel lower on the totem pole, of course. Their reward will be that they have many "parents." They will learn so much from their older siblings. No parent need feel guilty about what they themselves can't give to younger ones. In a tightly knit family, third and fourth children have a rich variety of mentors.

If the last child is treated as "the baby," she is likely to be indulged, and it will be necessary to be sure to expect as much of her as of the others. If she is overindulged and stands out in the family for it, she will devalue herself as "spoiled." It is wise to point out to her that learning to share and to participate equally is very much to her advantage.

When older children continue to fight with each other and you feel exasperated, you can try to sit down with them at a tranquil time. Ask them to advise you about what you should do (though you may decide not to follow their recommendations). Should you intervene, or should you leave it to them? In this way, you can give them a feeling of being responsible for their own behavior, or at least think over the dilemmas that it presents.

Left alone, children will learn to respect and care for each other. The ultimate reward will come when they begin to be "pals." I remember hearing ours plot together against us. That seemed like progress! When squabbling gives way to a united front against "the ogres," siblings are on their way.

38. Sleep Problems

WHEN PARENTS CALL ME IN DESPERATION TO ASK HOW TO GET THEIR baby to sleep at night, I can anticipate the story they will tell. By the time my advice is sought, there has usually been a long history of nighttime turmoil: of the baby waking at 10:00 P.M. after having successfully fallen asleep earlier, of parents waking up to hear the child crying at 2:00 or 3:00 A.M., dragging themselves to her room, and then rocking, singing, and cajoling to try to get her back to bed. Parents also report that once they arrive in the child's room, she becomes winning, delightful, and full of charm; she has had some sleep and is ready for several hours of play. When her charm begins to fail in the face of her parents' desperation, she may fall back on whimpering or wailing as if in real pain. Or, she may stare accusingly at the parent with a look that seems to say, "How can you leave me alone when you can see how much I want you to stay?" At any level, the urgent message she conveys is that she has needs that have not yet been met. Her lament reaches across any self-protective barrier the sleepy parent may attempt to set up.

Parents tell me they "try everything." They even try letting the child "cry it out," but they give up this approach after a few nights when the crying goes on for one or two hours and shows no signs of stopping. They try giving the child a bottle (not a good idea, since bedtime bottles containing anything other than water can lead to serious tooth decay) and a night light, neither of which works. The only thing that works, they tell me, is to take her into their bed. She can sit there and play for an hour or two, and they at least can sleep. They know that this will make it even harder later on.

However, since, up until fairly recently, there had been an unwritten taboo in our mainstream culture against allowing a child into her parents' bed, many mothers and fathers work very hard not to do this. They have found that going to the child before she is upset saves a longer period of calming down afterward. They often tell me that they go to the child every two hours after 2:00 A.M., quieting her, giving her milk, rocking her for a period, and successfully keeping her in her room. They can time their intervention so well that they have to remain only thirty minutes out of every two hours, whereas if they wait until she is upset and wailing, the visit takes an hour!

What is going on here? Why don't all children make such demands? Why is it that in one family all but one child learns to sleep through the night? Is it a sign of insecurity on the child's part, or does it arouse guilty feelings in the parents, who fear that their baby may not have had enough love or attention during the day? Why is it that certain children who go to sleep at 6:00 P.M. continue to awaken and make demands on their parents at about 10:00 P.M. and again at 2:00 and 6:00 A.M.? Why do some parents give in and reinforce this waking by taking the child out of bed rather than urging her to find her own ways of getting herself back to sleep?

Understanding Sleep

Every infant has characteristic cycles of light and deep sleep. These cycles are already entrenched at birth and have been established in synchrony with the pregnant woman's own daily cycles. They are usually not parallel to the maternal cycle, since the fetus often seems to sleep while the mother is active and wakes when she lies down. The mother's activity period leads to the fetus' in the following period. Thus, the newborn infant already has a sleep-wake rhythm. After birth, the environment tends to press the new baby to more and more wakefulness in the daytime and to longer and longer sleep cycles in the night.

By the age of four months or earlier, the periods begin to get set into a pattern—usually a cycle lasting three or four hours. In the middle of the cycle is an hour to an hour and a half of deep sleep in which the baby moves very little and is difficult to rouse with any stimulation. For an hour on each side, there is a lighter, dreaming state in which activity comes and goes. And at the

end of each four-hour cycle, the baby comes up to a semi-alert state in which she is very close to consciousness and awakens easily. At these times, each baby has her own activity pattern—she may suck her fingers, cry out, rock herself, or bang her head rhythmically. Older babies may move around the bed, try out new tricks like pulling up to stand or walking, or fuss or talk to themselves.

All of these behaviors seem to be in the service of discharging energy stored up from daytime activities and getting back down into the next cycle of sleep. When these intervals of semiconsciousness can be handled by the baby to get herself back down to sleep, the sleep cycles become stabilized and the child begins to stretch them into longer cycles so that she finally manages to stay asleep for eight and even twelve hours at a time. The cycles to an alert, disorganized state are still there every three to four hours, but the baby has learned to handle them alone.

Research has shown that getting back to sleep between cycles depends on a kind of conditioning. If the infant is in an environment that reinforces each alert period with a response or by a feeding, she is not likely to fall back to sleep. But if there is no response, she will be pressed to find her own patterns for discharging activity and comforting herself back down into the next cycle.

In the first year, as mentioned in Part 1, there are predictable times when a baby is likely to start waking at night, even though she may have been sleeping through before. At eight to nine months and again at a year, there are rapid increases in cognitive awareness (of strangers or strange situations, of new places, of changes in the daily routine) that coincide with spurts in motor development (such as crawling and sitting at eight months, or standing, walking, and climbing at twelve to fourteen months). With this increased activity comes a new capacity for getting away from the safe base of mother and father. The excitement and fears generated by this new capacity may temporarily interrupt the child's sleep patterns. Another explanation for the predictable regression in stable through-the-night sleep patterns just before a baby learns to walk is that between roughly nine and thirteen months of age, infants spend more time than previously, or later, in light sleep rather than deep sleep. As a result, they are more prone to awaken during the night. Some researchers believe that the memory traces of the motor movements that the baby will soon put together in his first step are laid down in the baby's brain in light sleep during this period.

Most children who sleep through the night by six months of age do so because of a combination of influences: parents' slower response at night, the lack of other stimulation, and the child's own need to stretch out sleep in some part of the twenty-four-hour cycle.

Patterns of Night Waking

About 17 percent of babies, then, are not stretching out at night by six months, and 10 percent still aren't sleeping through the night at one year. Again, a combination of factors is probably involved. Prematurity and limits on the infant's ability to nurse may play a role. There may be parental factors such as a reluctance to encourage independence in the child and let her work her way back to sleep. These parents have often had experiences in their own childhood that make them vulnerable to the pain of separation at night. A mother might remember feeling deserted by one or both of her parents in childhood. A father might remember night terrors when no one came to him. Some working mothers and fathers who are away all day need the closeness of the baby at night. A single parent who feels the loneliness of having to face the daily adjustments of parenting by herself might not want to give up any night feedings.

Issues of autonomy and independence are thus often at the root of sleep problems. Although there are many forces in our society that press a parent to feel guilty about holding a child too close or too long, most parents are not quite ready to push a baby of five or six months who cries out at night into self-comforting patterns. It is natural to want to cling and be clung to. Most parents secretly long for the lovely, warm comfort of a sleeping baby next to them. All this makes it hard for parents of babies who do not slip easily into sleeping through the night. They may need the guidelines that follow at the end of this chapter.

In my practice I've seen babies of three different temperamental types that seem prone to night waking. One kind is very active and intensely driving, with such excitement for learning that she is literally unable to stop herself when she is learning a new task. At night, the frustration of not being able to accomplish the task she's got in mind—usually a motor achievement—seems to drive her with the same intensity that drives her during the day.

This pattern may not subside after walking is achieved unless the parents begin to intervene by pressing her to master her nocturnal awakenings, for the child may be just as frustrated about other tasks and other steps toward mastery in the second, third, and later years. If her sleep has become an outlet for frustration in the first year, it may continue to serve this purpose.

Another group of infants who may wake at night and need to be comforted I have always thought of as "low motor expenders" during the day. They are the quiet, alert, watchful children who take everything in and think deeply about things, and they may not be very active. As they don't invest a lot of activity into their daylight hours, they may not tire themselves enough to sleep as deeply at night.

The third kind of child I've seen have difficulty settling down at night into a reliably prolonged sleep pattern is one who is sensitive and easily upset. Her sensitivity to new or strange situations makes her rather clinging, and her parents may play into this unknowingly. Around each new demanding situation—either a new developmental step or a demanding social situation—she is likely to regress in her behavior even more noticeably than most children. Since the parents of such a sensitive child want to help her, they may protect her from new and demanding situations. They are likely to hasten to comfort her when she is overwhelmed, often before she has had the chance to try out her own efforts at coping.

At night, this pattern of protection is likely to affect the behavior of both parents and child. The child demands their presence and comfort long after she may really need it, and the parents, in turn, find it difficult not to give in to her overly sensitive demands. They may take her into their bed or allow her to ask for and receive four or five nighttime visits from them. As they get exhausted and angry—with themselves and with her—her sensitivity to their ambivalence increases her misery, and this very ambivalence drives her parents to meet all her demands.

Co-Sleeping

Our mainstream culture has long held that to be able to sleep alone in childhood is part of being an independent person. Many other cultures, however, have always accepted co-sleeping unquestioningly, and as naturally as breastfeeding. In the past decade or so, more and more families in the United States have instituted the family bed. It seems to me that it is especially difficult for working parents to give their child up at night after being away all day, and that bed sharing helps them all feel close again. The American Academy of Pediatrics (AAP) has warned against co-sleeping, citing some studies that have shown an increased incidence of Sudden Infant Death Syndrome (SIDS), particularly in infants eleven weeks old and younger, among babies who sleep in a family bed. I suspect that other variables (for example, an intoxicated parent, or unsafe bedding) may have been involved in some cases of SIDS in these studies, but the AAP's position should be considered by parents making a decision about co-sleeping.

Parents who work away from home during the day often feel torn between putting a child to bed alone or keeping her close. Many parents now choose co-sleeping as a way to make up for missed times of closeness during the day. Apart from the controversy surrounding the relationship of co-sleeping and SIDS, I would urge parents to carefully consider the consequences of such a decision for another reason. A child who has not learned to sleep alone as an infant can be expected to have a harder time learning later on. When parents do decide it's time, pressing her to sleep through will require real purpose on the part of everyone in the household. Parents will have to be sure that they are ready to back each other up. They will also have to be sure that they believe it is an important, even a necessary, step for the child to take when they do decide to take it. A word of caution: Pushing a child out of the family bed when parents expect the next one is an especially tough time to choose. The older child already feels pushed out and wonders why she's being replaced, and she will need to regress temporarily to establish that she, too, can still be the baby when she needs to.

In my pediatric practice and in my hospital work, I have seen the problems that can be stirred up in whole families when a child is awake and demanding during the night. These families needed help, and I knew it would help their relationship with their child if I could give them a base for understanding the underlying issues.

Some parents, however, feel that sleeping alone is a custom our society unreasonably demands of its small children and that it may not be to the children's advantage. They feel that when a child needs them at night, it is more important to be with her than to worry about conforming to cultural expectations. They like being together as a family at night, and they feel that the child will outgrow the habit of sleeping with her parents—without psychological scars.

I have learned a great deal by listening to this point of view. I agree with the concern that sleep problems may indicate that the child is going through a time of stress and should not feel deserted at such a time. I also worry about whether our culture isn't demanding too much of small children in many ways. But I also believe that the needs of the parents at night have to be considered, and that learning to sleep alone can be an opportunity for a child to develop her ability to become self-reliant.

In considering whether to keep the child in their bed, parents would do well to consider some of the potential problems. Will the child be more dependent during the day if her parents keep her close at night? I'm not sure she needs to be—but that could be a pitfall, and one I'd urge parents to watch for. If a child is developing independence during the day, perhaps my argument for leaving her alone at night need not be taken as seriously. Will sharing her parents' bed as an infant and young child make it difficult to separate from them later on? To offset this tendency on the child's part, I would urge parents who want to continue the practice of sharing their bed to be sure that they agree that it is comforting *to them* as well as to the child. A child's presence can certainly come between them if she's allowed to continue to sleep there; and if one of them resents this, the child will suffer more than she might from being weaned to her own room. Hence, if both parents are not comfortable with this practice, and it is allowed to cause friction in a family, I'm sure it will be destructive to a child's future development. For this reason, parents should discuss the arrangement openly and reasonably at regular intervals. A good relationship between her parents is probably more critical to a child's development than her sleeping arrangements.

Parents must also watch the child for any signs of tension about sleeping with them. Eventually, she will begin to show that she no longer needs their comfort at night and will express a need for independence. If we can extrapolate from other cultures (India and Mexico, for example, where this is a common practice), it would seem that the third or fourth years would be the time to watch for signs of the child's readiness to sleep alone, even if she hasn't been able to do this before. It will probably be up to the parents to help her make the transition gently, gradually, and respectfully—talking to the child as she goes to bed, providing her with a beloved toy for company, and giving her a night light. It may help to start by shifting the child to a separate bed next to the parents'.

I would worry about an older child's image of herself if she still needs to be close to her parents at night, and wonder whether she might have a more difficult separation later in childhood. In the end, whether a child sleeps alone or with her parents may not be as critical as whether she is learning how to cope with her own needs and managing to get herself back to sleep when she comes to awakening periods during the night.

Bedtime Rituals

Many parents have a difficult time separating from their small children after they have settled cozily with them. A book, the potty, the "kiss me one more time" can stretch out and out. And yet, a bedtime ritual of cuddling and reading a favorite book is such a delicious time to get close with each other after a hard day. We used to sing and dance slowly at bedtime holding our babies. Then, as the children quieted down and we all felt close, we could put them down still awake but quiet. Each of them "learned" to go to sleep on her or his own. It was a lovely transition.

When parents are having a difficult time separating for their own reasons (for example, being away all day, feeling that the child is too vulnerable to leave, remembering being left as a child, and so on), the child senses it all too easily. "Don't leave me yet. I need to tell you something. I *need* to go to the bathroom. I *need* another story. You promised!" I would urge parents to set limits on the child, and themselves. "One more time and that's it!" Otherwise, the buildup from the struggle can interfere with the child's ability to settle down to sleep—at bedtime and even later when roused. Sleeping alone, as pointed out earlier, is a separation issue for parents, and an autonomy issue for the child.

Guidelines

When night waking continues to be a problem, the following suggestions might help parents teach a child how to get back to sleep by herself. Bear in mind that they are dependent on the individual situation, and particularly on the child herself. Each of these steps should be taken singly and slowly over time.

- Be sure you and your spouse both agree on the program. If you, her parents, disagree, the child will sense your ambivalence.
- Have a look at the child's day. Does she sleep too long and/or too late in the afternoon? For most babies more than a year old, naptimes should be started early (by 1:00 P.M.) and last only one to two hours at most. Many children over two give up their nap entirely, though some children who still need an afternoon nap will actually sleep worse at night without it. Any rest or nap after 3:00 P.M. will certainly break up the cycle of activity and diminish the need for continuous and deep sleep during the night.
- Be sure you have instituted a relaxing, nurturing routine at bedtime. If the child is old enough, talk to her at this time about the steps you are about to take toward helping her sleep alone and through the night. Roughhousing and play should be followed by a calming, quiet ritual time. A bedtime story is a wonderful routine. Television is not.
- Let the child learn to get to sleep when you put her down at night. Don't put her to sleep in your arms or at the breast. Help her quiet down but then put her in her crib and sit by her to help her learn her own pattern. Give her a lovey or her fingers. Pat her down soothingly. If she protests, assure her: "You can do it yourself."
- For a baby under a year old, some parents find it helpful to wake her at night before their bedtime. At that time, the bedtime routine can be repeated—talk to her, hug her, and give her a bottle or a feeding if that has been part of the routine. In this way, parents can ease their own consciences and not lie awake wondering, "Is she okay? Is she hungry? Have I done enough?"
- Reinforce a particular lovey—a blanket, an animal, or a doll—as part of her self-comforting routine. (But, as mentioned in earlier chapters, do

not allow a child to sleep with a bottle of milk in her mouth; this contributes to serious tooth decay.) Many toys in bed are in no way as good as a single beloved one. They dilute the sense of value and meaning that a child can have with one special lovey.

- At first, expect a child to rouse and cry out every three to four hours—at around 10:00 P.M., 2:00 A.M., and 6:00 A.M. After you have prepared her for the program and are really ready to start it, respond to her at these times with as little stimulating intervention as you can. If you have been taking her out of bed to rock her, don't; soothe and stroke her with your hand, but leave her *in bed.* She won't like it, but she'll understand. Stand by her crib and tell her that she can and must learn to get herself back to sleep.
- After a period of going to her each time, begin to stay out of her room and instead just call to her. Tell her that you are there and that you care about her, but that you are *not* coming, and remind her of her lovey. It amazes me that a child can begin to accept one's voice for one's presence.
- Finally, let her try all of her own resources. Wait at least ten or fifteen minutes before you respond. If you do go into her room, deal with her perfunctorily, repeating the unexciting regime just outlined and again pressing the lovey on her. Wait longer each time and make clear your resolve.

After forty years in the practice of pediatrics, I became convinced that while a child's independence may not be easy for parents to accept, it is an exciting and rewarding goal for the child. It seems to me that being able to manage alone at night helps a child develop a positive self-image and gives her a real feeling of strength, particularly when such independence is valued by her culture. You can further encourage this feeling of achievement by shoring the child up emotionally during the day. Once she becomes independent at night, she deserves all of the credit and loving praise that you can give her. (See also *Sleep—The Brazelton Way* in *Further Reading.*)

39. Spacing Children

In the course of routine office visits, I find I can expect a question about when to have a second child at certain times in the first child's development. These times are related to the first child's spurts in independence. After the initial adjustment to the baby, and when the first few months of sleepless nights and erratic schedules are over, new parents begin to experience the pure euphoria of being in love. Every time they look at their four-month-old, he smiles back at them adoringly. A vocalization from parents produces a sigh or an "ooh" in response. The baby wriggles all over as he attempts to communicate with his devoted, hovering parents. Few moments in life are as delicious as these minutes of reciprocal communication with a communicative, vocalizing infant. A parent feels competent, even masterful, in these brief exchanges. But it is hard to be head-over-heels in love without the nagging fear that sooner or later it must come to an end, or at least be diluted as the child grows up. Such moments may seem too perfect to last.

Considering a Second Child

Sometime during the first year, a parent may ask about the "best" time to have another baby. The timing of this question seems incongruous if one looks at the baby. He is round, soft, and dimpled. As he lies on the examining table, he looks carefully around the room, his face serious as he surveys each new object. Every minute or so, he glances back at his mother or father, who both lean on the table near him, talking to me. As he looks at them, they look back reassuringly. His face crinkles, his eyes soften, and he smiles gratefully up at them, his legs and arms wriggling as he thanks them with his whole body. This lasts only a few seconds. He returns to his job of processing the information about the strange place. They return to their job of communicating with me.

In that moment, I have witnessed an example of the depth of their attachment to each other. Each of them has felt a surge of loving feeling, and each has felt deeply the importance of the other's presence. The baby has said with his eyes, "You are my anchor, and I can afford to be here in such a strange, exciting new place because I can look back at you and you'll be there!" The parents have had a chance to feel the depth of their own importance to this new individual. Doesn't it seem amazing that, at that point, one of the parents asks, "What would be the best time to have another baby?" Or, a breast-feeding mother may ask, "When should I wean him?" If I pursue either of these questions with the parents, it will become apparent that they don't actually want another baby yet, nor does the mother want to wean this one. But the questions guard them against caring too much and help to balance the overwhelming attachment.

As we saw in chapter 6, at four or five months, a baby shows a first ripple of independence. He interrupts a feeding over and over—to look around, to listen to a door close in the next room, to stop to gurgle up at his mother, to smile brightly across the room at his father. For a mother, these may be the first signals that the baby doesn't need her as much anymore. For the baby, these represent a burst in his awareness of things and people around him. For enraptured parents, they may seem to be a reminder of the future when the child will indeed become independent of them.

For breast-feeding mothers, this can also be a physically vulnerable time for conceiving the next pregnancy. I have seen many instances of unexpected second pregnancies that were started at this time because the mother thought she was protected by lactation. Even though her periods had not returned, however, she was ovulating again. If a new mother is not using adequate contraception, she may start the second baby before she is ready.

Having two children as close together as fourteen to eighteen months is as challenging as having twins. Raising them successfully certainly can be done, and it can even be fun at times, but it is hard work while they are little, and a major stress on parents. Having two highly dependent individuals of different but close ages is demanding both physically and emotionally. The danger for the babies is that a physically exhausted mother is likely to make one of two unconscious choices. On one hand, she may lump the children together, treating them as if they were babies who were the same age. On the other, she may press the slightly older toddler to grow up too quickly. As the toddler resists by acting just like the baby, a mother unconsciously resents the demands on her and presses the older one to take more responsibility than he is ready for.

In planning for a second child, parents should try to keep in mind their own energies and tolerance. Their own reasons for hurrying or delaying in spacing children may be the best guidelines they can follow. A mother who is able to take time off for each baby, but wants to have her family quickly so that she can get back to work, may resent being kept at home for too many years and indirectly take it out on her family. Parents who feel they need time between each child to get in a better position financially may feel that they can assimilate only one child and one responsibility at a time. The problem for most families is that they can't anticipate their own reserves and their own tolerance.

Guidelines for Planning

There are a few guidelines that I've learned from my own experience over the years that may be helpful to young families who are trying to plan intelligently.

First, assume that it will be hard to give up the intense, reciprocally rewarding relationship with your first child. It's hard for a baby and it's hard for you, his parents. If you have enough time to begin feeling that you've really done all you can for him, it becomes easier. In other words, if you can feel that you've really belonged completely to your first baby, and that he is becoming independent, it becomes easier to share yourself with the next baby. Inevitably, the new baby will demand time and emotional energy. Almost as inevitably, a mother will push the older child to grow up quickly when the new baby arrives. In traditional cultures, there is usually a ritual associated with weaning the older child when the mother is expecting a new baby. She will openly push the responsibility for the older child onto another member of the family—a grandmother, an aunt, or an older sibling. Through this symbolic act, she will be saying, "Now I must turn my back on you so I can devote myself to the new one." Although this is often done in a harsh way, I have seen the anguish that the mother hides as she gives up her child. But given her heavy responsibilities, she knows she must force herself to "turn her back," or she won't have the energy available to nurture a new baby.

Also important as you plan for a second child is the normal but passionate mix of independence and negativism in the toddler. As a toddler embarks on the second year, he needs time to sort out his choices. Does he really want to be independent? Does he mean no when he says it so forcefully, or did he really mean yes? After a flaming tantrum that leaves him exhausted, who besides his parents can help him sort out the reason for the tantrum, the limits on himself that he must learn? Who else can refuel him to go on searching for the boundaries and the strengths that will help him become an independent person?

If parents cannot be available to a toddler and cannot see this struggle for independence as critical and exciting, both they and their baby will feel stressed and frustrated throughout the second year. Instead of seeing this year as a rich period of learning and testing, they may lose their sense of humor, which they sorely need to give them some perspective. Ideally, then, parents might plan for the second child to arrive after some of this second-year turmoil has had a chance to become resolved.

Parents who are considering this kind of two-and-one-half to three-year spacing between their children wonder whether the children will be too far apart to be friends as they get older. My own experience has led me to the feeling that, if the parents can enjoy the spacing of the children, the children will be better friends for it. If parents are stressed by children who are too close in age, the children will spend most of their childhood in competitive rivalry. For, as we saw in chapter 37 on sibling rivalry, these squabbles are aimed at parents. Children are inevitably rivalrous, and they will sort out their competitive feelings by themselves if parents are not involved. When parents feel that they may not have been adequate parents to each child, they get involved, and the feelings of rivalry are reinforced. In other words, children had better not be planned to please each other, but to suit the parents' requirements for available energy.

Helping Your Child Adjust to a Sibling

By the age of two or two and a half, most toddlers are independent in important new ways. Their mobility is established, their play is rich, and they can play on their own. By now, they should have established autonomous eating and sleeping habits, and many of them are beginning to want to be toilet trained. In addition, by two years of age, children are ready for group play with others their own age. A peer group can be the highlight of a toddler's week. The learning that occurs from each other and the discharge of tensions and sorting out of negativism that can take place in a small play group demonstrate the marvelous availability of children of this age to each other. This means that parents can set up regular play groups with other parents, or they can feel comfortable about placing their toddler in a day care or group setting. This is both for the toddler's *own sake* and for the parents' sake, for they can then be available to a new infant. Spacing children two or three years apart can be made to benefit each person in the family.

By the age of four or five, a child is ready to participate in the care of a new baby. An older child can feel the baby belongs to him. He can learn to feed, hold, rock, diaper, comfort, and play with the new baby. Once he recovers from the initial disappointment that the new baby isn't his own age and an equal in the games he's planned, he can begin to participate with his parents in the game of learning about the new baby and in watching the baby acquire each new developmental step.

I remember a five-year-old boy who came bursting into my office saying, "Dr. B., you should see my baby walking! He doesn't fall down anymore!" With that, he rushed over to his eleven-month-old sibling and held out his hands. His brother grinned all over at this attention from his hero. He gratefully and greedily grasped the older boy's hands to pull up to stand. Barely balancing, he held tightly to his brother's outstretched arms to teeter across the room. As the older boy backed up to lead his brother on, he chortled with delight, "Look, look at that!" As I watched this elegant example of an older child not only teaching the baby to walk but passing on to him the excitement of learning, I thought to myself, Isn't a younger child fortunate to have such an opportunity for learning about the thrill of living? These brothers are not only acquiring learning skills from each other, but they are learning what it means to be deeply dependent on each other.

At four and five, a child is naturally ready to care for and teach a smaller individual. Margaret Mead, the eminent anthropologist, said to me once that one of the most serious deprivations in our culture is that children ages four to seven so rarely have the opportunity to care for smaller children. She pointed out that in most cultures around the world, older siblings are expected to be responsible for younger ones. In this way, they learn the skills of nurturing and are more prepared when their time for parenting comes.

A space of several years between children automatically provides this kind of experience for the older child. And, for the younger, the opportunity to learn from an older sibling is a real privilege. Our last child acquired many of his skills and learned many of his values from the careful, patient teaching of his older sisters. A child's hunger to learn from an older sibling is founded in a kind of blind adoration. This is quite different from the more charged situation when we as parents try to teach the same tasks. I have always been struck with the eager, longing looks with which a baby or toddler watches an older child. And I am amazed at the speed of the imitative learning that goes on when an older sibling stops briefly to teach a small child a new skill.

When you are expecting a new baby, prepare the older child for the separation and for the invasion of your relationship. Let him learn to participate with you and identify with you as a caregiver for the new baby. Instead of pushing him away "to protect the new baby," let him learn how to be tender and gentle, how to hold and rock and feed the baby. Bring home a baby doll for him that he can feed and nurture while you attend to yours. Then, let him test it out safely with the new baby, while you are there observing.

After the new baby is at home and too many things demand your time and energy, be sure you save a special time for the older child *alone* and without the new baby nearby. This is a time when grandparents and other close relatives can really help. Each older child deserves a small segment of protected time with each parent. The amount of time is less important than making the time reliable and one to one. Though this can be especially tough for single parents, an hour a week per child per parent can be like pure gold in maintaining your relationships. Remind the older child about this time often. "Even though I don't have time to stop feeding the baby right now, remember that we *will* have our time together later. It's my time with just you because you are my first baby. It's our time. I will *always* care about you."

Affirming Individuality

Another issue that may trouble you, if you have more than one child, is your awareness of not feeling the same about each child. Parents will automatically feel like protecting the baby and pushing the older child to grow up. They may wish to push a daughter to be responsible and a son to be adventurous. They may have different dreams for each. These feelings cause guilt and resentment. It is my belief that parents do not feel equally about each child. Each one is bound to affect you differently, based on unconscious, past experiences. "She looks like my brilliant sister" or "He's a powerhouse like my brother" are valid reactions. If you face these responses honestly, recognizing where they come from, the child can benefit. If you try to hide them, any deviation from these images will disappoint you and undermine the child. However close in age or far apart, and however different from one another, children deserve to be seen as competent and loved for their differences.

40. Speech, Language, and Hearing Problems

THE LOSS OF ANY SENSORY MODALITY, SUCH AS HEARING OR VISION, DISorganizes the child's development. Other modalities are affected, speech and language skills may be delayed, and the child must learn to reorganize her nervous system to adapt. The other senses must make up for it, and it becomes costly to the child. But the wonder is—she can do it! Her parents become even more important in this adjustment, which can have a positive effect on their relationship.

Hearing Problems

Lack of hearing can have major implications for a baby's development. Although two-thirds of children with hearing loss are otherwise medically and neurologically healthy, profoundly deaf babies can be slowed down in all spheres. Without early detection and intervention, they will develop delays in their capacities for communication and social interaction.

Babies whose severe hearing loss has not been identified are likely to appear depressed and unreactive—slow to develop motorically and to react to parents' attempts to elicit an interaction. They may lie in their cribs passively, or they may develop repetitive, self-stimulating behaviors—such as head rolling—as if to fill up empty space. At the same time, the other sensory modalities, such as sight and touch, become heightened. This can make a baby hypersensitive and easily overwhelmed. Even a mild hearing impairment can interfere with language development, so the American Academy of Pediatrics advocates formal hearing screenings for *all* newborns. Early detection makes a big difference because many causes of hearing loss can be treated, and early intervention, including the use of sign language, can help stimulate language areas in the brain even when hearing cannot be restored or can be only partially restored.

One method I have used to get a rough idea of a newborn baby's hearing is more likely to work when she is asleep or as she is just rousing. I use a soft rattle and a bell in a quiet room. After several startles in response to the sound of either of these, a baby with normal hearing will shut out or habituate to the rattle or bell (see chapter 2). If I test a baby in a noisy environment, she may already be filtering out auditory input and may not attend to the sounds I introduce. Then she can appear to be deaf even though she's not. The reason for the two stimuli is to sample the range of her hearing. Another simple way to get a general impression is to give the baby a chance to respond to my voice when she's awake and looking away rather than at my face. If she quiets and slowly turns to my voice, I know that she hears me. If her mother and I compete on either side of her, she should choose the higher-pitched female voice. But my techniques often prove more effective in helping parents of hearing babies see how ready their newborns are to communicate, and how sensitive they are to unnecessary sounds, than in clearly establishing a problem with hearing.

Since "tests" like these are often inaccurate (they can't tease out whether one ear or both are affected or how severe the problem is) and sometimes even misleading (a baby who seems to hear may actually be responding to a visual cue), all newborns should receive a formal hearing screening. In addition, the primary physician should always refer a child for whom there is any concern about hearing to an audiologist specializing in children to further assess the baby's hearing, and to a pediatric otolaryngologist (a doctor who is an ear, nose, and throat specialist, or ENT), who can examine the ears and upper respiratory tract in greater detail. Depending on the nature of the condition, a team of specialists may be able to help improve or restore the child's hearing (for example, through the use of hearing aids or cochlear implants for babies as young as twelve months, or, later on, special amplification and communication strategies in the classroom). Universal newborn screening can be carried out with otoacoustic emissions (OAE) testing, which noninvasively measures the response of a new baby's inner ear to clicking sounds. Brain auditory evoked response (BAER) testing can also be used in young babies and provides additional information about pathways for hearing beyond the ear, in the brain. As a baby gets a bit older, by one to three months, she can be tested by so-called "paired techniques," which offer her a different sound on each side.

Otolaryngologists and audiologists can detect lack of hearing in infancy, before it interferes seriously with the child's development. If there is any indication that a baby is not hearing, or hears in certain ranges but not in all, or only at higher decibel levels, or more with one ear than the other, I'd suggest getting a complete evaluation. Hearing loss in only one ear is especially likely to go undetected—even for years—unless formal testing is done. When a hearing problem is identified, it is important to have the child's eyes checked as well, by a pediatric ophthalmologist, for two reasons. First, there are some rare causes of deafness that are associated with progressive vision problems. Second, a child without fully functional hearing will be more dependent on sight for communication and understanding. For this reason, she will need regular eye checkups.

In the second year, even a mild degree of hearing loss may become more obvious as the child garbles words in a regular fashion. Always suspect the possibility of hearing problems in a child who is not developing properly, particularly in the area of communication.

Otitis media (infection of the middle ear) can also threaten a child's hearing. Many infants develop a tendency to chronic otitis media. After an acute earache, the pressure from fluid accumulation in the middle ear seems to linger despite antibiotics, sometimes even after the infection is resolved. Otitis media has been called "glue ear"—as if the ear contained glue that was hard to mobilize. Chronic infection or fluid accumulation in the middle ear can cause hearing impairment. Infants in group care or with older siblings in school who are exposed to many different infections are particularly vulnerable. Ear infections may follow colds as often as every two weeks. Each ear infection can become more difficult to treat than the last, and parents and physicians get discouraged. The baby's general condition is often affected; she seems to become rundown and vulnerable to everything. At this point, an ear, nose, and throat specialist should be consulted. It may be necessary to use ear tubes in the child's eardrums. They allow drainage, reduce pressure in the middle ear, and prevent hearing loss.

Following the development of language is another important way of determining whether there is hearing loss, though earlier detection and treatment may prevent significant delays in speech. With an older child, if you have a question about hearing, a simple way to get a rough answer is to try whispering in one ear or the other, though this is far from a complete or reliable assessment, and it may be hard to tell what you can conclude from it. Be sure to whisper something to which you know the child will want to respond. There are many periods in a child's development when "selective attention" can be operating. Whisper a welcome question, such as, "Do you want to go to town with me?" or "Do you want a cookie?" Inattention peaks at four, five, and six. I would never expect to determine a child's ability to hear by asking him to get dressed or pick up his toys!

In my office, I put my finger in one of the child's ears and whisper in the other, "Do you want a lollipop?" If there are no responses, and/or speech is developing inappropriately, I refer the child for evaluation by an otolaryngologist or testing by an audiologist.

Speech and Language Delays

Speech and language delays are the most common developmental problems of early childhood. Unless carefully watched for, they will rarely be obvious until age two or later, even though the foundations of communication are laid in early infancy. In the first weeks, a baby is learning to differentiate between important and unimportant sounds. She shuts out an intrusive or unimportant sound that is repeated, and alerts to an important or interesting one. By seven days of age, she will choose her mother's voice over another female voice when presented with both at once. By two weeks, she will choose her father's voice in preference to another male voice. By six weeks of age, she will demonstrate predictable behavioral patterns for each of these important persons. She will, by her behavior, communicate to them that she recognizes them. In an experimental situation we set up, with the baby in a baby chair and the parent leaning over her to communicate, we showed that by three months, a baby will have learned an attention-inattention rhythm. In the periods of attention, she will alert, vocalize, and smile. When parents fit their own communication into this rhythm, the baby is able to imitate their vocalizations, facial movements, and movements of their heads and bodies almost precisely.

Parents tend to adjust intuitively to this pattern. They will imitate the baby almost precisely, matching her inflection and motor behavior as well as the attention-inattention rhythm. In the process, they are reinforcing her attempts at communication as well as the rhythms that underlie language later

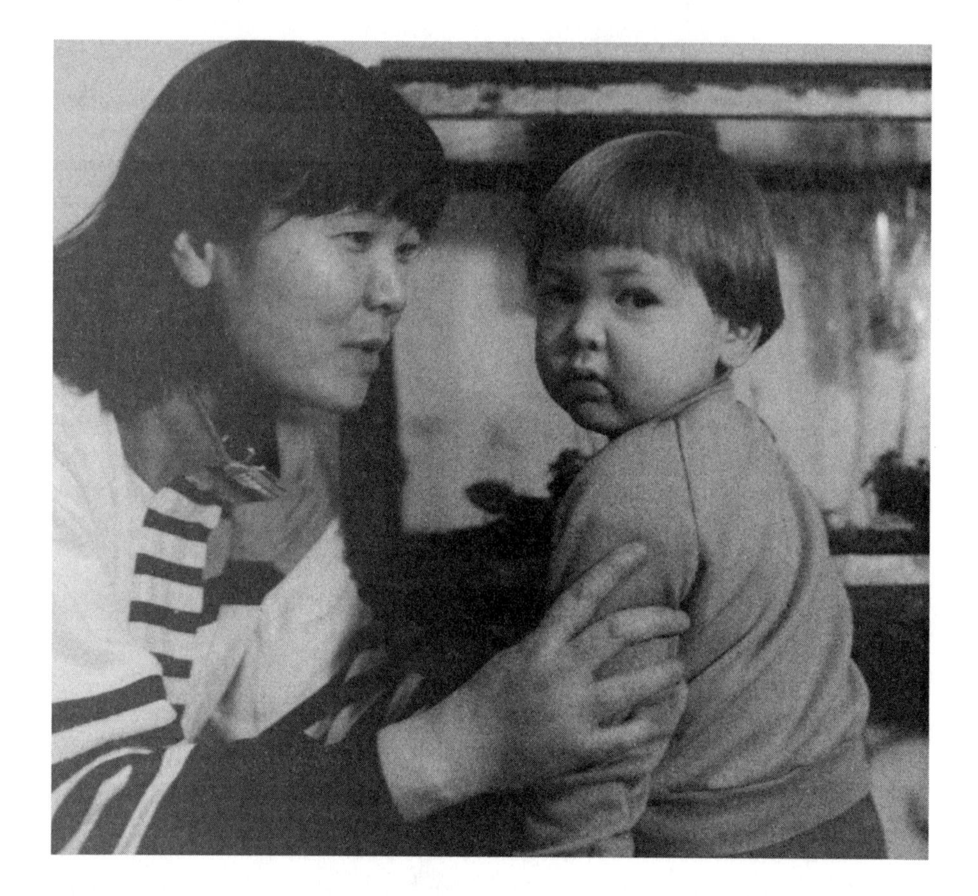

on. As adults match the baby's behavior, they add a little extra onto it. The baby tries to live up to the slight added difference—to match it and to imitate them. Parents pitch their voice differently to babies—not only with baby talk but with slowed rhythms and simpler words. This baby talk, sometimes called "motherese," has the significance of saying, "Now I'm talking to you." These special features of baby talk tell the baby that the talk is directed at her, and she'll know when to listen. At all other times, adults are speaking over the baby's head. So, the baby talk takes on a special connotation. The baby tries to respond—with a smile, a vocalization, or an arching forward with a wriggle of the whole body.

The following are signs of language development for which parents can watch.

- In the first weeks and months, the baby will show the rhythmic participation in communication just described.

- By three months, a small baby will be making vowel sounds like "ooh-agoo." These are likely to be responses at playtimes or feeding times, but they also occur at diapering and while she is lying in her crib talking to herself.
- At six to eight months, inflections and speech rhythms begin to be richer. A baby will continue to test vocalization and has a few consonants, including "mamama" and "dadada." These are not yet attached to the appropriate person.
- At about nine months, a baby will use her index finger to point. With this gesture she is able to say, "Look at that!" or "I want this!" or "Get me that!" She will also follow a parent's finger to look at whatever they are pointing to. Already she understands that this gesture is a symbol of sharing attention.
- At one year, a baby will talk a stream of gibberish but will usually attach "mama" and "dada" to the right person. She can respond to one-step commands, such as "Give it to me."
- At fifteen months, a baby will continue to emit completely unintelligible gibberish, but with more actual words immersed in it. Words for giving and taking are important. Her receptive language will be richer, that is, she can understand more commands. A baby of this age may have ten or more words, but there is immense variation in this.
- At eighteen months, a toddler will probably be able to say words like "ball," "doggie," names of special people, action words such as "up, up" when she wants to be picked up, and "bye bye." "Yes" and "no" are very important. Both nouns and verbs will be represented in her speech. She will also use complex nonverbal gestures for communication. Many toddlers can handle two commands ("Go in the other room and get me my slippers"), which shows their increasing level of receptive language and memory.
- At two years, a child can start combining words. She may put nouns and verbs together: "Mommy go," or the more complex "Daddy home," in which the noun "home" has become a verb! Her receptive language—understanding suggestions, questions, and warnings—shows that development is progressing. Even if children are not combining words, rich and appropriate gestural speech means that verbal speech is likely to follow.

If these signposts are delayed, a child should be evaluated for auditory impairment and other causes of speech delay—for example, dysarthria or oral apraxia, which is sometimes thought of as a discoordination of the mouth and tongue muscles used in speech, and may sometimes be tipped off by a child who drools excessively or who has trouble moving foods of different textures from the mouth to the throat. Mental retardation can be another cause of speech delay.

Lack of ability to use nonverbal gestures to communicate, or to understand nonverbal communication, and lack of understanding of the social conventions that underlie communication can be signs of an autism spectrum disorder. In children with some of these disorders, speech may also be lacking, minimal, or have an unusual, sing-song quality.

At the same time, parents can evaluate their efforts to encourage speech. Here are some questions I explore:

Do you speak to the child, or do you talk over her?

Does everyone in the family rush to the child before she needs to verbalize?

Do you read to her?

Do you enlarge slightly on her speech? This leads her on to learn new language skills.

Do you offer encouragement, responding to her words with your words and with your gestures?

Other ways to encourage speech include speaking directly to the child, then waiting until she has a chance to speak back, and assuring the child that she has plenty of time. You can also ask her siblings to help; she may learn more easily from them by imitation than from adults. If the child is stuttering or stammering, don't push her; encourage her by waiting patiently.

In bilingual households, speech may seem to come more slowly, but the total number of words a child can say in each language, when added together, are roughly the same as the number of words a monolingual child of the same age can speak in one language. The maximum number of words she can string together in a sentence will also be similar, but her speech may seem delayed because she may mix together words from both languages. By about age three, a child raised in a bilingual household will be speaking both languages. Before that, she will understand which language goes to which person.

Although many healthy children are "late bloomers" as far as speech goes, don't wait past age two to find out. Though patience and the encouragement just mentioned will usually be rewarded in a "late-blooming" speaker, early evaluation and intervention are critical to be sure that speech is not simply late. Here are a few signs that should prompt a speech and language assessment:

- No intelligible speech by two years
- Little or no ability to understand and use nonverbal gestures and facial expressions to communicate
- High-pitched or nasal quality to utterances
- Dull look as the child tries to speak
- No rhythm of communication or turn taking
- Evident overload or inattention when the child is spoken to or looked at
- Incessant repetition of adult speech, without variations or combinations on the child's part

Different aspects of speech may be affected. The *fluency* of speech can be disrupted, as in stuttering. Stuttering is normal and inevitable as children begin to speak. Only when it continues or is combined with other speech problems should parents seek help. A child can also have problems in *articulation,* that is, in producing sounds correctly. A nasal quality to the voice can mean a problem with *resonance,* and there can also be difficulties with the *pitch, loudness,* or *quality* of the voice, as in hoarseness or shrillness.

If you notice any of these problems, or if a doctor does, the child can be referred to a speech and language pathologist, and other specialists as well, when needed. If the doctor feels that the cause has to do with structural problems (as in a cleft palate affecting resonance), he or she will refer the child to a plastic surgeon or other specialist. The earlier that speech therapy or other treatments are started, the better this will be for the child's overall development. (See *Further Reading* and "Professional Associations" in *Useful Addresses and Web Sites* for more information.)

41. Stomachaches, Headaches, and Stress

All of us respond to tension and unusual pressures in our own way. This is true even in children. Some have a flare-up of asthma when they are tired or upset (see "Allergies and Asthma"). Others get stomachaches or headaches. Parents need to be aware that these can be symptoms of stress, though they should consult with their child's doctor about possible medical causes before assuming they are. Once they've established that there are none, they can look for pressures that may be unnecessary and overwhelming to the child. They can also begin to point out to the child the reasons for this "psychosomatic" response, without ever suggesting that their symptoms are less real or important because of their origin. In this way, the cycle of uncontrollable symptoms can be broken, and the child can eventually learn to be more in control.

Stomachaches

Stomachaches without medical explanation, despite careful pediatric evaluation, often occur in four- to six-year-olds as pressures from school and peers increase. This is also a stage when the child is beginning to be aware of aggressive feelings. Stomachaches are a sure way to get the attention that a stressed child needs.

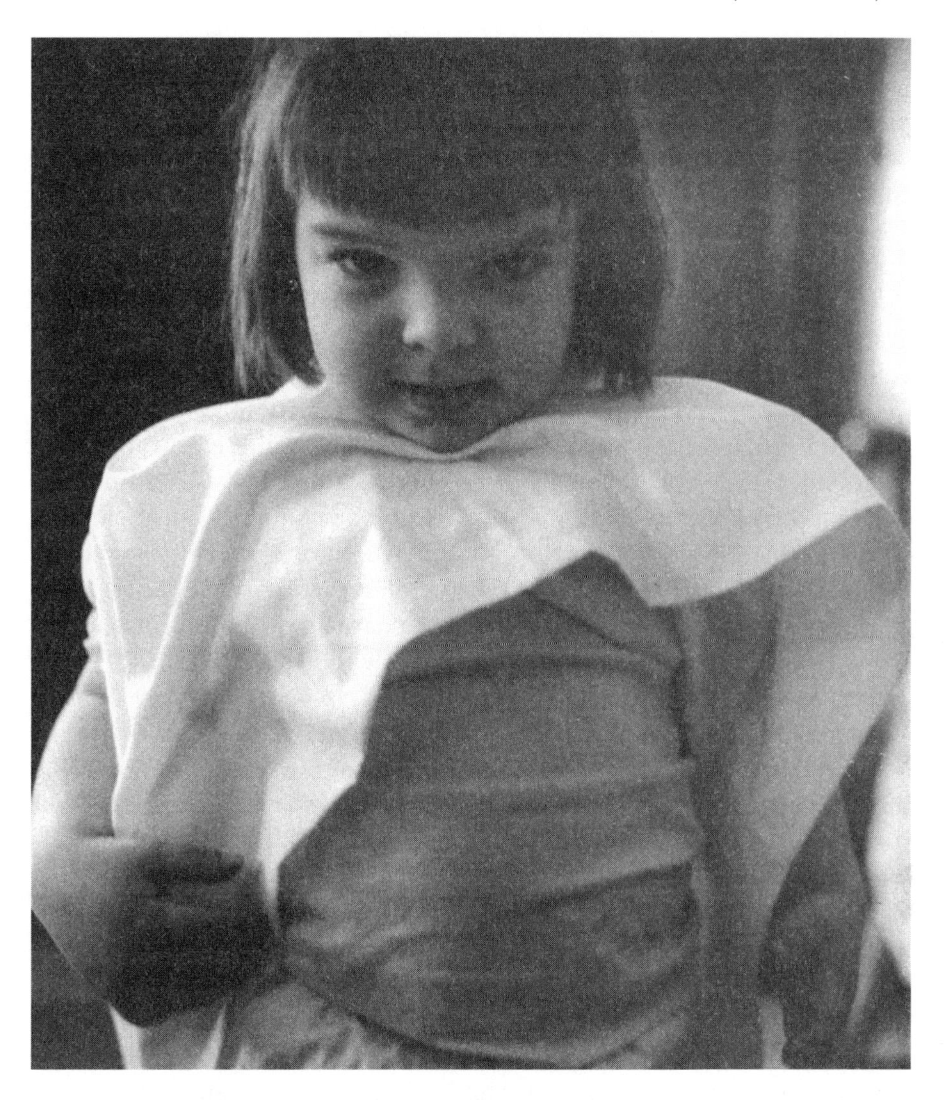

When a child complains of stomach pain, you should first consult the child's doctor to rule out other serious causes. To determine how urgently you need to act, you can check for an acutely painful area. Distract the child, then place your hand on his belly to press gently throughout. If the abdomen is board-like, or you cannot press over the inflamed area without causing extreme pain, or if you are uncertain about whether this is the case, the child should see a doctor right away. An inflamed appendix or an intussusception (an intestine that has telescoped onto itself) must be ruled out. A physician can feel for an acutely tender area and can use a stethoscope to listen for bowel sounds. An "acute abdomen" (such as an inflamed appendix or a blockage) will have a silent area around the inflamed, blocked organ. High-pitched bowel sounds may be heard in other parts of the abdomen.

If it is not acutely tender, you will be successful in pressing all through the child's abdomen without finding a tender spot—*as long as* you distract him. Focus his attention on something else and press all through his belly. If an area is painful, he is bound to guard it. Be sure to check the child's temperature as well, for a child with fever and severe abdominal pain will need to be evaluated by a doctor right away. When you talk with the doctor, he or she will also want to know if the child has been vomiting or having diarrhea.

No bowel movement in twenty-four hours or more can be another common symptom of obstruction when a child is suffering from severe, acute abdominal pain. If there has been one, the doctor will ask whether you have checked for blood, usually blackened blood. Although most children with constipation do not develop bowel obstruction—which does require emergency medical attention—the doctor will also ask if your child has been constipated. Many children this age forget to have bowel movements, or they may be holding them back. They get chronically constipated. Then, they produce a liquid stool from around the hard stool. No one thinks they are constipated. The hard b.m. hurts the anal sphincter, so it tends to hold back the b.m., and the constipation worsens. A stool softener, or a suppository to help the child produce the hard stool, may become necessary as a last resort, but only if the doctor recommends it. To prevent chronic constipation, include plenty of fruit, fiber, and fluids in the child's diet.

If the stomachache does not seem acute, you can try acetaminophen (such as Infants' or Children's Tylenol in the proper dose for your child's age and weight). This will not affect an obstructed or inflamed intestine. Wait an hour to see whether the pain diminishes. If it does not, call the doctor. If the pain goes away, or a doctor finds no problem, you can reassure the child. Your anxiety and the child's can be allayed. That is always an important first step.

If stomachaches are not acute and recur over and over, check to see whether they are related to any special foods. Keep a diary of foods eaten from day to day. Many children are mildly sensitive to milk and milk products. At times of tension or fatigue, this sensitivity may surface. Under normal conditions, it may not. Eliminating milk for a period can help you determine whether your child has this sensitivity, but the nutrients it supplies (such as protein, calcium, and Vitamin D) will need to be replaced if this period is prolonged. A diary of the foods the child eats just before the stomachaches occur can turn up such a common denominator.

If the stomachaches are related to mealtime, check with the doctor. Ulcers or colitis may be more likely to flare up at regular times closer to meals. If there is urinary frequency or burning, there could be a urinary tract infection. The doctor will want a urine sample to be tested.

Does this stomachache occur on school days—not on weekends? Does it occur when the child is stressed by any particular event? If it occurs each morning before school, try to rule out contributing factors. At breakfast, feed the child light foods that he can digest easily. Have him get up a little earlier with you and try not to rush. Then, he may be able to face the stress of school more easily.

Learning to live with stomachaches that have no medical explanation may be necessary, but such causes should be thoroughly explored. If none are found, the stomachaches should improve if the child's anxiety can be diminished. At each episode, reassure the child and offer an explanation of why stress brings the symptom out. When the stomachache goes away, remind him that you and he knew what to do about it.

Headaches

Rarely does a toddler or preschool child complain of a headache. If he does, I would certainly have him checked out by a doctor. Eye exams, including looking in the pupils with an ophthalmoscope, will be part of the checkup. A careful and complete physical examination is an important part of ruling out certain medical conditions that can lead to headache, though in most cases there is no serious, underlying disease. Depending on his or her findings, and on the nature, severity, duration, and frequency of the headaches, your pediatrician may recommend a neurological exam and additional testing to make sure the headaches are not a sign of a more serious problem. Often, though, special tests are not needed.

Migraine headaches have a genetic component, usually occurring in families in which other members have experienced them. There are likely to be many triggers for migraine. Certain foods (even chocolate), food additives, mothballs, cleaning fluids, stress, fatigue—even flashing lights—can be triggers for them. Any one trigger alone may not contribute to a migraine, whereas two or three together will. If you can't be sure, keep a diary of all the foods, events, and stresses that occur around the time of the headaches. Migraine sufferers soon build up a dread of headaches, which adds to the stress that helps to trigger them.

There are specific medications that may prevent a migraine headache if they are taken early enough. Their use should be explained to the child. If these headaches occur in spite of the preventive medication, the physician can prescribe more potent medicines.

Headaches can be a sign of a serious condition requiring prompt medical attention. For example, after a blow to a child's head, a headache is one sign that the child needs to be medically evaluated as soon as possible. A headache accompanied by fever and a stiff neck may mean that the child has meningitis, a serious infection that also requires immediate assessment and treatment. If headaches are associated with visual changes, nausea and vomiting, fatigue, or sleepiness, parents should also be sure to consult a physician.

Headaches that are not serious are likely to occur at special times—in the morning when the child's blood sugar is low, and in the evening before supper, when fatigue and low blood sugar couple to bring on such a symptom. These can be treated by raising the child's blood sugar with orange juice before he gets up or with a snack in the afternoon before he begins to feel cranky or upset.

If the headaches are mild and without a treatable medical explanation, I would follow the same guidelines indicated for stomachaches. Respect the child's need for loving attention; let him rest while you talk to him soothingly to reduce stress. Reassure him that the doctor did not find anything wrong, and help him try to understand what is behind the headaches. Gradually, explain whatever you have observed about his symptoms and when and why they occur. Help the child learn to live with his headaches. Like all problems with a psychosomatic component, they are likely to improve when the child feels more in control and less anxious about handling a recurrence.

42. Television

OTHER THAN A CHILD'S FAMILY, THERE IS NO FORCE TODAY WHICH INFLUENCES behavior as powerfully as does television. The average child spends more time in front of a TV set than she does studying in school or attending to parental instruction. In other words, a majority of children learn more about the world and values from television experience than from family or community. This places enormous responsibility on the media and on concerned parents.

Several organizations have been influential in limiting commercials aimed at children and in improving the quality of children's programming. Various devices are now available that enable parents to block inappropriate programs. But most of the responsibility for choosing programs and limiting time spent watching TV still must be taken by parents.

My cable television show, *What Every Baby Knows,* linked me to more families than my books and articles could ever have done. The intimacy that viewers feel is very precious, and I respect it. But it also frightens me, for it represents the power of that medium. Adults are affected at all levels by viewed experiences on television. When these are positive, they are grateful. When the experience is negative, they can be passionately angry. It is clear that television has the power to invade our personal feelings. Adults may be able to express those reactions and to defend their inner core from this invasion. Can children do the same?

Stresses of TV Viewing

Eyes glued to the screen, a small child sits in front of the television set. Her face and her body are immobilized. Any sudden loud noise on the program makes her startle, showing how deep is her concentration. Noises in the room around her don't penetrate her isolation. If parents want her attention and touch her on the shoulder, a startle, then a weeping protest, may greet this interruption of her mesmerized attention. At the end of even a half-hour's viewing, a child who is pressed into another activity is likely to dissolve in tears or in hysterical screaming. After this tantrum allows release of the tension she has built up, she can be docile or sullen. But at least she can be reached.

I worry about the cost of such intensity. A child's entire physical and mental capacity is involved in watching television. Her body is passive but tense. Muscle tension reflects a stressed child, not a relaxed one. This combination of inactivity and tension is physiologically demanding. Psychologically, the cost to her is reflected in the way she disintegrates afterward, or in the other ways she may demonstrate the price of her concentration. In small children, under age four, this price needs to be questioned. Preschool children have a limited capacity for heightened experience. For some children, television watching is one of the peak experiences of their day. Parents of a child of this age should weigh this against the other influences in their child's development. When they do, few parents continue to use it as an automatic babysitter.

Children between four and six years old concentrate on important adults, imitating their speech, their movements, and their ideas. Of course, they will identify with a television star. Children in my office would sometimes speak softly and tenderly, imitating the late Mr. Rogers. Three- and four-year-olds chanted the songs of *Sesame Street* that accompany the *A*s and *E*s as they read my eye chart.

But the hosts and actors on children's shows are not always so benign. Many children's shows now portray parents as distant, insensitive, unreliable, or odd, drawing them into a world where the commercial sponsors are the only trustworthy authority. Often, the characters that children identify with on these shows get what they want by begging and whining. Thankfully, there are still some alternatives to such programming. Commercials, too, however, have a powerful impact on small viewers. Until at least age six, many children can't distinguish shows from ads, and most don't understand advertisers' motives. Parents need to be aware of this. Do you want to reinforce this impact? Do you really want to buy a particular cereal just because it is being promoted with a clever commercial, or because your child has learned to pester you for it in the supermarket?

Many researchers, including, early on, psychologist Albert Bandura of the University of California, have demonstrated that five- and six-year-olds model themselves on the activity they have viewed on the screen. If it is violent, they are more likely to engage in violent behavior in the period immediately following a program. If the program contains sexually explicit language, children will test it out afterward. By the same token, a gentle, nurturing program can lead a child to model herself on the nurturing behavior she has viewed. More recently, efforts have begun to understand the effects of television on much younger children—ages two or three and under—including work by Daniel Anderson and Tiffany Pempek and by Darcy Thompson and Dimitri Christakis. But these have been dwarfed by the massive efforts to market television and other screen-based media to infants. Some studies have found a correlation between excessive TV watching between the ages of one and three and attentional difficulties at age seven. One, for example, found a correlation between excessive television watching (defined as three or more hours per day) in children under age three and symptoms consistent with attention deficit hyperactivity disorder (ADHD) detected at age seven. A number of other studies have questioned the ability of such young children to learn from these two-dimensional media. (See *References* for more information.)

TV Messages and Peer Pressures

Helping small children become skeptical of commercials and the other messages of TV will have benefits down the line. As they get older, the pressure to conform to a peer group intensifies. Children feel the "need" for the latest trendy toy, often a spin-off from the latest TV hit. They "need" to wear the same clothes that their friends are wearing. Advertisements aimed at older children are designed to make them feel that they will be unacceptable to their peers without the product being peddled. Frequent exposure to media conveying these messages has been shown to correlate with symptoms of anxiety and depression in older children.

A parent can have a balancing influence, but not without taking into account the importance of the child's need to feel part of her group. With an open discussion of current fads, you can work out where to draw the line. If you think that the accessories that are promoted are junk, you can make that very clear. If you can't afford them, say so. If the child is old enough to work to pay for them, let her decide whether to use her money this way. If she has learned to think independently, she is more able to make a thoughtful choice. A child who learns she doesn't have to conform to TV's commercial messages is ready to learn to lead, rather than follow.

In the middle years and in adolescence, the power of television as a shaper of children's thoughts and beliefs continues to grow. If TV is allowed to be the main influence in their lives, children learn behavior, language, and thought processes from television actors or celebrities as well as from their peer group. Most parents will want to balance these influences with their own and to foster independent thinking in their children. While respecting the child's need to establish her own territory and identity, you can express the values you believe in most and those that are important in your own family.

Limits on Viewing Time

As to hours of television viewing, I firmly believe that there need to be limits. The American Academy of Pediatrics urges that children aged two and under not watch TV at all, and that children over age two watch no more than one or two hours of television per day. (This is a maximum, and in some children it will be too much.) In addition to the quantity of TV watching, the quality must be supervised by parents. Besides the correlation with ADHD mentioned above, the amount of time a child spends watching TV is also a major risk factor for childhood obesity—a widespread and growing threat to children's health. A television set located in a child's room is another important predictor for obesity and should be avoided at all costs.

The physical and psychological demands on a child of any age help determine what further TV-viewing limits need to be imposed. For example, a child with a short attention span needs time out after a very short period. In general, I would urge parents to have a cap on the amount of time that children of all ages are allowed to watch. One hour a day during the week and not more than two hours on weekend days seems a reasonable goal. (Under age two, I would urge greater caution.)

Half of this viewing time should be "family time" in which the adult members watch, too. After it is over, there is an opportunity to exchange ideas and

to discuss the programs and what the commercials are trying to do. In this way, television becomes a shared experience. The child can be allowed to help decide which programs she will choose to watch. Choosing them each week can be a time when parents participate in choice making, to help the child sort out values. There are some good programs that deserve to be watched. They can be used as special family events.

Children will haunt you with: "Everyone else's parents let them watch TV. Your rules are mean. My friends don't even want to come to our house." These statements will shake your conviction. Then, you must remind yourself that the demands of this medium on the child's physiological and psychological capacities are enormous. Think of all the other ways she can relate to children of her age, such as sports, hobbies, excursions, or camping. Can you invest extra time and energy in them?

You will need to have your answers worked out. "I know that many of your friends can watch television for several hours a day. I'm afraid I don't believe in that, for you miss too many other fun things to do. In our house, an hour's television on weekdays is it. Two hours a day on the weekends, and you and I can choose them. If there is a great special, we can always make an exception. But these are our family's rules. I want you to understand why we have them and why they are important. But whether you do or not, they are the rules of this house."

However eloquent this little speech, nothing will undermine, or reinforce, your position more than your own viewing habits. In families where parents are enthusiastically involved with their children—in cooking, playing games, exploring the outdoors, or relaxing and chatting—the lure of the screen will be reduced. Parents who turn on the TV only to watch chosen, unusual programs, and who otherwise are available to their children (or plead for a peaceful moment with a book), will find that their views on television watching carry more weight.

Video Games

Computer and video games are less passive than television watching, but too much time spent sitting in front of a screen, and viewing destructive content, is just as much of a problem. Parents who want to familiarize their children with the operation of a computer, keyboard, and simple software should be wary of the claims made for the programs they acquire and personally review their contents. While there are more and more computer games for children that are fun and educational, there are still far too many that encourage and reinforce violent behavior. There are others that subtly promote gender stereotypes that may offend some parents, and others still that promote products children don't need. The Internet is a major challenge for parents to supervise, though there are programs and devices that can be used to limit a child's access. One children's cable TV Web site once offered a downloadable game in which sugary cereals made by one of the network's sponsors furtively appeared from behind rocks and bushes along the virtual jungle path each player was to navigate. And of course, the Internet has also been used by disturbed adults to lure unsuspecting children into more direct contact with them. My advice to parents of young children is to keep any computer within a child's reach disconnected from the Internet except when a parent can be present to participate.

43. Toilet Training

THE STEPS PARENTS CAN TAKE ONCE A CHILD HAS SHOWN THAT HE IS READY and wants to begin using the toilet were outlined in chapter 12. Parents who are able to be patient until their child shows the signs of readiness that I have spelled out in that chapter—usually between two and three years of age—are unlikely to run into serious problems.

The Danger of Too Much Pressure

Problems in toilet training nearly always arise because of an asymmetry in the parent-child relationship. When parents are unable to wait, and they impose toilet training as their idea, the child will feel this as an invasion.

All parents, of course, want their child to grow up and prove that he can maintain control over his bladder and bowels. Also, pressure on parents to get the child to conform comes from many sources. Their own wish to see him as advanced makes them want to compete with other families. Preschools often insist that a child be "trained" before he comes to school. Other parents may offer advice and condescending comfort when their children are already trained. Grandparents may imply that toilet-training success is a measure of successful parenting and of a child's overall competence. The entire second year may be felt by some families as preparation for success in this area.

Parents' own experiences play an enormous role in their attitudes toward toilet training. If they have memories of early and strict toilet training, they will find it difficult to conform to the relaxed child-oriented program that I have suggested. They may try to understand my point of view, but memories will keep haunting them. "My mother had me all trained at a year. She told me how hard I tried to avoid mistakes. Why can't my child try that hard?" Memories of punishments that parents or their siblings received may seem terrible when considered rationally, but they can undermine a parent's conviction that it's all right to let a two- or three-year-old make his own decisions in this area. The experiences of two parents may have been similar or quite different. Unless both parents want to leave it to the child, the one who wants to start training before the child has made *his* decision may raise doubts in the other. Should they be pushing or at least reminding the child to try?

A toddler for whom independence is a passionate issue anyway will have his own struggles. He may stand in front of a potty, screaming with indecision. Or, he may crawl into a corner to hide as he performs a bowel movement, watching his parents out of the corner of his eye. It is a rare parent who will not feel that such a child needs help to get his priorities straight. When a parent steps in to sort out the guilt and confusion, the child's struggle for autonomy becomes a power struggle between them. Then the scene is set for failure.

Most of these power struggles will simply make the period of training stormy, unpleasant, and much longer than it needs to be. However, when parents really lock into the struggle, serious problems can result. A child can withhold stools, causing chronic constipation, perhaps even leading to an enlarged colon (megacolon). As mentioned in earlier chapters, soiling occurs when a child inadvertently but regularly leaks into his pants around a retained, hard stool. The soiling may seem like diarrhea, but the basic problem is constipation. This is confusing to the parent and to the child, who is unaware of the reason. Control issues mount and increase the depth of the problem. A bowel softener to soften the stool so it won't hurt needs to be coupled with a letup on pressure—both from within the child and from without. This will be necessary before he will want to work on training himself again.

Some children may leak urine, especially when they are under stress. Parents complain to the pediatrician, who then feels the necessity to test whether the bladder and urinary sphincter are intact. Imaging studies, catheters, and invasion of the genitals result. The child is frightened. If his anxiety becomes fixated on this area, he can become more vulnerable to chronic incontinence.

Tension in the environment, not necessarily about toilet training, may be reflected in abdominal pains, cramps, and loose bowel movements. If the child then has difficulty in maintaining control, the tension will mount. Toilet training then becomes highly charged and adds to the stress on the child. Bedwetting (nocturnal enuresis) becomes an embarrassing problem for many children, especially boys, by the ages of four and five, because of societal pressures (see "Bedwetting"). If it continues, the child will avoid sleepovers. He dares not admit to himself or to anyone else that he's so inadequate at night. Parents become desperate about such a failure, which they see as their own.

Whether hushed up or treated as a reason for punishment, bedwetting can make the child feel hopeless and helpless. He will say he doesn't care and will develop all kinds of strategies for hiding his failure each morning.

In bedwetting, as in many of the problems encountered with toilet training, a child's need to become independent at his own speed is at stake. Though the reasons may be physiological, such as an immature bladder that empties frequently, or too-deep sleep (the result of an immature signaling system), the issue of who will control the solution is there. As parents and physicians begin to investigate reasons and institute measures (such as alarms, punishments, or signal devices that go off when he wets), the child's need for autonomy and control may be neglected. He sees himself as a failure —immature, guilty, and hopeless. The effect of this damaged self-image on his future will be greater than that of the symptoms themselves.

Why do parents become so concerned about toilet training that they invade the child's privacy and even his body in their quest for "solutions"? Given that this is a developmental process that the child will ultimately master at his own speed, why do parents feel they must control it? My experience has led me to the conclusion that it is very hard for parents to be objective about toilet training, as I've said before. Our culture demands that parents feel responsible for the child's success, and the childhood experiences of many adults in this culture add more pressure to this demand. Any failure in the child is felt as a reflection on their poor parenting. The child becomes a pawn—to be "trained." It may take us another generation before we can see toilet training as the child's own learning process—to be achieved by him in accord with the maturation of his own bladder and central nervous system. (See also *Toilet Training—The Brazelton Way* in *Further Reading*.)

When Problems Exist

The steps that I outlined in chapter 12 are preventive steps, ways of leaving the job of training to the child and avoiding future problems. If a problem has already arisen, I ask parents to try the following.

- Discuss the problem openly with your child. Apologize and admit you've been too involved.
- Remember your own struggles, and your eventual successes, so that you can let the child see that there is hope ahead.
- State clearly that toilet training is up to the child. "We'll stay out of it. You're just great, and you'll do it when you're ready."

- Let the child know that *many* children are late in gaining control, for good reasons. If he wants to hear the reasons, explain them.
- Then, let him alone. Don't mention it again.
- Keep the child in diapers or protective clothing, not as a punishment, but to take away the fuss and anxiety.
- Don't have a child under age five tested unless the pediatrician sees signs of a physical problem. A urinalysis can be done harmlessly, but invasive tests and procedures—enemas, catheters, X rays, and so on—should be reserved for children who clearly need them.
- For the child who is withholding stools, keep bowel movements soft by using fruit and fiber in the diet and stool softeners. This way, you can reassure the child that they will stay that way.
- Make clear to the child that when he achieves control, it will be his own success and not yours.

Parents who feel they are too involved might seriously consider counseling for themselves in order to relive and understand their reasons for being so concerned and so intrusive. They need to agree with each other about their handling of toilet training so that their conflict does not affect the child at a level that carries a serious cost for his future—his self-image. Controlling these areas to conform to a rigid society is not worth the price a child must pay.

If the child continues to have problems that bother him or interfere with his adjustment at school or with his peers, I would seek medical advice and help.

part three

Allies in Development

44. Fathers and Mothers

EVEN AFTER THE REEVALUATION OF GENDER ROLES BY WOMEN'S AND MEN'S movements, so much emphasis is still placed on mothers and their roles that it seems only fitting to ask again what the modern father contributes that makes him so special both for the baby and for the family's cement. For he is. In a few decades, the roles of fathers have undergone tremendous changes. Most fathers of a generation ago still saw themselves only as supplements to mothers. Now, stay-at-home fathers—often by choice—have become primary caregivers. But in the not-so-distant past they participated only when their wives told them to. The participation was almost always in sports or other "masculine" activities. They were also disciplinarians, called in when a mother was not being obeyed. Many people of earlier generations hardly knew their fathers as they were growing up. I felt that my own father allowed his role to be designated by my mother, rather than following his own inclination to be really involved in his children's activities. We ended up as rather uncomfortable pals in my adolescence, trying to talk "man to man." Neither of us knew enough about the other to make this work, and I longed to know him better.

Toward Shared Parenting

Although stereotypes of male behavior have begun to break down, it may take several generations before they really change. I have had primary caregiving fathers in my practice. They were pioneers who had to work things out for themselves. I remember one full-time father who would bring his daughter to all her checkups. I marveled at his skillful participation and was also impressed by his wife's ability to step back to let him take over. When I saw them together, I noticed that she did not tell him how he might have done something better or hesitate before she handed the baby to him. However, I also found myself worrying about her own attachment to the baby. Later, I realized that this reaction came from my stereotyped expectation of what mothers should do.

Once, when I asked this same father how things were going, he replied, "Okay." "Just okay?" I asked. "That doesn't sound so great. What keeps you from feeling better?" "My daughter calls me Mama when I give her the bottle and Daddy when she wants to play." Clearly, his daughter had learned to express her desires effectively! I congratulated him for being able to play both roles for her. He went on to explain how embarrassing it was when his daughter clung to him in front of his male friends. His remark made me realize how deeply our past affects all of us, including these male friends. I also wondered whether these friends might be jealous, seeing the lovely, close relationship he had with his daughter.

Even fathers who do not assume full responsibility for a child, and whose wives take off some time from work, have an increasingly vital role to play. When a new baby is coming and when the baby arrives, new parents are faced with the enormous responsibility of wanting to provide the best environment they can. In an extended family, the cushion of an experienced older generation acts as a buffer—even if parents decide that they certainly won't do it their own parents' way. A new mother is likely to be immersed in indecision and anxiety as a natural reaction to her caring so much. She will need another adult to share decisions and give support. If she has no one else to turn to, a husband becomes an even more important counterpart to his wife—not as a secondary "mother," but as a balance, a sounding board, sometimes a compass. Even when parents disagree, he is serving a major purpose in this balance. The mother is not isolated in the inevitable doubts and uncertainties of raising a child. At times, he can give the mother perspective in her fierce new attachment to a baby. His role can be both fluid and vital to all members.

Studies of the effects of the increasing involvement of fathers in their babies' caretaking point to the gains in the babies' development. Not only do school-aged children whose fathers were involved with them as infants demonstrate significant gains in their IQ, but they show more sense of humor, longer attention spans, and more eagerness for learning. These studies show that fathers who are available to their children expand their horizons—there are two important adults for children to identify with instead of just one. They also point out that a father's involvement contributes to more stable family support for the child. One study even demonstrates that father involvement gives the adolescent a surer sense of her own values and improves her ability to resist peer pressure. Single mothers can fill in for the lack of fathering by involving their own fathers and brothers as well as reliable male neighbors, coaches, and sitters. A divorced mother will do well to recognize the continuing importance of the father in the child's life, despite shortcomings as a parent she perceives in him (see *Further Reading* and *References*).

Competition Between Parents

The change in attitudes is reflected in the fact that it's no longer a mother's job to "tell" her husband when to be available. Fathers expect to participate and have their own motivation to make time in their busy lives for their children. The problem is now more likely to be one of competition between parents and perhaps gatekeeping by the mother. These are universal feelings that exist in every adult who cares about children. The more you care, the more you want that child for yourself. This natural feeling of possessiveness makes parents unconsciously competitive with each other. Each one can see the mistakes the other makes as he or she fumbles to learn the new role of parenting. Since learning to parent is learning from mistakes, not from successes, when each parent is ready to identify with and to back the other up, the job ends with multiplied benefits for the child. Learning to accept one's own mistakes makes it easier to be tolerant of the other parent's mistakes.

Children don't need parents to agree with each other on everything or do things the same way. Babies learn very early to expect different things from each parent, though it becomes confusing for them when parents actively undermine each other. What they do need is a sense of commitment from each parent and a lack of tension around them. Competition for the baby is a sign of intense caring, not a sign of deep disagreement. Rather than allowing these competitive feelings to cause anger with each other, parents need to use them to sort out the jobs to be done. There is plenty for both of them. Competition can be a strong source of motivation for each parent to do his or her best with the baby. I recommend that when parents sense this competition, they sit down together to discuss it. It then loses its power.

Fathers and Newborns

A father can begin learning his role very early on—starting in pregnancy. He can play a vital and supportive role for his wife during childbirth and enhance the outcome for his baby. Meanwhile, he shares in the thrill of having produced that baby! As mentioned in chapter 3, studies have shown that during labor a supportive figure called a *doula* can reduce the mother's need for medication, the length of her labor, and the chance of having a cesarean section. A doula can also help a father become comfortable with his new role. (See Klaus, Kennell, and Klaus in *Further Reading.*)

Fathers report that they feel a surge of euphoria when they see the new baby in the delivery room—akin to that reported by mothers who have been awake and actively participating in the delivery process. When the delivery team hands the father the baby to hold right away, he gets a chance to see that this is really a baby—and when the baby is healthy, intact after all the fears. This kind of experience, shared with the mother, brings to a peak all of the waiting, the wondering, and the self-questioning a man often has about whether he can really become a father. One study has shown that fathers who are present during their partners' pregnancies and births have an increase in their prolactin levels and a decrease in testosterone—hormonal shifts that are thought to support a male nurturing role.

At Children's Hospital in Boston, we studied the effect on fathers of showing them their babies' behavior in the newborn period (see chapter 3). Together, several of these studies show that, as a result of this early opportunity to learn to observe and understand their newborns' behavior, new fathers are eager to get to know their new babies and become significantly more sensitive to their cries. They respond more quickly to the behavior of the baby. They soon know when to burp her, when to talk to her, and when to change her diaper. In other words, the behavioral cues of the newborn shared in this first exciting period reinforce a new father's feeling of importance to his baby, and he demonstrates it by learning his baby's "language." The belief that men don't understand babies gains no support from these studies. They each show that what men need is permission to learn their new job. One interesting aspect of the research is that when fathers learn about their newborns, they are significantly more involved in supporting their wives. I would like to see all newborn nurseries try to include every father in the demonstration of his new baby's care and in a shared observation of all the wonderful things a newborn can do—such as turning to her father's voice, following his face with her eyes and head, cuddling into the corner of his neck, and so on. Fathers, in turn, should learn to expect to be included when the baby is being examined before discharge. Fathers need to make clear that they *want* to be present for checkups. Then the pediatrician or nurse will see to it that they are included in the discussions. Don't wait to be asked!

One question often raised by new parents who want to share equally in the baby's care is: How can a father share in feeding the baby if his wife is nursing her? As soon as they all return home, the father can play a major role in helping the mother position herself comfortably for nursing and in fetching the baby from her crib for her feedings. This interruption of his sleep is made up by the importance of his support to his wife's recovery and recognition of his central role. Later, after the mother's milk supply is established, I suggest that fathers use a supplementary bottle to feed the baby. The best time for this is after the baby has learned her role in nursing—lactation consultants recommend waiting four to six weeks before bottles or pacifiers are introduced, except when a mother can't breast-feed. (In my experience, many babies can be introduced in this limited way to the bottle at three or four weeks without experiencing "nipple confusion" or other disruption of breast-feeding, and it seems reasonable to do so for babies who are already avid and adept breast-feeders. Though I share the concerns about protecting breast-feeding as much as possible, I have seen some babies refuse bottles and pacifiers when they are introduced after four weeks of age.) The bottle may contain the mother's milk or formula. If it is given at the end of the day or in the middle of the night, a bottle will offer the mother a needed rest. And the chance for the father to get to know the baby all alone at the time of a feeding is such a delicious opportunity. It more than compensates for the misery of getting up in the middle of the night. Shared roles in caregiving not only allow a father a better chance to know his baby from the first, but also give him a chance to begin to understand himself and how he can unfold as a person who cares for a helpless, dependent new being.

By the time a baby is two weeks old, she will have learned her father's voice and be able to distinguish his from another male's voice. By four weeks of age, as we have seen, a baby will have expectable and predictable behavior that is different for each of her parents and for a stranger. Without knowing to whom she's reacting, we can watch a baby's behavior and successfully guess whether she's interacting with her mother, her father, or a stranger. With a father, the baby's shoulders hunch, and her whole face gets a look of eager anticipation, of wanting to play—her eyebrows pop up, her mouth opens, her eyes flash brightly. Even when she hears her father's voice in the distance, she has this eager look. By four weeks of age, she will have learned to expect her

father to talk to her in more excited tones. When a father looms into sight, the baby's special body behavior says, "There you are! Let's go!"

The Value of Two Models

A father can also temper the intensity of the mother-infant relationship when the child needs to become independent. In every area —learning to sleep alone at night, to feed oneself, to become independent in the second year—it helps when a father can say, "Aren't you going to let her go? Let her make a mess and learn to feed herself." This role isn't necessarily popular. No mother likes to think of herself as hovering. And to be reminded that she is will inevitably set up her defenses. But a father's involvement can help her to relax, pull back, and even examine her own behavior. Single mothers often have difficulty in allowing a baby to separate and to develop independence. Of course, if a father overreacts to mealtime messes or to fussing at night, his involvement may only add to his wife's concerns.

Fathers, like mothers, treat boy and girl babies differently. A father is much more likely to be active physically with a boy and to push him to learn new motor developmental steps. With girls, fathers are likely to be gentle, slowed down, even protective. They may cuddle and carry them more. Although a father may be unable to tell you that he feels differently, he becomes the conveyor of defined gender roles for his baby.

In the aftermath of the women's movement, some parents have felt that they can and should avoid "imposing" stereotypical gender roles on their children. But both mothers and fathers are bound to have different expectations and different relationships from the first with sons and daughters. Rather than being ashamed of this, parents can see that, in this way, each child learns about himself or herself as a unique individual. If both parents can be open and honestly involved with each child, each sex will have models to follow. A boy will pretend to shave and to wear a tie or a hat "like Daddy" in the second year. He'll even begin to walk like him. In the fourth and fifth years, he'll begin to tease Mommy "like Daddy does." He'll also compete with him for Mommy's attention at critically important times. A girl will see how her mother behaves when her father is around. She may imitate her mother in order to capture him at the end of the day. She can successfully ignore Mommy's orders to "get to bed and leave us in peace" after a long day of teasing negativity at the age of four or five. When Daddy says, "Okay, let *me* take you to bed," she suddenly becomes acquiescent and delightful. What more could any father need to show how critical his role is as a balance for the family? He need no longer be told that he's a good substitute for mother. He knows he's more important than that!

Boys whose fathers have been nurturing are more likely to be more nurturing themselves as they develop. They have identified with their fathers' style of participation. If a boy sees his father helping out by cooking and cleaning, he will grow up to feel comfortable in these roles as well. Children whose fathers have shared custody—or of course those raised by single fathers—will have examples of male nurturance in abundance.

Few people, men or women, start out with knowledge of how to be a good parent. They must learn by trial and error. For parents who have learned to be perfectionists in the workplace and who have learned not to make mistakes, parenting can be a frighteningly uncharted role. It may be extra hard for fathers to live up to the conviction that quality of life is more important than just being successful in the workplace, but today more fathers keep that in mind.

45. Grandparents

A CHILD WITH GRANDPARENTS WHO ARE AVAILABLE FOR CLOSE RELATIONSHIPS already has an opportunity to experience the importance of the past and to see his own parents in a matrix of other caring adults. For a grandparent, however, finding the right balance of helping and supporting without interfering takes sensitivity and diplomacy.

After I'd been in practice for thirty years or so, most of my patients were "grandchildren"—I had known many of their parents as babies and children themselves. In fact, I knew these former patients—and their parents, now grandparents—very well, and I knew the kind of child rearing they had experienced. When they came to me for a prenatal visit, in those days before the current obsession with confidentiality, I offered, jokingly, to share some of my memories with the new spouse. Sometimes, with their permission, we did share a few, but in general, both my patients and their spouses preferred not to relive their childhoods at that critical time. It is as if they wanted to enter parenthood free of any baggage from the past. They would often say, "I don't want to be like my parents," or even, "Help me to be a different kind of parent." These statements seemed to focus on the memories of failure or of painful experiences. During these months of pregnancy, none of the good times seemed to be remembered.

The Power of the Past

Is this necessary? In order to find an identity as a parent, perhaps there is an important purpose in trying to dissociate yourself from the past—your own past. The effort to be different and independent, the urge for a fresh start, is an important one. But it can work only partially. For the "ghosts" from your own past, the memories from your own nursery, have been deeply influential in shaping you. Painful childhood episodes are only part of your past. Being cared about, nurtured, loved passionately—despite your parents' mistakes—are equally powerful influences on the parent you are becoming. Learning and adaptation to stress are also a major part of your experience, part of the deep-seated behavior patterns with which you are bound to react when something your child does brings back your own experience.

When I followed these next-generation families, they, like all families, were likely to have times of crisis or problems in their child rearing. I could then look back at my record of these parents' own childhoods, and often I found the same difficult times or the same issues of parenting. This is confirmation to me of the power of past experience.

Patterns of behavior in new parents that mimic their own parents' responses are universal and are to be expected. From the records I could sometimes predict the times when the new parents would experience difficulty. It was rather eerie, and when I saw potential trouble ahead, I wished I could help families avoid it. But at the same time, there is a kind of intergenerational strength in learning from past crises and early experience that is marvelous. When I saw one of my former patients parenting his or her own offspring with skills and approaches familiar from their parents' behavior, I was awed and thrilled. This is the way parenting is handed on from one generation to another.

The power of the past is what makes grandparents' wisdom and memories both painful and supportive for parents. Their criticism can be powerfully undermining because it strikes at the effort to escape old ghosts. Grandparents who want to be truly helpful will do well to keep their mouths shut and their opinions to themselves until their help is requested. At that point, if their ideas can be discussed—not as formed opinions but as suggestions to be taken or disregarded—they can be helpful. If grandparents can honestly relive their frustrations as well as their longed-for goals, this will be far more helpful to new young parents than advice.

Parents who are struggling with issues of separation from their own parents will naturally find it hard to turn to them at the time of a new baby or a crisis with their children. Grandparents will be wise to see their children's re-

sistance to consulting them as part of a necessary struggle for independence. But that is not easy, either, at a time when grandparents want so much to be of help and to be part of the small child's life.

The vacuum that is created around a nuclear family without contact with grandparents can be lonely and sad. Grandparents and an extended family offer a sense of continuity to new parents. When they say, "We always did it this way," they are offering a solution from the past, adaptive patterns that have been tried and found to work. If offered as suggestions, such experience in grandparents, and in extended families, can give us some of the answers we all need. Family and cultural traditions can be an important base for a child's self-image. I would urge new parents to treasure traditional ways. The value systems that strong families pass on are important to individuals as well as to our society. Traditions from the various African, Asian, Caribbean, European, Latin American, and Native American cultures have enriched this country and strengthened families as well. Grandparents are the vital link in the continuity. Our dominant culture in the United States has failed to value the role of its elders, and as a result, lost much of this continuity. Without it, individuals have become isolated, and our culture has become a me-focused and greedy one. Self-interest thrives, but at the expense of strong bonds and a sense of responsibility for children's future.

Grandparents can convey family lore and expectations to their grandchildren. Whenever they tell a story from the past, they are giving the child the sense of a whole new dimension. Our culture and our values are often more easily handed on by grandparents than by parents, whose role is so charged as day-to-day disciplinarians. Children are readier to listen and to conform to grandparents, whom they may see as less judgmental. Continuity with their own heritage is linked into all the stories only grandparents can tell. As children discover their connections to the past, they learn to value the future. As they learn to treasure their extended family relationships, they learn to put their own needs into perspective. In offering this continuity, grandparents would do well to remember that grandchildren learn more from modeling than they do from advice.

Competition

Natural competition for the child can invade parent-grandparent relationships. (We have seen this already between parents and between parents and caregivers.) If this is understood and aired, it needn't be a problem. Mothers and daughters may need to watch for this especially. With in-laws, it is easier to anticipate it, due to the mythology surrounding relationships with in-laws. In some way, the better the grandparent was as a parent, the greater the perceived threat to children as parents. As children pass in and out of stranger anxiety—accepting, rejecting, and then accepting grandparents again—these competitive feelings may be rekindled.

Grandparents can all too easily challenge young, vulnerable parents. In their intensity, they can undermine the very values they want to perpetuate. A new parent learns more from mistakes than from successes. Learning their role themselves is more valuable as they grow as parents than being told what to do. Softly expressed, firm convictions that are given when they're asked for are the most helpful. Critical statements are bound to be rejected. Parents can be deeply hurt if they feel that grandparents don't see them as caring enough about the child. No grandparent or parent can prevent painful mistakes. A grandparent who wants to be helpful can be ready to listen and especially to provide parents with a safe haven to sort out their mistakes. It is hard to sit by and watch problems develop. It's all too easy to remember how you made it work and to rub in your own success. If you want your children to learn their parenting roles, sympathetic support will do a lot more than advice or criticism. The best thing about being a grandparent is the change in relationship between parents and children. Once they both are parents, they are equals.

The Gift of Grandparents

Families need families. "If only I had someone to turn to" is a common complaint in my office. Parents need to be parented. Grandparents, aunts, and uncles are back in fashion because they are necessary. These days, a rising number of grandparents are actually raising their grandchildren almost single-handedly. And stresses on many families are out of proportion to anything even two parents can handle. With both working, the responsibilities for providing child care and for maintaining family values can be overwhelming. The situations of the increasing number of single parents and of blended, remarried families add new burdens for those who are trying to provide for and find stable values for their children. Grandparents and extended families offer a cushion for some of these stresses. Increasingly, they are stepping in to fill in the gaps for nuclear families that aren't making it alone.

Grandparents, however, are too often far away. If they are nearby, they may both be working and find it hard to stand in on short notice. Unspoken differences of opinion may easily lead to resistance on the parents' part to turn to their own parents for advice or help. The fear of appearing intrusive or of being rejected may make grandparents wary. Yet children who have the luxury of relationships with grandparents, aunts, uncles, and cousins win out in many studies of child development. Maybe the nuclear family will turn out to have been a social experiment that can no longer thrive under current conditions. The opportunity for experiencing many models for learning about life adds to the child's potential. Parents offer a child a firm base, while grandparents and aunts and uncles offer options. Their presence implies an important past, and their beliefs are a part of the family's belief systems. All of us today are hungry for values. Religious beliefs and ethnic values have been undermined in our society. Strong values are at risk for too many families. Who else but grandparents can keep them alive?

At the time of birth or of a child's illness, or when a mother first goes back to work, grandparents can cushion the stress if they have been incorporated into the nuclear family and effectively extended it. When both parents must work, they will be fortunate indeed if they can have grandparents nearby to back them up in emergencies and to offer support when problems arise. However, given declining purchasing power and the increased challenges of ensuring one's own retirement in the United States, more grandparents than ever before continue to work, often full-time, and are less available than grandparents in earlier generations. As a result, there are limits on the help they can offer these days, but emotional support is as important as ever. Grandparents who are available can provide the parents with an opportunity to be with each other. They can give parents a safe night out or a weekend away together.

Grandparents can also help in the stormy times when a child is fighting for autonomy and parents are trying to maintain control. This help does not consist of grandparents taking sides. If they do, neither parent nor child will have the same opportunity to work out the conflict. A grandparent can help in *only one way:* by listening to both sides and clarifying the reasons for the struggle, without taking sides. For example, they can help parents express their own reasons for needing to feel in control. A chance to air feelings about family fights with grandparents or relatives might be an opportunity to defuse conflicts, but only if the grandparents and other family members can listen in a respectful and kindly way. A judgmental grandparent will only compound the issues. While grandparents may bring the wisdom of experience and a more objective view of the child's issues, they still must respect the parents' concerns first. Being a grandparent involves a great deal of diplomacy that is acquired on the job. In my own case, I gradually learned that to be of any real help, I had to be more aware of my children's concerns and not focus entirely on my grandchild's. The hardest and most important job of all, though, is learning when to stay out of it. When? Most of the time.

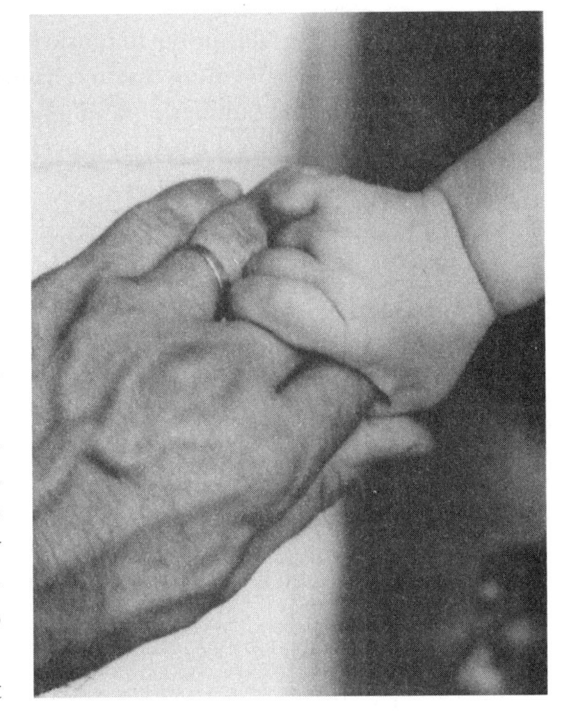

The most important gift a grandparent

can bring is unconditional, undemanding love. A grandparent can enjoy a baby without having to worry how he behaves or when to be firm. After years of parenting, grandparents are relieved just to be loving caregivers, not disciplinarians. They also offer a continuity of caregiving styles, of rhythms, of ways of behaving that are familiar to the child. As opposed to a caregiver outside the family, grandparents are like an extension of the parent. Grandparents show children the mountaintops; they pass on the dreams and goals of a family. Parents must show the children how to get there. My own grandmother gave me the inspiration to become a doctor for babies. She always said, "Berry's so good with babies." I wanted to please her more than anyone else in the world, so I learned how to be good with babies. Now, I hear her voice whenever I receive that compliment. Of course, my mother was jealous of my grandmother's influence on me. But she needn't have been. I needed them both—for different things.

Though sociologists seem to think they've exposed some unappreciated new trend, it will come as no surprise to grandparents that now, more than ever before, they are also, in increasing numbers, giving the gift of financial stability to their children. Given the decline in the actual earning power of the majority of Americans, grandparents—who benefited from better times—are stepping in to help their children provide everything from child care to a comfortable home to music lessons for their grandchildren. It used to be that parents of young children had to provide for their parents as well. Now, for a growing number of families, the flow of material aid is reversing—a sign, no doubt, that the heyday is over, and that harder times and scarcer resources are the current reality.

Guidelines for Grandparents

- Remember that you are not the parent; be a loving, delighted listener and hold back on advice.
- Don't rush up to small children even if they're your grandchildren unless you want them to withdraw. Never look a baby in the face at first; look just past him until he elicits your attention. Don't ever grab him away from his parent. Wait until he makes a reaching-out gesture toward you. Watch a small child's behavior. At the point where his face softens and he relaxes enough in your presence to begin to play with his toys, he is ready for you to join in.
- Make a ritual out of your meetings with grandchildren. Take them a toy

or a small present. Don't set up expensive expectations that must be lived up to later, however. Tell them stories about the "old days" when their parents were little.

- Don't try to treat each child alike, but try to make each one special. Have separate times for each—alone with you. Acknowledge that you will feel differently about step-grandchildren, but make a big effort to get to know them as people and as individuals.
- Agree ahead of time with your children about treats and indulgences so that you know where to stop. Consider consulting your children about presents for the holidays. You can overload small children and put too much emphasis on material things.
- Offer to babysit when you are not working and when they need you.
- Provide the focus for regular family reunions and for holiday events. Even if it seems like a huge effort and the event is fraught with charged emotion, the ritual and excitement of it will linger in children's memories. Include old friends from the parents' past.
- When you help financially or emotionally, be sensitive to how difficult it may be for your adult children to accept this help—particularly for a son- or daughter-in-law.
- Respect your children's efforts at discipline. They need your help. Don't undermine them. Don't tell your own children what to do, especially in front of grandchildren, or criticize your children in sensitive areas. Of course, you will want your grandchildren to be raised perfectly, but your criticisms of your children's parenting can do as much harm as good—or more—for you will undermine their self-confidence.
- Listen, but advise them only when they ask for your advice. Don't try to be a teacher for either grandchildren or children. You can offer much more valuable things—comfort, love, experience, hugs, and a sense of strength and stability. Be ready to offer it to both generations.
- When you are far away, stay in touch with postcards and letters, using drawings and large printing the grandchildren can read. Photos of parents when they were little are especially welcome, as are birthday cards and presents that fit the grandchild's stage of development and his interests. Videotapes can be another way to bridge the gap: Read a story or tell your grandchildren about when their own parents were their age.
- Use the telephone to say hello and congratulate your grandchildren for small triumphs. Your voice and the chance for interaction makes this a more satisfying option than e-mails, though these are a less expensive

way of staying in touch. Videotapes of yourselves and the children are a great way to bridge the distance, and of course communicating in real time with Web cameras can be even better.

- Regular visits for short periods are best. A three-day visit is likely to be enough. Help with housework and baby-sitting. Try to take everyone out on an excursion while you are there, or for a meal, to give the parents a break from their routine and briefly lighten their load. Before you arrive, offer to stay nearby in an inexpensive hotel if their quarters are cramped or if things tend to get tense when everyone is crammed together for a few days without a break.
- Tell your children when they are parenting well. Give them a pat on the back. Let them know that you admire their hard work in the ways it shows up in your grandchildren.

The best thing that has happened to me as a grandparent has been the chance for my children and me to have a whole new relationship. We are all adults, parents, on equal footing now. They can see my pleasure in the way they parent and in their children. They need me from time to time, and I revel in it. Each grandchild is a miracle, but a renewed relationship with your own children is an even greater one.

46. Friends

THROUGHOUT CHILDHOOD, FRIENDS OFFER OPPORTUNITIES TO A CHILD to try out different aspects of her developing personality, her interests, likes and dislikes, and ways of relating. She must learn how to socialize, how to give without expecting an equal return, how to share, how to elicit positive responses, and how to care about someone her own age. She can use these friendships as a safe haven in which to try out sides of herself and as a mirror. She can try out different styles and new adventures through the encouraging eyes of a friend. In the process, she is learning about herself. She is also learning how to attract and hold onto a friend. The necessary give-and-take of a friendship provides a child with opportunities for relationships that parents and siblings do not provide. A child without friends is a poor child indeed. When a child must learn to deal with her own temperament—for example, her shyness or high activity level—it is even more important for her to learn how to adapt to the demands of a group. A friend who is like her will help her do this. It has always intrigued me to watch two small children play and learn from each other.

First Friends

When should parents start introducing a child to other children outside the family? In the second year (twelve to twenty-four months) it becomes important for a child to learn how to cope with other toddlers. In a large family or in a busy neighborhood, she may already have begun to learn about sharing, rivalry, teasing, and coping with older children or a new baby. But the kind of relationships a child can make with children who are not her age are different from those she will make with her own age group. Older children tend to protect, to tease, or to overpower younger ones. In healthy peer relationships among toddlers, children first learn the give-and-take of equality. They learn the rhythms of reciprocity—when to dominate and when to submit. This is basic to important relationships in the future. A child learns which signals mean that she must give in and which ones mean that she can take the lead. As she learns these important signals, she learns how to relate to others. If she doesn't, she finds herself isolated. In the second year, children are both demanding of others and learning to be sensitive to their needs. It is wonderful to watch two-year-olds at play. If parents set up regular play groups of two or three toddlers, they can all learn about each other.

At this age, learning occurs by imitation. In so-called parallel play, two toddlers can putter alongside each other without ever appearing to look at each other (see chapter 11). And yet, they are already far more interested in and capable of learning from each other than the concept of parallel play would suggest. Each child imitates the other with entire hunks of behavior. This ability to pick up and imitate whole sequences of a peer's activity is astonishing at this early age. As one toddler stacks a row of blocks to make a skyscraper, the other will stack the same number of blocks for her building—using similar gestures as she does so. I have seen two-year-old children absorb whole new sets of behaviors from other two-year-olds and perform tasks to which they had never before been exposed.

Aggression

What if toddlers are not able to get along? What if one is too aggressive and overpowers the other, who is temperamentally a quieter, more reserved child? Is it healthy for either of them? Not really. The parents of these unequally matched children will likely be drawn into taking sides and risk reinforcing each child's imbalanced behavior. When parents of toddlers get into their children's play, they risk changing it entirely to an adult-oriented occasion. The opportunity for the children to learn about each other is diminished.

If the children cannot right the imbalance on their own, it is wise to find another child who is more your child's speed. If possible, find a playmate who is suited to your child in temperament. For instance, if your toddler is a quiet, thoughtful, rather sensitive child, try to find one like her. She'll learn a lot more from a peer who is learning to handle a temperament like hers than she will from your urging her to be more aggressive or gregarious. Though you mean to encourage her when you rally a hesitant child to fight back or to act differently, she will sense that you don't approve of her as she is. Her self-image is at stake.

If your child is aggressive and impulsive, look for another like her. They'll build up to peaks of frantic activity but will probably find ways of subsiding. In this way they will learn—gradually—about limiting themselves as well as about overreacting to their impulses. After playing together regularly two or three times a week, such children will eventually become bosom buddies and will be learning as much about themselves as about each other.

Teasing As a child gets older, she begins to use her friends for other important issues in her development. Some start teasing, perhaps reacting to and trying to resolve their own sibling rivalry. Others tease out of insecurity, unsure of their ability to make a lasting relationship. I would try to help a child who teases see that other children don't like to be teased. Although she may think this is a way to reach out, other children won't like it. They will reject the teaser and leave her alone. You might try letting a child who teases play with just one other child to learn about friendship that way. The absence of an audience of peers may reduce the teaser's insecurity as well as the impact of her teasing, but a parent will want to keep an ear open to be sure the other child isn't silently suffering.

Bullies A bully is an insecure child. She doesn't know how to deal with her peers or her aggressive feelings. All children run away from a bully. As she gets more and more isolated, the bully becomes even more insecure. Her bullying becomes an unsuccessful attempt to hide how vulnerable she feels. I would

try to bolster her self-image and talk about more acceptable ways of relating to her peers. When children are cruel, it is often when they are distressed. When one child touches a vulnerable point in another, that child lashes out. "You're stupid," "You're a sissy," or "You walk like an elephant" comes from a child who is struggling with her own feelings of incompetence. Counteract the bully's negative *feelings* with understanding and support, but let her know that her *behavior* is not acceptable.

To help the child who is being bullied or teased, you can reassure her that everyone gets teased and that it is a matter of learning to stand up to it. She certainly doesn't have to like or accept being bullied, but she'll have to assert herself in order to establish this. That's not so easy to explain. For a small child you might just say, "Don't let kids tease you. Tell them not to be mean and that you won't listen." To a somewhat older child (four years or older), you could explain that "Everyone has something she has to live with—maybe a birthmark, a limp, straight hair or curly hair, blue eyes or brown ones. Everyone needs to learn how to live with the way she was born. Other children tease when they are trying to understand you. They are trying to get to know you. But you need to show them that they can't hurt you by saying mean things. Once you decide that you are in charge of what to think about yourself, you don't need to pay attention to what teasers say about you. If you can take their teasing without getting upset, and stand up for yourself the way you are, they will respect you. And sometimes you may even end up being friends."

Parents should rarely interfere in peer relationships, but being bullied is a time when your child needs your support and help. The less adult involvement, the more children will learn about each other—and about themselves. If a relationship continues to be out of balance and becomes destructive, parents should advise a child to find other children. But the child may not follow that advice. Often the relationship is too important, even when it's out of balance. If a child truly is in danger—physical or psychological—then it is, of course, time for parents to step in.

Evolving Relationships

Children relate to other children differently at each age, and they work out different sorts of issues.

Two- and Three-Year-Olds As we have mentioned, this is a time for learning through imitation, learning about limits, and learning about language from each other.

Three- to Six-Year-Olds This is a time for learning about one's self and others, one's own emotions and others', about the connections between one's acts and the results, including one's effect on others. Conscience is dawning, and new understandings of aggression are possible. Little boys tend toward horseplay, locking onto each other to wrestle and roll around on the floor. They threaten each other with fists, though each one knows who is the stronger. Meanwhile, they are learning about their own aggression. Little girls tend to tease each other. They learn about provocative behaviors from each other. They giggle and often are incredibly silly. At these ages, a parent's role is to be sure there are opportunities for close playmates, chances for a child to learn how to make friends, to play and relate to others. If a child is isolated at this time, a parent should take it seriously and try to help her. This is the time to learn how to give and take with others. A spoiled or overprotected child won't make it.

The quality of a child's friendships is a good indicator to parents of a child's healthy development. Other children can be one of the most sensitive indicators of disturbance in a child. When I cannot be sure from the child's behavior or from the parents' report about the seriousness of a child's problems, I watch her with her peers or ask her teachers about how other children accept her. A child who is isolated in play groups or shunned in school is transmitting subtle messages to other children—of anxiety, self-doubt, inadequate social skills, or turmoil to which adults may not be attuned. Children will not accept these struggles in other children. They are too threatening. When other children shun a child, parents should take this as a warning that their child is struggling. A child with friends who is upset will have other children to turn to who may be sympathetic, understanding, and even protective. But children react differently to a child who has suffered a loss or who is temporarily upset and to one who is withdrawn because of deep-seated problems. Parents will want to take these signs seriously, both to get help for the child and to give her access to the world of experience other children can offer. (See our book *Touchpoints Three to Six* in *Further Reading.*)

47. Childcare Choices

LEAVING A BABY OR SMALL CHILD IN ANOTHER'S CARE IS NEVER EASY. IF the caregiver can be the other parent, a grandparent, or another close relative, it may be easier for the parent to share the child with them, for they have reason to care particularly about this baby, and the parent can be comforted by that thought. But it is still complicated. Caring parents will grieve about sharing their baby with another person, who may be the one to witness the first step, or the first word, while parents are at work. In several earlier chapters we discussed gatekeeping and the natural competition that evolves. This competitive feeling for the child is a normal, inevitable part of caring deeply. "Will he remember me? Will I lose part of his love—especially if the nanny (or other caregiver) takes good care of him?" Of course, parents will feel jealous. They will mourn the loss of their special times together and worry that they are no longer singularly important, even though, of course, they are. This mourning can be accompanied by three defenses: denial, projection of their feelings onto others, and detachment from the baby's care.

Denial is a defense that is critical to all of us. It is natural for grieving parents to deny their feelings as they separate from their child, and the younger the child, the more difficult it is to leave him. However, it tends to distort reality, and parents who are in denial may not recognize events—such as the cost of the separation for the child, and the parents—as they really are.

Projection occurs when parents blame others for events or developmental issues, or blame themselves and set the caregiver up as hero—temporarily, only to resent him or her later on.

Detachment from the baby and his progress doesn't mean that a parent doesn't care, but that it hurts so much to care. Parents who seem to be running away from caregivers, avoiding any real interaction with them, may be trying to handle this defense.

These defenses can interfere with the parents' relationships—with other caregivers and with their baby. Parents and caregivers who understand the defenses are less likely to distort their relationships.

Seeking a Nurturing Environment

We are all aware of how critical a nurturing environment can be to a small child, and that separation from a parent is traumatic in itself. When is it best done? Can the separation be softened? Can a small child adjust to more than one caregiver and not give up the primary attachment to his parents?

As far as we can tell, the answer to the last question is yes. Even a small infant will "remember" his parents' critical cues and will develop a set of expectations that will last and serve as "memory" for the parents' return. These expectations clearly develop in the first three or four months of life. When mothers and fathers have been consistently involved over the first few months, they will be remembered. In order to keep the relationship strong, they do need to be fully available when they return from work each day, to revive the important cues on which the baby depends.

I observed four-month-old babies in childcare situations for as long as eight hours at a time. They cycled at a low-grade level between waking and sleep states, never being very passionately involved with their caregivers. When a parent came at the end of the eight-hour stretch, the baby seemed to fall apart, crying and complaining. Someone on the staff always said, "He never does that to us." Of course not. He saved up his important feelings for his parents. If parents can take this type of comment the way it is no doubt meant—as reassurance that their baby is not crying all day—and also realize that it is a sign that *they* are the most important people in their baby's life, the baby's outbursts will be less painful to them. The reason parents feel all this so deeply is that the wrench of leaving their baby makes them feel vulnerable and guilty.

In evaluating center-based care, family-based care, or substitute caregivers in your home, you will want to watch for the consistency of caregiving behavior, the emotional investment from the caregiver, and the ability of each caregiver to respect the individuality of the baby. Warmth and empathy are critical in any supplementary caregiver. Does she respect each baby in her care? Watch her when she holds the baby to see if she observes and adjusts her rhythms to the baby's. Is she sensitive to each child's varying needs for food, a diaper change, sleep, and playful interaction? You'll also want to know more about her approach to small children. A simple question to ask that will help you determine whether you'll all be able to respect and live with each other's views is: "How do you go about toilet training a child?" From her answer you'll learn about how thoughtful she is, how experienced, how flexible or rigid, how much she must be in control, and how much she can yield when a child needs to experience mastery.

Next, I'd want to know whether the caregiver can also respect and nurture you as involved parents. Can she take the time to listen as you tell her what your baby has been like at home the evening before? Will she sit down to tell you about your baby's day when you come to pick him up? This is hard to tell ahead of time. But if a caregiver seems judgmental about your leaving your baby all day, I would look for a person who can understand your anguish and can accept your reasons for going back to work. The sort of person you want would say, "You know, I think he's about to start to walk," instead of, "He just walked for me today."

If you find a warm, caring person, you need to be aware of your competitive feelings and to talk them out from time to time. Give her your backing. If she does things slightly differently from you, don't worry. A child can adjust to several different styles and can learn to be flexible in the process. If you respect her ways of caregiving, the child will, too, as she gets older.

A person who can remain nurturing is likely to be one who is well trained in child development and who is not overloaded by too many other responsibilities and too many children to care for. But quality child care is not cheap, nor should it be. A good caregiver needs to be adequately paid. Early experiences shape your child's future. Giving him the best care and environment becomes an investment.

Kinds of Care

Child Care at Home If you can afford it for the child in the first year, at-home child care might be optimal. Your child will be in familiar surroundings. The separation from you and the accompanying bustle in the morning and evening can be somewhat less abrupt and hectic. This demands that you find a special person indeed. She must offer your baby an environment you would be proud of. This person must respect you and your household. She must have enough training and experience to understand babies, must be patient and respectful, and, above all, adjustable. She should be ready to respond to and prevent emergencies. She shouldn't be passive or depressed or in too much of a hurry. She should be full of ideas about what she can do with the baby all day and be ready to share them with you.

A nanny or mother's helper must be reliable and be able to make the baby her top priority. She mustn't have an unstable situation at home or other demands that might interfere with her dependability. Even in the best of circumstances, backup in emergencies had better be identified in advance unless your job is very flexible.

Family-Based Care Another form of care is offered by parents, usually mothers, in their own homes to a small group of children from infants through three or four years. By the second or third year, toddlers need other children to identify with and play with. They can profit from being with other children, especially those of their own age. Given an optimal situation, even younger children will as well. Hubert Montagner, a French researcher on infant behavior, has beautiful films of seven- to nine-month-old infants together who are already learning about and from each other. As early as seven months of age they can form deep attachments to each other. Home day-care or other group care *can* benefit infants in the first year. But it must be skillful and caring.

Family-based care is entirely dependent on the quality of the caregiver and her ability to relate to each child, although the safety of the physical environment is of course also a basic consideration. A ratio of more than three or four babies to one caregiver is expecting too much. More than four toddlers per adult is hopelessly chaotic. The children are then either "on their own" or parked in front of a TV. The child-to-adult ratio and the personality and character of the caregiver are the first considerations, but there are many others to be taken into account as you choose a home for care. Often, these parents are also caring for one or more of their own children. This can make things more complicated, as their children may vie more intensely for attention when other children are present, and favoritism is also obviously a risk. Many of these caregivers, though, are savvy about these issues and skillful in handling them. Though such home care is sometimes licensed and subject to regulations and monitoring, this is rarely the case. In the absence of independent monitoring and supervision, you will need to make careful observations and be alert to your child's reactions if you choose home care.

As with a caregiver in your own home, a single family-based caregiver is vulnerable to her own emergencies, so you will want to know in advance about her backup plans. If she or her family is ill, what will happen?

Family-based care, like the other forms of early child-care, has pros and cons. It is up to you to monitor it. Linger at drop-off and pick-up times, and watch the caregiver's interactions with the children. Notice their activities and how they spend their time there. What happens with other children may happen with yours when you are not there. Drop in at unannounced times to observe. You do not have to act like you are suspicious of the caregiver—just say you unexpectedly had some free time from work and decided to stop in and enjoy being with your child. Offer to help from time to time and then observe the caregiver's techniques, rhythms, and sensitivity. And, above all, watch your child for signs of neglect or depression.

Center-Based Care Licensed childcare centers must now meet certain standards in order to retain their license to operate. The National Association for the Education of Young Children (NAEYC) is a large organization of early childhood teachers who are trained and supervised. They developed a set of criteria for Head Start and later began applying these to childcare centers in an accreditation program. These standards can protect you and your child and increase the chances that your child's need for nurturing and early learning opportunities is fulfilled. Check to see if the center you are considering is accredited or seeking accreditation. (See *Useful Addresses and Web Sites.*)

Teachers at childcare centers should be well trained, supervised, caring, and well paid. We believe that the child-to-adult ratio should not exceed three to one for infants, four to one for toddlers, and six to one for three-year-olds. Teachers should be backed up for illness and other absences by trained substitute caregivers.

The atmosphere of a center is critical. A center in which the teachers are

happy, work as a team, and enjoy each other is ideal. If childcare teachers only see themselves as babysitters, or are treated that way, they will miss the rewards of nurturing and educating young children and soon become bored and withdrawn. Even very young children are sensitive to this. Test the atmosphere yourself. If the caregivers all congregate at one end of the room and leave the children to themselves, watch out! A ratio of three or four infants per teacher is no good if three teachers leave twelve infants alone. Look for teachers who seem to like children and who want to play with them. Watch to see whether they get down on the floor to play. Do they engage in playful interaction while diapering a baby? If every bid from the baby is treated as a chore rather than an opportunity, watch out. A baby lover reacts to each cry or diaper change as a reason for interaction. Babies need this kind of responsive environment. If a caregiver is too overwhelmed or too distracted, the infant will recognize it and withdraw or become depressed.

Monitoring Care

Having found a warm caregiver or a well-run childcare center, you will still want to watch how your child is responding. The child is the best guide to the atmosphere in which he is receiving care. If he looks happy and is thriving physically, you can be pretty sure he is in good hands. Of course, he will and should protest your leaving and, as we said, save complaints for your return. An older child will be likely to "tell tales" when he wants to retaliate against his caregivers. You can't always go by what he says. But you can by how he behaves. I would observe him in the center. Watch him at critical times in addition to drop off and pick up, such as mealtimes, free play, transitions from the playground, and naptime. Drop in unexpectedly if you can.

You can learn a lot by watching a caregiver and child together. Does one imitate the other? Do they adjust to each other's bodily positions, to the sensory modalities (visual, auditory, motor) that the other prefers? When a baby's face softens, does the caregiver's face soften too? Do *you* feel good about their interaction as you watch them?

A small child will usually show signs of distress if he is in a truly depriving environment. But his behavior may not adequately reflect an abusive experience. He may become sensitive to your raised voice or to your raised hand, but he may not. If you ask him whether he ever gets spanked or "touched," he will answer you in the way he thinks you want him to. You may not be able to tell for sure by his behavior. But if his behavior changes and he regresses to an earlier stage of development, you will want to learn why. And if he becomes depressed or withdrawn, I'd certainly take it seriously. Sadness, lack of responsiveness, and delays in responding to positive or negative stimuli can be warning signs. If he winces when you change his diapers or covers himself when you change his clothes, your index of suspicion might go up.

Evaluate such signs calmly and carefully. It's all too easy to overreact these days. If a child regresses to earlier behavioral patterns—losing toilet training, waking at night to cry out, or beginning to use babyish behaviors—watch to see if these are transient. If so, they may be due to the transition from your care to substitute care, or to a temporary upset or a touchpoint. If they are more long lasting, they can be a cause for concern. You should talk over his adjustment at the center and see whether the caregivers are concerned or whether they are defensive.

If a child is depressed or fails to thrive—losing weight, appearing sad, or refusing food—I would worry more. Then, I'd have an assessment by his physician. Include your assessment of the center in your history to the physician.

If you have specific reasons to suspect abuse, every state has a child protective services agency that should be contacted. But be as sure of your suspicions as you can. It is easy for a parent to feel guilty and project these feelings onto caregivers, accusing them unnecessarily.

The following is a checklist of other things to look for in choosing or monitoring day care.

Are the staff members attentive to the children's safety?
Are emergencies planned for and handled well?
Is good nutrition promoted?
Is the atmosphere bright, pleasant, and fun, or is it tense and glum?
What are the rhythms of feeding, sleeping, and diapering? Do these seem based on the children's needs or on a rigid schedule?
How does a teacher leave three to attend to one?
Are there signs of individual attention for each child?
Would *you* want to stay there?
How does the staff or home childcare provider recommend that you separate? Can you stay for the first week?
Can you visit at any time without advance notice?
Can you explain the child's needs in the morning and get a report at the end of the day?
What about sick children? How long before they let a child with a fever return?

Is there an emphasis on early learning? I feel that a center that respects the child's stage of emotional development and is ready to encourage it seems preferable to one that imposes a heavy curriculum without taking into account a child's readiness. High-quality childcare centers today can foster the emotional development of young children while offering them early learning opportunities that are stimulating, reward their curiosity, build experiences of success, and motivate them to become lifelong learners. While a focus on preliteracy is important, it is of little value if these other skills are not carefully nurtured as well.

No matter how fortunate you may be in your choice of care, we should all realize that today in this country, a large majority of working parents of young children are having to leave their children in care that you or I wouldn't trust—*nor do they.* There is not enough affordable, quality care available now, and most childcare professionals are not paid enough. Think what it must mean to a parent who has no choice but to leave a baby or small child with someone who is underpaid, burned out, and planning to quit in a few months, or even someone who they fear might abuse, neglect, or molest him. What does that do to the grief a parent feels anyway in entrusting a child to another person? We need national, state, and local funds to improve and assure quality child care for children all over the United States. Otherwise, we risk watching much of a generation grow up without nurturing care, and a whole generation suffers the consequences. Why haven't we already made the needed investments in quality early child care when we know that for every dollar spent, many times that amount will be saved later in social services, remedial education, and even in the criminal justice system?

48. Your Child's Doctor

"How do I get my pediatrician to listen to my questions? She's a good person, and I know she's good at diagnosing diseases in my children. But she's always in such a rush, and when I ask her questions about my child's development, she either ignores my questions or tells me not to worry. 'It's normal—he'll grow out of it,' she always says. But I do worry. What parent doesn't? Shouldn't I expect her to take my questions seriously, even if she doesn't always know the answers?"

These are the kinds of questions I hear quite often from concerned parents. The brave ones, those who express these concerns and know that their child's doctor needs to be more responsive, have a better chance of finding help. Many parents today are desperately seeking support in raising their children and don't know where to turn. In today's world, where grandparents work and other extended family members are often far away, stressed parents are at a loss for other sources of advice and support. One place they are likely to turn is to the pediatrician, family physician, or nurse practitioner who has shown an interest in their child's physical health. They hope for a similar concern about the child's mental health.

Pediatric Training

Most physicians are likely to be trained with a purely medical model—of disease and technology. The four years of medical school are crammed with ever-expanding knowledge of basic science, of disease and its treatments. Pediatric training is packed with still more technology and disease. As a result of the huge strides in pediatrics, better treatments than ever are available for an increasing number of diseases, even if we still haven't figured out how to provide them for the millions of uninsured children in our country. But because of the unavoidable pressure to master this always growing body of knowledge, little attention is paid to child development or to the art of listening and responding to parents' concerns. Now, it's beginning to change, and pediatric training requires a (still too brief) time devoted to learning about child development.

I am convinced that if we made more room for teaching basic communication skills in medical schools, doctors would be even more effective in identifying disease early and in helping their patients understand what they must do to fight it. Of all the medical specialties, it may be the family physicians who are most attuned to the importance of these relationships, since they take care of all members of a family. Few pediatricians are taught about forming relationships with parents and children. Because most pediatricians choose the field because they like caring for children, they may experience the participation of parents as an intrusion, and one that they certainly receive little or no formal training for. Many unconsciously blame parents for whatever is wrong with a child. This blame may be the result of their concern about the child and their own feelings about not being able to make her better. Training in developmental issues of the kind I describe in this book can help pediatricians better understand the experiences of parents as their children grow. Those who have such training will find that their efforts to build valuable relationships with parents can make pediatrics a tremendously rewarding field in which to work.

Since, at the present time, too few pediatricians get such training, they often feel uncomfortable when parents ask questions about behavior and emotions. Often, they don't know the answers—nor have they learned to acknowledge what they don't know. Instead, they may fall back on their own past experiences: "My wife (or my husband) and I found this," or, "My children got over this when they were three years old. Wait it out and don't worry." They might put you off with "Don't worry. She'll outgrow it." Although these answers are ways of saying, "I really don't know," they are also usually expressions of caring on the doctor's part, ways of trying to help.

Choosing a Doctor for Your Child

First of all, check the physician's credentials. Is he or she well trained, with access to a good hospital? Is she or another competent healthcare professional available when you need her? Does he have twenty-four-hour, seven-days-a-week coverage? Most physicians practice in a group, so that one member is available at all times. I do not believe that quality medical care can be provided to families of young children when they must switch from one doctor to another for every routine visit. I would urge you to choose a practice that is set up to give you your own doctor—the same one to see for each well-child visit, and for urgent visits whenever possible. When you are worried and your child is sick, your familiarity and relationship with the doctor will be more important then ever. Your doctor is your "medical home"—a safe, reliable base for you and your child to count on. Your doctor should know you and your child so that he or she can provide the kind of continuity of care that you couldn't possibly expect from a succession of new, unknown ones, the kind of care that all too many health maintenance organizations are demanding that we put up with. After regular office hours and on weekends, of course, it certainly is critical to have someone on call, and only fair to expect that this won't always be your child's doctor. It would be unreasonable to expect a single doctor to be at the mercy of night calls all the time. If your pediatrician is well trained and available, you are halfway there. You should be able to call him or her after an emergency to review what has been done and to find out what else he or she might advise.

Also, take the time to think about what type of doctor is best suited to the needs of your family—a pediatrician, or a family physician? Family physicians are trained to provide primary care to adults as well as to children, and some families prefer to share the same doctor.

You may want to ask others in your community about the doctor's personality. One of the best ways to find out about whether you will "click" with a new doctor is to resort to scuttlebutt. Do friends whom you respect seem to like this doctor? You might call the doctor's office and ask if he or she would be willing to meet with you for an interview. Many doctors don't like to be "looked over," but some do not mind. I've always preferred to have prospective patients know about me and come to me with their eyes open. This gives me the chance to be sure I can work with them, too. A parent-doctor relationship should be a mutual one. Each party should respect the other and be ready to work things out when the relationship becomes stressed.

Pediatricians who have been trained in child development sometimes teach in a medical center and conduct clinics to which parents bring their children for developmental assessment. In this way they can recommend early intervention when there are problems, physical or psychological. If you have concerns that are not being addressed by your physician, you might consider using one of these child development clinics or set up a referral through your doctor to gather information to supplement your doctor's medical advice.

Some pediatric groups now have the advantage of a nurse practitioner or a child psychologist in their practices who can help with behavioral "problems." If so, you should be able to arrange to see this specialist periodically—either to arrange for an assessment of your child or to get answers to your stored-up questions. The opportunity to get to know and observe your child will enable these members of the medical team to help you in any decision making.

Having a primary physician keeps you from having to rely on the staff of an emergency room for problems that are not emergencies. The ER doctors and nurses won't know you or your child and will only address your child's most urgent need—often only with a short-term solution—before rushing off to the real emergencies. A regular pediatrician of your own should offer far more than this to foster your child's well-being and healthy development. Regular checkups with such a primary physician mean that he or she will know you and your child when something goes wrong, and in a crisis, can benefit from prior knowledge of you and your child. Ask your doctor to tell you how to reach his or her backup when you have an emergency.

When It's Time for a Change

What if the relationship with your physician is deteriorating? I can recognize this when parents begin to be late for each visit or miss several appointments. When I see this happening, I ask them to come in specifically to discuss our mismatch, or I suggest that they might be happier elsewhere. It's a painful way to part, but it's better for the child than maintaining an ambivalent relationship in which neither of us is comfortable. The child's welfare is really the goal of a pediatric relationship, and sooner or later, a poor match is not in the child's best interest.

If, however, you want to try to work things out, ask for a special time for a consultation. When you do go in, remember that the doctor may be on the defensive and will be sensitive to the fact that you are dissatisfied. Let the doctor know that you respect and admire him or her, and acknowledge the efforts that he or she has made on your child's behalf. Perhaps you might try to meet the doctor halfway by apologizing for needing more than the doctor may have realized. Then, do your best to outline your needs. You are trying to get to know the doctor better and to let him or her know you better, so that he or she can help you with your child. A powerful way to rebuild your relationship is to recognize together that you both have the child's best interests as a common goal. A mutual understanding should achieve that, or it is time to change doctors. One question always worth asking yourself is: Have you done your share to make the relationship work? If you have and it is not possible, then it is better to get into another physician's hands before the child suffers.

Building a Trusting Relationship

There are many ways to make a good working relationship. One of the most important ones is for both of you, the parents-to-be, to go in to meet the physician during pregnancy. You can discuss your wishes and goals *before* the baby arrives. I have found that a prenatal visit can be a wonderful opportunity for us to get to know each other. Then, we can start with the baby together as old friends.

It is important for both parents to come for checkups whenever possible. Even though many fathers today are more involved in raising their children than in recent generations, some may still feel uncomfortable and practically say nothing. Even so, they can feel a part of the teamwork when they come. The physician will be pleased to have both parents present. The chance to know both of you is "money in the bank."

Try to find out when the physician is most available. Some doctors have a call hour—a regular time every day, usually first thing in the morning, when you can call in with a question. If your child is sick, but you are not sure whether to make an appointment for her, this is a good time to talk with her doctor about her symptoms and determine whether you need to bring her in to be seen. If there is no call hour, you might even suggest one, as a time-saver for everyone.

Most physicians basically like to be needed and do not mind responding to reasonable requests for help and advice. If you call at a convenient time or allow the physician to choose the time, it needn't be an intrusion. But save night calls for real emergencies. I have always had a call hour each morning, and at that time I expected to be available for all sorts of questions, unimportant as well as important. This took the pressure off for me. If parents saved minor stress until that hour, I respected them and knew that they respected me. We developed a basic trust that helped in more stressful times.

If the practice has a nurse who answers minor questions, use her as much as you can. But if you still have questions after talking your concerns over with the nurse, I'd make this clear. Ask the nurse to have the doctor call you. Explain that you are still anxious and need to talk to the doctor directly. If the nurse doesn't understand, continue to insist, politely.

Your child's doctor should be available for explanations of every medical problem or treatment, and I'd let him or her know that you want to be told as much as possible. When doctors withhold information, it is usually because (1) they are afraid you'll misuse it, (2) they want to protect you, or (3) they aren't sure of the diagnosis. In a warm, sharing relationship, a doctor can be honest with you in each case.

Parents can ask a physician questions that anticipate the difficulties that may arise later. "How can I treat this when she first starts to wheeze?" "How long should I wait?" "Is there anything I can do to prevent these recurrent earaches? I hate treating them after they're already full-blown." "How long should it take for this to heal? Should I call you again if it doesn't heal by then?" "How will I know if the fever is turning into an emergency? When should I call you?"

Parents can also ask for anticipatory guidance about child rearing and development from their pediatrician. Developmentally trained pediatricians are particularly well suited for this. Other physicians may be excellent in the physical sphere but may flounder and defend themselves in the area of child development. There is far too much to know for any single physician to master it all. In this case, as we said, use other sources, and don't be angry for what the pediatrician isn't equipped to do. You'll endanger your chances of getting the best medical care possible.

Most important of all is that the child feels that "this is my doctor." I have found that the most rewarding experience in pediatrics is for a *child* to want to see me and to trust me to help her with her illness. My day is made when a child calls me herself or when a mother calls to say that "Emily wanted me to call to find out what to do about her problem." Whatever her disease or problem, the child is bound to have feelings about it. Sometimes these can aggravate her condition, or at least interfere with her quality of life. A child is naturally frightened when something is wrong with her. If she can feel that "her doctor" will know what to do, she will feel a sense of trust and of belief in her own ability to handle the disease. Whenever I prescribe medication or make suggestions for children four years old or more, I am sure to include them in my instructions. For I want them to know what we are doing and why. After they are recovered, I try to say to them, "See, we (you, your mommy, your daddy, and I) knew what to do, and now you're better!" This implies that the child has had a part in mastering the disease, and it will reduce anxiety in the future.

The Doctor-Child Relationship

Routine visits are opportunities for me to make a relationship with the child right from the first—as well as to enhance it with the child's parents. As indicated earlier, I never expect a baby between the ages of nine months and three years to leave her mother's lap for an examination. When I recognize the child's need to be close to a parent, the child knows I respect her. I never look her directly in the face or ask for her to accept me. In this period, I gradually approach her, using a doll or teddy and her parent to show them all what I am about to do—stethoscope, otoscope, exam of the throat, or of the abdomen, and so on. By the time I examine her, she's seen the maneuver. I have watched her face and body for permission. When she relaxes, it means she has accepted me and is ready. Weighing her in her mother's arms is another sign of respect. It is easy to subtract the mother's weight to determine the baby's. In this way she will begin to trust me.

I make a big effort to get a slightly older child to want to come to my office—loading it with toys, a fish tank, a climbing gym, a flexible cloth tunnel to crawl through, and a rock collection, and I offer stickers and plastic rings (for children old enough not to swallow them) that they can show off proudly as tokens of their bravery. Children see these as my attempt to be an ally. When they can leave their parents in my office to play in my waiting room under the receptionist's watchful eye, I know the children have accepted me. (See chapter 12 for suggestions about strengthening this relationship.)

I am always looking for ways to make a special relationship with a small child. As she comes into my office, I watch to see how comfortable she is. If she is frightened about me, I know that. Giving her time to get used to me is respectful. I wait until she is willing to leave her parent's lap. As she eyes my toys, I shove one of the trucks in her direction, carefully. But I don't let her catch me looking at her. As she begins to play with the truck, I push another close by. If she looks up at me, I can look back toward her, but still won't dare to look her in the face. All of this time, I am talking to her parents, so I am actually not spending much extra time in this attempt to solidify our relationship. The time it does take is well worth it. She'll be far easier to examine. Her parents will be less hesitant to warn me of potentially serious problems—early—once they've seen this demonstration of my concern for their child's comfort, and it only takes two or three minutes.

By the time I must examine her, we have begun to push trucks back and forth between us. If she is ready, we can exchange comments on the trucks. As I examine her *in her parent's lap,* I urge her to listen to my chest and to examine me. We are sharing the experience and she knows it. She also knows that I respect her privacy and her natural anxiety about being examined. We are setting the stage now for a long future relationship.

With her in the room, I comment on her temperament and mode of play. She knows I understand her. She listens. Anything her parents and I need to discuss is talked about in front of her, and I try to put it in her terms. I want her to understand what we are talking about. No secrets! I prepare her for a shot, honestly, and urge her to cry and to protect herself. After it's over, I congratulate her on her success.

As a child gets older, at four, five, and six, I may even urge her to ask her own questions and to call me on the phone. She won't yet. But by six or seven, she will. We can discuss her illness between us, though of course I won't leave the parents out. In later years, and when she'll let me see her alone, we can share confidences without it being a triangle, though she, her parents, and I all know that I will help her to tell them what she needs to. If she still needs her parents present, that should be respected. But, even if her parent is in the office with her, I talk to *her,* and she knows I am *her* doctor.

At four, five, and six, I never ask a child to remove her underpants. With her permission, I can briefly pull them down to inspect the genital area, but I know how intrusive it is to be examined carefully at that time. By the same token, I do not use a vaginal speculum for adolescent girls, unless there is some urgent medical reason to do so, and whenever possible, I ask them in advance if they would prefer to switch to a female doctor, at the very least for gynecological care. Examining the throat with a tongue depressor is another intrusive manipulation. I can see the nasopharynx well if the child imitates my "Ahh" and can use a spoon or a less symbolic instrument to check the sides of the mouth.

As indicated in chapter 14 on "Allergies and Asthma," I believe in sharing all I know about each illness with the children themselves. My goal is to help them take an active role in conquering their own diseases. If they can call or talk with me, and carry out my advice, this lesson will stay with them. When they recover, I can congratulate them: "Look how you knew what to do—and it worked!"

During a school-aged child's visit, I always ask her something about her school. For example:

> "What is your teacher's name?" No answer.
> "Is she a girl or a boy?"
> "A girl, silly."
> "Does she ask you questions?"
> "Of course."
> "Do you know the answers?"
> "Sometimes."
> "Are you ever scared?"
> "Uh huh."
> "What do you do?"

"I cry." That tells me a lot.
"Do you have a best friend?" No answer.
"Is it a boy or a girl?"
"A girl, silly."
"Is her name Andrea?"
"No, it's Susie."
"Does Susie like to go to her doctor?"
"No!"
"I'll bet Susie won't talk to her doctor either." Laughter.

Then we can start to communicate, not with words, but with play and with gestures.

At each visit, I look for an entry into my patients' lives. I try to talk about their siblings, their teachers, their close friends, their school. As they get to the age of sports or music, we talk about these interests. I am not exploring for information, and I try to make that clear by my interested but unintrusive questions. I am concerned with making a relationship and letting them know that I care about them as people. I make a note on my chart about any area with which they are concerned. If I can use that as an opener on the next visit, it can ease the way to resuming our relationship.

In these visits, I am also aware of the child's experience of the touchpoints of her own development. When I can use my understanding of these, and their meaning to her, I can make each touchpoint a step toward closeness, so that a child will begin to see me as "hers." That is my goal.

Often, after a question or a bid for a confidence, the shy child will shake her head to say no. I then can say, "Your head says no, but your eyes say yes. Can you tell me which I am to believe?" Then, I try to shut up to listen. Waiting to get an answer from a child takes enormous patience and many failed attempts. But they know I'm on their side. As they get older, they show me how much they've appreciated this caring approach.

When children must go to the hospital, it becomes even more critical that a physician explain the reasons and the procedures in front of the child. We have found that preparation for acute or chronic hospitalization cuts down on the child's anxiety in the hospital, shortens the child's recovery time, and reduces the symptoms of anxiety afterward (see "Hospitalization"). Most parents dread the separation and trauma so much that they need a physician's help to face it themselves as well as to prepare the child. Of course, I feel pediatricians should fight to see that parents are allowed to accompany and stay with their child in the hospital. Even though the child will be under the care of various specialists, I always go to visit her and to interpret—for her and her parents—the illness, tests, and treatments.

In my office practice, the best reward for me at the end of a busy day always came when I heard a child's chortle of delight as she rushed in to see me and my familiar toys. Then, I knew we were off to a good start.

Sharing Responsibilities

I would urge you to seek to establish this kind of trusting, respectful relationship between your child and her doctor. You must do your part, as well. It is no help to enter the office saying, "He's going to cry," or, "She hates coming to see the doctor." That is sure to undermine both the child and the doctor as they struggle to make it with each other. Instead, prepare the child ahead of time, truthfully, and with reassurance about what is likely to happen. Remind her that you will be there, that it's her own doctor who wants to be her friend. The doctor knows how to help her when she's well and when she's not. It is surprising to me how much it helps a child's self-esteem to learn to trust her physician. In my book *Going to the Doctor,* illustrated by my grandson, Alfred, from a child's point of view, I suggest ways both parents and doctor can encourage this relationship.

Working with a pediatrician is a mutual job of learning what you can—and cannot—get from each other. You must demonstrate respect, and you deserve respect in return. Both of you have the same goal—a healthy, competent, confident child!

further reading
references
useful addresses and web sites
videos
index
about the authors

Further Reading

Alexander, Terry Pink. *Make Room for Twins.* New York: Bantam Books, 1987.
American Academy of Pediatrics Guide to Your Child's Allergies and Asthma. New York: Villard, 2000.
Ames, Louise Bates, et al. *The Gesell Institute's Child from One to Six.* New York: Harper and Row, 1979.
Ayres, Jean. *Sensory Integration and the Child: 25th Anniversary Edition.* Los Angeles: Western Psychological Services, 2005.
Bardige, Betty. *At a Loss for Words: How America Is Failing Our Children and What We Can Do About It.* Philadelphia: Temple University Press, 2005.
Bauer, Ingrid. *Diaper Free! The Gentle Wisdom of Natural Infant Hygiene.* Saltspring Island, BC, Canada: Natural Wisdom Press, 2001.
Brazelton, T. Berry. *Going to the Doctor.* Reading, Mass.: Addison-Wesley/Merloyd Lawrence, 1996.
———. *On Becoming a Family: The Growth of Attachment Before and After Birth,* rev. ed. New York: Delacorte Press/Merloyd Lawrence, 1992.
———. *Toddlers and Parents: Declaration of Independence.* 2d ed. New York: Delacorte Press/Merloyd Lawrence, 1989.
———. *Working and Caring.* Reading, Mass.: Addison-Wesley/Merloyd Lawrence, 1985.
———. *To Listen to a Child: Understanding the Normal Problems of Growing Up.* Reading, Mass.: Addison-Wesley/Merloyd Lawrence, 1984.

———. *Neonatal Behavioral Assessment Scale,* 2d ed. Philadelphia: Lippincott, 1984.

———. *Infants and Mothers: Differences in Development,* rev. ed. New York: Delacorte Press/Merloyd Lawrence, 1983.

Brazelton, T. Berry, and Bertrand Cramer. *The Earliest Relationship: Parents, Infants and the Drama of Early Attachment.* Reading, Mass.: Addison-Wesley/Merloyd Lawrence, 1990.

Brazelton, T. Berry, and Stanley I. Greenspan. *The Irreducible Needs of Children: What Every Child Must Have to Grow, Learn, and Flourish.* Cambridge, Mass.: Perseus Merloyd Lawrence, 2000.

Brazelton, T. Berry, and Joshua D. Sparrow. *Mastering Anger and Aggression—The Brazelton Way.* Cambridge, Mass.: Da Capo/Merloyd Lawrence, 2005.

———. *Understanding Sibling Rivalry—The Brazelton Way.* Cambridge, Mass.: Da Capo/Merloyd Lawrence, 2005.

———. *Feeding Your Child—The Brazelton Way.* Cambridge, Mass.: Da Capo/Merloyd Lawrence, 2004.

———. *Toilet Training—The Brazelton Way.* Cambridge, Mass.: Da Capo/Merloyd Lawrence, 2004.

———. *Calming Your Fussy Baby—The Brazelton Way.* Cambridge, Mass.: Da Capo/Merloyd Lawrence, 2003.

———. *Discipline—The Brazelton Way.* Cambridge, Mass.: Da Capo/Merloyd Lawrence, 2003.

———. *Sleep—The Brazelton Way.* Cambridge, Mass.: Da Capo/Merloyd Lawrence, 2003.

———. *Touchpoints Three to Six: Your Child's Behavioral and Emotional Development.* Cambridge, Mass.: Perseus/Merloyd Lawrence, 2001.

Carey, William B. *Understanding Your Child's Temperament.* New York: Simon and Schuster, 1997.

Cath, S., A. Gurwitt, and J. M. Ross. *Father and Child.* Boston: Little, Brown, 1982.

Chess, Stella, and Alexander Thomas. *Know Your Child.* New York: Basic Books, 1987.

Children's Hospital Boston. *The Children's Hospital Guide to Your Child's Health and Development.* Edited by Alan D. Woolf, Howard C. Shane, and Margaret A. Kenna. Cambridge, Mass.: Perseus/Merloyd Lawrence, 2001.

Coll, Cynthia Garcia, Janet Surrey, and Kathy Weingarten. *Mothering Against the Odds: Diverse Voices of Contemporary Mothers.* New York: Guilford, 1998.

Comer, James P., and Alvin F. Poussaint. *Raising Black Children.* New York: Penguin, 1992.

Curtis, Glade B., and Judith Schuler. *Your Pregnancy: For the Father-to-Be.* Cambridge, Mass.: Perseus, 2003.

Dunn, Judy, and Robert Plomin. *Separate Lives: Why Siblings Are So Different.* New York: Basic Books, 1990.

Eisen, Andy, and Linda Engler. *Helping Your Child Overcome Separation Anxiety and School Refusal: A Step-by-Step Guide for Parents.* Oakland, Calif.: New Harbinger, 2006.

Eisenberg, A., H. Murkoff, and S. Hathaway. *What to Expect.* New York: Workman Publishers, 1994.

Elkind, D. *Ties That Stress.* Cambridge: Harvard University Press, 1994.

———. *The Hurried Child.* Reading, Mass.: Addison-Wesley, 1981.

Emmons, F., and L. Anderson. *Understanding Sensory Dysfunction.* London: Jessica Kingsley, 2005.

Erikson, Erik. *Childhood and Society.* New York: Norton, 1950.

Ferber, Richard. *Solve Your Child's Sleep Problem.* New York: Simon and Schuster, 1986.

Fraiberg, Selma M. *The Magic Years.* New York: Scribner's, 1959.

Galinsky, Ellen. *Ask the Children.* New York: Morrow, 1999.

Gardner, Howard. *Frames of Mind: The Theory of Multiple Intelligence.* New York: Basic Books, 1983.

Gilman, Lois. *The Adoption Resource Book,* 4th ed. New York: HarperCollins, 1998.

Glenmullen, Joseph. *The Antidepressant Solution: A Step-by-Step Guide to Safely Overcoming Antidepressant Withdrawal, Dependence and "Addiction."* New York: Free Press, 2004.

Goleman, D. *Emotional Intelligence.* New York: Bantam Books, 1997.

Golinkoff, Roberta, and Kathy Hirsh-Pasek. *How Babies Talk: The Magic and Mystery of Language in the First Three Years of Life.* New York: Penguin, 2000.

Gopnik, Alison, Andrew N. Meltzoff, and Patricia K. Kuhl. *The Scientist in the Crib: Minds, Brains, and How Children Learn.* New York: Morrow, 1999.

Greenspan, Stanley. *Engaging Autism: Using the Floortime Approach to Help Children Relate, Communicate, and Think.* Cambridge, Mass.: Da Capo, 2006.

———. *The Four-Thirds Solution.* Cambridge, Mass.: Da Capo, 2000.

Greenspan, Stanley, and Nancy Thorndike Greenspan. *First Feelings.* New York: Viking, 1985.

Greenspan, Stanley, and Serena Wieder. *The Child with Special Needs: Encouraging Intellectual and Emotional Growth.* Reading, Mass.: Addison-Wesley, 1998.

Hannibal, Mary Ellen. *Good Parenting Through Your Divorce.* New York: Marlowe, 2002.

Harris, Robie, and Michael Emberley. *Hi New Baby!* Cambridge, Mass.: Candlewick, 2003.

———. *Go! Go! Maria! What It's Like to Be* 1. New York: Margaret K. McElderry/Simon and Schuster, 2002.

———. *Hello Benny! What It's Like to Be a Baby.* New York: Margaret K. McElderry/Simon and Schuster, 2002.

———. *It's So Amazing!* Cambridge, Mass.: Candlewick, 1999.

———. *Happy Birth Day.* Cambridge, Mass.: Candlewick, 1996.

Hetherington, Mavis E., and John Kelly. *For Better or For Worse: Divorce Reconsidered.* New York: Norton, 2002.

Hirsh-Pasek, Kathy, and Roberta Michnick Golinkoff. *Einstein Never Used Flash Cards: How Our Children Really Learn—And Why They Need to Play More and Memorize Less.* Emmaus, Penn.: Rodale, 2003.

Holt, John. *Learning All the Time.* Reading, Mass.: Addison-Wesley/Merloyd Lawrence, 1989.

Huggins, Kathleen. *The Nursing Mother's Companion: 20th Anniversary Edition.* Boston: Harvard Common Press, 2006.

Johnson, Robert L., and Paulette Stanford. *Strength for Their Journey: 5 Essential Disciplines African American Parents Must Teach Their Children and Teens.* New York: Harlem Moon, Broadway Books, 2002.

Klaus, Marshall H., John Kennell, and Phyllis H. Klaus. *The Doula Book: How a Trained Labor Companion Can Help You Have a Shorter, Easier and Healthier Birth.* Cambridge, Mass.: Da Capo/Merloyd Lawrence, 2002.

———. *Bonding: Building the Foundations of Secure Attachment and Independence.* Reading, Mass.: Addison-Wesley/Merloyd Lawrence, 1995.

Klaus, Marshall H., and Phyllis H. Klaus. *Your Amazing Newborn.* Reading, Mass.: Addison-Wesley/Merloyd Lawrence, 1998.

Konner, Melvin. *Childhood.* Boston: Little, Brown, 1991.

Kornhaber, A. *The Grandparent Solution.* San Francisco: Jossey Bass, 2004.

Kranowitz, Carol Stock. *The Out of Sync Child.* New York: Harper Collins, 1998.

Krulik, Tamar, Bonnie Holaday, and Ida Marie Martinson, eds. *The Child and Family Facing Life-Threatening Illness.* Philadelphia: Lippincott, 1987.

Leach, Penelope. *Child Care Encyclopedia.* New York: Knopf, 1984.

———. *Babyhood.* New York: Knopf, 1976.

Lerner, Henry M. *Miscarriage: Why It Happens and How Best to Reduce Your Risks.* Cambridge, Mass.: Perseus, 2003.

LeShan, Eda. *Learning to Say Goodbye: When a Parent Dies.* Boston: Atlantic Monthly Press, 1986.

Levine, A. I. *The Complete Lesbian and Gay Parenting Guide.* New York: Berkley Books, 2004.
Levine, Mel. *A Mind at a Time.* Simon and Schuster, 2002.
———. *Educational Care: A System for Understanding and Helping Children with Learning Problems at Home and at School.* Princeton, N.J.: Educators Publishing Service, 1994.
Linn, Susan. *Consuming Kids: Protecting Our Children from the Onslaught of Marketing and Advertising.* New York: Anchor, 2005.
Lobato, D. J. *Brothers, Sisters—Special Needs.* Baltimore: Paul Brookes Publishers, 1990.
Lopas, J., and D. Sova. *Step-Parenting.* New York: Kensington Books, 1985.
Mason, Diane, and Diane Ingersoll. *Breastfeeding and the Working Mother.* New York: St. Martin's Press, 1986.
McCollum, Audrey. *The Chronically Ill Child: A Guide for Parents and Professionals.* New Haven, Conn.: Yale University Press, 1981.
Nakazawa, Donna Jackson. *Does Anybody Else Look Like Me? A Parent's Guide to Raising Multiracial Children.* Cambridge, Mass.: Perseus, 2003.
Neifert, Marianne. *Dr. Mom's Guide to Breastfeeding.* New York: Plume Books, 1998.
Nelson, I., C. Erwin, and R. Duffy. *Positive Discipline for Pre-schoolers.* Rocklin, Calif.: Prima Publishers, 1994.
Nilsson, Lennart, and Lars Hamberger. *A Child Is Born,* 4th ed. New York: Delacorte Press/Merloyd Lawrence, 2004.
Osofsky, J. *Young Children and Trauma.* New York: Guilford Press, 2004.
Pruett, Kyle. *Fatherneed: Why Father Care Is as Essential as Mother Care for Your Child.* New York: Free Press, 2000.
———. *Myself and I: How Children Build Their Sense of Self.* New York: Goddard Press, 1999.
Queenan, John T., and Kimberly K. Leslie, eds. *Preconceptions: Preparation for Pregnancy.* Boston: Little, Brown, 1989.
Ricci, I. *Mom's House Dad's House.* New York: Fireside, 1997.
Rodriguez, Gloria G. *Raising Nuestros Ninos: Bringing Up Latino Children in a Bicultural World.* New York: Fireside, 1999.
Rosen, M. *Stepfathering.* New York: Ballantine Books, 1987.
Rosenberg, Ronald, Deborah Greening, and James Windell. *Conquering Postpartum Depression: A Proven Plan for Recovery.* Cambridge, Mass.: Perseus, 2003.
Sadeh, Avi. *Sleeping Like a Baby.* New Haven, Conn.: Yale University Press, 2001.
Samalin, N. *Loving Without Spoiling.* New York: McGraw Hill, 2003.

Schor, Juliet B. *Born to Buy: The Commercialized Child and the New Consumer Culture.* New York: Scribner, 2004.

———. *The Overworked American.* New York: Basic Books, 1991.

Schorr, Lisbeth. *Within Our Reach: Breaking the Cycle of Disadvantage.* New York: Doubleday, 1989.

Schreibman, Laura. *The Science and Fiction of Autism.* Cambridge: Harvard University Press, 2005.

Segal, Marilyn. *Your Child At Play: One to Two Years—Exploring, Daily Living, Learning, and Making Friends.* New York: Newmarket, 1998.

———. *Your Child At Play: Two to Three Years—Growing Up, Language, and the Imagination.* New York: Newmarket, 1998.

Shaywitz, S. *Overcoming Dyslexia.* New York: Knopf, 2003.

Shelov, Steven, ed. *Your Baby's First Year.* American Academy of Pediatrics. New York: Bantam Edition, 1998.

Siegal, Daniel J., and Mary Hartzell. *Parenting from the Inside Out.* New York: Penguin, 2004.

Small, M. E. *Our Babies Ourselves.* New York: Bantam Doubleday, 1998.

Spock, Benjamin, and Robert Needleman. *Dr. Spock's Baby and Child Care,* 8th ed. New York: Pocket Books, 2004.

Stern, Daniel. *Diary of a Baby: What Your Child Sees, Feels, and Experiences.* New York: Basic Books, 1998.

———. *The First Relationship.* Cambridge, Mass.: Harvard University Press, 1977.

Stern, Daniel, and Nadia Bruschweiler-Stern. *The Birth of a Mother: How the Motherhood Experience Changes You Forever.* New York: Basic Books, 1998.

Thompson, C. E. *Raising a Handicapped Child.* New York: Morrow, 1986.

Thompson, Michael, and Lawrence J. Cohen, with Catherine O'Neill Grace. *Mom, They're Teasing Me.* New York: Ballantine, 2002.

Thompson, M., and Catherine O'Neill Grace. *Best Friends, Worst Enemies.* New York: Ballantine, 2001.

Trozzi, Maria. *Talking with Children About Loss.* New York: Harper Collins, 1999.

Viorst, Judith. *Necessary Losses.* New York: Simon and Schuster, 1986.

Weissbluth, Marc. *Healthy Sleep Habits, Happy Child.* New York: Fawcett, 1999.

Wilens, Timothy. *Straight Talk About Psychiatric Medications for Kids.* New York: Guilford Press, 2004.

Wolman, David. *A Left-Hand Turn Around the World.* Cambridge, Mass.: Da Capo, 2005.

Zigler, Edward, and Mary Lang. *Child Care Choices.* New York: Free Press, 1991.

References

Abel, Ernest L. *Fetal Alcohol Syndrome: From Mechanism to Prevention.* New York: CRC Press, 1996.

Als, Heidelise. "Individualized Developmental Care for Preterm Infants." In *Encyclopedia on Early Childhood Development.* Montreal: Centre of Excellence for Early Childhood Development, 2004.

Als, Heidelise, B. M. Lester, E. Z. Tronick, and T. B. Brazelton. "The Assessment of Preterm Infants' Behavior: Furthering the Understanding and Measurement of Neurodevelopmental Competence in Preterm and Full Term Infants." *Mental Retardation and Developmental Disabilities Research Reviews* 11 (2005): 94–102.

Als, Heidelise, et al. "A Three-Center Randomized Control Trial of Individualized Developmental Care for Very Low Birth Weight Preterm Infants: Medical, Neurodevelopmental, and Parenting Effects." *Journal of Developmental and Behavioral Pediatrics* 24, no. 6 (2003): 399–408.

American Academy of Pediatrics, American Academy of Allergy, Asthma and Immunology, NIH-National Heart, Lung and Blood Institute, National Asthma Education and Prevention Program. *Pediatric Asthma: Promoting Best Practice—Guide for Managing Asthma in Children.* Milwaukee, Wis.: American Academy of Allergy, Asthma and Immunology, 1999. Available online at www.aaaai.org.

Amy, Eileen. "Reflections on the Interactive Newborn Bath Demonstration." MCN, *The American Journal of Maternal/Child Nursing* 26, no. 6 (2000): 320–322.

Anderson, Daniel, and Tiffany Pempek. "Television and Very Young Children." *American Behavioral Scientist* 48, no. 5 (January 2005).

Bandura, A., D. Ross, and S. A. Ross. "Imitation of Film-Mediated Aggressive Models." *Journal of Abnormal and Social Psychology* 66 (1963): 3–11.

Bowlby, John. *Attachment and Loss.* 3 vols. New York: Basic Books, 1969, 1980.

Brown, Roger. *A First Language.* Cambridge: Harvard University Press, 1973.

Brazelton, T. Berry, and Bertrand G. Cramer. *The Earliest Relationship: Parents, Infants, and the Drama of Early Attachment.* Reading, Mass.: Addison-Wesley/Merloyd Lawrence, 1990.

Bruner, Jerome. *Child's Talk: Learning to Use Language.* New York: Norton, 1985.

Bruner, Jerome, A. Jolly, and K. Sylva. *Play: Its Role in Development.* New York: Penguin, 1946.

Burns, Catherine E., et al. *Pediatric Primary Care: A Handbook for Nurse Practitioners,* 3d ed. St. Louis: Saunders, 2004.

Cardone, Ida Anne, and Linda Gilkerson. "Family Administered Neonatal Activities." In *Neonatal Behavior Assessment Scale,* edited by T. Berry Brazelton and Kevin Nugent Kevin. London: MacKeith, 1995.

Carey, William B., and S. McDevitt. *Coping with Children's Temperaments.* New York: Basic Books, 1995.

Caton, Donald, Maureen P. Corry, et al. "The Nature and Management of Labor Pain." *American Journal of Obstetrics and Gynecology* 186, no. 5 (May 2002).

Chantry, Caroline, et al. "Full Breastfeeding Duration and Associated Decrease in Respiratory Tract Infection in US Children." *Pediatrics* 117, no. 2 (February 2006).

Christakis, Dimitri, et al. "Early Television Exposure and Subsequent Attentional Problems in Children." *Pediatrics* 113 (2004): 708–713.

Dershewitz, Robert A., ed. *Ambulatory Pediatrics,* 3d ed. Philadelphia: Lippincott-Raven, 1999.

Dixon, Suzanne, and Martin Stein, eds. *Encounters with Children.* St. Louis: Mosby, 2000.

Field, Tiffany, et al. "Prenatal Cortisol, Prematurity, and Low Birthweight." *Infant Behavior and Development* 29, no. 2 (2006): 268–275.

Greenspan, Stanley. *The Growth of the Mind and the Endangered Origins of Intelligence.* Reading, Mass.: Addison-Wesley/Merloyd Lawrence, 1997.

Gross, Ruth T., Donna Spiker, and Christine W. Haynes. *Helping Low Birth Weight and Premature Babies: The Infant Health and Development Program.* Palo Alto: Stanford University Press, 1997.

Heimann, Mikael, ed. *Regression Periods in Human Infancy.* London: Lawrence Ehrlbaum, 2003.

Hoekelman, Robert A., ed. *Primary Pediatric Care,* 4th ed. St. Louis: Mosby, 2001.

Kagan, Jerome. *Three Seductive Ideas.* Cambridge: Harvard University Press, 1998.

———. *The Nature of the Child.* New York: Basic Books, 1984.

Kagan, Jerome, and Nancy Snidman. *The Long Shadow of Temperament.* Cambridge: Harvard University Press, 2004.

Kaiser Family Foundation. "A Teacher in the Living Room? Educational Media for Babies, Toddlers and Preschoolers." Washington, D.C., December 2005.

Karl, Donna. "Principles of Newborn Behavioral States Organization to Facilitate Breastfeeding." *Maternal Child Nursing* 29, no. 5 (2004): 292–298.

———. "The Interactive Newborn Bath: Using Neurobehavior to Connect Parents and Newborns." *Maternal Child Nursing* 24, no. 6 (1999): 280–286.

Kessler, Daniel B., and Peter Dawson. *Failure to Thrive and Pediatric Undernutrition: A Transdisciplinary Approach.* Baltimore: Paul H. Brookes, 1999.

Lester, Barry, and C. F. Boukydis. *Infant Crying: Theoretical and Research Perspectives.* New York: Plenum, 1985.

Lewis, Michael, and Lawrence Taft, eds. *Developmental Disabilities: Theory, Assessment and Intervention.* New York: SP Medical and Scientific Books, 1982.

Levine, M. D., W. B. Carey, and A. C. Crocker. *Developmental Behavioral Pediatrics,* 3d ed. Philadelphia: W. B. Saunders, 1999.

Lieberman, Alicia, et al. *Losing a Parent to Death in the Early Years: Guidelines for the Treatment of Traumatic Bereavement in Infancy and Early Childhood.* Washington, D.C.: Zero to Three Press, 2003.

Mahler, Margaret, Fred Pine, and Anni Bergman. *The Psychological Birth of the Human Infant.* New York: Basic Books, 1975.

Mohrbacher, Nancy. *Pocket Guide to the Breastfeeding Answer Book.* Schaumberg, Ill.: La Leche League International, 2005.

Nathanielsz, P. W. *Life Before Birth.* Ithaca, N.Y.: Promethean Press, 1992.

Nelson, Katherine, ed. *Narratives from the Crib.* Cambridge: Harvard University Press, 1989.

Parker, Steven, Barry Zuckerman, and Marilyn Augustyn. *Developmental Behavioral Pediatrics: A Handbook for Primary Care.* Philadelphia: Lippincott, Williams, and Wilkins, 2004.

Rudolph, Colin D., et al. *Rudolph's Pediatrics,* 21st ed. New York: McGraw-Hill, 2002.

Shonkoff, Jack P., and Samuel J. Meisels, eds. *Handbook of Early Childhood Intervention,* 2d ed. Cambridge: Cambridge University Press, 2000.

Shonkoff, Jack P., and Deborah A. Phillips, eds. *From Neurons to Neighborhoods: The Science of Early Childhood Development.* National Research Council Institute of Medicine. Washington, D.C.: National Academies Press, 2000.

Sorce, James F., Robert Emde, Joseph Campos, and Mary Klinnert. "Maternal Emotional Signaling: Its Effect on the Visual Cliff Behavior of 1-Year-Olds." *Developmental Psychology* 21 (1985): 195–200.

Stern, Daniel. *The Motherhood Constellation: A Unified View of Parent-Infant Psychotherapy.* New York: Basic Books, 1995.

———. *The Interpersonal World of the Infant.* New York: Basic Books, 1985.

Thompson, Darcy, and Dimitri Christakis. "The Association Between Television Viewing and Irregular Sleep Schedules Among Children Less Than 3 Years of Age." *Pediatrics* 116 (2005): 851–856.

Van de Rijt-Plooij, Hedwig, and Frans Plooij. "Distinct Periods of Mother-Infant Conflict in Normal Development: Sources of Progress and Germs of Pathology." *Journal of Child Psychology* 34, no. 2 (1992): 229–243.

———. "Mother Infant Relations, Conflict, Stress and Illness Among Free-Ranging Chimpanzees." *Developmental Medicine and Child Neurology* 30 (1988): 306–315.

Wallerstein, Judith S., Julia M. Lewis, and Sandra Blakeslee. *The Unexpected Legacy of Divorce: The 25 Year Landmark Study.* New York: Hyperion, 2000.

Weissbourd, R. *The Vulnerable Child: What Really Hurts America's Children and What We Can Do About It.* Reading, Mass.: Addison Wesley, 1996.

Westman, Jack C. *Parenthood in America: Undervalued, Underpaid, Under Siege.* Madison: University of Wisconsin Press, 2001.

Williamson, Gordon, and Marie Anzalone. *Sensory Integration and Self Regulation in Infants and Toddlers: Helping Very Young Children Interact with Their Environment.* Washington, D.C.: Zero to Three Press, 2001.

Winnicott, D. W. *Talking to Parents.* Introduction by T. Berry Brazelton. Reading, Mass.: Addison-Wesley/Merloyd Lawrence, 1993.

———. *Babies and Their Mothers.* Introduction by Benjamin Spock. Reading, Mass.: Addison-Wesley/Merloyd Lawrence, 1988.

———. *The Child, the Family and the Outside World.* Introduction by Marshall H. Klaus. Reading, Mass.: Addison-Wesley/Merloyd Lawrence, 1987.

Zeanah, Charles H. *Handbook of Infant Mental Health.* New York: Guilford, 1993.

Zimmerman, Frederick, and Dimitri Christakis. "Children's Television Viewing and Cognitive Outcomes." *Archives of Pediatric and Adolescent Medicine* 159 (July 2005).

Zutavern, Anne, et al. "Timing of Solid Food Introduction in Relation to Atopic Dermatitis and Atopic Sensitization: Results from a Prospective Birth Cohort Study." *Pediatrics* 117, no. 2 (February 2006).

Useful Addresses and Web Sites

Child Advocacy

Alliance for Education
509 Olive Way, Suite 500
Seattle, WA 98101–2556
www.alliance4ed.org.

Campaign for a Commercial-Free Childhood
53 Parker Hill Ave.
Boston, MA 02120
(617) 278–4172
www.commercialfreechildhood.org

Children's Defense Fund
25 E. St., NW
Washington, DC 20001
(206) 343–0449
www.childrensdefense.org

Educare
5150 Ashley Phosphate Rd., Suite 100
North Charlestown, SC 29418
(843) 760–6064
www.educareinc.com

Every Child Matters
440 First St., NW
5th Floor
Washington, DC 20001
www.everychildmatters.org

Fight Crime: Invest in Kids
1212 New York Ave., NW, Suite 300
Washington, DC 20005
(202) 776–0027
www.fightcrime.org

InterNational Association of Parents and Professionals for Safe Alternatives in Childbirth
Route 4, Box 646
Marble Hill, MO 63764
(573) 238–2010
www.napsac.org

Kids First
112 W. San Francisco St.
Suite 305A
Santa Fe, NM 87501
(505) 989–8076
www.kidsfirst.org

National Alliance for Breastfeeding
Attn: Marsha Walker
254 Conant Rd.
Weston, MA 02493–1756
www.naba-breastfeeding.org

National Safe Kids Campaign
1301 Pennsylvania Ave., NW,
Suite 1000
Washington, DC 20004–1707
www.safekids.org

Ounce of Prevention
122 S. Michigan Ave., Suite 2050
Chicago, IL 60603–6198
(312) 922–3863
www.ounceofprevention.org

Parent Action
1875 Connecticut Ave., NW, Suite 650
Washington, DC 20009
(202) 238–4878
www.parentsaction.org

Parents as Teachers
2228 Ball Dr.
St. Louis, MO 63146
(314) 432–4330
www.parentsasteachers.org

Stand for Children
516 SE Morrison St., Suite 420
Portland, OR 97214
(503) 235–2305
www.stand.org

Zero to Three
National Center for Infants, Toddlers and Families
2000 M St., NW, Suite 200
Washington, DC 20036
(202) 638–1144
(800) 899–4301
Western Office
350 South Bixel, Suite 150
Los Angeles, CA 90017
(213) 481–7279
www.zerotothree.org

Environmental Health

Center for Children's Health and the Environment
Mount Sinai School of Medicine
Box 1043
One Gustave Levy Place
New York, NY 10029
(212) 241–7840
www.childenvironment.org

Children's Environmental Health Network
110 Maryland Ave., NE, Suite 505
Washington, DC 20002
(202) 543–4033
www.cehn.org

Environmental Working Group
1436 U. St., NW, Suite 100
Washington, DC 20009
(202) 667–6982
www.ewg.org

Institute for Children's Environmental Health
1646 Dow Rd.
Freeland, WA 98249
(360) 331–7904
www.iceh.org

Mount Sinai Pediatric Environmental Health Program
One Gustave Levy Place
1190 Fifth Ave.
New York, NY 10029
(212) 241–6500
(866) 265–6201
www.mountsinai.org/msh

Physicians for Social Responsibility
1875 Connecticut Ave., NW,
Suite 1012
Washington, DC 20009
(202) 667–4260
www.psr.org

U.S. Environmental Protection Agency (EPA)
Children's Health Protection
1200 Pennsylvania Ave., Room 2912
Washington, DC 20004
(202) 564–2188
www.epa.gov

Parenting

Birth and Life Bookstore
141 Commercial St., NE
Salem, OR 97301
(503) 371–4445

Centers for Disease Control
NIP Public Inquiries, Mailstop E–05
1600 Clifton Rd., NE
Atlanta, GA 30333
www.cdc.gov/nip

Childbirth Connection (formerly Maternity Center Association)
281 Park Ave. South, 5th Floor
New York, NY 10010
(212) 777–5000
www.childbirthconnection.org

Depression After Delivery
www.depressionafterdelivery.com

Good Grief Program
1 Boston Medical Center Place, Mat 5
Boston, MA 02118
(617) 414–4005

International Childbirth Education Association
ICEA Bookstore
P.O. Box 20048
Minneapolis, MN 55420
(952) 854–8660
www.icea.org

International Lactation Consultants Association
1500 Sunday Dr., Suite 102
Raleigh, NC 27607
(919) 861–5577
www.ilca.org

Kid's Turn
1242 Market St., 2nd Floor
San Francisco, CA 94102–4802
(800) 392–9239
www.kidsturn.org

La Leche League International
1400 N. Meacham Rd.
Schaumberg, IL 60173–4808
(847) 519–7730
www.laleche.org

Lamaze International
2025 M St., Suite 800
Washington, DC 20036
(800) 368–4404
www.lamaze.org

National Headache Foundation
820 N. Orleans, Suite 217
Chicago, IL 60610
(888) NHF–5552
www.headaches.org

National Safety Council
1121 Spring Lake Dr.
Itasca, IL 60143–3201
(800) 621–7619
www.nsc.org

Putting Kids First
(888) 300–4707
www.puttingkidsfirst.org

Professional Associations

American Academy of Audiology
11730 Plaza American Dr., Suite 300
Reston, VA 20190
(800) AAA–2336
www.audiology.org

American Academy of Child and Adolescent Psychiatry
3615 Wisconsin Ave., NW
Washington, DC 20016
(202) 966–7300

American Academy of Pediatrics
141 Northwest Point Blvd.
Elkgrove Village, IL 60007
(847) 434–4000
www.aap.org
asthma Web site:
www.aap.org/schooledinasthma

American College of Obstetricians and Gynecologists
409 12th St., SW
P.O. Box 96920
Washington, DC 20090
(202) 638–5577
www.acog.org

American Speech-Language-Hearing Association
10801 Rockville Pike
Rockville, MD 20852
(800) 498–2071
www.asha.org

Bright Futures
Georgetown University
Box 571272
Washington, DC 20057–1272
(202) 784–9556
www.brightfutures.org

Healthy Beginnings
210 William Howard Taft Rd.
Cincinnati, OH 45219
(513) 861–8430
www.healthybeginnings.org

Healthy Families America
200 S. Michigan Ave., Suite 1700
Chicago, IL 60604
(312) 663–3520
www.healthyfamiliesamerica.org

National Association for the Education of Young Children
1509 NW 16th St.
Washington, DC 20036
(202) 232–8777
www.naeyc.org

National Black Child Development Institute
1101 15th St., NW, Suite 900
Washington, DC 20005
www.nbcdi.org

National Head Start
1651 Prince St.
Alexandria, VA 22314
(703) 739–0875
www.nhsa.org

Society of Developmental and Behavioral Pediatrics
15000 Commerce Parkway, Suite C
Mt. Laurel, NJ 03054
(856) 439–0500
www.sdbp.org

Special Needs
(see also Professional Associations)

Alexander Graham Bell Association
3417 Volta Place, NW
Washington, DC 20007
(202) 337–5220
www.agbell.org

American Society for Deaf Children
ASDC Headquarters, 3820 Hartzdale Dr.
Camp Hill, PA 17011
(717) 703–0073
www.deafchildren.org

Autism Society of America
7910 Woodmont Ave., Suite 300
Bethesda, MD 20814
(301) 657–0881
www.autism-society.org

Child Anxiety Network
www.childanxiety.net

Childhood Apraxia of Speech
1151 Freeport Rd., #243
Pittsburgh, PA 15238
(412) 767–6589
www.apraxia-kids.org

Deafness Research Foundation
2801 M. Street, NW
Washington, DC 20007
(202) 719–8088
www.drf.org

Exceptional Parent
EP Global Communications
65 East Route 4
River Edge, NJ 07661
www.eparent.com
(800) 562–1973

Interdisciplinary Council for Developmental and Learning Disorders
4938 Hampden Lane, Suite 800
Bethesda, MD 20814
(301) 656–2667
www.icdl.com

National Alliance of Autism Research
New England Office
124 Watertown St., Suite 3B
Box 6
Watertown, MA 02472
(617) 924–3300
www.naar.org

National Association for the Deaf
8630 Fenton St., Suite 820
Silver Spring, MD 20910
(301) 587–1788
www.nad.org

National Dissemination Center for Children with Disabilities
P.O. Box 1492
Washington, DC 20013
(800) 695–0285
www.nichcy.org

National Institute of Mental Health (NIMH)
Public Information and Communications Branch
6001 Executive Blvd., Room 8184, MSC 9663
Bethesda, MD 20892–9663
www.nimh.nih.gov
(301) 443–4513
(866) 615–6464
(301) 443–8431 (TTY)
(866) 415–8051 (TTY)

National Institute on Deafness and Other Communication Disorders
3440 Market St., 4th Floor
Behavioral Health Center
Philadelphia, PA 19104
(215) 590–7440
www.raisingdeafkids.org

National Mental Health Association
2001 N. Beauregard St., 12th Floor
Alexandria, VA 22311
(703) 684–7722
www.nmha.org

National Stuttering Association
119 W. 40th St.
14th Floor
New York, NY 10018
(800) 937–8888
www.nsastutter.org

National Tourette's Syndrome Foundation
42–40 Bell Blvd.
Bayside, NY 11361
(718) 224–2999
www.tsa-usa.org

Obsessive Compulsive Foundation
676 State St.
New Haven, CT 06511
(203) 401–2070
www.ocfoundation.org

Sign Media
4020 Blackburn Lane
Burtonsville, MD 20866–1167
(800) 475–4756
www.signmedia.com

Videos

Touchpoints Videos
ConsumerVision, Inc.
66 Newtown Lane, Suite 3, East Hampton, NY 11937
(800) 756–8792
E-mail: ConsumerVision@aol.com

Breastfeeding, The Art of Mothering
Maurice Teitel and Sylvia Delaney
Port Washington, NY: Alive Productions, Ltd.

Fragile Beginnings: Postpartum Mood and Anxiety
Injoy Videos
(800) 326–2082

Index

Bold numbers indicate photographs.

About the Authors

T. Berry Brazelton, M.D., founder of the Child Development Unit at Children's Hospital, Boston, is clinical professor of pediatrics emeritus at Harvard Medical School. Currently professor of pediatrics and human development at Brown University, he is also past president of the Society for Research in Child Development and Zero to Three: The National Center for Infants, Toddlers, and Families. A practicing pediatrician for over forty-five years, he introduced the concept of "anticipatory guidance" for parents into pediatric training. The author of over 200 scholarly papers, Dr. Brazelton has written thirty books for both a professional and a lay audience, including the sequel to this book, *Touchpoints Three to Six*, as well as the now-classic trilogy *Infants and Mothers, Toddlers and Parents,* and *On Becoming a Family.* His television show, *What Every Baby Knows,* has run for twelve years and won an Emmy and three Ace Awards.

To continue his important research and implement its findings, Dr. Brazelton founded, and codirects, two programs at Children's Hospital: the Brazelton Institute (furthering work with the Neonatal Behavioral Assessment Scale) and the Brazelton Touchpoints Center (training healthcare and childcare professionals in over seventy centers across the country in the Touchpoints preventive outreach approach).

Dr. Brazelton, who has served on the National Commission for Children appointed by the U.S. Congress, is the recipient, among his very numerous awards, of the C. Anderson Aldrich Award for Distinguished Contributions to the Field of Child Development, given by the American Academy of Pediatrics, and the Woodrow Wilson Award for Outstanding Public Service from Princeton University.

Joshua Sparrow, M.D., child, adolescent, and general psychiatrist, is assistant professor of psychiatry at Harvard Medical School, outpatient supervisor at Children's Hospital, Boston, and director of special initiatives at the Brazelton Touchpoints Center. Dr. Sparrow's work with the Brazelton Touchpoints Center has included consultation on child development and parenting to the Harlem Children's Zone and to Native American Early Head Start Programs.

Dr. Sparrow has coauthored eight books with Dr. Brazelton: *Touchpoints Three to Six: Your Child's Emotional and Behavioral Development,* and the Brazelton Way Series on *Calming Your Fussy Baby, Discipline, Sleep, Toilet Training, Feeding Your Child, Understanding Sibling Rivalry,* and *Mastering Anger and Aggression,* and together with Dr. Brazelton writes a weekly *New York Times* Syndicate column, "Families Today."